From Servant to Savant

From Servant to Savant

Musical Privilege, Property, and the French Revolution

REBECCA DOWD
GEOFFROY-
SCHWINDEN

UNIVERSITY PRESS

Oxford University Press is a department of the University of Oxford. It furthers
the University's objective of excellence in research, scholarship, and education
by publishing worldwide. Oxford is a registered trade mark of Oxford University
Press in the UK and certain other countries.

Published in the United States of America by Oxford University Press
198 Madison Avenue, New York, NY 10016, United States of America.

© Oxford University Press 2022

All rights reserved. No part of this publication may be reproduced, stored in
a retrieval system, or transmitted, in any form or by any means, without the
prior permission in writing of Oxford University Press, or as expressly permitted
by law, by license, or under terms agreed with the appropriate reproduction
rights organization. Inquiries concerning reproduction outside the scope of the
above should be sent to the Rights Department, Oxford University Press, at the
address above.

You must not circulate this work in any other form
and you must impose this same condition on any acquirer.

Library of Congress Cataloging-in-Publication Data
Names: Geoffroy-Schwinden, Rebecca Dowd, author.
Title: From servant to savant : musical privilege, property, and the French
    Revolution / Rebecca Dowd Geoffroy-Schwinden.
Description: New York : Oxford University Press, 2022. |
Includes bibliographical references and index.
Identifiers: LCCN 2021033795 (print) | LCCN 2021033796 (ebook) |
ISBN 9780197511510 (hardback) | ISBN 9780197511534 (epub)
Subjects: LCSH: Music—Social aspects—France—History—18th century. |
    Musicians—France—Social conditions—18th century. |
    Musicians—France—Economic conditions—18th century.
Classification: LCC ML3917.F8 G46 2022 (print) | LCC ML3917.F8 (ebook) |
    DDC 306.4/8420944—dc23
LC record available at https://lccn.loc.gov/2021033795
LC ebook record available at https://lccn.loc.gov/2021033796

DOI: 10.1093/oso/9780197511510.001.0001

To Chris and Dad, with love and gratitude

CONTENTS

Preface xi

Acknowledgments xiii

Abbreviations xix

Note on Translation of Sources xxi

Introduction 1
   On Privilege, Property, and
      Professionalization 3
   The Abolition of Privilege 7
   The Politics of Historiography and the
      Archive 10
   Chapter Summaries 15

Part I Musical Privilege

1 Legal *Privilège* and Musical Production 21
   The Privilege to Perform 24
   Musical Privilege in Publishing, Commerce,
      and Manufacturing 33
   Privilege as Property 38
   The "Dilution" of Privilege 42

2 Social *Privilège* and Musician-Masons 51
   French Masonry, Music, and Parisian
      Sociability 53
   Brother Servants and Occasional Brothers 56
   Talented Brothers, Architects of Music, and
      Free Associates 63
   Fellow Professionals and Savants 70
   "A Little Lesson in Social Harmony" 74

Part II Property

3 Private Property: Music and Authorship 79
   Proprietary Tremors on the Eve of
      Revolution 82
   From Musical Privilege to Musical
      Property 87
   The "Declaration of the Rights of
      Genius" 104

4 Public Servants 112
   From Pleasing Paris to Serving the
      Nation 113
   An Institution of Their Own 121
   Patriotic Servants 123
   Professionalization and Public Patronage 129

5 Cultural Heritage: Music as Work of Art 132
   Music and the Fine Arts under the
      Revolution 134
   The Conservatory's "Museum" of Musical
      Works 144
   The Museum's Imperial Agenda 149
   "The Edifice Is Rising" 155
   Cultural Property and Artworks for the
      Future 162

6 National Industry: Music as a "Useful" Art and
   Science 165
   Music, the Useful Arts, and Mechanical
      Invention 167
   Interlude: A Method in the Madness 180
   Mechanical Innovations: Useful to
      Whom? 181

The Conservatory's Design for a "Romantic
     Machine"   188
  Postlude: A "Detractor" Breaks His
     "Silence"   206

Conclusion: Privilege by Any Other Name   208

Appendix   211

Notes   213

Bibliography   277

Index   297

PREFACE

The place of "privilege" in this book's title requires immediate contextualization given the word's ubiquity in twenty-first-century discourse. It appears here in a strictly historical sense; *privilèges* were legal or social permissions granted to subjects in Old Regime France. I nevertheless encourage the reader to heed the resonances that you may hear between privilege then and privilege now. The following introduction illuminates how revolutionary historiography is always also about the present. The coupling of "privilege" and "property" in 2020, a year that brought to the fore the troubled history of race in America and more broadly in the modern West, calls to mind "possessive investments," a term George Lipsitz uses to describe the ways in which whiteness collects and protects privilege like a kind of property.[1] Music scholarship has tended to accept the French Revolution's motto of "liberty, equality, fraternity," without consideration for the exclusions left in the conflict's wake. A reexamination of the French Revolution therefore affords an opportunity to scrutinize our own moment and to measure ourselves against the long shadow cast over modern democracies by the mythical Age of Revolution. Collusion at the level of law, policy, and individuals renders privilege invisible in both its historical and contemporary manifestations, so that unremarked on it cements together the stones of institutional walls. Institutions have long, sometimes hidden histories; if we do not bring them to light, then we cannot dismantle their more insidious legacies for the future.

Rebecca Dowd Geoffroy-Schwinden
Denton, Texas, USA
February 2021

ACKNOWLEDGMENTS

Research for *From Servant to Savant* received generous financial support from the University of North Texas (UNT), including a CREATE award from Faculty Success, two Scholarly and Creative Activity Awards, and a Junior Faculty Summer Research Support Award. The American Musicological Society's M. Elizabeth C. Bartlet Grant for research in France funded the archival research for Chapter 6. I am grateful to archivists and librarians who aided in my research, especially Michel Ollion at the Archives nationales de France, Pauline Girard and Juliette Jestaz at the Bibliothèque historique de la Ville de Paris, and Sophie Leroy, Karine Raczysnki, and Isabelle Taillebourg at the Centre de documentation du musée des arts et métiers.

A number of people facilitated the production and publication of this book. Suzanne Ryan and Mary Horn at Oxford University Press shepherded this project through the contract phase, and Norm Hirschy and Zoe Barham kindly stepped in to see it through to completion. I appreciate the friends who helped me to prepare the manuscript. Meticulous developmental and copyediting by Matt Somoroff improved this book in its earliest stages. Bryan Stevens created the musical examples. Dan Ruccia designed Figure 2.2 and arranged all of the figures and images into production-ready formats. Denise Carlson expertly prepared the index, and Koperundevi Pugazhenthi and Leslie Johnson oversaw production.

Short excerpts of my previously published work appear here in significantly revised form. Liverpool University Press has graciously permitted me to reprint selections from my chapter "The Revolution of Jommelli's *Objets d'art*: Bernard Sarrette's Acquisition of Musical Manuscripts for the Bibliothèque du Conservatoire" in *Moving Scenes: The Circulation of Music and Theatre in Europe, 1700–1815*, Oxford Studies in the Enlightenment, eds. Pierre-Yves Beaurepaire, Philippe Bourdin, and Charlotta Wolff (Oxford: Voltaire Foundation, 2017), 61–76. *Transposition: Musique et sciences sociales* has allowed the reproduction of portions of my article "Music, Copyright, and Intellectual Property: A Newly Discovered Letter from André-Ernest-Modeste Grétry," Le prix de la musique, *Transposition: Musique et Sciences Sociales* 7 (2018).

This book benefited from extensive feedback, questions, and discussions. My dissertation defense at Duke University with Annegret Fauser, Louise Meintjes, William M. Reddy, and Philip Rupprecht transformed my thinking about the framework for this project. Jacqueline Waeber has remained a brilliant and lasting advisor. Many fruitful exchanges about my research took place at conferences, including the Society for Ethnomusicology preconference symposium "Music, Property, and Law" held at the University of Texas at Austin; the "Music History and Cosmopolitanism" conference held at the Sibelius Academy at the University of the Arts Helsinki; the "France: Musique, Cultures, 1789–1918" conference held at the Bibliothèque historique de la Ville de Paris; and two panels at the Annual Meetings of the American Musicological Society: "Rethinking Enlightenment" in San Antonio organized by William Weber, and "Political Revolutions and their Musical Outcomes" in Boston organized by Glenda Goodman and Kay Kaufman Shelemay. Jonathan Huff and Clare Siviter organized a conversation with the Revolutionary Researchers network at King's College London which reshaped my approach to musicians' professionalization. The final section of Chapter 6 was nuanced by conversations with Peter McMurray, David Trippett, and Bettina Varwig, who generously welcomed me into the sound studies community at the University of Cambridge.

I am grateful to this incomplete list of friends and colleagues who commented on portions of the manuscript or book proposal at various stages of its inception: Annelies Andries, Rafe Blaufarb, Mark Darlow, James Q. Davies, Julia Doe, Glenda Goodman, Katherine Hambridge, Mary Caton Lingold, Darren Mueller, Andrei Pesic, William Weber, and Shaena Weitz. Beverly Wilcox suggested useful sources. Annelies, Julia, and Katherine provided quick and rigorous responses to all of my obscure questions about eighteenth-century French opera and theater. Chapters 3 and 6 received the generous critique of my writing group: Alexandra Apolloni, Zeynep Bulut, Stephanie Doktor, Sarah Gerk, Kristen Turner, and Jillian C. Rogers. I am fortunate to belong to a brilliant, generous, and fun community of scholars in musicology; in addition to those already mentioned, Rachel Bani, Karen Cook, Evan Cortens, Alison DeSimone, Katharine Ellis, Mark Everist, Sarah Eyerly, Kimary Fick, Sarah Fuchs, Ashley Greathouse, Fanny Gribenski, Sarah Hibberd, Hedy Law, Guido Olivieri, Jann Pasler, Jennifer Ronyak, Braxton Shelley, and Laurel Zeiss, among others who I have embarrassingly omitted, have made conference meals, workshops, and other exchanges both productive and pleasurable as I researched and wrote. Time spent in Paris with many of the colleagues named here not only improved my work but also provided me with very happy memories.

Mark Darlow welcomed me to the University of Cambridge for a month to workshop this book. Plans for one-hour meetings extended through entire afternoons of lunch and tea. His authoritative knowledge of eighteenth-century French culture and incisive historical thinking improved this book in countless ways. I owe him a debt of gratitude for the time that he has spent offering reading suggestions and providing detailed feedback on the manuscript. Most importantly, he taught me the significance of words and language, and that one should never take their meanings for granted. I am a more meticulous scholar for having worked with him and I now cherish his friendship, too.

A lovely group of colleagues and students at UNT support me. Benjamin Brand and Hendrik Schulze have provided both mentorship and friendship for which I will remain eternally grateful. Peter and Dayna Mondelli faithfully checked in on my well-being, whether through texts, phone calls, or delicious meals (some even in Paris!). April L. Prince, Sean Powell, and Jamey Kelley kept me showing up to Harvest House to write during hot Texas summers; I am thankful to the Harvest House staff, as well, for providing such a welcoming workspace. Many more colleagues in the UNT College of Music, too many to name here, made time-intensive committee work fun and provided a welcome respite from the sometimes isolating writing process. My students' insightful perspectives have greatly impacted how I think about professional musicianship; they opened my eyes to the lasting legacy of the Paris Conservatory and helped me to think from a musician's perspective. Discussions in my fall 2015 doctoral seminar Music and Social Institutions in Eighteenth-Century Paris clarified this project in many ways. Thoughtful conversations about monumentalism with Peter Kohanski influenced my final revisions of Chapter 5. My adventures in Paris and Belgium with Jennifer Youngs during her dissertation research brought some much needed joy to my summer archival work. Along with Julia Doe, we saw Grétry's heart and touched Rousseau's piano, and in accordance with genuine eighteenth-century sensibility, it brought us to tears!

Leisure time with friends in Dallas has helped to counterbalance the intensive labor that went into this book. I appreciate the caring community we have found among my husband's colleagues at Site Selection Group, especially Josh and Carrie Bays, Jenna and Teddy Cunningham, Beth and Philip Land, Carly Fritts, and Alison Boden. We are fortunate that my own colleague Vivek Virani and his family, Ria and Prema, are now our neighbors with whom we enjoy game nights, house concerts, pool time, and meals. I always look forward to book club brunches with Andrea K. Barreiro, Karisa Cloward, K. Ann Horsburgh, Jill E. Kelly, Bianca Lopez, and Elizabeth Russ. Benjamin Brand, Jill E. Kelly, Alexandra Letvin, and Brandon G. Miller have made Dallas home. Jill has provided expert advice on book writing, grant applications, and beyond. Hikes and backyard pizzas with Jill and Brandon sustained me through the final year of preparing this manuscript in the age of social distancing.

I am particularly grateful to four people who carried me through the more challenging moments of writing: James Q. Davies, Darren Mueller, April L. Prince, and Jillian C. Rogers. When I did not feel like showing up to write, Jill and I scheduled video chats to hold each other accountable. She offered generous feedback on almost every chapter and has been a constant companion since the moment I began archival research in 2012. April spent many evenings listening to my concerns about this project; her amazing ability to empathize and to laugh heartened me constantly. April and Jill have shared much with me both professionally and personally, and cheered me on relentlessly for years. I treasure my friendships with each of these strong, brilliant women. Darren's constant reassurance and sage advice always helped me to regroup. This book would not exist without his signature level-headed pep talks. He remains my trusted sounding board. Exchanges with James spanning three years and as many countries inspired the form this book has taken. He encouraged me to focus on property, patiently listened to the evolution of this project, and fueled the thinking that led to Chapter 6. This book would not be what it is if I had not gotten a bit lost in his musings about air and embraced his suggestion to take a bolder stance.

It is a unique gift to have friends and family who faithfully inquire about what must seem to them like hopelessly esoteric work. I am deeply grateful for my Penn State and Scranton friends—Sam and Corey, Ande and A.J., Carrie and Michael, Leslie and Chris, Patty, Professor Ronald McKinney, S.J., Joe Moore, Michael Popick, Wayne and Robin, and the Ryders (who now number in the dozens!). Caroline Erol makes every trip to France feel like a homecoming, and her parents, Isabelle and Pierre, always welcome me to Carnac as if I were part of the family. Quiet reflection and evening conversations in their yard yielded many of my arguments. I am grateful to my own family for their love and for their support of my academic pursuits, especially Matt Daigle; Chris and Allan; Mimi and Uncle Bob; Mare, Tim, and Ella; Morrie and Cathy Schwinden; the Walters; Lisa and Hilary; Aunt Bernie and Joe; and Aggie and Dad. This book exists because my parents, Gerard and Anne Geoffroy, provided for me in every way imaginable since the beginning. I come from a long line of women teachers and writers who inspire my career; the musical inspiration, however, came largely from the country and western piano of my Uncle Rick.

My husband, Chris Schwinden, and our foxhound, Hayley, were by my side at every stage of this project. Chris moved wherever my career necessitated and patiently tended to every high and low. His generous spirit, selfless sacrifices, and astounding work ethic gave me the time, space, and resources necessary to be myself, which at times became inextricable from this book. He also knew precisely when I needed some "Daily Affirmation" during moments of self-doubt. Hayley's scratches at the back door and her demands for treats pulled me away from my desk chair daily, reminding me of what really matters in life—my loved ones.

ABBREVIATIONS

BHVP   Bibliothèque historique de la Ville de Paris
F-Pan Archives nationales de France
F-Pn   Bibliothèque nationale de France
L.A.   Lettres Autographes
CNAM   Archives historiques, Musée des arts et métiers, Saint-Denis

NOTE ON TRANSLATION OF SOURCES

Many of the documents consulted for this project bear the orthographic and diacritical inconsistencies of eighteenth-century French writing. These have been maintained and labeled "sic" only where meaning may be obscured or where an error appears in a published source. Translations are my own unless otherwise indicated, and the original French is provided in the endnotes.

Introduction

During the promising early years of the French Revolution, the piano maker Tobias Schmidt wanted to be useful. He was likely motivated more by opportunity than altruism. His utilitarian resolution just happened to coincide with new property laws that granted valuable rewards and patents to "useful" inventions.[1] But Schmidt did not rely on his usual trade in keyboard instruments to pursue utility. Instead, he turned to a "rudimentary submarine" that he had been developing.[2] When two scheming competitors duped him into divulging the machine's secrets and patented it for themselves, Schmidt was left furious and empty-handed. He filed a complaint about the theft only days before the revolutionary law on inventions officially passed.[3]

Schmidt's workshop stood on the bustling Cour du Commerce Saint-André, a narrow alley of shops that still attracts tourists hoping to catch a glimpse of revolutionary Paris. Schmidt was alleged to struggle with alcoholism and, if so, he must have found it difficult to resist slipping through the back door of the passage's lively Café Procope, where famous one-named revolutionaries like Danton and Marat hatched their political plans over beverages late into the night. Their carousing probably hindered the sleep of another famous revolutionary living just across the way, Joseph-Ignace Guillotine, who in 1792 identified a perfect opportunity for his neighbor, Schmidt, to be useful.

As a representative in the revolutionary government, Guillotine found himself among a group of doctors seeking a more humane execution method. (The Revolution's *égalité* knew no limits.) At the time, the contraption used to separate human heads from bodies employed a curved blade and clunky mechanism that caused brutally cruel inconsistencies. A new design by the inventor Antoine Louis boasted a more efficient triangular blade and yolk promising a quicker, less painful demise. Schmidt proposed a far lower fee

From Servant to Savant. Rebecca Dowd Geoffroy-Schwinden, Oxford University Press. © Oxford University Press 2022.
DOI: 10.1093/oso/9780197511510.003.0001

to build Louis's improved execution device than the royal carpenter initially approached for the job and his technical skills in crafting smooth, heavy piano actions offered a perfect solution to Guillotine's problem. On April 17, 1792, enlightened doctors and surgeons gathered outside Paris to test Schmidt's work. After slaughtering live sheep and decapitating human corpses to their satisfaction, "the machine" soon began its famed revolutionary career. Although Guillotine would try to dissociate himself from the invention that came to bear his name, Schmidt attempted to capitalize on it by applying for a patent. The government rejected his request, reasoning that "It is humanly distasteful to grant a patent for an invention of this kind; we have not yet reached such a level of barbarity. While Monsieur Schmidt has produced a useful invention of a lethal kind, since it can be used only for carrying out legal sentences he must offer it to the government."[4] According the Revolution's new property regime, an individual could not own a macabre public "good" like the guillotine however "useful" it may have proven.

Schmidt's ordeal might seem like a mere amusing if somewhat ghastly anecdote of history. Yet it perfectly illustrates what this book reveals as a much broader and significant phenomenon. People working in the Parisian music world, from instrument builders to composers, tested the limits of the modern property regime born of the French Revolution. In the process, they began to establish professional and epistemic practices that would come to define modern professional musicianship and music historiography. Schmidt will not appear again until Chapter 6, but by the time he does it will be abundantly clear that his revolutionary frustrations occurred amidst an unimaginable complexity of laws and policies intended to delineate music as a form of private and public property. If before the Revolution music was an activity that required legal permissions (called *privilèges*), after the Revolution, music had evolved into an object that could be owned.

Musicologists agree that a tectonic musical shift occurred "around 1800."[5] Widely accepted historical narratives precede the seismic date. Over the course of the eighteenth century, the social status of musicians in Europe elevated from servants to artists as they found livelihoods outside the court and church. Music transformed from a form of monarchical representation into a commercial product consumed by a paying public and an aesthetic object contemplated by philosophers. As instrument technologies advanced rapidly, allowing for ever more nuanced musical expression, audiences began to revere the virtuoso performers and orchestras who mastered them with technical precision. Together, these novelties could be summarized succinctly as a change in musical production, put differently, a change in the way that people in Europe created, circulated, consumed, and consequently, conceived of music.

Despite its reputation as a global capital of literature and fashion at the time, France is often portrayed as an anomaly in this trajectory, as a place where heavy-handed absolutism prohibited the benefit concerts and generic experimentation that led to the musical innovations embraced in other cosmopolitan centers. Yet Paris nevertheless beckoned to professional musicians pursuing fame during this period. Mozart was dismayed by Paris's initial indifference toward him. Haydn conquered her remotely. Later, she tempted a Vienna-trapped Beethoven. Paris presided over Europe as its music publishing capital. And while in retrospect Paris seems to have taken up new performance models more slowly than her European peers, a single event forced Parisian musicians to confront their long-standing, ostensibly antiquated music world—the 1789 French Revolution.

In this book, I argue that the French Revolution was fundamental to these changes across cosmopolitan Europe because it abruptly ended a privilege-based system of musical production and set in its place a modern property regime. Almost quite literally overnight, music transformed from an activity requiring permission to an entity that could be possessed. When the New Regime required a strict delineation between private and public property,[6] musicians claimed music as their unalienable personal expression while the French nation appropriated it as the collective product of cultural heritage and national industry. Meanwhile, musicians' gradual, century-long professionalization became codified into revolutionary laws and institutions. From these circumstances emerged three lasting musical values: the composer's sovereignty, the work's inviolability, and the nation's supremacy. Although the appearance of these concepts "around 1800" is often attributed to Austro-Germanic philosophy and composers, here I reveal how they took shape in revolutionary Paris among a prolific cast of characters. Far from mere bystanders to the changes sweeping eighteenth-century Europe, Parisian musicians stood at the vanguard of musical production models and values that would come to dominate not only their profession but also the writing of music history. The Revolution may have abolished *privilège*, but revolutionary musicians replaced it with a more modern form of privilege predicated on property ownership and reliant on an exclusive class of individuals who held the right to evaluate music and control its production.

On Privilege, Property, and Professionalization

To comprehend how Parisian musicians contributed so significantly to changes in European musical production "around 1800," we must consider the coevolution among privilege, property, and professionalism first. Although this is a story about musicians in revolutionary Paris, it requires situation within a much longer history. The pre-1789 society of orders in France rigidly defined distinctions among the kingdom's subjects. In a population of around 27 million, about 150,000 clergy made up the First Estate,

350,000 nobles occupied the Second Estate, and everyone else, an overwhelming majority of the population (approximately 98%) constituted the Third Estate. The Third Estate was by no means homogeneous, it included well-off doctors, lawyers, and merchants as well as workers and starving peasants. And "Privilege," writes historian Jeff Horn, "was the beating heart of . . . Bourbon France;"[7] it shaped the conduct of everyone, including professional musicians.

The "privileged" enjoyed certain advantages distributed primarily in the form of legal exceptions that were called "privileges." Indeed, the word connoted both social and legal powers. Of the five entries for *privilège* in the 1694 Académie Française dictionary (the authoritative dictionary of the French language) the first entry defines it as "the faculty accorded to an individual, or to a community to do something at the exclusion of all others."[8] The second entry describes the legal acts by which these exceptions were granted, as well as the "rights, prerogatives, and advantages"[9] that came along with certain positions. The privileges granted by the monarch to individuals and groups ranged from tax exemptions for the church and nobility to craft monopolies for guilds or exclusive trade rights for particular communities. Members of the Third Estate usually accessed privilege collectively through social institutions like guilds or, later in the century, by purchasing offices that came along with certain privileges.[10] Eighteenth-century France inherited this interdependency between social and legal privilege as a vestige of feudalism, the medieval socioeconomic structure through which people protected their land, kin, and limb, by exchanging objects and rights across networks of unequal power relations.

Privilege colored everything from leisure activities to financial matters, reaching widely and deeply into everyday life, even into music. Musical privilege, as I call it in Chapter 1, similarly extended from the trivial to the prodigious. In a small town in southern France, a noblewoman held the legal privilege to dictate when the violin could be played in the streets,[11] while the Ballard family maintained an exclusive privilege to print music in France for nearly 200 years. An exclusive privilege granted rights to do something at the exclusion of all others. Such a privilege protected three royally sanctioned stages in Paris until the Revolution: the Opéra, the Comédie-Française, and, later, the Comédie-Italienne. It is precisely this theatrical dimension of privilege that tends to receive emphasis in musicological studies. I suggest here, however, that privilege demands a much wider investigation in the world of Old Regime musical production.

Over the course of the eighteenth century, slight changes to the definition of privilege associated it more palpably with property. The 1694 dictionary's primary definition of property, which persisted through the 1798 edition, described it as, "the right, the title by which a thing belongs to someone."[12] This distinction must be emphasized: In eighteenth-century France, one did not truly own or possess property so much as one held a right to use it. Ownership, use rights, and power were thus inseparable in prerevolutionary France.[13] If the king was sovereign over France and its subjects then one needed a powerful position with privileges attached to it in order to enjoy the use of the kingdom's bounties. The 1762 dictionary linked privilege to property in legal terms, where privilege might refer to one's preference in a mortgage agreement.[14] By midcentury, French subjects understood privilege as a right to some aspect of a "property;" this usage indicates a much broader phenomenon. The system of rights to lands and immovable properties became so complex by the end of the eighteenth century in France that the phrase "fiefs in the air" came to describe properties for which privileged individuals high up in a mortgage chain collected revenue even while hardly owning them.[15] Whether legally accurate or not, privileges had come to be perceived as a very close corollary to or in some cases even synonymous with private property.

By 1789, the *Dictionnaire critique de la langue Française* replicated, in concise form, all of the previous definitions of privilege, but coupled it with the term *privilégié*: one who possesses a privilege, a "privileged person."[16] Although *privilégié* appeared in previous dictionaries, in 1789 the two words appeared within a single entry. By linking privilege, property, and "the privileged," the dictionary revealed the system's dark underneath, where revolutionaries would soon shine a light, setting it ablaze. The final definition of privilege, consistent from 1694 to 1798, seems to warn of such combustibility, "a liberty that one has or gives oneself to do things that others would not dare to do."[17] Only some individuals, usually those from the First and Second Estates, dared to endeavor certain activities. They granted themselves permission to do as they liked, an arbitrary advantage that would soon bring down a nearly millennium-old political system.

Scholars identify two of the French Revolution's defining legacies as the Abolition of Privilege and the birth of modern property rights, yet the authoritative French dictionaries' definitions of privilege and property remained remarkably stable throughout the eighteenth century.[18] Dissonance between the record of meaning and the reality of evolving concepts stemmed at least in part from the fraught political project of defining words. For example, in 1798, as revolution waned and the French government remained in flux, one new dictionary acknowledged that some concepts associated with corporate privilege like *corporations*, *jurande*, and *maîtrise*, had been abolished, while its definition of other Old Regime words, such as "king," remained largely unchanged, even after France had committed regicide.[19] Such lexical discrepancies demand a turn to the lived experiences of privilege and property as a means to understand their fundamental place in this musical story. After all, "the term 'property,'" explains historian Rafe Blaufarb, "was an empty signifier, a battleground, not a solid concept with a fixed definition."[20]

It is precisely this battleground, in musical terms, that this book sets out to examine.

The Old Regime privilege system required professional musicians to affiliate and collaborate with privileged institutions like noble households, the royal court, theaters, publishers, and guilds, in order to maintain legal and social status as well as economic agency. Such dependency has led scholars to describe early modern musicians as "servants." Part I, "Musical Privilege," shows that professional musicians in many ways succeeded in acquiring both legal and concomitant social privileges under the Old Regime through fissures created by the growth of liberal professionalism, economic deregulation, and collective aristocratic patronage over the course of the eighteenth century.[21] Musicians eventually came to consider themselves not as servants, but as professionals—experts who received specialized education requiring both theoretical and practical knowledge to enhance discrete technical skills. I define "professional" musician here as a person who secured their livelihood primarily from money earned through some aspect of musical production. This definition productively opens up the category "musician" from narrower definitions like composers and performers to a wider "music world," in Howard Becker's sense of the phrase, including publishers, concert managers, instrument builders, and others.[22] I frequently maintain contemporaneous terminologies employed by historical subjects to emphasize the diverse kinds of professional musicianship that emerged in eighteenth-century Paris. Oftentimes one individual fulfilled numerous musical roles.

It is enlightening then to consider musicianship alongside a number of other fields that also professionalized in eighteenth-century France, from more obvious corollaries like writing and painting, to surgery, dentistry, pharmacy, cooking, architecture, the military arts, and engineering.[23] Although the field of sociology offers extensive literature on theories of professionalization, these tend to presume an industrial or capitalist system anachronistic to the prerevolutionary context. Musicological studies usually address professionalization either in the generalities suggested by the opening narrative of this chapter or in detailed chronicles of particular cosmopolitan contexts that differed greatly from Paris.[24] A set of common parameters by which fields including musicianship professionalized in eighteenth-century France prove more instructive in unpacking the significance of the Revolution to music history. The criteria for professionalization traced throughout this narrative include enhanced legal recognition of professional practices and products; wider social acceptance among peers in other fields; standardization of techniques, training, accreditation, and tools; and increased public authority. These changes arise in every chapter of this book. The degree of authority that some musicians managed to achieve before the Revolution gave them the opportunity to negotiate certain aspects of their changing field after 1789. As shown in Part II, "Property," professional changes straddled the revolutionary fault line and crystallized under the New Regime. The coevolution of music alongside other professions significantly impacted musicians' epistemic practices.[25] Moreover, musicians offer a poignant example of how a specific profession weathered the revolutionary tides, an upheaval that ravaged some workers and professionals even as it raised others.

In secondary literature, the professionalization of musicianship during the eighteenth century tends to be taken for granted and at face value. Even when it serves as a focus of study, composers usually enjoy the spotlight. Recent musicological studies, however, have shown the significance of amateur musical practice during this period.[26] One cannot understand professionalism without amateurism and vice versa because these categories continually defined one another.[27] As professional musicianship took hold in Europe, new standards prevented those who lacked credentials from securing a place in the world of musical production regardless of their talents. A widening schism between amateur and professional music-making, naturalized during the nineteenth century and institutionalized by organizations like the Paris Conservatory, led to an understanding of musicianship itself as inherently professional, and therefore as gendered (male) and raced (white). By exposing this process of professionalization then, I also historicize the construction of what remains by many measures a prohibitively exclusive profession.

My title signals a transition "from servant to savant." The term "savant" in the early eighteenth century referred to a person typically within an academy who developed abstract theories and established the rules of their art or science.[28] Over the course of the century, savants began to engage with a wider Parisian public and therefore exhibited a kind of sociability distinct from the detachment of their seventeenth-century predecessors.[29] By 1789 savants in the old sense of the term came to be viewed as pedantic, antiquated, and perhaps even oblivious to reality. This perception proved all the better for musicians who had rarely if ever been considered savants anyway. Composers like Étienne-Nicolas Méhul and François-Joseph Gossec found prestigious positions in national institutions formed under the Revolution precisely because they represented a new kind of savant, with reverence for the practicalities of economic necessity and the mysteries rather than the rules of artistic genius. A unique professional trajectory allowed some musicians to transform into the epitome of postrevolutionary savants while others remained servants to the nation.

The Abolition of Privilege

Despite the many continuities between the Old and New Regime described throughout this book, the night of August 4 represented a notable rupture when France suddenly abolished privilege.[30] It occurred amid a succession of dramatic political events that took place during the summer of 1789. A confluence of challenges prompted the king to reconvene the Estates General, an advisory group made up of representatives from all three estates last called on by Louis XIII in 1614. Nearly two centuries later, Louis XVI urgently needed input on how to salvage his sinking ship. A fiscal crisis arose after supporting the American Revolution. An economic calamity seemed to loom as fear of famine spread. Since the early eighteenth century the Crown lost ever more control over a Parisian culture that critiqued the monarchy. All the while, religion's promise of salvation became less appealing than the possibility of material fulfillment in this life. Desacralization weakened the king's God-given authority. If only one facet of the French nation had wavered—fiscal, economic, cultural, or social—perhaps the monarchy could have remained afloat. Instead, representatives from near and far traveled to Paris carrying their constituents' *cahiers de doléances*, their "lists of grievances," and prepared to offer suggestions for the kingdom's improvement. The Estates General opened on May 5, 1789.

Its Third Estate representatives were largely moderate men.[31] But they faced a highly charged environment in Paris and arrived ill-prepared to face the shouting throngs, brutal working hours, and seemingly insurmountable complexities cobbled into the French system over centuries of dysfunction. Deputies began by debating the custom of voting by estate—each estate cast one vote agreed on by its members collectively, a practice which gave an unfair advantage to the mutual concerns of the First and Second Estates. The Third Estate requested double representation to rectify the disparity. In his pamphlet *What Is the Third Estate?*, published only five months before the Estates General convened, the Abbé Emmanuel-Joseph Sieyes proposed that although the Third Estate was "nothing" in France, it deserved to be "something."[32] The Third Estate, he argued, not only produced the most wealth but also contributed to the collective good more than the other two estates, thus, it represented "everything" to the nation.[33] On June 20, the Third Estate found itself locked out of the Versailles hall where the Estates General had been scheduled to gather. Presuming themselves purposely excluded (a misunderstanding, it would turn out, of epic proportions), they met instead on the indoor Versailles tennis court, joined by a few priests who had defected from the First Estate. There, they pledged to remain, by virtue of their sovereignty as the true nation and vowed to work together to establish a new constitution. They recast themselves as the National Assembly, and the king, the other estates, and all of France eventually accepted them as such. On July 14, the fall of the Bastille prison symbolically destroyed a system of abstract justice that had dictated every aspect of French subjects' lives for centuries, what the musicologist Olivia Bloechl calls the "traumatic structure of life in the ancien régime."[34] That summer, the French began to reimagine their nation.

On August 4 the National Assembly met to continue their exhausting deliberations.[35] As the evening wore on, a revolutionary spirit fueled by liberty, equality, and fraternity, apparently moved representatives to stand up one by one and renounce their many individual privileges. Yet, as could be inferred from the above descriptions of privilege, a renunciation of privilege relinquished much more than mere titles. By the morning of August 5, the rubble of a feudal socioeconomic system smoldered around the representatives. They had created a momentous task—to construct new legal foundations where privileges once stood.

A French acquaintance recently described the night of August 4 to me as "the *real* Revolution." It is easy to comprehend why the night's mythic tale of self-sacrifice continues to shine in French national memory. As Blaufarb succinctly puts it, until that fateful night, the Old Regime legal system had coupled property with power.[36] Put simply, people earned access to use certain property from the monarch by virtue of the power they held personally through legally privileged positions. Rather than owning property outright, French subjects until 1789 held the rights to *use* property—usufructuary rights.[37] Titles and offices were (or at least seemed to be) bought, sold, and inherited, granting personal access to this powerful sphere.[38] This was even true for musicians, who could arrange the inheritance of friends or family members' lucrative positions at court. Privileges therefore defined property's uses under the Old Regime. When privilege was abolished, property remained, but it had to be allocated differently.

The Declaration of the Rights of Man, published two weeks after the Abolition of Privilege, attempted to decouple property and power by granting everyone sovereignty over their personal domain.[39] This meant that rights to property no longer emanated from the monarch alone. The Declaration has since been drawn on exhaustively in debates about property and human rights in the modern West: "Since property is an inviolable and sacred right, no one shall be deprived thereof except where public necessity, legally determined, shall clearly demand it, and then only on condition that the owner shall have been previously and equitably indemnified."[40] This mandate necessitated a stricter delineation between private property and public goods like bridges, roads, and water (and apparently, guillotines), which, according to the New Regime (and as we saw in the case of Schmidt), individuals could not own. The revolutionary government replaced the formerly royal domain with a national domain intending to empty it; the plan was to sell all government-held properties, thereby placing all property in the hands of private individuals except for public utilities.[41] But the Declaration made two conflicting priorities clear: individual and national rights. Philosophical debates about natural rights have long questioned the extent to which an individual suspends their personal rights upon entering political society. The French like the Americans, Dan Edelstein explains, settled on a "preservation regime," which preserves individuals' rights in society.[42] This concern for the individual led to the legal dismantling of corporate privileges like guilds early in the Revolution.

Under the New Regime, individuals, institutions, and the nation all hoped to gain something from owning music: a livelihood, fame, a legitimizing cultural heritage, or a commercially competitive industry. Part II, "Property," chronicles Parisian musicians grappling with the new policies and laws affecting their profession. Music, like other cultural products, complicated the New Regime's separation of public and private property. Divorced from privilege, music became a legally delimited entity that could belong to individuals as personal property (Chapter 3) or to the nation, as a cultural heritage (Chapters 4 and 5) and a national industry (Chapter 6). While it may be tempting to explain music's public capacity as a simple conversion from monarchical to national political representation, this change in proprietary logic had profound consequences for modern musical production.[43] Although revolutionary music has long been interpreted as a manifestly cultural or political phenomenon, when situated in a longer history of privilege, professionalization, and property, Parisian musicians' activities during the 1790s appear remarkably more complex and meaningful than zealous singing at the barricades.

The Politics of Historiography and the Archive

Scholarly focus on the politics of revolutionary musicians has deflected attention from the politics of the historiography and archives from whence their story came. The unique disciplinary turns of both French revolutionary studies and musicology have until recently obscured the Revolution's formative effects on modern musicianship and music historiography. Here I weave together a tale of two historiographies in order to demonstrate how their entwined legacies now allow for a productive reassessment of music and the French Revolution.

To begin with, the French Revolution's history is always also about the present, reaching as far back as Alexis de Tocqueville's *L'Ancien Régime et la Révolution* (1856), which cast the Revolution as the ultimate triumph of Louis XIV's project to centralize France. De Tocqueville's interpretation reflects the apparent failure of the republican agenda under Napoleon III's Second Empire (1848–1870). When revolutionary historiography was institutionalized at the Sorbonne, Alphonse Aulard, the first Chair of History of the French Revolution, saw the "republicanism and positivism" of the First Republic (1792–1804) reanimated in his own historical moment—the birth of the Third Republic (1870–1940).[44] Forged from the fall of Napoleon III and the Franco-Prussian war in 1870, the Third Republic looked back to the Revolution in an attempt to finally cast aside the tyranny of monarchy.[45] This period, not coincidentally, also saw the first significant wave of musicological research on the Revolution, most notably in publications by Constant Pierre and Marie Bobillier, a woman who worked under the male pen name Michel Brenet.[46] Jann Pasler elucidates in exacting detail how the First Republic's legacy contributed to music's expansive role in Third Republic politics and citizen formation.[47] Pierre and Bobillier's catalogs and chronicles, based on the robust archival record of Old Regime and revolutionary music, provided a tremendous foundation for future researchers. Yet Pierre's particular focus on materials from the Paris Conservatory and its contributions to revolutionary festivals seemed to cast revolutionary musicians as overtly political—a decided virtue for Third Republic purposes, but an interpretation that has disproportionately shaped subsequent understandings of music in the revolutionary decade.[48]

The twentieth-century revolution that led to the formation of the Soviet Union recast the French Revolution's "present" yet again, prompting Aulard's student, Albert Mathiez, to consider it through a "popular, socialist, and Leninist" lens.[49] Mathiez's contemporary, Georges Lefebvre, who became the Sorbonne's Chair in the History of the French Revolution in 1937, furthered this reading in his focus on sociology and social structure, ultimately developing a "Marxianized republican interpretation" of the Revolution.[50] Lefebvre's student Albert Soboul ascended to his mentor's position in 1967 and insisted on this account of the Revolution as a bourgeois class struggle necessary to the "transition from feudalism to capitalism."[51] Historian François Furet, however, soon outwardly rejected this Marxist socioeconomic interpretation. Furet initiated what came to be known as a revisionist historiography, which read the Revolution as a political and cultural phenomenon born of a "constitutional crisis that paralyzed the Old Regime monarchy."[52] (Some might wonder whether Furet's historiographic turn was equally rooted in his disagreements with the Communist Party, a possibility that shows revolutionary historiography as not only perpetually presentist but also personal.[53]) The Marxist interpretation of the Revolution indeed cast an anachronistic industrial-capitalist framework onto a crumbling mercantilist, emergent free market system, and attributed monolithic class allegiances onto people who in historical reality carried far more complex identities. Identity soon became a central focus for historians who had come to agree that the French Revolution represented a primarily political and cultural conflict. Lynn Hunt, among others, insisted on the coconstitution of politics and culture in seminal revisionist work.[54] So vast and diverse is the revisionist historiography and the new cultural history of the French Revolution that followed in Furet's wake that I could not possibly account for this body of scholarship here.[55]

Revolutionary historiography's cultural turn will sound familiar to historical musicologists, who at the same time during the 1980s and '90s began to consider culture as their primary object of study, a disciplinary turn dubbed the New Musicology. This methodological change decentered composer biographies and scores, and consequently, included diverse people and traditions into a historiography previously dominated by white, Austro-Germanic, or, when most generous, European men. Opera and popular music consequently became prominent topics of study; revolutionary music lent itself to both emergent subfields.

Music seemed a natural fit for studies of revolutionary political culture because it provided fertile ground for the analysis of identity formation, expression, and representation, or, more insidiously, propaganda. A number of edited volumes about music during the French Revolution appeared around the bicentenary.[56] Two seminal monographs, written by historians rather than musicologists, soon followed. Laura Mason demonstrated that popular singing became a legitimate form of political activism during the early Revolution before it hid from censorship in the sociopolitical underground of nineteenth-century Paris.[57] James H. Johnson speculated that revolutionaries' belief in the power of music contributed to Parisians' subsequent adoption of absorbed listening practices.[58] His instinct to connect the Revolution to musical romanticism was not isolated. And yet a decade earlier the prominent German musicologist Carl Dahlhaus, who like the revisionists rejected Marxism, had already resisted accepting the Revolution as a musical fault line.[59] Even as some scholars ultimately heeded Dahlhaus's warning by correcting foundational claims that the Revolution represented a distinct rupture in musical style,[60] French music from the 1790s has struggled to shake its propagandistic reputation. As the musicologist Michael Fend has explained, the French Revolution posed a "problem" for musicologists' traditional methods.[61] With the exception of opera and popular song, the revolutionary decade has been treated as a curiosity in music studies, more relevant subsequently for what it inspired rather than holding any intrinsic value for music historiography more broadly. Scholars outside of musicology have trumpeted the Revolution's significance for music far more.[62] For musicologists at a remove from the discipline's French niche, if the Revolution's political ideals of individualism provided a convenient shorthand to herald romantic subjectivity among the likes of Beethoven, its music less gloriously granted composers license to be loud, pictorial, and overtly political, or even, in Haydn's estimation, downright "trashy."[63] Musicology has therefore acknowledged the Revolution's simultaneity with the discipline's "seismic date," 1800, yet continues to consider it more as a harbinger than a watershed.

In many ways this book reassesses the foundations of music history; I do not wish to construct a new master narrative but rather to historicize and critique an influential one that still haunts the discipline. Revolutionary music comfortably lent itself to opera and popular music studies, both considered acceptable Others to the long dominant historical narrative of

Viennese Classicism rooted in philosophy and built upon the legacies of Mozart, Haydn, and Beethoven. By maintaining distinctions among cultural, social, intellectual, and all manner of music histories, the discipline's Austro-Germanic interpretations covertly retained dominance of the "high art" version of music history that many musicologists now experience as the elephant in their classrooms. A number of studies address the construction of this narrative in Austria and Germany,[64] but few expose its other continental origins. It remains admittedly taboo to return to discourses about "genius" composers and their "masterpieces" since the risk of reifying these problematic terms lurks around every corner. Silence around these concepts, however, prohibits a more robust understanding of how musicology ever arrived at such an apparent historiographic crisis in the first place and how professional "Classical" musicianship continues to reflect and perpetuate now troubling Enlightenment and "Romantic" values.[65] Certain legacies can only be dismantled by scrutinizing the history of how they came into being.

This book therefore collapses received distinctions among cultural, political, social, legal, economic, and technological histories of music, to reveal a material rather than philosophical origin of concepts like the sovereignty of composers, the inviolability of musical works, and the supremacy and centrality of the nation over cultural and industrial realms. Musicological studies have increasingly turned to the varied material conditions of musical production.[66] In this study, "material" refers to infrastructure, policy, law, and institutions, as well as to musical scores, manuscripts, methods, and instruments; in other words, the materials and the material realities of professional musicianship. I show how the navigation and negotiation of these conditions gave rise to discourses and epistemic practices that later came to characterize musical production models under capitalism. Although I corroborate, in the case of France, some of the musical changes around 1800 already identified by philosopher Lydia Goehr,[67] I more importantly provide nuanced evidence for how musical "works" and composers became centered in a modern system of musical production destined to support nationalist, imperialist, and colonialist endeavors, even before discourses about genius and masterworks had ossified.[68]

Institutional histories of revolutionary music, especially those in opera studies, successfully resist one-dimensional political readings of the Revolution and thus represent a significant predecessor to my work.[69] Scholars have given nuanced attention to eighteenth-century French opera as a genre within its institutional contexts.[70] Mark Darlow's extensive archival research on the Opéra's administration during the French Revolution proves it impossible to attribute any coherent political agenda to repertory choices. Julia Doe has recently shown that the politics attributed to revolutionary musical "canons," and even entire genres, tend to overlook prerevolutionary origins and practical reasons for the success of certain works.[71] In the case of *opéra comique* Doe provides a perfect example of how a genre's history was conscripted for political purposes during the nineteenth century.[72] French scholars have similarly given careful attention to venues outside the operatic context such as concerts and instrumental genres like the *symphonie concertante*.[73] The Paris Conservatory has for obvious reasons earned its own body of scholarly literature beginning with Pierre's early archival work during the Third Republic.[74] Indeed, in Jean Mongrédien's estimation, institutions constitute the Revolution's defining musical legacy.[75] I mostly sideline discrete genres and venues in this book precisely because these detailed studies are so authoritative; *From Servant to Savant* complements this rich body of literature by focusing on how individuals navigated their professional work across institutions.

My methodology therefore puts pressure on the archival logic that underlies institutional and genre histories. French revolutionaries and their successors cultivated archives with the express purpose of writing a certain version of their own history; the revolutionary archive quite intentionally conceals as much as it discloses because its original mission was to constitute a new future for the French nation.[76] Thus, by pushing against archival organization and expanding outside the silos of institutions and their genres, I have uncovered the competing agendas that animated the Parisian music world during the Revolution.[77] I identify the complexities of the revolutionary music project by probing the relationality between institutions and individuals rather than the coherent narratives that neat document collections seem to suggest. I returned to archives that had been partially or seemingly wholly published in order to reappraise their physicality and as a result found evidence that had been overlooked or excluded because it did not fit particular narratives or institutionalized memory. In some cases, documents simply eluded clear classification and therefore went unnoticed, for example, a letter from the composer André-Ernest-Modeste Grétry left to linger among the personal papers of Sieyes.[78] My archival research always originated with questions about how musicians navigated the shifting socioeconomic and legal terrain beneath them and what they did on the "battlefield," in Blaufarb's words, to generate meaning around an "empty signifier"—property.

A precedent for my methodology can be found not only in the histories of eighteenth-century French music institutions cited earlier but also in recent revolutionary scholarship that has successfully synthesized earlier political and cultural turns in the field to reassess the significance of economic and legal experiences of the Revolution. William H. Sewell Jr., who pioneered the cultural turn in the 1980s, has recently called for scholars to return their attention to socioeconomic aspects of the Revolution.[79] Rebecca Spang redeemed economics from its Marxist historiographic shame by revealing daily struggles around currency during the Revolution.[80] And Katie Jarvis's research on market women during the Revolution takes an "experience-centered" approach to the economic conditions that women faced, and the politics and sociality that arose around these material concerns.[81] Blaufarb meanwhile confirmed a long-held belief: the Revolution's lasting legacy was the establishment of a modern property regime, what he calls "the great demarcation."[82] After years of the bewildering volume and diversity of revisionist historiography, Paul Cheney found solace in Blaufarb's work, where historians of the Revolution could finally identify the delineation of "state and civil society" as a convincing and coherent revolutionary project.[83] Blaufarb's conclusions about land and real estate can be extended and translated to other realms of revolutionary experience. I address how the reckoning between state and civil society through property affected musicians and ultimately music history.

This book thus contributes to new hybrid material-cultural histories in both musicology and French revolutionary studies. Property is coterminous with the history of rights. From the perspective of discourse analysis, Edelstein has demonstrated that the Enlightenment individualist understanding of natural rights which preceded the Revolution "were essentially, and almost wholly, property rights."[84] By relating material conditions to arguments about rights, historians have begun to reconsider the Revolution's socioeconomic effects independent of Marxist interpretations. Carla Hesse and Katie Scott have both addressed professionalization and cultural products through property. Hesse showed how legal changes around author's rights during the Revolution situated authors in an interstitial place in revolutionary society.[85] Scott brings together the history of property and aesthetic theory to argue that visual artists transformed from patronized court artists into "bourgeois entrepreneurs" through emergent intellectual property rights.[86] I, too, return to production and to labor in search of professional musicians' lived experience of a new, modern property regime. Experience paints a blurrier picture of political identities and implicates music in domains beyond aesthetics (style) and activism (politics). I maintain the revisionists' faith in culture as a conduit to understanding human agency in times of political upheaval. Yet I remain vigilant to the reality that Spang made abundantly clear—individuals struggled to maintain control over "stuff and money"[87] through everyday revolutionary politics, and this negotiation was the very basis for survival during the fitful emergence of modernity.

Chapter Summaries

To focus solely on the Revolution would imply only rupture where many long and contiguous progressions merged. The background provided in Part I, "Musical Privilege," sets forth important precedents for my 1790s chronicle.

Chapter 1 supports a basic claim: musical production in eighteenth-century Paris was deeply embedded within the Old Regime system of legal *privilèges*. This assertion must strike specialists of the period as quite obvious. Extensive scholarship elucidates how the privilege system inflected music publishing and theatre in particular and life under the Old Regime more generally. In this chapter I shift focus, however, from the effects of privilege on discrete sectors of musical production to the ramifications of privilege as the dominant infrastructure through which musical production took place until 1789. In short, privileges provided a paradoxical conduit to professionalization before the Revolution. In the second chapter, "Social *Privilège* and Musician-Masons," I illuminate the social status of musicians in the context of Parisian Masonic Lodges during the 1770s and '80s. A series of significant phenomena coalesced in Masonic lodges. Instrumental music, known to take hold slowly in Paris, became a popular form of entertainment, placing composers and performers center-stage. Musicians gained opportunities to fraternize among one another in lodges and also among other professionals outside of royal or religious organizations. Composers connected with writers, whose professional advances they would draw on, as shown in Chapter 3. And finally, as in other sociable spaces like salons, lodges exposed musicians to talk of natural rights and social utility.[88] Musicians essentially gained an opportunity to take part in what the historian Kenneth Loiselle has termed an apprenticeship in classical republicanism.[89] Masonic lodges provided a social privilege distinct from the legal privileges found in the guilds and academies discussed in Chapter 1. Part I reveals the interdependency of social and legal privilege under the Old Regime and contends that professional musicians were well positioned when the Revolution began to make authoritative claims in their changing field.

Part II, "Property," explores the contradictory claims to musical proprietorship that emerged after the Abolition of Privilege. Chapters 3 through 6 are therefore arranged thematically around the competing conceptions of musical property that coalesced under the New Regime. At the heart of each chapter lies revolutionary policies, legislation, and laws: The Le Chapelier Laws and the "Declaration of the Rights of Genius" in Chapter 3; government rewards made available to struggling artists in Chapter 4; legislation founding the Paris Conservatory in Chapters 4 and 5; laws legalizing the confiscation of church and *émigré* property and treaties permitting the acquisition of foreign cultural property in Chapter 5; and laws on inventors' property rights in Chapter 6. Chapter 3 finds composers beginning to claim legal sovereignty over their expression, as those associated with the printing and sale of music tried to establish a system of production that made works alienable for commercial gains. Assertions about works' inviolability came from composers' claims to authority and were only exacerbated by imperatives to preserve music as a kind of cultural heritage discussed in Chapters 3 through 5. Chapter 4 shows how musicians became public servants, and their work the nation's property. Chapters 4 and 5 illuminate the standardization of techniques, training, and accreditation, in the Paris Conservatory, legally established in 1795, which consummated the professionalization begun a decade earlier. As the Conservatory set about establishing its curriculum, Chapter 5 exposes a concern for collecting and displaying musical works by "great masters" that motivated the French to confiscate scores and instruments from *émigré* households and enemy territories for a "museum" housed in the new institution. A complex logic of musical universalism and French exceptionalism fueled an imperial appropriation of cultural property for the nation, in the process, objectifying musical works and prioritizing composers in order to write a new music history for a future, regenerated French society. Chapter 6 reveals that performers' technical skills and instrument technologies gained increased attention once music was legally conceived of as a national industry necessary to economic revitalization. As music entwined with technical education, technological innovation, and scientific experimentation, it joined a national domain of public goods that individuals could not possess, a development that supported the nation's, and especially the Conservatory's bids to own French music.

The professional gains traced here should not be mistaken for liberation. The fiction of musical "triumph" during the Revolution is crafted from facile equations between revolutionary political rhetoric and myths of romantic freedom.[90] Over the course of this narrative, music becomes a material resource collected, measured, valuated, divided, and possessed. It hangs in the balance as both a tangible object for national exploitation and an intangible expression, the composer's (and sometimes the performer's) inalienable property. Competing property interests exacerbated chasms among actors in the Parisian music world. Conflicting views of musical proprietorship crystalized rigid conceptions of composers and their works, which in turn became deeply embedded within nineteenth-century nationalism, imperialism, and colonialism. This book reveals material realities of musical production and epistemic practices that made so-called musical Romanticism possible.[91]

PART I

Musical Privilege

1 | Legal *Privilège* and Musical Production

On a crisp Saturday morning in January 1708, Suzanne Peigné, the widow of a Parisian book seller, purchased music from a mysterious "man wearing a scarlet cloak."[1] The score, *Proserpine*, was a nearly three-decades-old opera composed by Jean-Baptiste Lully and authored by Philippe Quinault.[2] Their 1680 collaboration resurrected Quinault to royal favor after King Louis XIV's mistress, Madame de Montespan, had banished the librettist from court. But by the winter day when Suzanne placed the volume for sale on the River Seine parapet, both men were long dead and even the king's fallen lover had been laid to rest one year earlier. The legal *privilèges* dictating the text's circulation, however, continued to haunt the streets of Paris.

Later that same afternoon the deceased composer's son, Jean-Baptiste de Lully *fils*, happened upon Suzanne's display during his walk along the quai de l'École. An adamant defender of his family's hard-won status, Lully *fils* retained the nobiliary particle "de" in his surname, an honor that his father had initially feigned and eventually earned upon ennoblement as a *conseiller-secrétaire du roi*.[3] Contemporaries and historians alike have disregarded the contested syllable. Yet such quibbles mattered deeply to Lully *fils*. He became distressed upon realizing that the *Proserpine* score lacked an imprint of his father's official signature to confirm its compliance with a contract signed in 1680 by Lully, Quinault, and the music printer Christophe Ballard.[4] The agreement divided revenues from the sale of Lully-Quinault publications three ways among the signatories. No official signature meant no guarantee that Lully or his heirs had received their share of the profits. After an ordeal involving the dramatic seizure of Suzanne's score and a heated series of interrogations at the Châtelet courts, Lully *fils* failed to convince officials of his familiar claim; he had doggedly initiated and lost similar cases in those years around 1700, causing Christophe to incur steep legal fees in the process.

Their long-running generational dispute opens a revealing window into the power of musical privilege in Old Regime France.

Although the term did not exist during this period, "musical privilege" succinctly describes how many types of legal *privilèges* interlocked under Louis XIV's reign to secure a small group of individuals and institutions into control over Parisian musical production, from printing and selling scores to organizing performances and inventing new music technologies. Before the French Revolution, music-making was by and large an activity that required some form of *privilège*, which granted the legal permission to do something at the exclusion of others. Privileges thus generated a paradoxical mode of governance through simultaneous liberty ("you may do this") and restraint ("and no one else may"). Fiscal privilege came in the form of tax exemptions;[5] economic privilege in the form of trade or manufacturing monopolies;[6] political privilege in the form of powerful positions within the increasingly complex bureaucracy spreading from Versailles throughout the provinces;[7] and social privilege in the form of honorific allowances such as the right to carry a sword.[8] The bidding wars waged for privileges among guilds, towns, and individuals financially benefited the Crown. All privileges were in essence legal as well as royal—juridical formalities confirmed them and the monarch could revoke them, though on occasion it required him to spar with the French courts. Some historians have compared the system to England's constitutionalism even as others warn against such conclusions given the divided decisions of the French courts, called Parlements, which confirmed various royal decrees.[9] As this chapter and the next illuminate, all types of privilege affected professional musicians because these legal permissions inflected almost every aspect of musical production, from patronage to performance, publishing, and technical innovation.

During Louis XIV's reign, musical privilege concentrated in the church and court among members of the First and Second Estates, respectively. Musicians often negotiated or purchased positions within these institutions then passed them on through family and kinship networks.[10] Securing a position at court, while costly, could prove massively beneficial.[11] Despite all their differences, Lully *fils* and Christophe Ballard shared this advantage: their aging fathers had carefully arranged for their children to receive certain privileged positions. Prior to Lully's demise, the king granted the twelve-year-old Lully *fils* an appointment in a Carcassonne abbey. Even though the position "assured him a cozy income,"[12] the savvy heir found a way to trade this position up to an even more lucrative ecclesiastical post. Music hence did not belong to musicians so much as musicians themselves belonged to legally privileged institutions.[13]

Musical production in this context could therefore be described as relatively feudal or more specifically what Alain Viala calls *clientélisme*, a patronage relationship characterized by service.[14] Members of the Second Estate paternalistically cared for "their" musicians because musicians counted among the loyal servants who lived in noble households.[15] Lines blurred between domestic servants and musicians, two distinct roles sometimes fulfilled simultaneously by the same individuals.[16] Music patronage signaled social and political exclusivity. French music patrons formed part of a group described by Hilton L. Root as "the very privileged," who enjoyed legal privileges coterminous with their status.[17] Because privileges granted some individuals freedom by restricting others, they enhanced monarchical control and created a "fountain of privilege" most concentrated at the top of society.[18] Ordained by God, the king passed privilege down through an ever-expanding pyramid of people and institutions below him.

Musical privilege flowed from the Crown through many channels. The processes necessary to obtain a privilege varied as widely as the activities that required permission, from implementing a new music-printing method to establishing a concert series. A privilege may have been granted directly from the monarch as a royal grace such as the Opéra privilege bestowed on Lully. It could have come along with a purchased or appointed office like the one Lully *fils* occupied. Some privileges were partially leased from someone who already held it, as in the case of the Concert Spirituel. Alternatively, a privilege might have originated from an intricate series of highly regulated formalities. The complex web of Crown administration and guild bureaucracy that distributed printing privileges provides just one example of the system's labyrinthine networks.[19] And distinct networks indeed formed once Louis XIV's administration opened the privilege tap, hoping to generate revenue and control.[20] Eventually not only the nobility but also those with lesser titles or no titles at all could enjoy fiscal privileges that drew in expendable income to patronize music. As privileges continued to regulate music-making, opportunities nevertheless arose for professional musicians to work more autonomously from privileged individuals and institutions. This chapter demonstrates that paradoxically the influx of privileges from the late seventeenth century onward contributed to the professionalization of Parisian musicians and to their rise from servitude. Parisian musicians elevated from court servants to cosmopolitan artists by obtaining expanded legal rights, professional autonomy, and institutional authority through the many channels forged by privilege. Consequently, professional musicians found themselves well positioned when the French Revolution began in 1789 with an astonishing, unimaginable event—the Abolition of Privilege.

Historians in recent decades have more closely scrutinized privileges because of the fundamental role they played in the Crown's fiscal and political crisis during the 1780s. Musicologists have mostly taken privileges for granted as the price of entry into Old Regime music-making rather than as a significant object of study in their own right; consequently, they have focused quite narrowly on theatrical privilege. I do not delve into the intricate business of negotiating, securing, and leasing musical privileges here because each case would require its own detailed study due to the idiosyncrasies of every transaction. My goal is more modest: To expose the privilege system as the primary framework for musical production in prerevolutionary Paris.

The Privilege to Perform

Parisian musicians long accessed collective or corporate privilege through a guild called the Confrérie de Saint-Julien-des-Ménétriers. The *ménétriers* evolved from the fourteenth to seventeenth centuries into a powerful corporation that looked remarkably similar to French craft and trade guilds. It required apprenticeship, a qualifying examination adjudicated by a jury of the guild's top leaders, and a *lettre de maître*, which officially sanctioned musicians to perform at various events outside of court, such as balls, banquets, weddings, town festivals, and other civic events.[21] A struggle between the *ménétriers* and court musicians, particularly Lully and the organist François Couperin *le grand*, has been well documented in music historiography. What remains to be considered is how their dispute sheds light on the many ways that privilege came to dictate musical production in eighteenth-century Paris, the bureaucratic capital of corporatized musicians. Musicians' pursuit of privileges indicate that the system provided them both individually and collectively with a valuable source of professional security, agency, and authority.

The infighting among professional musicians described here symptomized a much broader trend. Professionals in early eighteenth-century Paris began to distinguish themselves from both the lowly artisans affiliated with guilds and the abstract thinkers affiliated with academies.[22] Historian Paola Bertucci has shown that from this evolution emerged an ethnographic category, the artist. She calls these categories "ethnographic" rather than "epistemological" because they are based on discourses, practices, and experiences, in early eighteenth-century France.[23] While savants worked exclusively in the realm of the mind and artisans created products manually according to rules that they could not articulate, artists—such as composers and organists, as I will argue—used their minds to create beautiful things according to rules that they were able to explain.[24]

Unlike the centuries-old guilds, the realm of savants was established in France primarily during the seventeenth century in the form of an academy system intended to improve and protect French culture.[25] Such institutions had long existed in Italy, but a glaring difference characterized the French system. While academies sprang up across Italy and coexisted within individual cities, French academies shared rather more features with the native craft and trade corporations that preexisted them; territorial, monopolistic, standardized, and hereditary, both guilds and academies in France promoted exclusivity and protectionism.[26] The French academies were part of a comprehensive royal agenda. Feudalism in France had given way to a mercantilist economic system as royal bureaucracy centralized from the sixteenth century onward, most notably under Louis XIV. Although mercantilism's definition remains notoriously vague, it benefited the absolutist state through protectionist economic policies specifically regarding trade. In the case of France, the term "mercantilism" is sometimes used interchangeably with "Colbertism," after the minister Jean-Baptiste Colbert, who fostered centralization during the Sun King's reign. Some historians correctly label mercantilist policies as "illiberal" in the sense that they imposed strict regulation, yet perhaps surprisingly privileges seem to have counterbalanced such ostensibly restrictive policies.[27] Colbert sought to center the king not only within this economic system but also among fiscal, legal, political, social, and cultural realms as well; this interdependency formed the very foundation of Colbertism. The royal academy system constituted one part of his agenda and included the institution that would come to be known as the Opéra.

Pierre Perrin established the original Académie d'Opéra through a privilege granted to him in 1669. The Opéra differed markedly from the other academies that closely preceded it, including Painting and Sculpture, Inscriptions, Dance, and Sciences. Perrin's academy would neither codify the art nor educate its practitioners, but rather it would present public performances.[28] Other academies, to the contrary, purposely excluded the public from their activities.[29] Nor did academies maintain salaried employees or a hierarchical organizational structure as Perrin planned to implement. At its inception Perrin's academy represented an unusual marriage of academic prestige and commercial structure.[30] This origin would come to affect musical production in eighteenth-century Paris because it firmly situated music-making as an activity regulated by legal permission, a practice already implemented by the musicians' guild, the *ménétriers*, which itself faced persistent juridical battles against the new academies. Problems had already begun for the musicians' guild upon the founding of the Royal Academy of Dance in 1662. Until then, dancing masters fell under *ménétriers'* jurisdiction because of the presumed symbiosis between music and dance. The "king" of the *ménétriers*, Guillaume Dumanoir, had fought the Academy of Dance's establishment on legal grounds and failed.[31] The guild thus lost control over one key aspect of musical productions, dance, to the academy system.

As Perrin tried to establish his Académie d'Opéra, he soon found himself imprisoned for debt in the Conciergerie on Paris's Île de la Cité. In this quite inglorious context Lully supposedly "transact[ed] some undeniably shady business" to acquire the Opéra privilege.[32] At the time in 1672, "two different teams of operatic impresarios claimed" the privilege.[33] Apparently acting under Colbert's direction, Lully wrested the privilege from the unfortunate Perrin, changing the institution's name to the Académie Royale de musique,[34] a semantic difference that from a legalistic perspective notably widened the scope of Lully's rights. He planned to incorporate a music school into his new academy. With this, Lully became perhaps the most famous example of a musician who enjoyed an incredibly powerful royal privilege.[35] Lully's privilege is frequently referred to as the "patent" to the Opéra, a term from the French *lettre patente*, a published ruling, edict, or privilege by the king.[36] The privilege granted Lully the exclusive right to produce through-composed music and dance within the kingdom's borders and caused fair theater impresarios to develop amusingly clever workarounds such as audience singalongs and singing marionettes.[37] Louis XIV's ruling on the Opéra privilege explicitly notes that Lully earned the patent by virtue of his talent as a musician; expertise made Lully an appropriate candidate to lead the new academy, technically the realm of savants. The social elevation here could not be denied, a fact that certainly did not escape Lully (or his scheming heirs). Academies garnered a symbolic prestige and tangible legal power that no mere commercial theater could have offered to the composer: a legal monopoly on public music-making throughout the kingdom.

Lully collected a constellation of privileges in addition to Perrin's in order to safeguard his monopoly over multiple musical genres and institutions, a power that he ultimately secured through lawsuits.[38] When the playwright Molière died the following year, Lully lobbied hard to minimize the number of musicians who could perform at the Comédie-Française and "progressively strangled music in spoken plays."[39] The composer seemed to enforce his privileges only selectively, however, ignoring musical activities in the king's brother's household, even when those performances clearly infringed on his monopoly.[40] The privilege system's most pernicious feature of all was that only a "privileged" few among the First-Estate clergy and Second-Estate nobles could easily thwart legal privileges. In the words of musicologist Patricia Ranum, "nobles could do as they wished."[41]

Having identified legal privileges as the best path to self-preservation, Lully pursued them aggressively wherever he could. Soon Michel Dumanoir ascended to his father's position as "king" of the musicians' guild. King Michel questioned whether the "academicians" belonging to Lully's Académie Royale de musique were legally required to obtain a *lettre de maître* from the guild before performing outside the court. Lully provided a salty retort to Michel's inquiry, arguing that because the very best instrumentalists served the king they should not be subjected to guild scrutiny in order to perform in public.[42] Lully refused to see less talented "fiddlers" infringe on his musicians' performance rights. He ultimately defeated Michel and won the privilege for his instrumentalists to perform outside the academy without guild-granted *lettres*. With that, the *ménétriers* definitively lost a corporate monopoly on public music-making, which began a long history of the Académie Royale de musique's dominance over the Parisian musical landscape, requiring contracts and fees at the whim of its directors from any institution that hoped to produce music.[43]

Lully's case offers an intriguing though not singular anomaly to the ways that privilege usually regulated the Old Regime economy. Privileges upheld a corporate structure that simultaneously fostered productive competition and protected labor.[44] Lully capitalized on the former, using his own privileges to dismantle corporate privilege among performing musicians and to consolidate those permissions into the hands of private individuals. These individuals were primarily concentrated in the court and church, evinced most saliently by a simple glance through the legal protections registered in favor of musicians throughout Louis XIV's reign.[45] Lully thus paved the way for future generations of musicians to dissociate themselves from the musician-artisans in the *ménétriers* and to instead work as artists (in Bertucci's definition of the term) or liberal professionals free from guild regulations. Might they even have been defined as savants at this point? I think not. Although Lully led an academy, it did not function like the others. Moreover, the work of academy musicians was neither abstract nor exclusively practiced in the mind.

Soon the dance academy echoed Lully's critiques of the *ménétriers*-trained performers and requested the exclusive rights to teach dance, claiming that those who held a *lettre de maître* from the musicians' guild lacked skill and consistently ruined performances.[46] The *ménétriers* lost once again. In 1683, Louis XIV resolved by *arrêt* that "ménétriers" referred only to violinists (a lexical truth) and so dancers were once again exempt from guild regulation. Despite a 1692 decision that technically retracted the 1683 one permitting both the academy and *ménétriers*-affiliated masters to offer dance lessons, the guild nevertheless began to change as a result of these 1690s legal proceedings. Michel relinquished his seat as king of the *ménétriers* and the corporation replaced its "royalty" with a *collège* of four *jurés*, or officers, perhaps in an attempt to appear on pace with academic trends.

After Lully's death, the *collège* of *ménétriers* officers brought a well-known legal case against a group of composers, organists, and harpsichord instructors including François Couperin *le grand*, all of whom refused to join the guild's corporate ranks. The guild officers attempted to legally compel all composers and keyboardists to affiliate with their corporation by citing the original patent that defined the profession as an "art and science."[47] The officers argued that in order to maintain a "liberal profession" among musicians, this legal definition needed to be respected. To achieve this end, they wanted the keyboardists and composers who practiced the science of music to be subjected to the same legal standards as the monodic instrumentalists who practiced its art.[48]

The stratification of social prestige among professional musicians widened as monodic instruments such as the violin, flute, and horn took on diabolical and sensual associations in opposition to more learned, polyphonic instruments.[49] According to Luc Charles-Dominique, Orpheus's lyre and Apollo's harp had become savant.[50] While *ménétriers* "played" their instruments, harmonists "touched" theirs, anticipating perhaps the sensationist epistemology soon adopted by French thinkers, which located knowledge formation in the senses.[51] As keyboardists came to be regarded as learned individuals who took many years to master their instruments, violinists or "fiddlers" were considered a collective, less prestigious band.[52]

Other professionals, most notably in medical fields like surgery, dentistry, and pharmacy, similarly began to distance themselves from guilds during this period in order to exercise more individual freedom and to gain social prestige through liberal education. The keyboardists argued that because their work was "enclosed in the mind," it should not be submitted to the same corporation as performers and dancers whose labor represented only "bodily dexterity."[53] Rote physical tasks did not fall into the realm of liberal professionals. Surgeons and violinists alike tried to dispel reputations as mere automata until at least the mid-eighteenth century.[54] Three aspects of professionalization were thus deeply entwined: professional practices, the laws governing professionals, and their social status.

Although the musicians' guild lost yet another legal battle against the keyboardists in 1695, Louis XIV overturned all of the previous decisions made against the musicians' guild in 1707.[55] But the composers, organists, and keyboard instructors managed to prevent the king's decision from being registered into law through the Paris Parlement—the most powerful of the French courts, which over the course of the eighteenth century increasingly acted as a kind of check on monarchical authority. The court and church musicians thereby maintained their legal victory despite Louis XIV's change of heart, a revealing demonstration that the king could not always get his way with the privileges that formed a complex system of governance rather than unchallenged absolutist control. The harmonists succeeded in disempowering the *ménétriers* by the turn of the eighteenth century, and consequently, music fractured into an art regulated by an academy privilege and a *métier* regulated by guild privilege.[56] Instrument builders, for example, maintained a firm guild structure and music printing remained under the purview of the larger Paris Book Guild and its bureaucracies. Florence Gétreau claims that Couperin, like Lully, sought a "new status for the artist"[57] and she describes this victory as an "ennoblement . . . a definite consecration in this battle for artistic liberty."[58] But liberty from what and for whom? While composers, keyboardists, and court musicians indeed enjoyed a newfound freedom from the guild and protection under the academy, Lully and Couperin had degraded nearly all of the guild musicians' corporate monopolies, the only privilege that most musicians had ever possessed.[59]

A composition by Couperin provides evidence of the professional distinctions that emerged among musicians at this critical juncture. Couperin attacked the guild musicians in a five-movement keyboard suite titled "Les Fastes de la grande et ancienne Mxnxtrxndxsx" (The Splendors of the Great and Ancient Ménétriers, 1716).[60] The suite's five acts seem to refer sarcastically to the five-act *tragédie lyrique*, the quintessential form of the Académie Royale de musique. It thus depicts a pathetic attempt at *académisme* by a paltry guild ensemble. The suite simultaneously takes on the character of medieval civic processions as each movement represents successive groups of guild members perhaps passing by a stationary listener. The most prominent members of the guild, the "officers," lead the procession in the suite's "First Act," followed by the "hurdy-gurdies" and "beggars" in the "Second Act," the "jugglers, jumpers, and acrobats" alongside "bears and monkeys" in the "Third Act," the "invalids" and "cripples" wounded in service to the guild in the "Fourth Act," and finally, the "drunks" and animals who cause complete chaos among the rag-tag procession in the "Fifth Act." By superimposing an academic musical form onto a civic guild ritual, Couperin conjures a carnivalesque scene.

The difference between academy and guild musicians is depicted explicitly with acerbic titles and expressive markings and more subtly with harmonic and rhythmic choices. Since musical *académisme* was equated with harmonic thought,[61] the *ménétriers'* lack of harmonic ingenuity resounds throughout the suite by never leaving a C tonal center; it alternates between the major and minor mode throughout. Although nearly all of Couperin's *Ordres* are crafted within a single major-minor tonal center, in this suite he sardonically adheres to simple tonic-dominant harmonic motion. Couperin not only imitates the feigned harmonic capabilities of instruments like the "hurdy-gurdy," but he also reenacts the *ménétriers'* rudimentary contrapuntal knowledge. Despite the binary structure of each movement in the keyboard suite, these are a far cry from the courtly French forms soon adopted by Johann Sebastian Bach. They lack the pleasing variety, chromatic inflection, and melodic ornamentation expected of musicians with "good taste."[62] Recordings of the piece by Olivier Baumont provide an ideal performance interpretation to foreground the present analysis of Couperin's programmatic musical attack on the *ménétriers*.[63]

The stately dotted rhythms of the notables and officers' march proceeds in a mock ceremonial manner. Among the few other marches that appear in Couperin's *Ordres*, its character might be contrasted with the more tasteful march, "Les pélerines," found in the *Troisième Ordre*. Couperin identifies the street instruments in the second movement of "Les Fastes" as the bourdon and the hurdy-gurdy (*vielle*).[64] "No musical instrument," according to Robert A. Green, "has suffered so grievously from changes in social status" as the hurdy-gurdy in eighteenth-century France.[65] In this suite, it falls to an all-time low. The simple mordents and trills on the first beat of each measure thwart any expectation of learned musicianship. Each half of the two binary-form airs in the "Second Act" are precisely the same length, emphasizing their mechanical nature. The ornamentation devolves into formulaic inflections that become absolutely comical by the third and fifth movements. By incorporating uncourtly entertainers like "jugglers, tumblers, and acrobats" into the procession's "Third Act," Couperin invokes the controversy surrounding the Academy of Dance and the poorly trained guild "dancers."[66] The dancers' act in fact flows seamlessly from the second, highlighting their mere physical rather than mental dexterity as they fall easily into step with the mechanical street instruments. Animals join the band in the Third Act, emphasizing the musicians' low status and rote practices—even bears could be trained to execute such entertainments.

The "Fourth Act" furthers Couperin's depiction of the guild musicians as physical laborers who feel the toll of their trade with age. The dotted rhythms from the first movement return with the "invalids and cripples" wounded "in service to the great Mxnxstrxndxsx." According to Couperin's markings, in this act the right hand depicts the "dislocated," and the left hand, the "lame." The "lame" in the bassline lumber upward until the double bar line and then downward until the movement's end. The *ménétriers* are incapable of thinking vertically and struggle to keep two monodic lines together. The result in mm. 9–11 is what sounds like a failed harmonic sequence (Example 1.1). Meanwhile the "lame" seem to lose another limb in the bassline anacrusis to m. 8, when the octaves that had proceeded since the beginning of the movement lose their bottom note. The lowest member struggles to return before m. 9, yet the "lame's" grounding limb is lost definitively for the remainder of the A section. Most jarring are the descending melodic tritones performed by the "dislocated" in mm. 14–20. Harmonically hopeless, the guild veterans appear hardly capable of achieving a rudimentary melodic perfect fifth without the drone of street instruments to support them. The trills on the strong beat attempt to mask woefully wrong notes. Couperin suggests a "small reprise, if wanted," perhaps only if the wounded are capable of continuing at all. The guild members' apparent disabilities implicate their profession as manual rather than intellectual. Years of physical labor have left them maimed.

In the final "Fifth Act," even the young guild members' bodily dexterity fails. Among the "disorder, and collapse of the entire troop caused by drunkards, monkeys, and bears," the ensemble implodes metrically under a "very fast" tempo marking. The meter switches from simple to compound in the B section, but on the second beat of m. 32, one part of the group seems to forget the change and lapses back into triplet divisions on the level of the

EXAMPLE 1.1 In the Fourth Act of Couperin's keyboard suite, the "lame" lose a bottom limb and fail to achieve a harmonic sequence in mm. 9–11. In mm. 14–20 the "dislocated" poorly mask melodic tritones with embellishments.

beat (Example 1.2). The duple and triple divisions compete and contrast through the remainder of the movement, finally succumbing in m. 44 to a reliance on "crutches," represented by octaves in the left hand that seem to keep the ensemble together. Although the guild officers from the "First Act" believe that they are leading a stately, serious procession, the extremely slow fourth act and far-too-fast fifth depict the utter chaos left in their wake. Couperin's suite provides musical evidence of the complaints that guild-trained performers ruined performances.

LEGAL *PRIVILÈGE* AND MUSICAL PRODUCTION | 31

EXAMPLE 1.2 In the Fifth Act of Couperin's keyboard suite a metrical collapse in m. 32 eventually requires "crutches."

Charles-Dominique and Gétreau agree that the legal struggle between the musicians' guild and the composers, organists, and keyboardists jettisoned performed, oral music from written, academic music, and caused a professional schism—what Gétreau calls two "classes" of musicians—that would continue to diverge until the Revolution.[67] Keyboards represented the epitome of individuality and expressivity.[68] Increasingly, individual artists did not need to rely on guilds; they were, "free" or "liberal" professionals. Both the guild and academy musicians claimed the term "liberal," but disagreed on whether freedom came from corporate protection or individual agency before the law. The *ménétriers* continued to fight the Académie Royale de musique's exclusive privileges, but an *arrêt* passed in 1728 and renewed in 1732 legally forbade the *ménétriers* from infringing on the academy musicians'

rights. A hierarchy among monodic and polyphonic instruments translated into a social hierarchy constituted by legal privileges.

Privilege ordered Colbertism, and Colbertism ordered France. Artists, according to Bertucci, affiliated with *"lieux privilégiés"* like academies to secure corporate privilege outside guilds.[69] Colbert designed these new royally sanctioned institutions dedicated to the arts, crafts, and sciences to improve the French political economy and to cultivate cultural heritage for the glory of the monarch.[70] French Enlightenment tenets would extol both the arts and sciences as engines of human progress when practically applied.[71] And so eventually the work of mechanical artists earned respect, too, even as their privileged protections deteriorated.[72] A practice or product was deemed useful to the nation if it contributed to the greater good.[73] The Académie Royale de musique and the Academy of Sciences, the privileged institutions that monitored the performance and theory of music, respectively, represented but two nodes in a vast system of knowledge production dedicated to the nation's overall health. As early modern France instrumentalized professionals' expertise toward commercial and imperial interests, diverse professions earned prestige as useful members of the French nation.[74]

The struggle between harmonists and monodists described here reveals how musicians joined this stratified system by securing what I call musical privilege. Keyboardists and composers like other artists emphatically claimed their work was born of *l'esprit*, the mind, to resist subjugation to the musicians' guild. Application of *l'esprit* to mechanical production distinguished artists from the rote physicality of artisans, the kind of mechanical physicality harshly critiqued by Couperin in his keyboard suite. As shown in the case of the guild musicians versus the court and church musicians, these distinctions were not theoretical categories but social and legal ones that dictated how a person's professional practices would be judged before the law.

Musical Privilege in Publishing, Commerce, and Manufacturing

Music publishing sat at the intersection of many privileged institutions and individuals, among them, the Paris Book Guild, the Royal Administration of the Book Trade, the Ballard family, and the Academy of Sciences as well as individual composers, engravers, and entrepreneurs. The musical privileges regulating music publishing were not wholly separate from performance rights. Lully, for example, acquired a separate privilege to sell his opera scores at the entrance to performances, and the privilege to print and sell music performed at the Opéra eventually became a standard consideration in negotiations of the institution's privilege.

Extended privilege language on musical publications persisted into the early eighteenth century as a vestige of an earlier gift economy; see, for example, the general privilege found at the end of Couperin's *L'art de toucher le clavecin* (1716) shown in Figure 1.1. As Stephen Rose has argued in the case of German principalities, at one time privileges enhanced princely authority.[75] Privileges evolved from a benevolent gift between sovereign and author into a legal transaction, yet privileges' monarchical source never changed and they remained a mark of prestige for the recipient.[76] Even as privileges on printed music dedicated less space to praising the author and the composition over the course of the eighteenth century, musicologist Marie Bobillier contends that musical "privilege maintained its character as a favor" granted at "the pleasure of the king."[77] This is partially true. A 1726 legal brief demanded by the Paris Book Guild clarified that "a privilege was not a royal 'grace' to be conferred or revoked at the king's pleasure but rather a royal confirmation of an anterior property right."[78] Ironically, the statement was intended to affirm the guild's ownership over privileges ceded by authors by affirming their status as property. As we shall see, the Crown eventually reversed this position later in the century as it tried to rein in rampant privileges.

Among a variety of music-printing privileges, the more powerful ones required higher fees. A simple permission cost only five *livres* because it granted only the right to print and did not affirm any kinds of ownership over the materials published. Rights of the seal granted legal claims over a printed work and cost 60, 120, or 240 *livres* per volume, depending on the time period that the privilege covered. A general privilege was the most expensive kind because it afforded exclusive rights.[79] Musical entries in the privilege registers from 1653 to 1790 provide an incomplete picture of music publication because registration of primarily musical texts was not compulsory.[80] Permission to print was in part a mode of royal censorship crucial to the book trade; music did not require mandatory registration because without text it appeared less threatening to the Crown's interests. For this reason, many music methods are found in the registers simply because they contained extensive prose. For example, on October 3, 1687, a registered privilege states, "M. Jean Rousseau presented us with a privilege . . . for the printing of a book titled *Traité de la Violle* that contains a curious dissertation on its origin, etc., for ten years."[81] The author had the rights to dictate the printing of his work for ten years, at which time he would need to renew the privilege in order to maintain exclusive rights to its circulation. Such exclusive privileges were costly, prohibitively so for average musicians.[82]

Indeed, privileges better protected music printers, engravers, and publishers than composers. Most famous among the privilege-holding printers was Christophe Ballard's family, who held a monopoly on music printing in

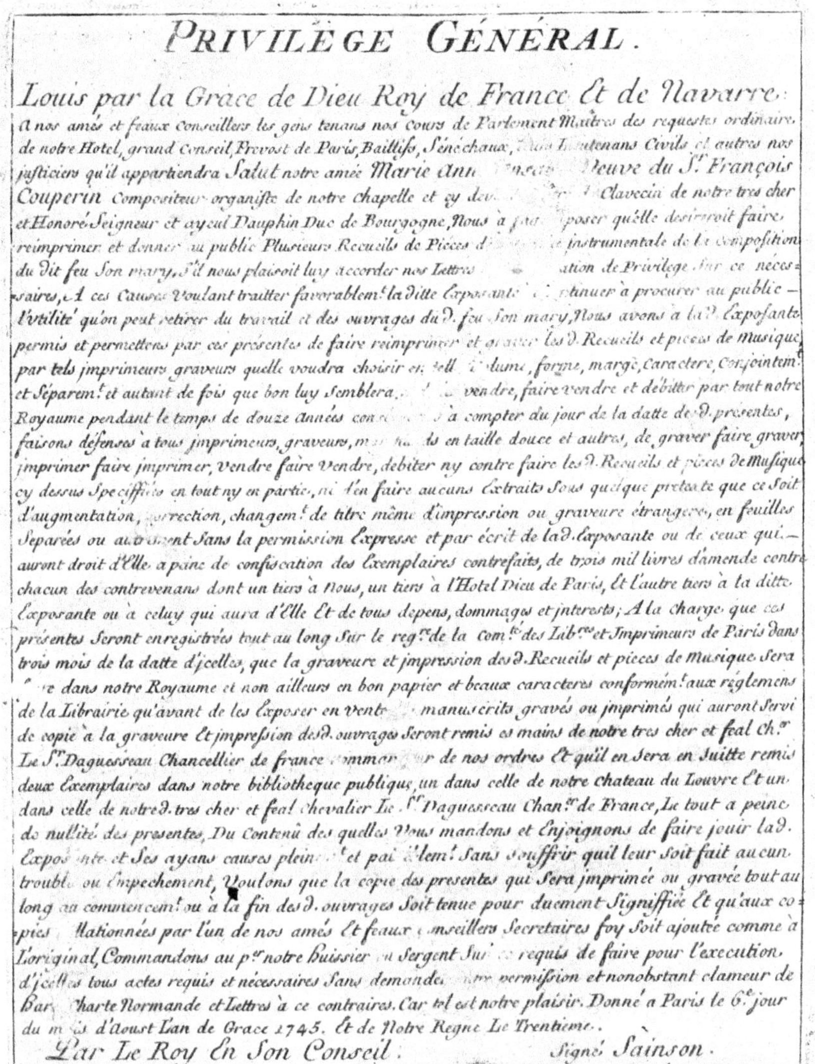

PRIVILÈGE GÉNÉRAL.

Louis par la Grace de Dieu Roy de France Et de Navarre:
A nos amés et feaux Conseillers les gens tenans nos Cours de Parlement Maîtres des requestes ordinaire
de notre Hotel, grand Conseil, Prevost de Paris, Baillifs, Sénéchaux, [illegible] Lieutenans Civils et autres nos
justiciers qu'il appartiendra Salut notre amée Marie Ann[illegible] Veuve du S.r François
Couperin Compositeur organiste de notre chapelle et cy dev[illegible] Clavecin de notre tres cher
et Honoré Seigneur et ayeul Dauphin Duc de Bourgogne, Nous a fai[illegible] poser qu'elle desireroit faire
reimprimer et donner au public Plusieurs Recueils de Pieces d[illegible] instrumentale de la composition
du dit feu Son mary, s'il nous plaisoit luy accorder nos Lettres [illegible] ation de Privilège sur ce nécessaires, A ces Causes Voulant traitter favorablem.t la ditte Exposante [illegible] ntinuer à procurer au public
l'utilité qu'on peut retirer du travail et des ouvrages dud. feu Son mary, Nous avons a lad. Exposante
permis et permettons par ces présentes de faire reimprimer et graver lesd. Recueils et pieces de Musique
par tels imprimeurs graveurs quelle voudra choisir en telle [illegible] lume, forme, margè, Caractere, Conjointem.t
et Séparem.t et autant de fois que bon luy Semblera, [illegible] vendre, faire vendre et débitter par tout notre
Royaume pendant le temps de douze Années con[illegible] à compter du jour de la datte desd. presentes,
faisons défenses à tous imprimeurs, graveurs, m[illegible] ds en taille douce et autres, de graver faire graver
imprimer faire imprimer, Vendre faire Vendre, debiter ny contre faire lesd. Recueils et pieces de Musique
cy dessus Speciffiés en tout ny en partie, ni d'en faire aucuns Extraits Sous quelque pretexte que ce Soit
d'augmentation, correction, changem.t de titre même d'impression ou graveure étrangere, en feuilles
Separées ou autrement Sans la permission Expresse et par écrit de lad. Exposante ou de ceux qui
auront droit d'Elle a peine de confiscation des Exemplaires contrefaits, de trois mil livres d'amende contre
chacun des contrevenans dont un tiers à Nous, un tiers à l'Hotel Dieu de Paris, Et l'autre tiers à la ditte
Exposante ou à celuy qui aura d'Elle Et de tous depens, dommages et interests; A la charge que ces
présentes Seront enregistrées tout au long Sur le reg.re de la Com.té des Lib.res et Imprimeurs de Paris dans
trois mois de la datte d'icelles, que la graveure et impression desd. Recueils et pieces de Musique Sera
[illegible] dans notre Royaume et non ailleurs en bon papier et beaux caracteres conformém.t aux réglemens
de la Librairie qu'avant de les Exposer en vente [illegible] manuscrits gravés ou imprimés qui auront Servi
de copie à la graveure Et impression desd. ouvrages Seront remis es mains de notre tres cher et feal Ch.er
Le S.r Daguesseau Chancellier de france [illegible] de nos ordres Et quil en Sera en Suitte remis
deux Exemplaires dans notre bibliotheque publique, un dans celle de notre Chateau du Louvre Et un
dans celle de notred. tres cher et feal Chevalier Le S.r Daguesseau Chan.er de France, Le tout a peine
de nullité des presentes, Du Contenu des quelles Vous mandons et Enjoignons de faire jouir lad.
Expos[illegible] et Ses ayans causes plein[illegible] et pai[illegible] lem.t Sans Souffrir quil leur Soit fait aucun
trouble ou Empechement, Voulons que la copie des presentes qui Sera imprimée ou gravée tout au
long au commencem.t ou à la fin desd. ouvrages Soit tenue pour duement Signiffiée Et qu'aux copies [illegible] llationnées par l'un de nos amés Et feaux Conseillers Secretaires foy Soit ajoutée comme à
L'original, Commandons au p.er notre Huissier ou Sergent Sur [illegible] requis de faire pour l'execution
d'icelles tous actes requis et nécessaires Sans demander [illegible] permission et nonobstant clameur de
Haro, Charte Normande et Lettres à ce contraires. Car tel est notre plaisir. Donné a Paris le 6.e jour
du mois d'Aoust l'an de Grace 1745. Et de Notre Regne Le Trentieme.

Par Le Roy En Son Conseil. Signé Sainson.

Registré Sur le Registre Onze de la chambre Royale et Syndicale de la Communauté des Libraires et
Imprimeurs de Paris N.o 475. fol. 411. conformem.t au Reglement de 1723. à Paris le 20. Aoust.
1745. Signé Vincent Syndic. Les Exemplaires ont été fournis.

Gravé par L.s Hue.

FIGURE 1.1 Extended privilege language on music publications in the early eighteenth century like the one from Couperin's *L'Art de toucher le clavecin* (1716) still conveyed its status as a royal grace. Courtesy of the Bibliothèque nationale de France.

Paris from the sixteenth- to the mid-eighteenth century. Engravers, however, were not beholden to a guild, and so they could reproduce any music they owned without infringing on the Ballard privilege.[83] When music was engraved, then the composer or publisher could register a privilege for it.[84] Composers usually earned money by either selling their scores to printers and publishers or by self-publishing.[85] Advertisements for new musical editions available *chez l'auteur* provided an opportunity for composers to assert an authority to their works outside the expensive privilege system.[86] As one example among many, Le Sieur Lanzetti alerted "the public" through the *Mercure de France* that the "cello sonatas engraved in Paris under his name and without him knowing [were] full of errors."[87]

The privilege registers inherently represent an advantaged group of musicians who possessed the financial means to pursue the costly formalities necessary to attempt protecting their music from *contrefaçon*, a term from criminal law meaning "infringing copy."[88] As early as 1670 the keyboardist Jacques Champion de Chambonnières claimed in the preface to his *Pièces de clavecin* that he had published the pieces in part because of the "counterfeit" copies of his music that already circulated throughout Europe. "I should voluntarily give what has been violently taken from me," he decided, "and myself put into the light of day what others have already half done for me."[89] In reality, privileges had only a limited ability to prevent piracy and instead held a more symbolic role since "a privilege could enhance the commercial value of a published book."[90] Enduring names from French music history happen to be those who proved most assiduous at renewing privileges for their works. An overwhelming number of printing privileges from the late seventeenth century protect keyboard works composed by musicians affiliated with the court or the church, among them, Marin Marais, Lully, Couperin and his descendants, and Rameau.[91] Indeed, a critique that would arise in literary property debates during the Revolution was the fact that Old Regime publication privileges seemed to be inheritable in perpetuity.[92] Couperin's privilege registered on May 14, 1713, was renewed by his widow and later his descendants in 1733, 1745, and 1757.[93] Women, including the court composer Élisabeth Jacquet de la Guerre, are found throughout the registers as both composers and engravers, albeit less frequently than their male counterparts.

The privilege system thus set people in the music publishing world into competition with one another. In one case, music publishers stymied the establishment of a Parisian music lending library during the 1760s and prevented it from distributing scores until publishers' privileges expired.[94] During the legal battles between music publishers and the lending library's subscription office, composers variously allied with each side, unable to decide whether it was in their better interest to protect legal privileges or to gain popularity through lending subscriptions regardless of piracy risks.[95]

Entrepreneurial musicians like Charles Nicolas Le Clerc, a member of the king's prestigious "twenty-four violins," capitalized by purchasing the rights to reproduce extensive foreign catalogs in France.[96] A few foreign composers like Johann Stamitz and Christoph Willibald Ritter von Gluck obtained privileges to their works before clever Parisians like Le Clerc took action. Le Clerc purchased general privileges from the 1730s through the 1760s for wildly popular works including Jean-Jacques Rousseau's *Le devin du village* and Giovanni Battista Pergolesi's *La serva padrona*, as well as compositions by other well-known European composers including Corelli, Geminiani, Handel, Hasse, Locatelli, Quantz, Scarlatti, and Vivaldi, among others.[97] Foreign musicians had to be careful about advertising their works in Paris, since a work was considered in the "public domain" outside its original political boundaries and thus could be legally printed and sold.[98] Symphonies by Parisian composer François-Joseph Gossec accompany more famous composers on Le Clerc's list. Gossec appears nowhere on the register as having purchased his own privilege.[99] While composers primarily applied for privileges around 1760, from the 1770s onward publishers populate the registers far more.[100]

Extended privilege language was soon replaced with a terse abbreviation, "A. P. D. R.," for "Avec privilège du roi," a practice that symptomized privileges' increasing ubiquity. Not all scores bearing this abbreviation had necessarily passed through the process of registration; they appeared simply to stave off would-be counterfeiters or because the printer failed to remove the "A. P. D. R." from a previous setting.[101] It was not the restrictiveness of privileges that caused musicians to disregard them but rather their inconsistent implementation and weak protections.

Because the privilege to print music intersected with the privilege to invent music technologies, craft guilds and the Academy of Sciences competed to regulate the sector. Early in the eighteenth century the Academy of Sciences seriously considered music as a mode of scientific inquiry that married theory and practice. In addition to reports on acoustics, phonation, and audition, its members evaluated mechanical inventions like musical instruments, protometronomes, and eventually music-printing and -engraving methods. The Academy assessed these objects to consider endorsing a royal privilege that would grant its builders or inventors exclusive production rights. For instrument makers, this proved particularly beneficial. A *lettre patente* issued by the Parlement as a result of an Academy of Sciences recommendation provided its recipient with a legal exception from what Albert Cohen describes as the, "jealously guarded . . . commercial prerogatives and techniques" of instrument builders' guilds, which, like the printer's guild, "were quick to resort to litigation to preserve" their "economic monopoly."[102] People with patents were exempt from guild restrictions and were thus held to different legal standards, much as the musicians in Lully's Académie Royale de musique were exempt from *ménétriers* oversight. The Academy of Sciences granted musical innovators a valuable exception from corporate privileges.

Recognition from the Academy of Sciences not only served as a conduit to legal protections but also "enhanced reputation," provided "public recognition," and improved sales of a given product.[103] It is such acknowledgment that Rameau sought when he submitted his theoretical treatises to the Academy.[104] A music method praised by the Academy meant an authoritative stamp of approval for its writer.[105] Such approbation from the Academy of Sciences was on occasion also noted in printing privileges as a means of further advertisement. The privilege received by M. Jean François Demoz on July 12, 1726, for example, noted that his method for teaching plainchant was "approved by messieurs the Academy of Sciences . . . to be without comparison easier, shorter, and clearer to learn and to put into practice than all others that preceded it."[106] Demoz received a general privilege—the most expensive kind.

The Academy's reviews eventually contributed to the degradation of the Ballard family's monopoly. After the Printers' Guild rejected a new music-printing method proposed by Pierre-Simon Fournier precisely because it competed with the Ballard patent, Fournier submitted it to the Academy of Sciences instead. The Academy of Sciences praised his work's precision and economy, and soon after, Parlement also found in favor of Fournier, demoting Ballard simply to music printer for the king. With a deregulated print market and a proliferation of engraving, the Parisian music market became a publishing capital of Europe.[107]

The ubiquity of privilege still permitted a rich, cosmopolitan musical life to take root in Paris.[108] Foreign composers and musicians flocked to Paris for professional opportunities to perform and to publish.[109] French instrument builders thrived. Musical privilege was not the unequivocal mark of heavy-handed absolutism. Yet its inherent complexities profoundly dictated musical production.

Privilege as Property

The concentration of musical privilege at the very top of society diluted as privileges proliferated throughout the eighteenth century.[110] Meanwhile, those who benefited from the "fountain of privilege"[111] began to misunderstand their legal permissions as property, eventually prompting the Crown to reduce its generous flow. In the process, musicians found themselves in favorable positions either in the flexibility that they enjoyed working among a variety of institutions or in the authority that they earned within privileged institutions. At mid-century, however, musical privilege attracted criticism from all sides.

The first "public" concert series in Paris, the Concert Spirituel, provides a useful example of how musical privilege flowed—in this case from the Crown, to the Opéra's privilege holders below it, and still lower down to the entrepreneurs who ran the enterprise.[112] In 1714 the Académie Royale de musique officially received permission to lease the rights to song and dance, a "venal extension of the Opéra's privilege."[113] Although according to David Charlton the Opéra "amounted to the monarch's personal property" because its "legal status presumed that [it] existed to entertain his family and guests in the first instance, and anyone else on an incidental and contingent basis,"[114] we have already learned that privilege rendered this arrangement quite complex. Before the concert's entrepreneurs could open their doors, they were obligated to lease a portion of the Opéra director's privilege in order to secure the permission to perform music. Despite this agreement, when it opened in 1725 the Concert Spirituel remained forbidden from infringing on the Opéra's exclusive right to stage music sung in French, technically restricting the concerts to evenings when the Opéra was closed and to a repertoire consisting of Latin sacred music. The Concert Spirituel soon paid "a huge price" to expand its repertory permissions from the Opéra.[115] Within two years of its opening, infractions caused the Concert Spirituel entrepreneurs to clash intermittently with the Opéra's directors, less so when the two institutions were run simultaneously by the city of Paris. Beverly Wilcox notes that the entrepreneurs' privilege was "a modification to the Opéra's privilege," therefore any change in the Opéra's direction by the Crown affected the Concert Spirituel.[116] Ripples in the "fountain of privilege" reached far and wide. For example, the king unilaterally revoked Maximilien Claude Gruer's Opéra privilege after the director held a lascivious gathering during which he "forced three singers . . . to show the guests what they wanted to see."[117] This change in Opéra direction required the concert entrepreneurs to renegotiate their privileges with a new director, and different directors guarded their privilege with varying degrees of stringency. In 1732 alone the Opéra legally pursued two different Parisian concerts, the Harmoniphiles and L'hôtel Longueville, for infraction on its privileges.[118] François Berger, as Opéra director in 1744, became infuriated when the Comédie-Italienne had employed in addition to its six legally sanctioned violins, "several basses, bassoons, flutes, and flageolets."[119] It was not until 1761 that the Comédie-Française and Comédie-Italienne received privileges of their own.[120]

The Concert Spirituel entrepreneurs Jean-Joseph Cassanéa de Mondonville and Gabriel Capperan (a bassist described by Wilcox as "treacherous"[121]) found themselves threatened with legal action in 1758, surprisingly not by the Opéra but by a violinist from their own orchestra named Louis-Antoine Travenol. While court-connected musicians in the tradition of Lully saw privileges as an opportunity for advancement, less fortunate working musicians like Travenol only felt the injustices that swirled at the bottom of the "fountain of privilege." Travenol suffered the reputation of a diabolical fiddler, a label perhaps more self-inflicted than stereotypical. He attracted ire from freemasons after publishing a pamphlet supposedly divulging the brotherhood's secret rituals at a time when Masonry endured extensive scrutiny by the monarchy and church.[122] The same year, in 1748, Travenol circulated an anti-Voltarian tract. When Voltaire retaliated, a vaudevillesque case of mistaken identity landed Travenol's sick elderly father in prison at the hands of the eminent philosopher. An extended legal battle ensued and wound its way through the Châtelet courts to the Parlement of Paris, ultimately leaving Voltaire looking rather petty and Travenol even poorer than when the debacle began.[123] No one had really expected much more from a violinist; the public saw Voltaire as the villain in the affair. As a man of letters and the wealthier party, Voltaire's pursuit of a poor musician in court was in extreme distaste. Although legal proceedings had offered an acceptable conduit to professional agency in Lully's day and legal disputes for privileges served as a way to resist excessive monarchical power,[124] it had become decidedly less honorable for courtly writers and artists to engage in such affairs. And so when Travenol published yet another inflammatory pamphlet, this time threatening legal action against the Concert Spirituel, he posed a potential source of embarrassment for the concert's entrepreneurs.

Privilege was at the heart of Travenol's critique. The subtitle of his publication, *Les entrepreneurs entrepris*, identified the essay as a "complaint" from "a musician oppressed by his comrades."[125] After losing his positions in both the Opéra and Concert Spirituel orchestras, Travenol hoped to garner support among influential patrons in the Parisian music world and threatened court proceedings if he did not soon receive compensation for past performances described in the pamphlet. He had, in his own words, "plenty of time to pursue a trial" having been recently relieved of his duties.[126] Travenol acknowledged outright that he sought justice in an atypical format by citing poetry and verse rather than legal authorities to support his claims, and he conceded his own social limitations: "I am not, like [Mondonville], a man of the court. . . . I speak and write as I think, especially to my colleagues."[127] Admitting the social stratification between himself and Mondonville, Travenol took it as a point of pride to reject a courtly status and subtly diminished Mondonville by calling him an "equal." They were both, after all, just musicians. Travenol's complaint posed a shockingly complicated question: Who "owns" the seats in an orchestra? While Travenol treated his orchestra seat like personal property, Mondonville contended that Travenol merely enjoyed the privilege of sitting there, a privilege that could be granted and revoked only at Mondonville's discretion.

Travenol's mock-legal writing genre and appeal to social superiors underscores the persistent interdependence of legal and social privilege. He organized the pamphlet in imitation of contemporaneous judiciary memoirs, presenting first the "facts" and then the "means."[128] Yet the pamphlet begins with an epistle "to the protectors and protectresses of the sciences and fine arts,"[129] and it seems to have circulated among the precise milieu Travenol had hoped. The handwritten nameplate on one copy of the pamphlet reads "À Madame la Marquise de Flavacourt, Dame du Palais de Reine," a famous courtier during Louis XV's reign. Travenol maintained consistency with the older courtly epistles that depicted musicians as servants.[130] Such epistles had largely disappeared in Paris by the early eighteenth century, and so his rhetoric cynically underlines the very privilege system he sought to contest.[131] Fallen from favor, and "exiled from the Court of Apollo" by his fellow musicians,[132] Travenol felt particularly spurned by Capperan because the bassist sided with the privileged Concert Spirituel rather than his fellow string player:

> We are all children of the divine Apollo
> Thus, our nobility is equal
> And the bass, following musical rules,
> should take and treat with affection the interests of the violin.[133]

Travenol accused Capperan of being more familiar with "Gregorian" and "Hermogenian codes," the Roman law that structured the French legal system since the twelfth century, than the "musical code," a metaphorical social code among fellow musicians that subordinated the bass part to the violin.[134]

Personal woes led to Travenol's dispute with the Concert Spirituel entrepreneurs. Left to care for two ailing, octogenarian parents, he had been saddled with his father's debt upon the elderly man's death. Travenol soon became ill himself, forcing him to take leave with half of his usual pay from the Opéra.[135] At the same time, the Concert Spirituel "removed" him from his place in its orchestra.[136] Travenol wanted 54 *livres* that he believed were owed to him by the concert administrators because François Francœur, born to a dynasty of court musicians, had substituted for Travenol at seventeen concerts.[137] Mondonville told Travenol "that it wasn't right" to pay him because he "hadn't played."[138] Mondonville argued that Francœur should receive at least half the compensation because he was the one who actually performed; Travenol's duty was technically fulfilled, but not personally. Mondonville claimed that Francœur already served as a supernumerary at the time anyway, and so only Mondonville himself had the right to engage him as a substitute. Travenol pointed out what he considered a logical fallacy in Mondonville's argument: if Travenol could not contract out to Francœur in the first place, then how could Mondonville force them to split the compensation? "Sieur Mondonville's arguments," Travenol jested, "are not as seductive as his motets."[139]

Their disagreement reveals the confusion around musical privilege at midcentury. Travenol viewed his seat as personal property believing that as long as it was filled then he deserved payment. Mondonville saw the seat's occupation as a privilege that only the concert's entrepreneur could manage. Travenol argued that it had always been an accepted practice for musicians to arrange their own substitutes at the Concert Spirituel. After speaking with a mutual acquaintance, Mondonville felt sorry for Travenol's state, and willingly handed over the 54 *livres*. Travenol published the letter that supposedly accompanied Mondonville's payment: "You have no right to demand payment for the fortnight since you did not serve, and that is an all-time rule; that one cannot send another subject in their place."[140] Mondonville insisted that charity, not justice, motivated the payment. Travenol penned an enflamed response refusing this "charity" and noting that as a young student he had filled in for M. Senaillé and M. Dupont. "I am not the only one," Travenol claimed, "to whom you have granted this privilege many times."[141] And here we see the weakness in Travenol's argument: It was indeed Mondonville who directed the flow of musical privilege.

Travenol made clear in the conclusion of his pamphlet that he detested the Opéra and the Concert Spirituel's power. Similar complaints were raised by boulevard theater playwrights and directors against the Comédie-Française during the same period.[142] Because privileged institutions thrived on arbitrary, royal privilege, "ordinary justice could not compel" them to treat their employees humanely.[143] With a disabled sister in his charge, and still sick and carrying his father's debts, Travenol despaired "the injustice and the inhumanity of these little tyrants of Parnasse," who ran Parisian orchestras "like the ancient Romans . . . sacrificing the particular good of the Musicians, to the general good of Music, or, rather, to their own interests."[144] Music was held in higher regard than musicians, who did not reap the benefits of its popularity among the privileged elite. Even other musicians, like Francœur, enjoyed hereditary positions at court and held privileges for their compositions, while fiddlers like Travenol served as pawns in their scheming. Travenol appealed to the "protectors and protectresses" of the arts closest to privilege's source—the king. Even while demanding fair treatment, he played the role of a lowly servant drowning at the bottom of the "fountain of privilege."

The "Dilution" of Privilege

The Italian violinist Jean-Pierre Guignon spent the final decades of his life attempting to resuscitate the feeble musicians' guild, seemingly the only privileged institution dedicated to "the good of the Musicians" rather than music's privileged patrons. Guignon had performed with great success at the Concert Spirituel since the series opened, and was even among the few musicians inducted into one of the first Parisian Masonic lodges, Coustos-Villeroy. Notorious not only as an exceptional violinist, Guignon's reputation, like Travenol's, preceded him. He drove Jean-Baptiste Anet and Jean-Marie Leclair from the king's service, incited the assault of another musician, and pursued legal proceedings over financial matters.[145] Despite these interpersonal calumnies, in 1741 King Louis XV had revived for Guignon the position of "king" of the *ménétriers*, last held by Michel Dumanoir in the seventeenth century.

The first item on King Guignon's agenda was to maintain more consistent standards among French string players by creating a hierarchy in which less qualified performers would only have the legal right to play three-stringed instruments like the rebec.[146] Implementing this new policy posed an inevitable challenge, because since the beginning of the century the guild, as discussed earlier in this chapter, consistently struggled to persuade musicians to obey its statutes. Guignon also divided France's local *ménétriers* branches into "major" and "minor" cities, leading to a total decimation of the system throughout France. Provincial musicians complained of the unfair centrality that Paris guarded and keyboardists once again protested registration of a legal motion that would force them to join their monodic comrades' corporation. The keyboardists triumphed and the ruling in their favor on January 22, 1750, delivered another blow to the already weakened guild. Despite his valiant efforts, by 1773, Guignon, the last king of the *ménétriers*, had no choice but to officially dissolve the long-fraught corporation. Guild musicians consequently lost any lingering hope of enjoying real corporate privilege, a privilege that they had never fully earned in the eighteenth century, especially in comparison to the strong, centuries-old trade guilds, or even their counterparts in instrument building.

As if to flaunt their victory, court musicians immediately published the legal precedents for musicians to pursue individual rights. From their perspective, it was the guild, not the royally sanctioned theaters, that had enjoyed unfair privileges. More than only a useful resource, the collection of legal documents flaunted the Academy musicians' many victories against the guild since the age of Couperin. It gathered all the decrees and rulings relevant to professional musicians that had been registered as French law since the late seventeenth century, a majority of which found against the *ménétriers*. The king's musicians collectively authored the publication's foreword, where they claimed that the *ménétriers* had long attempted to coerce musicians into joining their ranks and to pay for unnecessary legal rights in order to initiate superfluous court cases throughout France.[147] The publication was intended to grant musicians ready access to the laws assuring "the honor and liberty of the musical art."[148] Like their predecessors, these musicians defined "liberty" as freedom from guild regulation.[149] They hoped that, "it [would] provide [musicians] the means to defend themselves" if the *ménétriers* "were to attack again the liberty of their profession."[150] The collection ends with the king's edict suppressing the *ménétriers*, registered in Parlement on March 13, 1773. Just as Travenol, more than a decade earlier, had depicted institutions like the Opéra and Concert Spirituel as tyrannical, the court musicians' forward, following in Lully and Couperin's footsteps, portrayed the defunct guild as impeding on individual, professional liberty. The musicians who published the collection of laws positioned themselves as a greater utility to the nation when left to freely cultivate their talents, unfettered by complex regulations and corporate structures.

Many professional musicians had already learned to thrive along the margins of a semifree market without strong guild structure. The end of the musicians' guild coincided with broader changes in Parisian musical production identified by both Luc Charles-Dominique and David Hennebelle: musicians began to work more independently from institutions or more authoritatively within them and "semipublic" concerts proliferated, blurring the lines between a patronage and commercial system. Hennebelle describes this phenomenon as a "'dilution' of aristocratic musical patronage" into private, collectively patronized orchestras,[151] where musicians practiced together consistently away from the court and the church as colleagues rather than as servants, particularly as fewer musicians lived in the households of patrons. And within these new orchestras professional musicians mixed with accomplished amateurs, a change with social consequences revisited extensively in the following chapter.

A more dynamic and complex relationship emerged among professional musicians as well as between musicians and their patrons. In the dedication of his *Messe des morts*, Gossec addressed the Concert des Amateurs administrators who had subscribed to the publication, indicating a new kind of musician-patron relationship fueled by respect rather than money. The most "powerful" encouragement patrons granted to musicians was, according to him, "The noble distinction with which [patrons] treated them . . . elevat[ing] the artists' souls." He claims that a mutual interest in improving music had transformed patrons. This transformation is described by Viala and Hennebelle as an evolution from *clientélisme* (pay for service) to *mécénat* (support for art). Patrons no longer purchased music only to enhance their social status but also shared a genuine enthusiasm for musicians' talents. Gossec pejoratively employs the same term, "protectors," that Travenol had used only decades earlier, to deride patrons who were more interested in "purchasing" music than "deserving" it.[152] Gossec proudly casts musicians as "artists," unmistakably in the terms described by Bertucci. Rather than "amplifying the difference in status," between dedicator and dedicatee as composers had done in early eighteenth-century epistles, Gossec's dedication situates him on a social plane alongside wealthy connoisseurs and amateurs.[153]

These changes in musical production occurred amid a broader series of policy efforts intended to dismantle corporate privileges and to deregulate the economy. The Crown recognized a need to close the faucet of the no-longer-lucrative "fountain of privilege." The Controller-General of Finance Anne-Robert-Jacques Turgot espoused Physiocratic theories as the solution. Originally, staunch Physiocrats adhered to the proposals of the movement's founder, François Quesnay, who posited that economic prosperity could only come from a robust, deregulated agricultural system rooted in geometry and bordering on the mystical.[154] A "free market," after all, requires faith.[155] Physiocrats adapted Quesnay's rigid, sometimes esoteric conceptions to a more political proposition: the market would thrive if left to liberal individuals in competition with one another, free from the kind of regulation that privileges enforced.[156] In other words, the competition for privileges prevented a truly free market from forming. Only three years after the court musicians published their fatal assault on the *ménétriers*, the Parlement of Paris pleaded with King Louis XVI not to approve Turgot's "Six Edicts" abolishing the French corporate system. Turgot's fall from power in 1776 briefly spared the guilds from extinction, but he had nourished the idea that guilds were an unfair collective privilege that impinged on individual liberty.

Deregulation provided an opportunity to recast trades as professions and to elevate entwined legal and social status. The originally "illiberal" or protectionist mercantilist economic systems led to the liberalization of professions across Europe as monarchies began weakening guild restrictions to expedite trade.[157] Defining features of a liberal profession included freedom from guild regulation and specialized education rather than apprentice-based training.[158] An example of this process in practice was when the pharmacists' guild loosened its hold in 1777 to open a *Collège*, raising pharmacy to the status of a "public utility" and "art" based in scientific thought in the field of chemistry.[159] In this, musicians seemed to have pioneered a professional trend, even if it went unacknowledged. Like the court musicians, playwrights too distanced themselves from the writer's guild to dissociate from those who lacked "genius" and to wrest control over their plays from privileged institutions.[160] The privileged Comédie-Française had long claimed plays as its own property and stopped compensating authors once ticket revenue for a particular work sank too low. Pierre Beaumarchais created the Société des Auteurs Dramatiques as a guild alternative through which to seek a fixed social status in the institutional workings of the Comédie-Française. But such social status in Old Regime France could only be secured through a legally defined position.[161]

During this period a patriotic sentiment emerged which situated the good of the nation above individual interests in the commercial endeavors that had long benefited only legally privileged individuals and institutions.[162] "Patriotic" playwrights, for example, sought to direct their work toward the public by casting it as a good for the nation rather than the court.[163] They embraced legal means to professional ends as musicians like Lully had long done.[164] Other playwrights accepted courtly civility, just as Mondonville had while running the Concert Spirituel. We shall see in Chapter 3 that composers for the dramatic stage eventually divided along similar lines.

Paradoxically, as musicians advanced their social status their legal options in some ways narrowed. Legal pursuit of property rights went against courtly behavior because such actions belied a material disinterest expected of true "men of letters,"[165] an expectation that Voltaire thwarted when he pursued Travenol in court. It seems that some customs had changed since the time of Lully, when aggressive legal actions were a viable route to securing personal privileges. These tensions set significant precedents for changes in musical production shown in Chapters 3 through 6. Individual rights, deregulation, and the utility of the arts and sciences would become defining features of proprietary debates around music during the French Revolution. But as it stood in the late 1770s, guilds faced extinction in light of growing liberal professionalism and deregulation. Musicians perhaps surprisingly found themselves on the cutting edge of these changes.

The Crown sought two reforms around privilege to reconcentrate power with the monarch and to abolish any economic and fiscal privileges that hindered market competition or prevented lucrative tax revenue. These changes inevitably affected musical privilege. In 1777, the Crown reversed its earlier position on printing privileges and "reaffirmed the absolutist interpretation of royal privileges as an emanation of the king's grace alone and not the recognition of a property right," explains historian Carla Hesse.[166] This judgment effectively broke up the monopoly of the publishers' and printers' guild. Paradoxically, it granted ownership priority to individual authors even as it reversed the assertion that privileges affirm anterior property rights.[167] In May 1782, seeking to offset expenses from the Seven Years' War and American Revolution, Louis XVI turned his eye toward his *corps de la musique* and put forth an edict and new regulations that would dictate its activities.[168] He cut the *corps* budget nearly in half from 499,848 *livres* per year to 259,600.[169] The Opéra was soon reclaimed as the Crown's personal property, as well.[170] With a king from whom all privilege flowed, there was in reality no possibility of a "free" market. Because the prerevolutionary legal system remained indistinct from its political system and because all rights to property and power flowed through the king rather than through an open political market, only cronyism provided the opportunity to exchange rights beneficially outside "loyalty rights"—privileges that required loyalty to the king.[171] This political and socioeconomic structure generated confusion. Individuals believed they owned and traded privileges that oftentimes did not in strictly legal terms belong to them.

The reassertion of the Opéra's power over theatrical productions in Paris epitomizes the contradictory project of simultaneously strengthening and limiting privilege. The Opéra, once again the monarch's property as described by Charlton, was granted authority in 1784 over the establishment of all fair or boulevard theaters, which in the past had been regulated not by privileges but by police permits.[172] Such marginal industrial activity had long been allowed to take place among the loopholes of privilege in the faubourgs.[173] As part of these changes the Opéra granted the privilege to a theater called the Variétés-Amusantes to two entrepreneurs of its choice, leaving the theater's original director, François Duval Malter, disenfranchised and dispossessed. When Malter brought a lawsuit, the Council of State agreed that he should receive a small compensation for the movable property that he had lost, but otherwise they found in favor of the new entrepreneurs chosen by the Opéra. According to the Council, Malter had never owned the theater, only permission by police permit to run it. "Privilege prevailed over property," concludes Michèle Root-Bernstein.[174]

The Opéra provides a perfect replica in miniature of the governmental model that the Crown sought during this period. The reorganization in some ways generated a microcosmic free market under concentrated authority. The Opéra received revenue from lesser theaters, but as a result, those lesser theaters could openly compete with one another for privilege, even as the Opéra denied complaints about competition from the Comédie-Française.[175] A confusing state of affairs indeed. Ironically, the two entrepreneurs who had received the privilege in favor of Malter in 1784 published a memoir against exclusive privilege in 1785![176]

Musicologists have long noted how such contradictions in the late eighteenth-century Parisian music world affected music consumption. Although the Concert Spirituel saw some generic and programming innovations in instrumental music during the 1770s and 1780s, the fact remained that only an elite group of Parisians enjoyed access to performances of *musique moderne*. Private concerts became the vanguard of new music, where Italianate and instrumental genres thrived. Some scholars even cast these institutions, at least those that welcomed a broader bourgeois audience, as "semipublic,"[177] ultimately a way to circumvent musical privilege. Julia Doe argues that theatrical privileges frustrated attempts at generic experimentation except when permitted by the monarchs, rendering the system all the more arbitrary.[178] The Crown, despite its apparently progressive taste, hindered new musical genres from reaching a wider public even amidst a flourishing printed discourse and music print market that demonstrated the Parisian public's growing melomania. Disillusionment with privilege's protections caused the number of registered music-printing privileges to drop dramatically from the 1760s to 1780s: twelve registered between 1765 and 1769, nine during the 1770s, and only three from 1780 to 1786.[179] Although Jean Gribenski argues that the diminished faith in the power of privileges were the sign of a weakening monarchy,[180] privilege was always intended to be mutable in order to incite competition. Consequently, privileges proliferated to a point of obsolescence in music publishing. Despite these frustrations, professional musicians in many ways benefited from the bewildering privilege system because they had already adapted to a deteriorating corporate system. The 1780s reforms thus affected professional musicians in two ways—they not only saw a wider music market open but also found positions of authority within and around privileged institutions, including the most privileged theater in the kingdom, the Opéra.

A robust "gig economy" developed in Paris, illustrated most saliently on the eve of Revolution by the *Tablettes de renommée des musiciens*, a subset of the *Almanach général* published by Mathurin Roze de Chantoiseau from 1769 until 1791.[181] His goal was to directly connect merchants with artists.[182] De Chantoiseau's publication supported emergent free-trade ideologies by connecting craftsmen with the shopkeepers who could sell their products, necessarily surpassing guild restrictions. As Root points out, "once the buyer and seller are brought together, the middleman," in the case of France, the king, "is no longer needed."[183] The evolution of musicians' place in the *Almanach* is telling. In 1769, it included only around 100 musicians, primarily tutors and performers whose specializations ranged from the lowly musette and *vielle* to violins, keyboards, and voice. By 1791, the *Almanach* grew to include university faculties from theology to medicine and veterinary sciences, members of academies, painters, sculptors, and more. But by then the edition no longer included musicians because as early as 1785 their field had grown so large that it required an independent supplemental edition, the *Tablettes de renommée des musiciens*. Of the 800 musicians included in the 1785 edition, only 40 percent of their biographies note affiliation with one or more institutions.[184] This is remarkable because it indicates a profound change since the late seventeenth century, when musicians "belonged" to the court, noble households, the church, or a guild. Here, we find evidence of a robust market for freelance musicianship as aristocratic patronage "diluted."[185] Only about 25 percent of the *Tablettes* musicians listed affiliations with the court or church.[186]

Although Hennebelle highlights the equality that the *Tablettes* seemed to bestow on musicians, "fashioning a face of the dignified musician, where singularity prevails over anonymity, where successful composers and performers of the lyric stage do not eclipse the teachers of instrumental music, nor even orchestral musicians,"[187] a professional hierarchy harkening back to the days of Lully and Couperin *le grand* persists in the pamphlet. Hennebelle convincingly hypothesizes that the *Tablettes* does not even account for all professionals working in the Parisian music world at the time.[188] Instead, he proposes that, because its main criterion for inclusion was "notoriety," it represents primarily "the world of *savante* music . . . leaving in the shadows that of popular music,"[189] the music jettisoned from the Académie Royale de musique a century earlier. This is particularly notable when taking Bertucci's "ethnographic" categories into account. The *Tablettes* notes "savant" musicians, attributing this identity to a select few composers: Gluck, Niccolò Piccinni, and André-Ernest-Modeste Grétry, as well as to musicians who were members of the clergy, held high positions in the court, or enjoyed praise from the Académie Royale de musique. Musicians who composed for the stages (*auteurs*) and those affiliated with privileged institutions earned a higher social status in the *Tablettes,* seeming to complete the project begun by Lully over a century earlier.

Some musicians' autonomy and authority increased significantly in the new École Royale de chant et de déclamation, an institution founded in 1784 in response to a public demand for higher-quality performances at the Opéra. The Opéra needed to respond to public taste because, as Louis XVI noted in the 1780 edict reorganizing the institution under Papillion de la Ferté, it contributed to French commerce and industry.[190] Parisian audiences began to expect better singing and the "revolution" in music attributed to the arrival of Gluck, Piccinni, and Antonio Sacchini, fueled a French desire to compete with their peers, particularly the Italians.[191] This caused an outcry for a school where opera singers could train like the Italian music conservatories.[192]

The École offered at least a small group of musicians more agency in a privileged institution and began to standardize musicians' training within a broader curriculum, a notable feature of professionalization that resembled the standardization of education that many professionals from teachers to artists underwent during this period.[193] Michel Noiray compares it specifically to the education of painters and actors. Its contemporaneity with other new institutions like the *Collège* for pharmacy and the School of Mines should also be taken into account.[194] When Gossec took over as the École director in 1784, he hoped to offer a more "liberal" education including geography, history, and mythology, the kind of education that distinguished learned professionals from artisans.[195] Noiray delineates the École's academy-like training from the Opéra musicians who he describes as acting in a "corporate" manner, particularly in their animosity toward the new school's authority.[196] The Opéra technically had a singing school and offered some training in its *magasin*, but it did not employ a curriculum and merely targeted specific roles that singers were slated to perform. The *magasin*-trained singers were consequently critiqued as "automata," because they mimicked roles without careful thought or education.[197] These critiques relegated Opéra performers to Bertucci's category of artisans who performed rote tasks, just like the guild-trained musicians who fought Lully and Couperin in the seventeenth century.

From the construction to the crumbling of Colbertism, privilege defined musical production in Old Regime Paris. It created patrons, dictated performance, inflected publishing, and regulated technical innovation. But as the "fountain of privilege" diluted, musicians found new spaces for themselves. At the end of the eighteenth century, Parisian musicians had distinguished themselves in privileged institutions not as servants but as respected professionals who valued, like their peers in other fields, "education, personal dignity, and social utility."[198] Legal privilege was after all also a social concept; it is this aspect of Old Regime privilege that the following chapter illuminates.[199]

2 | Social *Privilège* and Musician-Masons

The beloved opera composer André-Ernest-Modeste Grétry claimed that in Old Regime Paris musicians felt "humiliated by the little consideration they enjoyed, not as artists, but as men."[1] The previous chapter revealed the improved professional opportunities musicians found during the eighteenth century, however, according to Grétry, they still failed to find social equality "as men" within Parisian society. As he rose to fame during the 1770s and became a favorite of Marie Antoinette, Grétry ostensibly detested the rigid stratification among court creatures even as he climbed their ranks. Yet slowly the composer witnessed a change in this state of social affairs. "I saw born and enacted a revolution among musical artists," he whimsically recounted around 1800, "which slightly preceded the great political revolution" of 1789.[2]

He supported this observation with an anecdote, alleging that "many similar scenes" took place among musicians on the eve of revolution.[3] One day in the waning Old Regime, Grétry chronicles, a musician presented himself on an opulent Parisian doorstep to challenge its occupant, a marquis, to a duel. The musician's orchestra colleagues encouraged him to confront the nobleman, whom they refused to admit into performances until he apologized for incessantly mocking their comrade's corpulence throughout an entire concert the prior evening. The marquis balked at the mere suggestion of dueling with a musician. "Nobility" prevented him from accepting such a socially uneven engagement. "It would be much more degrading to your nobility," the musician advised, "if you would allow me to give you a commoner's correction."[4] Fearing an embarrassing public display, the marquis reluctantly accepted. The musician demanded a *privilège*, "a liberty . . . to do [some]thing that others would not dare to do."[5] Dueling was not only illegal, but custom discouraged dueling with one's social superiors. Considered barbaric by the late eighteenth century, the practice had been quite unsuccessfully outlawed by Louis XIV a century earlier, yet "this privilege"—dueling—"endured, little daunted."[6]

While Grétry's story conveys a romanticized, perhaps even hypocritical postrevolutionary perspective, other literary depictions of duels published during this period also paradoxically reveal men "embodying freedom beyond the law yet subordinating [themselves] to cruelly inexorable rituals."[7] Grétry's duel conveys the musician's self-worth; duels represented a bourgeois assertion of merit that either "underscore[ed] specific sorts of professional rivalry" or served as "a vehicle of class sensitivity."[8] The marquis tacitly acknowledged his opponent's professional and social standing by accepting the musician's invitation. The composer's poetics astutely illustrate a musician navigating his evolving social status. Grétry's nameless musician performed in close proximity to the marquis in a setting like the masonic Concert de la Loge Olympique, an orchestra in which professionals, connoisseurs, and amateurs mixed, and where their class distinctions were temporarily suspended. Opera duets and "dueling" instrumental performances had recently aestheticized the duel as well, casting performers as transformed by their encounter.[9] In an enlightened duel like Grétry's, the two men would ideally walk away not simply alive but changed. Contemporaneous ideals of social harmony compelled the marquis to resolve the dissonance that he had struck with the musician.

Nowhere did metaphors of harmony imbue French discourses more pervasively than in masonic rhetoric. Musician-masons must have recognized the metaphor's irony all too well. While in the writings of Jean-Jacques Rousseau harmony symbolized a utopian equality, it in fact perfectly represented the hierarchical nature of lodge sociability and Old Regime society.[10] As the composer Jean-Philippe Rameau had proven earlier in the century, notes in a chord gravitate toward a root. Not only are individual chords stratified but also the entire harmonic system rests on a graded order of consonant, stable sonorities and dissonant embellishments. Although musicians simply ornamented masonic ritual when lodges were first established in Paris, they slowly came to play a more fundamental role in lodge life. Because French Masons concerned themselves with social status, lodge records provide an opportunity to examine professional musicians' evolving position within the privilege system of late eighteenth-century Paris. As the previous chapter demonstrated, legal and social status were deeply entwined in Old Regime France, and so they must be considered in tandem.

French Masonry, Music, and Parisian Sociability

Cosmopolitan Englishmen exported speculative Masonry to Paris from London, where it had originated in the Grand Lodge established there in 1717. The term "speculative," meaning theoretical, distinguished the new British Grand Lodge from the "operative" Masonry that had existed for centuries as a ritualized craft guild for men who actually practiced masonry. The transition from operative to speculative Masonry first occurred in seventeenth-century Scotland.[11] From its very inception, speculative Masonry prioritized music. The first masonic constitution, written by the British clergyman James Anderson, included a history of Masonry, an outline of the responsibilities and obligations of Freemasons, and a masonic songbook.[12] Music not only served masonic lodges during rituals and rites but also accompanied the conviviality of banquets and social events. Music and Masonry shared notable features, both required years of apprenticeship and revered Pythagorean theories. The masonic chapels that sheltered the brotherhood's secret ceremonies were even called "pillars of harmony."[13] Indeed, doctrines of physical and metaphysical harmony rested at the heart of masonic ritual.[14] It might be said that eighteenth-century speculative Masons used music to build the sacred spaces that operative Masons had once erected with stone and mortar.[15]

Masonic lodges proliferated as cultural life migrated from Versailles to Paris. Coincidentally, the first Parisian masonic lodge opened its doors in 1725, the same year that the city's first public concert series, the Concert Spirituel, was founded.[16] After Englishmen introduced speculative Masonry to France, it had a fitful start and was characterized by "factionalism [and] internal dissension."[17] During the 1730s, Parisian lodges received their patents from the Grand Lodge in London. Patents officially granted masonic privileges like freedom to affiliate with other lodges. This governance greatly resembled the French privilege system. Like all entities in France, lodges functioned through a highly centralized system of privileges that flowed from the top of its hierarchy. In 1738, the same year that Pope Clement XII condemned Freemasonry, French masons founded their first central administrative body, called the Grand Lodge like its British counterpart. (French Masons felt confident that the pope's edict did not apply to them.) Louis de Bourbon Condé, Comte de Clermont, was elected Grand Master of the French Grand Lodge on December 11, 1743. During the 1740s, investigations into rumored antireligious and antimonarchist plots plagued the new institutions. The Parisian Grand Lodge, known as the Grand Orient, was eventually reorganized in 1773 after much debate. A rival Scottish lodge had been a central antagonist in the mid-eighteenth-century French Freemasonry feuds. The Scottish rite recognized many more grades or membership ranks rather than the typical three, sometimes up to twenty-five. All French lodges received their foundational constitutions from the Grand Orient, however, the "mother" Scottish lodge began to grant constitutions to lodges that the central lodge had refused to recognize. But by 1781, the two "mother" lodges arrived at an understanding and coexisted peacefully until the Revolution. More aggressive counts estimate that about 600 lodges in France came under the Grand Orient's jurisdiction during the 1770s, rising to around 1,000 by 1789.[18]

Masonic lodges sat at the intersection of the growing public sphere theorized most famously by Jürgen Habermas and the more private world of aristocratic salons illuminated in great detail by Antoine Lilti.[19] In the public venues where Parisians began to exchange perspectives, they also exchanged money for goods and services. In other words, both social and economic conditions led First-Estate clergy and Second-Estate nobles to interact with Third-Estate bourgeois subjects in cafés, shops, and public gardens. More time spent people-watching sparked demand for affordable luxury goods like fashionable clothing and wigs, and as a result, it became increasingly difficult to discern individuals' social class based on appearances alone.[20] Mixing among social classes was facilitated in part by *politesse*.[21] "Politeness" did not erase inequality altogether, because it was fundamentally an aristocratic practice.[22] Instead, *politesse* encouraged Parisians to set aside inequality for the sake of civil discourse.[23] Because lodge culture traversed the boundaries between Old Regime hierarchy and budding republican equality, it vividly reveals the tensions that professional musicians experienced within this evolving socioeconomic context.[24]

Freemasonry helped to popularize such new modes of sociability.[25] Masonic brothers and sisters were forbidden from discussing their "civil status" once they crossed a lodge threshold. France was one of the few countries to permit female Masons, who joined affiliate "sister lodges" and cosponsored events with their male counterparts.[26] While Masons likely knew one another's real-world statuses, within the *temple* social distinctions were purposely set aside as the more democratic *politesse* eclipsed old forms of sociability like *honnêteté* (courtly manners).[27] By the 1770s it may have seemed like everyone had become a Freemason, however in reality only about 3 percent of the Parisian population belonged to a lodge.[28] Members came from across the First, Second, and Third Estates—from the king's immediate family to members of the military to merchants and lawyers. Even Marie Antoinette attended lodge events. Although at their inception few Parisian lodges counted professional musicians among their members,[29] later in the century, when lodges began to serve as centers of learning and culture, musicians were increasingly inducted as brothers.

Yet far from the masonic utopia depicted in Mozart's *Magic Flute* (1791), the brotherhood did not truly equalize social relations. Lodge leadership implemented strict membership hierarchies that in many ways mirrored not only the Old Regime estates and military but also craft and trade guilds, even adopting some of the medieval institutions' language.[30] The Grand Orient leadership had a markedly noble composition compared to Parisian Freemasonry in general.[31] Its grandmaster, Louis Philippe II, Duke d'Orléans, descended from Louis XIV's younger brother and was one of the closest blood relatives to the king. His son of the same name would later become king of France during the 1830 Revolution. Rarely had the French seen the royal family, nobility, or military socialize with members of the Third Estate as they began to in Parisian lodges, particularly among lawyers and financiers.[32]

Unlike the rising bourgeois professionals who infiltrated these aristocratic echelons, other groups did not receive such a warm welcome into the brotherhood. Lodge sociability depended on morality and loyalty, and inductees were required to prove "knowledge," "conduct," and "zeal" among other attributes in order to earn a voice within the fraternal harmony. Freemasons recognized a universal supreme being, yet Jews were sometimes denied admission to lodges simply because of "spiritual differences."[33] And local masonic authorities often refused membership based on professional class alone. Standards differed from one city or town to the next. Workers who received wages from traders were excluded from Bordeaux lodges, while tanners were shunned among Masons in Brest. Even as the Grand Lodge took great care to curate a mixed yet respectable social composition in lodges and generally supported exclusivity and hierarchy,[34] some provincial lodges accused it of maintaining lax membership standards.[35] The Grand Lodge denied constitutions to one lodge for admitting too many merchants and expressed dissent when an actor somehow earned a position of leadership in another.[36] Actors and servants were forbidden from the brotherhood throughout France because Masons questioned the former's morals and the latter's "dependency" or "subordination." Actors' morality had long been suspect as a result of their ability to behave in a manner that did not represent their true feelings, and servants were believed to prioritize loyalty to their master (their source of income) over their brothers. Servants could only join the lowest masonic ranks in order to perform domestic duties within lodges. This social threshold—what historians have called "the limits of salaried dependence and artisanal independence"[37]—represented a crucial standard that professional musicians needed to meet not only in lodge life but also in social life more widely. To be a "free" professional, they were expected to possess mastery over their own comportment. As shown in the previous chapter, musicians had only recently escaped servitude at the court and church to become "artists" in the eyes of the law.

Archival documents that remain from Parisian lodges thus provide an opportunity to test Grétry's plausible claim that during the 1770s and 1780s musicians corrected the "little consideration" they received "as men." Table 2.1 summarizes the lodges that serve as focal points in this chapter, which were selected because many musicians who populated them would later join

TABLE 2.1 Parisian lodges that serve as focal points for this chapter.

La Réunion des Arts	Originated with a group of violinists
La Candeur	An aristocratic, military lodge where musicians served
Les Amis Réunis	A large Parisian lodge known for its concerts
Saint-Jean d'Écosse du Contrat Social	Scottish Rite lodge where musicians held leadership roles
Olympique	Aristocratic and best-known musical lodge
Les Neufs Sœurs	Lodge founded as a learned society

the Paris Conservatory.[38] French historians have already systematically calculated the number of musician-masons in Paris and indexed the lodges to which they belonged, ultimately arguing that speculative Masonry granted musicians a bourgeois status by the time the Revolution began in 1789.[39] Their claim rests primarily on the fact that musicians gained access to new patrons through lodge affiliation. While these sociological conclusions about musician-masons are in many respects accurate, they require nuance. The term "bourgeois" fails to capture the multifarious statuses that musicians came to occupy.[40] Musicians' masonic rankings offer a framework through which to consider this social diversity in practice. As a cultural microcosm, lodge sociability indeed reveals that musicians distinguished themselves from servants. More importantly, masonic terminology articulates the varied ways in which musicians acquired social *privilèges* in the two decades prior to the Revolution.

Brother Servants and Occasional Brothers

The orchestra musician Georges Jacques Devaux provides an illustrative case of musicians' changing sociability in Parisian lodges. From the few historical traces left behind by Devaux, it seems he was neither famous nor wealthy; he was just a decent violinist who made his living as such. He performed in the orchestra at the Concert Spirituel, and in 1786 his name appeared as a tutor at the Opéra on the *Tablettes de renommées des musiciens*, discussed in the previous chapter. Devaux was in no way courtly like Mondonville or Grétry. Nevertheless, by the 1780s Devaux found a respected place for himself among the masonic lodges of late eighteenth-century Paris. Devaux's path to masonic glory, while relatively short, proved anything but easy.

Musicians were at first neither well represented nor well regarded in the Parisian lodges recognized by the Grand Lodge. Devaux and his brothers in the lodge La Réunion des Arts were painfully aware of this reality. To become a recognized lodge, gentlemen had to prove to the Grand Lodge that they desired membership in the brotherhood and had already been gathering regularly to participate in activities befitting Masons. When Devaux and his fourteen brothers at La Réunion des Arts first requested a constitution from the Grand Lodge in 1776, their membership was composed almost entirely of musicians with the sole exception of one priest, who may well have been musically inclined, too.[41] Eleven of the musicians (at least eight, violinists) listed their occupation as "Académie Royale de Musique" (the Opéra), and two simply as "music teacher."[42] In this, the musicians resemble other professionals who identified themselves in lodge documents primarily through the privileged institutions to which they belonged. From 1776 to 1778, the most notable commonality among the musicians who joined La Réunion des Arts was their membership in the orchestras at the Concert Spirituel and Opéra.[43]

When the Grand Lodge's Paris chamber unanimously denied the Réunion brothers a constitution in 1777,[44] it was the second time that their table had been rejected. Lodge tables listed the names, occupations, and masonic rank of each member. So it seemed to be the social composition of their membership that failed to meet the Grand Lodge's approval. The musicians of La Réunion des Arts persisted. Certain that their demonstrated "zeal" for Masonry would eventually find recognition in the form of a constitution,[45] they appealed the rejection to the Grand Lodge council. Devaux and his brothers demanded a prompt ruling about whether the chamber had perhaps misjudged their carefully compiled dossier.[46] The council, which essentially acted as the Grand Lodge's court of appeals, agreed to send the application for reconsideration in the chambers, a body that oversaw the establishment of new lodges.[47]

La Réunion des Arts must have received yet another rejection, because nearly one year later the lodge submitted a third request to the Grand Lodge. This time, a Brother Devillière from the lodge Caroline Louise Queen of Naples agreed to serve as an advocate for the brothers of La Réunion des Arts. Devillière's lodge affiliation was apropos, since the Queen of Naples (Marie Antoinette's sister) was known as a champion of oppressed Masons.[48] The new dossier included previously submitted records, showing lodge activities and membership from 1776 and 1777, and a new membership table, "to purify [their] lodge according to [the Grand Lodge's] desire."[49] It was this dossier that finally earned Devaux and his brothers a constitution. Two years after the first application, La Réunion des Arts finally celebrated its official installation as a constitutionally recognized Parisian masonic lodge in September 1778.[50]

Though none of the appeals explicitly reveal why the Grand Lodge rejected La Réunion des Arts, the lodge's difficulty in obtaining a constitution likely stemmed from its social composition: all musicians, mostly orchestra violinists, and not a single bourgeois subject, learned professional, or member of the military or nobility among them. The historian Gérard Gefen has suggested that the vulgar reputation of violinists in mid-eighteenth-century France, fueled by the court versus guild feuds discussed in the previous chapter, may have in fact inspired them to become Freemasons in an attempt to elevate their social statuses.[51] In 1777, La Réunion des Arts had made a seemingly desperate attempt to diversify its membership and satisfy the Grand Lodge's preferences by adding a seventy-five-year-old infantry lieutenant to its table, but the remaining twelve brothers (the oldest among them aged forty-one) were all musicians.[52] By 1778, however, the professions represented on La Réunion des Arts' tables changed. Alongside seventeen musicians could be found a customs director, a "bourgeois" from Paris, a draftsman, and an ex-infantryman who held a venal office.[53] This table contained more varied professions and the backing of Devillière, already a Mason. It was this table that eventually earned the Grand Lodge's approval. Devaux and his brothers enjoyed their very own lodge privileges only after diversifying their membership from a simple band of violinists.

During the time that La Réunion des Arts sought official recognition, in other lodges, musicians were still overtly treated as servants. The Parisian lodge La Candeur, for example, was decidedly aristocratic.[54] The highest ranks of the French nobility and military populated La Candeur, and its affiliated women's lodge boasted famous countesses and marquises, including favorites of Queen Marie Antoinette. The metaphors of harmony and the masonic canticles ornamenting La Candeur's ceremonies hid neither its members' aristocratic musical tastes nor their low regard for "brother musicians." The description of banquets held by La Candeur might easily be mistaken for an evening among Marie Antoinette's intimates at court.[55]

After opening one banquet with toasts to King Louis XV, La Candeur's brothers and sisters sang verses on themes of virtue, wisdom, charity, and joy. The verses, authored by the lodge's noble members, were set to well-known popular tunes and *opéra comique* airs. Many of the preexisting melodies came from the *opéra comiques* composed by the court-favorite composer Grétry. When the banquet concluded, lodge members mounted their very own production of his *L'ami de la maison* (1771). In fact, the only printed music in La Candeur's pamphlets from this period is an air from Grétry's *La rosière de Salenci* (1774). Both operas had been performed at court and at the Comédie-Italienne. By this time, Italianate French dialogue opera had become a marker of more progressive aristocratic taste, particularly because of Marie Antoinette's preference for the genre.[56]

Like Marie Antoinette's Trianon performances, the nobles at La Candeur's banquet entertained themselves by performing lighthearted music taken from their favorite court performances. Simple airs and popular melodies also promised to showcase aristocratic singers without revealing any lack of musical talent. A tune performed at the banquet, shown in Example 2.1, was frequently (and incorrectly) attributed to the master of comic opera, Giovanni Battista Pergolesi, who had famously composed *La serva padrona* (1733)—Parisians' first introduction to the genre.[57] The lyrics that the La Candeur brother Charles-Henri Ribouté authored for the "Pergolesi" melody carry a distinctly masonic message honoring universal, benevolent deities. Ribouté thwarts any overly optimistic expectations that listeners may have held for the performance, asking, "Is eloquence necessary when one has feeling?"

Although musicians were necessary to aristocratic lodges' festivities, tables evince their social inferiority in these spaces, where they were treated

EXAMPLE 2.1 A poem by La Candeur brother Charles-Henri Ribouté set to "Que ne suis-je la fougère?" exemplifies the musical tastes of an aristocratic social lodge.

as servants. La Candeur's banquet description does not mention André Jean Gallet, Jacques Schneitzhoffer, or Jean-François Veillard, three musicians who would later join the Paris Conservatory during the Revolution. Yet the three must have witnessed and accompanied the spectacle. Their names appear on La Candeur's membership tables among the lodge's "brother musicians," listed just above the final membership classification—"waged brother servants" (Figure 2.1).[58] This placement, separate from regular lodge brothers and situated near the messenger and concierge, indicates the low regard in which La Candeur held its musicians.[59] The musicians' masonic ranks appear alongside their name and instrument simply to confirm their affiliation, since the Grand Lodge forbade nonmasons, called profanes, from attending lodge events. The servants could only join the lowest rank, apprentice, to conform to these rules, and the table carefully notes that they are "paid." Brother-servant Richard is identified as *nègre*. The table thus reveals a constellation of aristocratic social values and prejudices.

The lodge's military roots are particularly evident even among its musicians; of the sixteen who appear on its tables, ten served the Gardes françaises, the infantry regiment of the king's household.[60] Most of La Candeur's regular members held honorary military titles as part of their noble lineage and, like military instrument ensembles, a typical lodge ensemble, called a *harmonie*, included only wind instruments.[61] Among La Candeur's musicians were clarinetists, oboists, flutists, hornists, and bassoonists. The choice to perform Grétry's *L'ami de la maison* makes sense in light of these performance forces, as the opera could have been easily executed by the small wind band.[62] The only La Candeur musician who did not come from a military background was the oboist Veillard, who came instead from Louis Philippe II's personal orchestra. All of La Candeur's "brother musicians" served the nobility, whether on the battle field or in their homes.

In an exclusively aristocratic and military lodge like La Candeur, which was dedicated to both charity and entertainment, musicians maintained a courtlike status as servants who executed practical duties. They played their instruments just as the messenger delivered messages: on command and at the pleasure of their "brothers and sisters." As at court, La Candeur's musicians neither composed banquet music nor starred in performances. The aristocratic lodge members sang; the musicians accompanied. As Grétry would complain years later, the musicians were treated as instruments, "to be dumped in the same case" after performing.[63] Unlike Devaux and his fellow violinists in La Réunion des Arts, Gallet, Schneitzhoffer, and Veillard simply ornamented La Candeur's revelry.

During the 1780s, larger lodges began to actively recruit musicians for their *harmonies* and orchestras.[64] Because the Opéra's privilege continued to hinder completely public concerts, lodges became "semi-public" venues for musical performance.[65] As instrumental music began to take on a more

(5)

FRERES MUSICIENS.

Noms des Freres.	Talens.	Grades.
GALLET.	Clarinette.	M∴
BONNAIRE.	Clarinette.	M∴
HARTEMANNE.	Clarinette.	Ap∴ Comp∴
LOUIS.	Clarinette.	Comp∴
LIX (l'aîné).	Clarinette.	Comp∴
LIX (le cadet).	Clarinette.	Comp∴
VÉLIARD.	Hautbois.	M∴
BRUAND.	Hautbois.	Comp∴
PINOTON.	Flûte.	Comp∴
FALCOZ.	Flûte.	Ap∴
BURRY.	Cor-de-chasse.	M∴
SERVETA.	Cor-de-chasse.	M∴
PFALTZGRAFF.	Cor-de-chasse.	Comp∴
SCHNEITZHOFFER.	Basson.	M∴
KOCH.	Basson.	M∴

| EVRARD, Tapissier. | Décorateur. | M∴ |

FRERES SERVANS GAGÉS.

| RICHARD (Nègre). | Messager. | Ap∴ |
| BATAILLE. | Concierge. | Ap∴ |

FIGURE 2.1 A membership table from La Candeur situates musicians apart from lodge members, just above the "waged brother servants." Courtesy of the Bibliothèque nationale de France.

prominent role in lodge life, Devaux, Gallet, Schneitzhoffer, and Veillard all joined more visible lodges, where musicians slowly climbed the masonic ranks from "brother servants," to "occasional brothers," and, for a lucky few, to the coveted ranking "free associate," a category that waived subscription fees for a select number of gentlemen who could not afford membership dues but possessed skills deemed valuable to a lodge.

SOCIAL *PRIVILÈGE* AND MUSICIAN-MASONS | 61

Parisian lodges maintained instrument ensembles to serve a variety of social, ceremonial, and moral functions: to entertain during lodge festivities, to enhance the solemnity of masonic rites, and to raise money for charitable initiatives. Lodges took on the title *société* when hosting profane, that is, nonmasonic events such as charitable, musical, or even political activities.[66] Along with the lodges Olympique and Les Neuf Sœurs, to which we shall return later, Les Amis Réunis emerged as a particularly musical lodge and maintained an orchestra called the Société des Amis Réunis.[67] The Société held around twelve concerts per year to raise money that would contribute to the lodge's various philanthropic endeavors.[68]

Performing in a lodge's *harmonie* or orchestra did not necessarily indicate that musicians fully participated in lodge social life. Les Amis Réunis initiated twenty-eight musicians as brothers and affiliated eight others, yet it also counted thirty-seven "occasional brothers and brother servants" among its ranks.[69] The lodge likely brought in "occasional brothers" only for performances, never initiating them as full members. Forty *aggrégés* positions accommodated professional and amateur musicians who already belonged to other lodges and performed in the Réunis orchestra at concerts and other events.[70] Because masonic policy mandated that all participants in lodge activities hold masonic status, it was far easier to "borrow" musicians from other lodges as necessary. The historian Pierre-François Pinaud postulates that many musicians, particularly foreigners, were likely forgotten in the records of Les Amis Réunis. His assertion rests on the fact that neither the forty *aggrégés* nor the "occasional brothers" are ever totally accounted for in the extant membership tables.[71] In most years, tables indicate that the lodge could have convened a small ensemble from among its own membership, but it likely relied on outside musicians to execute any major performances. A preponderance of the musicians officially inducted as Les Amis Réunis brothers identified professionally as either composers or violinists, an indication of their status compared to mere orchestra musicians, who were only required for a monthly concert and not for the social functioning of the lodge. By now, some violinists had become esteemed virtuosos, a welcome elevation from their monodic shame during the battles with Couperin discussed in the previous chapter.

Few musicians ascended the hierarchy of Les Amis Réunis, and only one seems to have earned a "free associate" position. In Les Amis Réunis, the free-associate positions were instead dominated by doctors, surgeons, medical students, and apothecaries. The prestige of all of these professions had recently been elevated due to their combination of practical, skilled work with liberal education. These gentlemen did not just use instruments, they were thinkers, too. The lodge valued scientific expertise above all else.[72] The violinist Jean Bitsch was the lone musician to attend the lodge's fabled international assemblies, apparently convened to hatch political plots to subvert the monarchy.[73] Bitsch was born in Cologne; fluency in German would have been a useful skill during the bilingual assemblies held with German-speaking delegates. And the cellist Gilles Louis Chrétien earned a free-associate membership likely due to his penchant for science not strings. Chrétien had developed a physionotype, a device that allowed artists to quickly sketch the contours of a human face.[74] His clear application of scientific inquiry to the arts likely drew the attention of his brothers in Les Amis Réunis. Neither Bitsch nor Chrétien climbed Les Amis Réunis' ranks for their musical merit. In this lodge, musicians were admitted primarily for their utility to mount concerts rather than any particular social prestige or musical knowledge that they might have contributed to the organization.

As "brother musicians" and "occasional brothers" in La Candeur and Les Amis Réunis, musicians continued to fulfill a more servile role, even as some like Bitsch and Chrétien earned regard for nonmusical talents. Musician-masons nevertheless began to see a gradual upward social mobility that would continue to rise during the 1780s, when their fellow musicians earned the coveted lodge positions once reserved for other learned professionals.

Talented Brothers, Architects of Music, and Free Associates

In Saint-Jean d'Écosse du Contrat Social, which boasted the largest membership of any Parisian lodge, musicians began to ascend to grades above the entry-level title "apprentice" (a term adopted from guilds).[75] As a Scottish lodge competing with the official Grand Lodge, Le Contrat Social's impressive orchestra fulfilled not only social, ceremonial, and moral purposes but also projected vitality and status to its rival "mother" lodge, the Grand Orient. The lodge actively recruited thirty-nine musicians into its ranks as *frères à talent*, "talented brothers," a membership category for those awarded lodge positions despite their inferior social status by merit of their desirable talents.[76]

The composer Étienne-Joseph Floquet was one of the first musicians to earn a prestigious masonic leadership position when he became Le Contrat Social's *architecte de la musique*.[77] Floquet had found success at the Opéra with his heroic ballet *L'union d'amour et des arts* (1773), however, at the time that he became architect, he was struggling in the shadow of Piccinni and Gluck's popularity in Paris. Floquet's nonmusician brothers depended on him to manage the orchestra and even to recommend new *frères à talent* when the lodge required more musicians. Two of Floquet's colleagues, the music publisher Jean-Jérôme Imbault and the singer Jean-François Laïs, soon shared his title and duties as fellow music architects. When Floquet died suddenly at the age of thirty-four (rumor had it that he succumbed to excessive carousing with less-than-reputable ladies), Le Contrat Social memorialized him with all the ceremony and sentiment reserved for well-respected brothers. Rather than appoint a new leader to the orchestra, Le Contrat Social's administrators invited the musicians to elect from among themselves a new trio of architects.[78] This privilege demonstrated a growing trust that musicians were dependable professionals capable of self-direction.

As some orchestra musicians earned self-direction, soloists meanwhile garnered celebrity-like status. Yet their notoriety became fraught as social class intersected with other factors like gender or race. For example, when the accomplished violinist and conductor Joseph Bologne, the Chevalier de Saint-Georges, attended one of the Contrat Social concerts at the end of 1780, he was apparently "introduced," upon entering the lodge, "with the honors due to his grade."[79] A Contrat Social brother alleged that, at the time of Saint-Georges's visit, he was a member of the lodge Les Neuf Sœurs—this is the earliest evidence of the virtuoso's highly rumored masonic affiliations.[80] Grétry credited musicians' social elevation during the 1770s and 1780s to Saint-Georges's "manly courage."[81] Indeed, as a virtuoso violinist, composer, and conductor, he offered an ideal avatar for Grétry's liberated musician: freed from the servitude of previous generations and accepted among the Parisian elite, including Marie Antoinette, Saint-Georges in some ways seemed to transcend through his superior talents in music, dance, and fencing not only his status as musician but also his heritage as the son of an enslaved woman. And yet Saint-Georges had been passed over in a bid for director of the Opéra because its leading ladies petitioned the queen and refused to work under a "mulatto." He also suffered more than one physical assault in the streets of cosmopolitan Europe. Although Saint-Georges was believed to have been a Mason and conductor of masonic orchestras, except for the letter mentioned earlier no lodge materials identify him as such. Some historians of Masonry suggest that Saint-Georges's race may have prevented him from being included on membership tables even if he were an active participant in lodge social life and a renowned musician.[82] Figure 2.1 shows that La Candeur's servant, Richard, is identified as *nègre* on the lodge's tables. Perhaps even attempting to list Saint-Georges on such an explicitly stratified table would have proven too complex for *politesse* to navigate.

Saint-Georges is fabled to have conducted the Concert de la Loge Olympique. Of all the Parisian lodge orchestras, Olympique is memorialized for its talented musicians and for the high commission that Saint-Georges supposedly negotiated for Haydn's Paris Symphonies, which the Olympique orchestra premiered.[83] Olympique membership tables remain extant only from 1786 and 1788, so it is entirely possible that Saint-Georges joined Olympique as early as 1779 and remained a member until 1785, the period when Haydn received the commission.[84] Olympique was after all founded to replace the Concert des Amateurs, the orchestra that Saint-Georges directed until its closure in 1781.[85] The Loge Olympique perhaps more than any other Parisian lodge exposes the paradoxes of musicians' rising social status on the eve of Revolution.

The Olympique's bylaws explicitly set forth its musical ambitions: "The origin and fundamental nature of the Olympic Lodge and Society is absolutely masonic.... Its primary purpose and interest for a large number of the Masons who formed it, and for those who have since joined, is the establishment of *a good concert* that could, in some respects, replace the loss of the Concert des Amateurs."[86] From 1786 until July 1789, Olympique held concerts in the Salle des Gardes of the Tuileries Palace. To reach the hall, Olympique concertgoers walked directly through the Salle des Cents Suisses, the former venue of the Concert Spirituel, which in 1784 moved to the Salle des Machines.[87] Apparently the neighboring Concert Spirituel had failed to fill the musical void left by the Concert des Amateurs—perhaps because of its haphazard programming in comparison to the Olympique's carefully curated and commissioned programs.[88] Privilege, remember, granted access to emergent musical genres.

Olympique's tables provide compelling evidence of the tensions in musicians' status. Olympique technically comprised three parts: the masonic lodge (Loge Olympique de la Parfaite Estime), the concert series (Concert de la Loge Olympique), and the social club (Société Olympique). There were three membership classes in the lodge, including administrators who directed lodge bureaucracy, subscribers who paid membership fees, and free associates. Administrators came from among the lodge's subscribers. Subscribers paid 120 *livres* for access to the lodge, its social events, and most importantly, the concert series.[89] Masonic affiliation was required to attend the twelve concerts per year, however, once inducted into the first degree members were not required to pursue further masonic grades. Olympique affiliated a women's lodge so that the fair sex could attend the concerts and lodge events.

The bylaws stipulated twenty-four free-associate positions for members invited to join without paying the subscription fee because of their utility to the society as "artist professors" or amateurs.[90] While some lodges like Les Amis Réunis reserved "free associate" positions for doctors and scientists, Olympique particularly targeted musicians for this membership category; they occupied half of the free-associate slots in 1786 and 1788. Unlike the *frères à talent* inducted into Le Contrat Social despite their inferior social status, Olympique's free associates were not required to perform in the orchestra, though some did.[91] Rather, free-associate musicians in Olympique earned their membership because they brought a certain prestige or expertise rather than only a service to the lodge.[92] Free associates enjoyed many of the same benefits as dues-paying members, but they could not hold offices in the lodge leadership and were submitted to a merit evaluation by the lodge administration before annual membership renewal. Many likely composed music for the lodge or advised in a musical capacity.[93] These memberships were enjoyed mostly by well-known composers, musicographers, and music entrepreneurs—Jean-Joseph Cambini, Nicolas-Étienne Framery, Louis Joseph Françœur, Nicolas-Marie Dalayrac, Étienne-Nicolas Méhul, and François-André Danican Philidor. Other free associates included a violinist who would lead the Olympique orchestra as its conductor in 1788 and 1789, Guillaum Navoigille-Julien, and the singers Pierre-Jean Garrat and Louis Augustin Richer. Despite the rumors surrounding Saint-Georges, Navoigille-Julien is the only musician definitively identified as a conductor for the Olympique orchestra by the extant membership tables. Anecdotal evidence suggests that the virtuoso violinist Giovanni Battista Viotti held the position as well.[94]

Olympique's tables display a clear social stratification among its musicians. The Olympique bylaws paradoxically specified that the lodge social hierarchy should maintain "perfect equality," even as "different obligations distinguish[ed the] three classes" of administrators, subscribers, and free associates.[95] Professional musicians appear among all Olympique classes, however only eight enjoyed the social life of the lodge as subscribers.[96] Like a majority of the musicians who earned free-associate slots, the three musicians who paid the 120 *livres* subscription fee to Olympique in 1786 were all composers. "Orchestra members" appear as a separate category on the lodge tables. Logically, they had no need for tickets to the twelve concerts because they performed in them; thus they paid no subscription fee. While the orchestra members' obligations are quite clear, their lodge privileges remain frustratingly ambiguous in the printed protocol. It is most likely that they performed and participated in the concert society, but not necessarily in lodge social activities. Amateurs and free associates who performed in the orchestra were listed both in the subscribing-member and free-associate sections of the lodge table, as well as in the orchestra list, thus, these members likely mingled socially in the lodge.[97] Amateurs, free associates, and members of the Opéra were identified in the orchestra list to distinguish their prestige among the other orchestra musicians.

It remains unclear whether only star performers and composers or the entire orchestra and chorus received compensation for their Olympique performances. Jacques Marquet de Montbreton Norvins, a politician and writer, claimed in his memoirs that Olympique's success was rooted in its ability to pay "great national and foreign artists" to perform at the concerts and compose for the orchestra.[98] There is no indication on membership tables that performers were paid as the "waged brother servants" had been in La Candeur, however the Olympique orchestra's roots in the former Concert des Amateurs indicates a possibility that this may have been the case, since the defunct series had boasted high-quality performances precisely because it could retain a stable orchestra membership through consistent pay.[99] One key distinction between artists and savants was the latter's disinterest in profit,[100] it therefore may not have befitted the musicians' evolving professional sensibilities to accept pay. Their exposure in the lodge nevertheless offered numerous means to circumvent the system of musical production restricted by legal privileges, providing a variety of financially lucrative possibilities.[101]

The Concert des Amateurs's precedent for payment and sociability unfortunately only opens up more questions than it answers. As mentioned in the previous chapter, the opportunities for musicians to fraternize in the Concert des Amateurs and to earn pay for their services in fact gave them a new sense of camaraderie and autonomy. And the "salaried dependence" that originally prevented servants from climbing the masonic ranks seemed not to apply to the diverse salaried professionals who enjoyed masonic comradery in Paris during the 1770s and 1780s. Moreover, while compensation might seem like a sign of persistent servitude, the contrary became increasingly true in light of new patriotic understandings of consumption and *mécénat* (patronage characterized by support of the arts rather than servitude).[102] An equalizing force animated the exchange of money for goods and services in the Parisian public sphere, leading to what William H. Sewell Jr. terms "interstitial capitalist abstraction."[103] Even a change in hiring conditions from court contracts at Versailles to positions in Parisian orchestras (or, for lack of a better term, "Paris gigs") would have contributed to an evolution in social dynamics for professional musicians. The emergence of interstitial capitalist abstraction complicated the belief that the pursuit of profit determined one's social status.

Regardless of pay, the Olympique orchestra incited other physical and conceptual changes in how musicians engaged with people whom they previously served at court. Veillard, the oboist in La Candeur, took up the bassoon in the Olympique orchestra. No longer an accessory to aristocratic leisure, he climbed the central platform with his colleagues as the attentive audience awaited another superb performance of instrumental music. Norvins claimed in his memoir that part of the orchestra "appeared dressed in embroidered costumes, in lace cuffs, sword on the side, and a plumed hat on the benches."[104] The question is, which part of the orchestra dressed this way? After all, one equalizing force in late-eighteenth-century Paris was the inability to distinguish social class by clothing—especially swords, the symbol *par excellence* of social *privilège*. The costume clearly granted a level of prestige to anyone who donned it, but it may also have distinguished amateurs from professionals or members of the nobility and military from those who lacked such distinctions.

Musicians became an institutional focal point and mingled with amateurs of a higher social status, much like the musician in Grétry's duel that opened this chapter.[105] Olympique's 1786 orchestra consisted of 66 percent professional musicians, 18 percent amateur musicians, and 16 percent musicians of unknown professional status.[106] Figure 2.2 is based on the orchestra arrangement proposed by Warwick Lister in his article about Olympique's first performance of Haydn's Paris Symphonies. Lister created the figure according to the 1786 lodge table, which specifies the instrument, part, and desk each musician occupied during performances. Figure 2.2 further specifies Lister's rendering by indicating the status of each musician. The first desk of the first violins, for example, included one free associate, two amateurs (one of them a tax collector), and one professional musician who was also a member of two other masonic lodges. Veillard shared a desk with his fellow

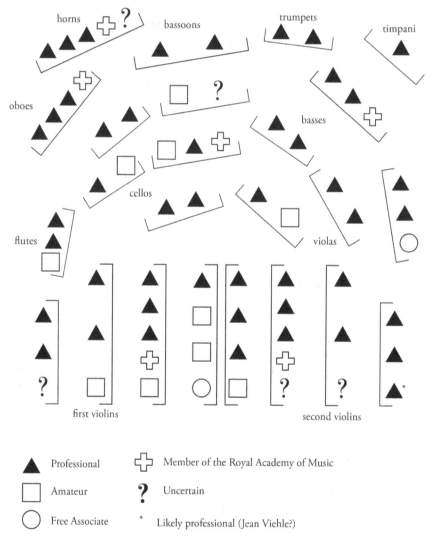

FIGURE 2.2 The Olympique orchestra arrangement incited physical mingling among professional and amateur musicians. Designed by Dan Ruccia.

68 | MUSICAL PRIVILEGE

professional musician, the bassoonist Étienne Ozi (who would also become a professor at the Conservatory), but the two were situated just behind the cello desks; perhaps directly behind some of the most prestigious nobles in all of Freemasonry: Claude-François-Marie Rigoley Comte d'Ogny, founder of the Olympique concerts, and Savalette de Langes, founder of the lodge Les Amis Réunis. It was unlikely that a musical logic motivated the decision to intersperse amateurs with professionals, since many amateurs possessed equal or sometimes even greater talent than professionals during this period.[107]

The byproduct of this spatial arrangement was a mingling of musicians with prominent lodge members, most notably those who worked in banking and finance. Music-making was one of the public activities that did not require subjects to relinquish their legal privilège, as was the case when a noble decided to engage in trade, for example. This particular professional group—tax collectors and financiers—had gained significant status over the course of the eighteenth century and became prominent Parisian cultural patrons as nobles lost the funds necessary to support artists.[108] By the 1780s, even the king was trying to curb musical expenditures.[109] Musicians began to experience a symbiotic social elevation alongside the professionals who gradually replaced the French court as arbiters of Parisian culture.[110]

Yet, unlike Le Contrat Social, Olympique's music direction remained in the hands of the noble amateurs who played in the orchestra, including post administrator and tax collector Étienne-Marie de La Haye, post general D'Ogny, and Court of Accounts officer Claude-François de Barckhaus. D'Ogny and La Haye's fathers had financially supported Olympique's predecessor, the Concert des Amateurs, and La Haye's father subscribed to the new concert series. Thus, Olympique maintained a semblance of the noble patronage that had migrated from Versailles to Paris over the course of the eighteenth century, and indeed it welcomed noble patrons, including Marie Antoinette herself, into its audiences.[111] But as an institution that arbitrated the vanguard of musical taste in Paris, the lodge nevertheless elevated musicians to a new, privileged position in cultural discourses about music.[112]

Despite its aristocratic leadership, in Olympique, musicians enjoyed a status as artists rather than as servants. Performers such as Veillard and Ozi contributed their exceptional talents to the execution of difficult orchestra works while composers like Luigi Cherubini produced works especially for Olympique's subscribers, such as his 1789 *Circé*. Musicians who were invited to become Olympique free associates traversed the categories of artist and savant, advising the lodge as experts in their field. Subscribing musicians had already garnered a high social regard, sufficiently accomplished and affluent to afford their own memberships as fellow Olympique brothers. Composer Méhul traversed these membership categories, a subscribing member in 1786, by 1788 he became a free associate, meanwhile his fellow composer (and famed chess player) Philidor consistently maintained a free-associate position.

The lodge hierarchy situated musicians in a structure established by talent and duty, not blood or birth. No longer contracted servants, musicians were members of a social system to which they provided a desirable specialized skill (as orchestra and chorus members), a degree of prestige (as famed composers and theoreticians), or both. Professional musicians were recruited into the Olympique orchestra for their outstanding talents regardless of social standing, and this made them, at least in this masonic context, equal in merit to their legally privileged counterparts who also performed in the ensemble. The Olympique musicians did not serve as mere accompaniment as in La Candeur or an embellishment of lodge prestige as in Le Contrat Social. In fact, it was by grace of the orchestra musicians alone that the Concert de la Loge Olympique could exist at all. Orchestral music endured a slow start in France. It was primarily in circles of connoisseurs like the Concert des Amateurs and Concert Spirituel where symphonies, symphonies concertantes, and string quartets gradually rose in popularity.[113] As instrumental music rose in regard, so too did orchestra musicians.

Across Paris, even mere orchestra musicians like Devaux began to enjoy mobility. After serving for six years as a violinist in the Contrat Social orchestra, Devaux's fellow musicians elected him to serve as one of the lodge's three architects of music.[114] In only a decade Devaux ascended from struggling to obtain a constitution for La Réunion des Arts to become an administrator in one of the largest Parisian lodges.

Fellow Professionals and Savants

Nonmusical lodges increasingly included musicians as fellow professionals, or as Grétry put it, "as men." The membership tables from nonmusical lodges reveal the various professionals who began to view musicians as equals by 1789. Musicians found themselves in lodges among merchants, visual artists, and dentists,[115] bourgeois and military classes, and architects, engineers, engravers, law students, and legal professionals from clerks to lawyers and bailiffs.[116] Such lodges never affiliated a sufficient contingent of musicians to form an ensemble. On occasion, perhaps Brothers Mazzuchelli and Chelard in the lodge Saint-Charles de la Parfaite Harmonie treated their brethren to a violin duo, or maybe Brother Tacusset sang a masonic hymn to the accompaniment of Brother Adam, but these performances would differ from the experiences of musicians who accompanied *opéra comique* in La Candeur or who participated in the formal orchestra maintained by Le Contrat Social. It is far likelier that the musicians in nonmusical lodges joined simply to socialize as masonic brothers among other professionals who also left their civil status at the threshold. In some lodges, musicians even seemed to enter as a predefined group. Musicians who belonged to Saint-Jean de Palestine, for example, came predominantly from the Théâtre-Italien, including the famed composer Luigi Cherubini.[117]

Acceptance within these Enlightenment institutions offers one piece of evidence that musicians enjoyed social advancement similar to that of other rising professionals in the period leading up to the French Revolution.[118] When a Brother Oudet gave an opening speech at the 1783 installation of Saint-Charles under its new Scottish name, Saint-Alexandre d'Écosse, he emphasized the "equal union" among the diverse professions represented in the lodge, and explained how each specialization—savants, artists, merchants, legal professionals, and members of the military—contributed a unique yet indispensable utilitarian service to civil society.[119] Musicians were considered professional equals who, like architects, dentists, and so many others, contributed to a secular humanitarian ideal.[120]

Musicians enjoyed social elevation, evinced by their positions as free associates and their participation in the learned and cultural agendas of many Parisian lodges. Knowledge of liberal studies and the application of its theories to practical ends had become a key attribute of "learned" professionals in eighteenth-century France. Surgeons, for example, and dentists, who had once belonged to the guild of barbers and wig-makers, rose in stature throughout the century because they began to enhance the practical service they provided with liberal education.[121] In other words, they began to learn their professions by studying rather than simply doing.[122] Their prestige rose as they provided utilitarian services by applying technical skills through instruments.[123] Studies in Latin and classics may not have affected how they pulled a tooth or repaired an injury, but they did enhance their ability to relate to other educated professionals in social venues like masonic lodges. This advancement can be seen in Les Amis Réunis, where doctors, surgeons, and medical students occupied many of the free-associate positions.

Certain Parisians, like Michel-Paul-Guy de Chabanon, proactively encouraged musicians to pursue such relationships with other professionals. Chabanon was a scholar of Hellenistic thought, elected to both the Académie des inscriptions et belles-lettres and the Académie française. As an accomplished musician, Chabanon had circulated and performed among professional musicians in Paris for decades.[124] He proposed that professional musicians pursue social advancement, as painters had, through dialogue with other artists and learned professionals.[125] His proposal even circulated as far as German lands, albeit attributed incorrectly to Chastellux.[126] One practical inspiration for his call was likely his personal experience in the Concerts des Amateurs and de la Loge Olympique, where he witnessed Parisian musicians circulating by virtue of their talents among elites.[127]

Masonry shared similar cultural characteristics to guilds and academies, particularly because they fostered professional interests and spiritual benefits.[128] Professional musicians sorely lacked such self-directed institutional structure in late eighteenth-century Paris. Chabanon hoped musicians would find authority in an academy dedicated to music. His tacit acknowledgment that the Académie Royale de musique—the Opéra—did not function as a true academy, implied that musicians deserved to recuperate authority in their field from the *lieux privilégés* populated by nonpracticing savants.[129] Who else, Chabanon asked, "outside of those who, all their life, have performed music" had a right to submit judgment on the art?[130] He considered the École Royale de chant a significant step toward this goal.

Professional acceptance among peers and calls for a musician-led academy both indicate the emergence of a privileged group of musicians considered "academic," learned, and savant.[131] These musicians typically identified as keyboardists, composers, theoreticians, and musicographers, and seemed to gain access more readily to nonmusical lodges, where they mingled socially rather than by virtue of a particular skill set. Les Frères Initiés, for example, was constituted predominantly by men who worked as merchants and commissioners, or in the Paris legal system, especially the Parlement de Paris and the Châtelet courts. Only three musicians participated in the lodge, which welcomed over 100 brothers from 1776 to 1792. All three composed, one was also a musicographer and theorist, and only two overlapped during their memberships.[132] Similarly, of the twelve musicians initiated into the lodge Saint-Charles des Amis Réunis during its eleven-year existence, the two for whom records remain extant were the composer-organist Nicolas Jean Lefroid de Mereaux and the theoretician Honoré François Marie Langlé—another Olympique free associate who taught at the École Royale de chant and would during the Revolution become a faculty member alongside scientists at the Lycée des arts discussed in Chapter 6.[133] Both De Mereaux and Langlé earned positions in the Paris Conservatory when it opened in 1795, De Mereaux as a professor of composition and Langlé as a professor of harmony and as the institution's librarian. Thus, as musicians joined lodges to socialize, it was composers, keyboardists, and those who wrote or theorized about music who predominated. Stratification among musicians persisted.

Lodges modeled on learned societies especially welcomed famed composers into their ranks. The astronomer Jérôme de Lalande founded the lodge Les Neuf Sœurs as a learned society that would facilitate fruitful dialogue among savants from the sciences, arts, and letters. It boasted famous members including Voltaire and Benjamin Franklin, who served as its Venerable Master from 1779 to 1781. Its namesakes were the daughters of Mnemosyne, the nine muses of Greek mythology who inspired the disciplines that the lodge sought to foster and advance. The lodge hosted academic festivals in which lectures and musical performances punctuated exhibitions of sculptures, paintings, drawings, and architecture. Balls and banquets permitting only the most notable minds in Paris followed each festival.[134] The events served as both venues for intellectual exchange and fundraisers, like the concerts held by Le Contrat Social. Attendees paid 12 *livres* (half-price for ladies) and confirmed their respectable civil status to receive a ticket with their name on it. Nontransferable tickets ensured that no undistinguished, nonpaying guests could enter the festivals. Les Neuf Sœurs' brothers not only cultivated theoretical knowledge in the privacy of their lodge but also hoped to improve society at large by bringing their knowledge to a wider albeit select public.

Les Neuf Sœurs imagined a new social hierarchy in which success in the sciences, letters, and arts demanded a commitment to future generations of learned men including musicians.[135] In Old Regime France, privilege had required duty to the Crown.[136] Les Neuf Sœurs' members envisioned a social structure in which privilege came from merit in the form of genius and talent. Duty was thus owed to the advancement of knowledge itself and not to a monarch who protected knowledge in his academies. The Neuf Sœurs also sought to use their knowledge for charitable good, and so they supported students and made contributions "to elevate children destined to be artists."[137] Neuf Sœurs brothers saw that artists often faced poverty and dedicated their efforts to nurturing the "genius" of young artists by providing them with financial security. This encouragement of the next generation of artists and students was predicated on a belief that the pursuit of knowledge in general benefited humanity and was consequently a utilitarian pursuit. To this end, the lodge founded an affiliate school—called a *musée*—to teach the liberal arts and to provide laboratory space for scientific experiments. The school's curriculum ranged from European literature to physics. Pilâtre de Rozier, the chemist who pioneered aviation with his hot air balloon, taught "ancient music" there.[138] The school even welcomed the public into lectures, demonstrations, and courses.

Euterpe, the muse of music, entitled musicians to participate in Les Neuf Sœurs' endeavors. The lodge maintained an orchestra for ceremonies, particularly its legendary academic festivals; however, few if any of the orchestra members were listed as brothers in the lodge tables.[139] Of the 258 Neuf Sœurs members from 1775 to 1792, 39 musicians were initiated or affiliated. This may seem an ample number to constitute an orchestra, until one considers that half were composers, and the other half, teachers, singers, keyboardists, a musicographer, and a music editor and engraver. Even the famous Saint-Georges was supposedly a member. These musicians may have performed together, but they certainly did not constitute orchestras for concerts. Only five musicians inducted into Les Neuf Sœurs identified solely as instrumentalists. This was, rather, an elite group of musicians.

These learned musicians took on a role in the social life of Les Neuf Sœurs. The composer Piccinni, who had been brought to Paris as Gluck's rival in the 1770s, was one of the lodge's most famous members and served as *premier maître des concerts* at the lodge ceremony memorializing Voltaire on November 28, 1778. He composed a variety of music for masonic ceremonies held at the lodge. The composer Dalayrac, a free associate at the Loge Olympique in 1788, had also held a privileged place in Les Neuf Sœurs since 1778 and composed music for the receptions of Voltaire and Benjamin Franklin into the lodge. Les Neuf Sœurs brothers prided themselves on the fact that their lodge had been the first truly founded on equality, granting entrance to musicians as a "class of citizens" based on their merits as professionals in the sciences and arts and recognizing musical achievements.[140] The synthesis of theoretical knowledge and practical application championed by Les Neuf Sœurs raised composers and other learned musicians above the status of instrumentalists to that of savants whose insight guided their professional field, just as Chabanon had prescribed.

"A Little Lesson in Social Harmony"

A focus on composers and their works began to crystallize in lodges, and as it did, the compositions written for lodges also evolved. Some lodge music contributed to well-established genres like the light-hearted operas and popular melodies performed in La Candeur or Cherubini's Loge Olympique cantatas, while other musical genres favored in lodges were relatively new to Parisian ears. Saint-Georges's concertos placed a focus on outstanding instrumental performer-composers. Piccinni's hymns transferred sacred forms into secular contexts. And Haydn's symphonies offered an ideal combination of popular and learned aesthetics.[141] As instrumental music elevated in popularity, so too did the composers and performers who brought it into being. Both composers and performers, like artists, created something beautiful through the application of rules, however, composers also possessed attributes of the savants who established those rules. During this period in France, musical aesthetics were still likened to language.[142] Because composers communicated through a medium akin to writing, they were more easily perceived as learned. The next chapter will explore how composers capitalized legally on their position as "authors of music."

On the one hand, musicians were elevated to a higher regard than they had previously experienced in Paris, and indeed, across France; no longer mere background noise, as Mozart had bemoaned during his first performance for the French nobility, instrumental music became something to which people listened.[143] By the eve of the Revolution, some musicians had achieved an elevated status even as social fissures widened within the profession.[144] The *frères à talent* in Le Contrat Social enjoyed a notable degree of self-direction; lodge officials solicited their suggestions for new inductees and allowed the orchestra to freely elect their leadership. Prioritization of high-quality orchestral performances in both Le Contrat Social and Olympique transitioned performers from background to center stage. At their Olympique orchestra desks, they literally rubbed elbows with financiers and nobles as they worked side-by-side in matching uniforms to constitute what came to be known as the best orchestra in Paris.

On the other hand, many performers were subsumed into an anti-individualist whole that left prestige to composers, virtuosi, and conductors. As instrumentalists became a single unit on stage, those who composed or explained music—the composer Méhul, virtuoso Viotti, and theoretician Louet—could afford to sit in the audience and enjoy concerts as subscribing members of the Société Olympique.[145] If musicianship gained professional prestige, it was indisputably composers, musicographers, and theoreticians who were leading the way. Lodge records chronicle musicians' rise from servants accepted only to provide basic support during lodge events to artisans inducted by virtue of their rote skills and finally to artists expected to create something beautiful using both their skills and minds. Finally, some musicians became respected savants—leaders and advisers in their area of expertise.

Rising social status was a key criterion for professionalization across fields during the eighteenth century.[146] Freemasonry colored musicians' relationship with other professionals and also provided them with an opportunity to engage one another in new contexts.[147] Musicians went from serving prestigious comrades to participating as fellow brothers and provided what came to be considered a social utility—music. Historians of Freemasonry agree that like other cultural institutions such as "colleges, academies, salons, and literary, learned, and agricultural societies," masonic lodges sought to develop an educational and cultural ideal that would unify the modern French nation outside of (or at least as a supplement to) the monarchy.[148] For this reason, it is important to remember that music and musicians served increasingly public roles in the years leading up to 1789.[149] As we shall see in Chapters 4 through 6, some musicians during the French Revolution would ultimately embrace an understanding of music as a form of public property protected by national institutions.

But Georges Jacques Devaux, the average orchestra violinist discussed throughout this chapter, did not live to see the Revolution. After his struggle to earn a constitution for La Réunion des Arts during the 1770s, he quietly continued to work his way up the masonic ranks.[150] When he died over a decade later, just before the French Revolution began in 1789, Le Contrat Social memorialized him, their *architecte de la musique*, with all the sentiments reserved for well-loved brothers.[151] One of Devaux's masonic brothers noted that although "Brother Devaux offered nothing by his birth," a mere "rung in society," his "genius"—which a "vulgar mind" might not suspect gave such "interest and charm"—"was known to find in private life, in talents, and in masonic virtues . . . an inexhaustible field of praise."[152] Like many musicians who became Masons during this period, Devaux elevated his social standing through his talents, and his case proves that it was not exclusively composers, virtuosi, and conductors who enjoyed access to new kinds of social *privilège* through Freemasonry.

Considering this warm masonic eulogy, it is tempting to imagine Devaux as the musician in Grétry's illustrative tale that opens this chapter. According to Grétry, the musician ultimately faced the marquis in the Bois de Boulogne, a traditional meeting place for duels. Upon piercing the terrified nobleman's arm with the tip of his sword, the musician gloated, "I do not wish to kill you, but only to give you a little lesson in social harmony."[153] This was not in fact a barbaric trial by combat like duels in the "Dark Ages," but rather, an enlightened demonstration of honor by a musician staking claim to his privileged status.[154]

PART II

Property

3 | Private Property: Music and Authorship

Many renowned librettist-composer pairs met in the Masonic lodges examined in the previous chapter: Marcouville-Favart, Méhul-Chénier, Philidor-Guichard, and Sacchini-Framery.[1] Although these composers embraced a social identity as "authors" of music, some believed that composers' legal rights seemed to lag behind those of their literary counterparts'. Public musical production continued to take place through institutions governed by privileges such as the court, theaters, concert series, or publishers, a reality less pernicious in itself than the system's impotence more generally, which bred the frustrations exposed in Chapter 1. Just before and especially during the French Revolution, the legal framework that assured profits from the circulation of musical works began to transition from a privilege system toward author's rights, a broad concept constituted by two distinct protections, printing rights and performance rights.

These protections tend to be treated discretely in scholarship even though the two realms were in practice interdependent for the musicians who made their livelihood from composition.[2] Printing rights could be transferred from an author to a publisher; performance rights could be transferred to theater administrators. Performance rights dictated whether theaters could produce a work depending on whether the author had granted permission, received compensation, or was deceased. In England, the 1710 Statute of Anne first guaranteed what is called copyright in Anglo-American law. This statute neither applied to music explicitly nor protected authors of printed works. Instead, it guaranteed publishers the exclusive rights to print any legally acquired work during a fourteen-year period. Composers began to enter English copyright debates later in the eighteenth century, most famously through the cases of Johann Christian Bach and Charles Frederick Abel.[3] Such protections began inconsistently in early America.[4] The strong French privilege system kept composers in France behind their British peers.

Four main differences distinguish modern copyright laws from protection by royal privilege. Privileges had to be requested and were not guaranteed. A privilege could be revoked at any time. For print, a privilege was granted not only for initial prints but also for reprints. And finally, privileges did not extend across state borders. This last feature caused numerous frustrations for music publishers throughout eighteenth-century Europe, as some composers used this loophole to their advantage.[5] All four hallmarks of privilege contributed to a precarious system because legal protections ultimately rested with the sovereign, a right that as we learned in Chapter 1 the French king reasserted at the end of the eighteenth century.[6] Because printing and performance rights guaranteed protection for a definite timeframe, they conflicted with a privilege-based system in which protection could be granted and revoked at will or renewed in perpetuity.[7] Thus, as Stephen Rose has cautioned, scholars must resist teleological equations between early printing privileges and more modern copyrights, especially because the ideologies behind these systems differed quite profoundly.[8] I would add to Rose's admonition that composers should not be too easily conflated with authors of literature because music began to acquire unique legalities. It is more productive to consider, as I do here, how musicians drew on rights already granted to authors in order to bolster their own claims to personal property.

Composers' pursuit of enhanced legal rights during the eighteenth century have been subject to at least two historical interpretations, one intellectualist, the other, materialist.[9] The intellectualist interpretation contends that a spirit of ownership motivated composers to insist on a moral right to dictate how their music circulated.[10] Ownership could be defined abstractly or tangibly. Consequently, from the late seventeenth to early nineteenth centuries, debates persisted about whether author's rights were constituted by an inalienable, natural right to self-expression or by wholly transferrable property rights.[11] The materialist perspective, primarily purported by legal scholars, posits that as the printed circulation of music became more lucrative than royal patronage and ticketed performances, composers increasingly pursued ownership rights to secure their share of profits from the sale of their works.[12] The transition from court to freelance musicianship occurred diffusely as public concerts and publishing gradually became, by the materialist logic, more profitable than contracted court positions.[13] In essence, the intellectualist interpretation understands property rights as moral, while the materialist interpretation views them as practical. Neither interpretation necessarily precludes the other, rather, proponents of each interpretation view one as more influential than the other in the evolution of composers' claims to property rights.

The rise of author's rights in Europe were directly linked to the transition away from protectionist economic policies and toward free market systems as described here in the Introduction and Chapter 1. As early as Adam Smith's *Wealth of Nations*, free market advocates in Britain identified copyright as a necessary evil to incentivize artistic production. In an ideal free market ideas would circulate unencumbered by property rights in order to fuel innovation. Yet without a legal guarantee to compensation, artists and inventors had little incentive to share their work with society.[14] The legislators who created the legal infrastructure for a free market therefore needed to consider art from a utilitarian perspective. Artists hoped to consider it through an individualist lens, emphasizing the moral dimensions of their rights. What Rose points out in the case of German principalities was for the most part true throughout cosmopolitan Europe and early America, "older and new viewpoints" on musical authorship, "were in constant dialogue."[15] Musicians' arguments for legal rights during the French Revolution centered these competing perspectives: materialist versus intellectualist and utilitarian versus individualist. A series of subsidiary tensions ran beneath these broader perspectives such as the balance between collective and individual legal protections, the relative tangibility or intangibility of musical property, and the extent to which music was alienable as a form of property.

During the Revolution composers agitated for and gained legal rights that under the Old Regime had remained inconsistent at best and nonexistent at worst. The Abolition of Privilege created a rupture in the French economic and political system, forcing legislators to confront the legalities of cultural production. Rhetoric set forth in the Declaration of the Rights of Man offered a new discursive framework for musicians to claim proprietorship.[16] As music circulated through diverse media its legal boundaries between print and performance blurred and new laws demanded a sharper delineation of music as a form of property. Music before 1789 had already joined a constellation of semipublic practices in the arts and sciences that were increasingly viewed as social, cultural, and industrial utilities. As the government crafted legislation to implement a modern property regime that strictly delineated public from private property, music's public utility conflicted with musicians' individual claims to personal ownership. Jann Pasler has shown music as a social and political utility capable of "composing" citizens, an ideology cultivated in Third Republic France by drawing on a rich revolutionary history.[17] In the First Republic, revolutionaries recognized music's multifarious utilities that served not only to develop a new citizenry but also to fuel a budding national and imperial agenda. Musicians and the French nation were forced to negotiate music's paradoxical nature as both a private property and public good. The second part of this book reveals how proprietary disputes exacerbated preexisting legal and social distinctions among professionals in the Parisian music world.

Proprietary Tremors on the Eve of Revolution

Following in the footsteps of playwrights and authors, Parisian musicians during the 1780s more deliberately pursued institutional roles and legal rights even as they obeyed the expectations of Old Regime sociability. Like playwrights who had sought a more clearly defined role in the Comédie-Française,[18] composers affiliated with the new École Royale de chant hoped to expand their authority. They used their new institutional position to advocate for formalities that would enhance for musicians the 1777 ruling that granted literary authors increased property rights over their work when the Crown broke up the Printers' and Publishers' Guild monopoly.[19] The École faculty requested from the Crown exclusive rights to print music, which "would counter the many inconveniences and abuses" that "authors [composers] experienced."[20] It is worth highlighting that musicians activated the moniker "author" as they sought rights that writers had already begun to enjoy.[21] The profits from the École's printing enterprise would then be reinvested in the school, particularly to pay pensions, some of which had been cut in a recent edict. The king approved the École's printing privilege request on April 25, 1784. This seemed to be a significant gesture that had the potential to shift privileges around music publishing to an institution governed by composers and performers.

In a *Mercure de France* advertisement for the piano arrangement of André-Ernest-Modeste Grétry's opera music, the journal noted the composer's frustration with piracy: "We often have cause to speak against musical arrangements, made without the author's participation, veritable robbery, by which the artists, and often even the public, are equally duped. M. Grétry has also recently complained publicly. It is hoped that by dint of complaints, a new order would be established to protect the property of authors."[22] Interestingly, the problem Grétry identified was not overt plagiarism but rather rearrangement. Grétry focused on the moral dimensions of unauthorized copies and arrangements; they dishonored composers and ultimately harmed the public. As director of the Queen's musical entertainments and a beloved court composer on a royal pension, it would have raised eyebrows in the *beau monde* if Grétry were to initiate legal action against the pirates who pawned off his melodies. Lawsuits were more common among workers affiliated with guilds, not men of letters and artists, because such maneuvering evinced a distasteful concern for money unbecoming of an "author." It was completely appropriate, however, for Grétry to defend his honor as a dramatic author in public forums. Grétry later complained that such social propriety had hindered composers' financial success under the Old Regime.[23]

Not until September 1786 did the government establish a legal process to combat "the piracy of which the composers and merchants of music were complaining was injurious to the rights of artists."[24] A new policy drafted by the Conseil d'État finally obliged engravers to participate in the privilege system that had long governed music printing, including new formalities requiring a record of author permissions and the deposit of protected works in public libraries.[25] Clarifying language from the 1777 ruling, the government committed to taxing imported scores, confiscating pirated ones, and fining the possessors of counterfeits. An office housed at the École would grant seals to all legally engraved or printed music intended for sale. Seals would distinguish between music printed before the court ruling (called *ancienne musique*) or after. And so *musique ancienne* and *moderne* took on a legal status. All proceeds from the new formalities would go to the École. The ruling required printers to receive permission from composers before printing or selling their works, thus granting French composers a degree of control over the circulation of their compositions that they had struggled to obtain since Couperin and Lully.[26] These formalities further entwined musical property rights with institutional bureaucracy. Unsurprisingly, none other than Grétry occupied the newly created role of the Royal Music Censor who administered the official seals.[27] If Grétry wanted to combat *contrafaçon*, the only viable way to do so was to obtain an institutional position that gave him access to printing and publishing regulation.

Yet musicians still worked according to the terms of privilege and music publishers still benefited most from these laws and policies.[28] It comes as no surprise that the very first score authorized for engraving and publication by Grétry in his capacity as Royal Music Censor belonged to Ignace Pleyel, who acquired rights ceded to him by Jean-George Sieber.[29] These were two of the biggest names in Parisian music publishing. Other than Grétry's few extant approvals,[30] there is no evidence of rigorous attempts to apply these new formalities; they never achieved uniform implementation.[31] The ruling nevertheless seemed to prompt a spike in privilege applications from three of the four major Parisian publishers during 1787 and 1788 even as privilege applications overall remained shockingly low—about 12 among at least 550 scores published that year.[32]

While Grétry maintained a courtly demeanor regarding property rights by appealing to their moral dimensions among a polite public, a composer named Stanislas Champein instead adopted what historian Gregory Brown identifies as a "patriotic" stance, popular among playwrights who were more concerned with the reception of their works and unashamed to appeal to legal authorities when necessary.[33] Champein felt he had not received just compensation from the Comédie-Française for the music in his *comédie-héroïque*, *Les amours de Bayard, ou Le chevalier sans peur et sans reproche* (1786). Rather than delicately maneuver around the *sociétaires* who ran the theater, he took his case to the Châtelet court in Paris.[34] The Châtelet court required an expert review of the score to advise its decision about Champein's claim. The resulting report brings together distinct aspects of playwrights' previous author's rights cases including aesthetic quality, labor value, public reception, and property rights. By connecting labor and musical works to critique and ownership, Champein's case evinces an emergent modern conception of musical composition that centers the composer's authority rather than the patron or venue.

On a Saturday morning in June 1787, Jean-Baptiste Rey and Jean-Baptiste Rochefort met at Rey's home in what is today Paris's second arrondissement to write the "expert report" on Champein's score.[35] Rey and Rochefort were both well known as conductors at the time, Rey as director of the Opéra orchestra and Rochefort its second conductor. Like other experts who evaluated visual and plastic artworks for the court, the two had the appropriate academic affiliation with the Académie Royale de musique. Customarily in such reports, experts from a given field opined on the contested value of artworks that had been brought before a judge or civil administrator.[36] A 1667 ordonnance established this juridical process, and so the reports offer an illuminating window into the legal definition of artworks over the course of the eighteenth century.[37] Most typically, a disagreement between a seller and buyer motivated one party to initiate the legal proceedings. If a tribunal decided after testimonies that a report was required, then a judge would assign experts to evaluate the work's value. The experts would make a "visit" to inspect the artwork while parties to the case removed themselves during their discussion. The experts' exchange would then be documented for the judge to review. The experts were not actually expected to offer legal advice, but rather to provide a specialized testimony, which the judge could then consider in his final deliberation.[38]

Reports were filed in regard to the fine arts as well as crafts and commerce.[39] Identification as a guild member or independent professional proved crucial to the procedure. Recall from Chapter 1 that in 1774 the king's musicians published a collection of laws on music precisely because they hoped to demonstrate their legal status as free professionals and artists, not guild members and craftsmen. In the case of expert reports, a party's professional title, their *état*, determined the set of laws to which their case would be subject. A "master metal engraver," for example, was subject to guild regulations. An "engraver artist" was "completely free" before the law.[40]

Painters, sculptors, and other visual artists wrote most reports for this court; however, other professionals also appear among the experts consulted, including architects, embroiderers, and paint manufacturers.[41] Musicians before Rey and Rochefort primarily appraised church bells. In a 1779 report, Armand-Louis Couperin, cousin of François from Chapter 1, opined that the Church of Saint-Merri's bells rang out of tune. He recommended lowering the tuning of the largest and second-largest bells.[42] An organist at the Church of Saint André des Arts visited the bells at the Church of Saint Barthélemy and found the middle bell sounded "a bit like that of a cracked vase," and the large bell created "an ugly harmony." He suggested bringing both into concordance with the two older bells, which were "very good."[43] In these cases, organists provided technical expertise to evaluate instruments. The report on Champein's case scrutinized neither instruments nor harmonics, rather Rey and Rochefort's report addressed the "author's rights" liable to Champein for his "score."[44] There seems to have been little if any precedent for their evaluation.

Champein's case drew directly on the author's rights that playwrights had pursued a decade earlier, even though it was primarily instrumental music that Champein had composed for the Comédie.[45] According to standard procedure, Rey and Rochefort received from the prosecutor, Collin de la Combe, the sentences and summaries already passed down by the civil chambers on Champein's case. When the eleven o'clock hour rang at Rey's home, Monvel (a pseudonym for actor Jacques Marie Boutet), the librettist, had still not appeared for the appraisal. Rey and Rochefort proceeded to determine the "price and estimate of the work of music."[46] They summarized that Champein had composed thirty-eight pieces of music for *Les amours* including "songs, pantomimes, ballets, an overture, entr'actes and choruses," and even extra music to accompany the production's extensive "pantomime action."[47] After evaluating the composition, Rey concluded, "considering the music by its own merit, by the labor price that it had to cost, by the beauties found in it, and finally by the success and applause that it has had and will have, I would estimate it in a noble and just manner and in relation to the profit that it must have produced for the author of the words."[48]

Rey cited an explicit legal precedent: article twelve of the Conseil d'État du Roi court ruling that specified the honorariums due to authors who wrote works for the Comédie-Française. The article set forth that authors would receive 142 *livres* and 16 *sols* for each 1,000 *livres* of receipts earned for a five-act production; for a three-act production, 107 *livres* and 2 *sols*.[49] Rey pointed out that Monvel, the librettist, had been paid for a five-act production, when in reality at least two acts consisted almost entirely of Champein's music accompanying action and dance. This ratio should have significantly changed their share of profits. He moreover suggested compensating Champein both for past and future performances. Rey also noted, though legally irrelevant, the unfair institutional privilege enjoyed by authors for the Comédie-Française. If Champein had composed the same amount of music for an opera at the Comédie-Italienne, his compensation would have been "three times" higher, most notably because composers for the Comédie-Italienne were always entitled to the same compensation for future performances, while, once a work entered the Comédie-Française repertory, that is, after it failed to sell a certain number of tickets, the author was no longer entitled to shares and the Comédie-Française took ownership over the work. Ultimately, like playwrights before them, Rey and Rochefort criticized the royal privilege of the Comédie-Française. Rochefort emphasized that the music accompanied nearly the entire production, concluding that Champein's work should consequently receive commensurate compensation. The two conductors in essence claimed recent author's rights for composers.[50]

Rey and Rochefort's report reveals the tensions between authorial privileges and nascent property rights on the eve of the French Revolution. They argued Champein's rights from two distinct and somewhat conflicting ideologies—inalienable intellectual property and property constituted by Lockean effort. They emphasized, on the one hand, the aesthetic value of Champein's work above and beyond its market worth, noting the music's "own merit" and the "beauties found in it."[51] Such a position draws on a belief that intellectual creations are worth more than their component parts. Author's rights, according to definitions that had circulated in France since midcentury, were rooted in authorial originality.[52] The philosopher Denis Diderot, who had been conscripted into a conflict around the Paris Book Guild's monopoly in 1763, defined ideas as the product of the soul, "the most inviolable form of property because they spring directly from the individual mind."[53] He reasoned, "What form of wealth *could* belong to a man, if not a work of the mind . . . if not his own thoughts . . . the most precious part of himself, that will never perish, that will immortalize him?"[54] Rey and Rochefort's findings in one sense supported a Diderotian perspective on author's rights. They also implied that Champein held inalienable rights over the composition by insisting on his entitlement to all future pay; even if the theater paid for his music as in a market transaction, they believed that Champein nevertheless remained eligible for proceeds from future performances by a logic that ascribed the composition to him morally, and thus, for his lifetime. The report contends then that ownership over music was neither wholly transferrable nor alienable.

They undermined this moral appeal to property rights, however, when they addressed in the same report Champein's labor and the audience's reception of his music. Rey and Rochefort noted the "labor price that it had to cost" Champein to compose the music, a Lockean perspective of value emanating from effort. French courts tasked with enforcing guild regulations would likely have been familiar with this slippery epistemological slope.[55] Some French thinkers like the Marquis de Condorcet had disagreed with Diderot's perspective, and asserted instead that ideas could not be owned precisely because they were not created from thin air but rather were discovered in "nature."[56] Diderot challenged Condorcet's perspective, asking, "What comparison could there be between a man, the very substance of man, his soul, and a field, a tree, a vine, that nature has offered in the beginning equally to all, and that an individual has only appropriated through cultivating it?"[57] Rey and Rochefort inadvertently supported the Lockean perspective further by situating the public as a necessary factor in legitimizing Champein's claims; they cited "the success and applause," that his music had received in his favor. This stance drew on an earlier French conception of genius as reliant on the public's endorsement rather than intrinsic value.[58]

Although Champein's case technically sought remuneration for performance rights—that is, proper payment for the performance of his composition—the case explicitly claimed "author's rights," and thus demanded for composers the protections that playwrights had already begun to enjoy. Rey and Rochefort made arguments in his favor that rested on his composition's intangibility and inalienability, both moral, intellectualist claims. Materialist concerns about musical ownership were nevertheless present in their attention to labor and reception. This report puts into relief the tensions around author's rights pinned between a crumbling privilege system and an emergent property regime.

From Musical Privilege to Musical Property

The same year that Rey and Rochefort evaluated Champein's score, Louis XVI faced the series of crises described in the Introduction, which led to the fateful night of August 4, 1789, when the National Assembly abolished privilege in France. Even though the abolition's tremors did not reach the world of musical production immediately, the dawn of August 5 brought with it a renewed opportunity for former members of a decade-old *société* of playwrights founded by Pierre Beaumarchais. When the group reestablished, it hardly resembled its prerevolutionary predecessor; Jean-François De La Harpe, a playwright who had overcome humble beginnings and championed Enlightenment philosophers, took Beaumarchais's place as its leader. Only a few of the original members joined.[59] Composers did not participate in the earlier iteration of the playwrights' *société*. Composers Grétry and Nicolas-Marie Dalayrac joined them in 1789 and became fundamental to the revolutionary reincarnation of "dramatic authors," as the group referred to itself. Throughout 1790 and 1791, the dramatic authors sought property rights by sending the revolutionary government petitions and letters. This time, composers participated in their campaign.

Distinctions between public and private property were central to the dramatic authors' rights because stakeholders debated, as the historian Gregory Brown puts it, "whether works in the existing repertory should be controlled by the heirs of the author; the troupe; the printer to whom the work had been sold; or the public."[60] These were precisely the rights Champein sought to claim in his 1787 case. While some parties claimed that plays housed within the Comédie-Française were public property, others felt that the Comédie held an unfair privilege over the works. Dramatic authors argued that their "genius" needed to be encouraged for the sake of national culture. Genius itself was cast as a public good.[61] As Mark Darlow has shown, playwrights benefited from walking a fine line between "private and general" good.[62] The Comédie countered the dramatic authors' individualist stance; by owning the French "classical" repertory, the Comédie considered itself better positioned to "defend the 'honor,' 'genius,' 'art,' and 'utility' of French theatre."[63] What came into question was whether private individuals or national institutions would own French works of art. Two different definitions of genius competed in these debates, one that identified it as an individual attribute and, the other, as a quality cultivated within an individual by a national, collective genius.[64]

Cultural products posed a considerable challenge to the revolutionary government's agenda to clearly delineate public from private property after the Abolition of Privilege.[65] The public domain of tangible property like land and buildings was created in order to be emptied of its contents,[66] but some revolutionaries argued that the public domain of more intangible, or movable property, like music and books, should not be controlled by private interests, which might prevent useful information and cultural heritage from circulating freely to the public.[67] It would not take long for legislators to realize that the didactic and pedagogical value of free knowledge was a somewhat false hope. Upon deregulation of the book trade, much to their dismay, low-brow literature proliferated and "valuable" literature had to be resuscitated by government intervention.[68]

Some writers and musicians drew on proprietary rhetoric to combat legislation that would facilitate a free marketplace of ideas. La Harpe, the dramatic authors' new leader, wrote a petition to the National Assembly in August 1790 to argue that the public could only be served by recognizing dramatic authors' individual rights first, because they would then be incentivized to write more plays. Author's rights would provide the freedom to "exercise talents," he claimed.[69] In accordance with the political thinker Abbé Emmanuel-Joseph Sieyes, La Harpe defined property as discrete from privilege and as a natural right sanctioned by law with no need for formalities to validate it.[70] La Harpe requested that authors be granted the right to associate, that the Comédie-Française's institutional privileges end, and that a public domain (rather than the Comédie's domain) be established. The dramatic authors' activities during these early days of Revolution drew on the dominant discourses of the time, "melding of personal and public interest . . . individual liberty, property, and the public domain and the need to regenerate culture."[71] The dramatic authors' detractors nevertheless felt that the public domain provided a necessary cultural heritage—the nation's masterpieces—which were threatened by claims to corporate power and individual property.[72]

Sieyes received La Harpe's petitions because he served on the Assembly's Committee on Liberty of the Press, which was considering printing rights at the time. As a clergyman, Sieyes had long enjoyed privileges of both the First and Second Estates.[73] He nevertheless harbored resentment toward the nobility who occupied the most prestigious positions of the First Estate, often at the expense of more deserving bourgeois clerics, who found themselves overlooked because of their meager social connections.[74] Sieyes exercised his assiduous study of philosophy and his critiques of Old Regime privilege when he wrote three pamphlets in reaction to the political, economic, and fiscal crises of 1788 and 1789. The publications earned him celebrity in Paris and invitations to salons, and by 1789 he found himself elected deputy to the Estates General as a representative of the Parisian Third Estate.[75] In *What Is the Third Estate?*, a pamphlet published six months before the storming of the Bastille, Sieyes critiques the Old Regime socioeconomic hierarchy that divided subjects into three classes—clergy in the First Estate, nobility in the Second, and everyone else in the Third. Instead, he proffered that the Third Estate, always treated as "nothing," was in fact "everything" to the French nation and deserved to become "something" politically.[76] He proposed that citizens instead be grouped into four classes based on their production of wealth for the collective good of the nation, his own idea of political economy combined Jean-Jacques Rousseau's social contract with Adam Smith's economic acumen.[77] In his position as deputy to the Estates General, Sieyes applied his acute political thought to suggest that the Third Estate held true sovereignty and could therefore declare itself the National Assembly without participation from the First and Second Estates. His leadership earned Sieyes appointment to committees that would draft the new constitution and the Declaration of the Rights of Man.

Sieyes seemed to seriously consider the requests submitted to him by dramatic authors. Grétry and Dalayrac both signed an undated petition, along with many librettists associated with the Comédie-Italienne, requesting a law to protect the property rights of writers and artists.[78] The two composers notably pursued rights from both the Comédie-Française and the Comédie-Italienne. They and their co-petitioners demanded that no copies of their works be printed or sold without explicit written permission from the author, and that, upon the author's death, his or her heirs would inherit rights to the work for a specified period of time. The suggestions outlined in the petition appear quite clearly in a report that Sieyes submitted to the National Assembly in January 1790. Though the legislation never passed in the form in which he presented it, the proposal is considered a milestone in French legal history. The language synthesizes competing intellectualist and materialist perspectives on creative work. Sieyes insisted "the property of a work should be assured to its author by the law."[79] It also outlines protection from counterfeit publications and unauthorized performances, explicitly stating that the articles apply equally to printed music and dramatic scores. The final paragraph of the petition Sieyes received from Grétry, Dalayrac, and their Comédie-Italienne associates reads: "Musicians, as talented associates with men of letters in the composition of works destined for the lyric theatre and in the community of work, interests, and rights with them, solicit from the National Assembly the same protections for their property and the same portion of profits from their operas in the provincial theatres."[80] And so composers officially situated themselves alongside "men of letters," and Sieyes, as a member of the National Assembly, incorporated this claim into his legislative drafts. The Revolution offered an opportunity to disentangle the Old Regime's tightly entwined legal and social categories that had plagued musicians for more than a century.

Pleased to see his own beliefs echoed in these proposals, Grétry wrote a letter to congratulate Sieyes about the implications that his recent work on liberty of the press held for dramatic authors.[81] Despite their revolutionary sympathies, Sieyes and Grétry both seemed to foster ambivalent views about the Old Regime privilege structures from which they had greatly benefited. Sieyes demonstrated open disdain for the Second Estate; he described the nobility as a lazy class that leached off the productive labor of the Third Estate. Yet his views about his own order, the First Estate, remained complicated. Sieyes viewed the clergy as a professional class that provided necessary services to the nation, particularly as educators. The clergy were useful, and anyone useful deserved a place in his vision for the reordered French social hierarchy. Grétry also openly critiqued the nobility in his postrevolutionary writings; until the Revolution, however, he never disparaged the monarchy or the pensions it provided him.[82] The two men undoubtedly shared a view of man as "*sociable* not servile,"[83] and therefore felt frustrated with the Second Estate's privileges. Grétry, like Sieyes, would later deride the servile status that professional musicians endured at the hands of the idle nobility even as he drank deeply from the "fountain of privilege" discussed in Chapter 1. When Grétry read Sieyes's legislative proposal to grant ownership rights to musicians, he likely recognized a kindred spirit who valued the industry of liberal professionals.

In his letter, Grétry contrasts Sieyes's proposals with those of the dramatic authors' leader, La Harpe.[84] Although Grétry participated in the group, he remained suspicious of La Harpe's true sentiments toward musicians, believing that La Harpe had a prejudiced view that "dramatic authors" included only "men of letters" who wrote for the Comédie-Française.[85] Painfully aware, or perhaps simply paranoid, that men of letters did not consider him a peer, Grétry complained to Sieyes about the Comédie-Française authors' condescension toward the Comédie-Italienne writers and composers. Grétry's music had enjoyed considerable success at the Comédie-Italienne. It is true that when La Harpe approached the legislature, he never addressed composers' rights directly even though composers signed his petitions.[86]

Grétry attacked institutional privilege, particularly the tensions between the privileged Opéra and Comédie-Française compared with the Comédie-Italienne and Théâtre Feydeau.[87] In the letter, Grétry highlights Beaumarchais's *Figaro* (1784) as an example of this inequity, claiming that the play generated more revenue in a few performances at the Comédie-Française than his own opera *Richard, Cœur de Lion* (1784) could ever earn at the Comédie-Italienne. It is unclear whether Grétry had a truly detailed understanding of the comparative financial benefits of producing with each theater, particularly when one considers that Rey and Rochefort had argued precisely the opposite in Champein's case. He likely sought to highlight the inequity between librettists and composers rather than the theaters. Nevertheless, Grétry's complaints echo those of Rey and Rochefort in their evaluation of Champein's score for the Châtelet court. Grétry argues that as long as laws favored librettos and scripts over scores, then composers who created successful dialogue opera would continue to struggle to survive with "no bread" on the table and "but an *écu* from performances throughout the kingdom."[88] Composers expressed aesthetic concerns for the inextricable relationship between music and text when they protested the setting of translated librettos to new music,[89] yet they clearly also had a more practical consideration in mind—their livelihood.

Performance rights remained a fundamental concern for composers. Provincial theaters maintained a long tradition of restaging *opéra comique* after they first appeared in Paris without requesting permission from the authors.[90] The increasing popularity of dialogue works and Italian translations coupled with the enhanced role of music in such productions (precisely the situation Champein had faced) motivated composers to join librettists in the struggle for ownership over stage works and also to challenge their perceived advantages. During the 1770s, tensions surrounding Italian translations had frustrated writers and composers of new French stage works who believed that translations of Italian works drew revenue away from the Opéra and Comédie-Française.[91] In fact, the composer Champein cleverly circumvented this system of language restrictions by composing *Le nouveau Don Quichotte* (1789) under an Italian pen name, Signor Zuccarelli.[92] By the 1780s another rivalry had arisen between the Comédie-Italienne and Théâtre de Monsieur (later Feydeau), which clearly infringed on the former's privileges to perform *opéra comique*. The year after his letter to Sieyes, Grétry wrote a pleading letter to Beaumarchais about Marsolliers de Vivetières and Dalayrac's *Nina, ou La folle par amour* (1786), which had been translated into Italian by Giuseppe Carpani and set to new music by Giovanni Paisiello. The Italian version of *Nina* received over two-dozen performances at the Théâtre Feydeau from September 1791 until August 1792 without permission from or compensation to its original authors.[93] Grétry had begged Beaumarchais, as he did Sieyes, to continue pursuing their "cause" to the authorities.[94]

The debate about rights to translations also symptomatizes an epistemological change. In mid-century France, originality had been defined as the ability to see "nature" or reality differently, and then to create art that helped others to experience this novelty.[95] By this logic, playwrights or librettists who set the same story or composers who composed new music for a translation therefore seemed to pose few problems. As ideas about originality changed, so too did moral, and consequently legal, perceptions of such creative works. As Michael McClellan explains, authors and composers like Grétry "believed an inextricable element of the original" French *Nina* "could not be transferred to a translation."[96] Thus, translations, parodies, and adaptations posed more challenges in 1790 than they had in earlier decades. The complications with *Nina* related more to the libretto than the music, a fact that from Grétry's perspective would have represented yet another slight to composers. Perhaps this focus on the libretto arose simply because *Nina*'s original composer, Dalayrac, was above such squabbles, at least until he joined them vocally during the Revolution.

Only weeks before the first law regarding performance rights passed, Grétry published a letter in the *Journal de Paris* continuing his earlier quest to quell counterfeit scores. If theaters were going to continue performing his works without permission, he quipped, then they should at least correct their scores using an authorized copy. "The hope that there will soon exist laws that make the property of artists respected makes me endure this last injustice with patience," he compromised in his old courtly way.[97] Use of an authorized score would guarantee compensation from publication even if the performance revenue never materialized. Grétry subtly staked a more intellectual claim here, too, one that had been veiled in his previous *Mercure de France* statement: performances should maintain fidelity to a composer-approved score.

The law anticipated by Grétry in the *Journal de Paris* did not pass quite as he had hoped. He presumed that the legislation would adopt the terms proposed by Sieyes in the 1790 report that Grétry had praised in his letter. Instead, the law of January 13, 1791, largely belonged to Issac René Gui Le Chapelier. Because its true purpose was to break up the theater monopoly, it explicitly protected only the rights of libretto authors and clearly refers to the Comédie-Française, in particular. Moreover, the author's rights implied by the decree resulted as a mere byproduct of the law and did not grant the exclusive property rights that Sieyes sought to provide to all artists.[98] It simply required an author's written consent in order for a work to be performed. Without consent, authors would become legally entitled to all profits drawn from performance of their works.[99] According to the legislation, works became public property five years after the author's death, until which time authors and their heirs held exclusive rights. Thus, the law acknowledged both the author's work as personal property and also that artistic works constituted a public good that should be openly accessible in perpetuity.

Although the January Le Chapelier Law represents the first performance right granting authors the authority to dictate performance of their works during their lifetime, this right was ultimately limited in time, like a legal privilege that required renewal.[100] An oft-overlooked passage by Le Chapelier concluded that once a work was "give[n] over to the public . . . by the nature of things, everything is finished for the author and the publisher when the public has . . . [through publication] acquired the work."[101] The law required permission from writers before their works could be used publicly, a moral authority providing them with a significant social standing in the reimagined French nation. [102] And yet, published work sooner or later belonged to the public.

Composers began to enjoy rights born of the legislation even though it did not address music explicitly. On February 4, 1791, Nicolas-Étienne Framery, a writer, music theorist, composer, and former brother in the lodge Les Neufs Sœurs, founded an agency to assist "authors"—librettists *and* composers, he specified—in collecting the compensation now legally due to them for works performed in France. He planned to monitor the implementation of these laws not only in Paris but also throughout the provinces. The *Moniteur du dimanche* advertised the agency on February 20, and explicitly noted that "authors and composers" should present themselves at the office to sign a procuration, which would grant Framery's agency the legal right to act on their behalf.

When the dramatic authors decided to elect a committee of ten from their membership to negotiate these new rights with the Comédie-Italienne, Grétry received the most votes, and Dalayrac tied for second place.[103] Grétry and Dalayrac, two composers, led the dramatic authors as they demanded recognition of rights now guaranteed to them by law. From March to July 1791, however, various legislations raised the threat that Framery's firm might suffer critiques as a workers' corporation—a vestige of Old Regime corporate privilege.[104] This was dangerous territory. Corporations were officially banned the month after Framery founded the agency, and (another) Le Chapelier Law, passed on June 14, 1791, championed private, individual interests.[105]

With the June Le Chapelier Law, the Abolition of Privilege finally extended directly to the music world. The remarkably short text had an immense impact on French society because after decades under fire it definitively abolished craft and trade guilds in France. Their abolition represented a firm stand for individual rights over collective privilege. Moreover, it held a variety of ramifications for musicians. "The freedoms granted to labor and industry" in the law ostensibly codified the free-market economic philosophy that had gained traction in France since midcentury. It also abolished the monarchy's monopoly over theaters; musicologists tend to focus narrowly on this aspect of the law. Theaters multiplied from three official sanctioned ones in 1789 to thirty-five in 1792.[106] Proliferating performance venues caused relaxation in royal censorship, since it was no longer the centralized authority representing the Crown that would determine repertoire choices. Theaters would instead negotiate repertoire decisions within individual institutions and among various municipal bodies. Darlow rightfully cautions against describing this as a "liberty" of the theaters, as many scholars have, since additional parties and bureaucratic levels participated in the negotiation of repertoire decisions now more than ever.[107]

The individual industry championed in Le Chapelier became even murkier when applied to those who executed musical works as singers and instrumentalists. Performers argued that the utility of their labor entitled them to government support. In debates about the Opéra's ownership, performers received mention, though it remains unspecified whether "performers" included orchestra musicians alongside singers, especially once instrumentalists mostly disappeared from the institution's administration. While under the municipality's governance the Opéra's administration included orchestra members as well as singers and dancers, by the summer of 1791 it included only singers and conductors—Rey and Rochefort, who had adjudicated Champein's composition for the Châtelet court. The two became the Opéra's *maître de musique* and assistant *maître*, respectively.[108] Performers' supporters argued that although the "'material rights' over the theatre (that is, as a building)," may have belonged to the nation, the "rights of performance," as Darlow explains, were "inalienable and personal and belong[ed] to performers."[109] Indeed, members of the Opéra demanded their share of performance profits, claiming productions as the fruit of their combined individual industry.[110] Singers and instrumentalists faced a difficult task as musical property was increasingly defined as a tangible, legally delimited object, especially in the form of scores. Composers pushed hard for a legal standard by which music remained the composer's creative work regardless of who performed it.

The idea at the heart of Le Chapelier—the abolition of collective privilege for the sake of individual enterprise—seemed to offer a profound opportunity for the dramatic authors. Because musicians had maintained only a weak guild organization dissolved decades earlier, as described in Chapter 1, they did not need to reorganize in the manner that more guild-dependent professions did in the wake of Le Chapelier. As performance venues multiplied, new theaters and revolutionary festivals would require more and new music, even if demand from the aristocracy and church waned.[111] This deregulation caused a flurry of unauthorized performances, which Framery's new agency planned to combat. Performance venues lacked the teeth of royal privilege and Framery was prepared to hold them accountable. Despite the fraught ramifications of the law, Grétry expressed a belief that M. Le Chapelier seemed to genuinely sympathize with the plight of "dramatic authors." And Grétry certainly considered himself a musical "author."[112]

In August 1791, Grétry teamed up with another Opéra composer, Jean-Baptiste Le Moyne, and two librettists, Marmontel and Guillard, to argue against the terms—the very word, in fact—that had defined their pay from the Opéra under the Old Regime. "The annual salary that the government pledged to authors for a specified number of works for the opera theatre," they argued, "was very improperly called a pension."[113] The authors argued that their royal pension had represented, in reality, "the agreed upon price of their work," in other words, a payment for the use of their personal property not their service. As the government reevaluated the system of royal pensions in light of new legislation and policies, these dramatic authors claimed that their payment had been improperly called "pensions," when the payments in fact represented remuneration for a product that they had provided to the opera to sell on their behalf. They insisted on being called "suppliers," drawing on the January Le Chapelier Law, they argued that:

> The law regarding pensions is all the less applicable to authors than article 4 of the decree of January 13th which concerns them. The Assembly expressly stated that the acts or deals agreed upon between authors and production administrators will be executed. It is precisely the case where authors find themselves. It is the execution of a deal that they demand. They claim the cost of a sale that they made. . . . This title of suppliers which they support is true in such rigor that the opera could not have and cannot yet sustain itself fifteen days without their works. The decrees of the Assembly themselves on the subject of this type of property give them the right to oppose performances of their works and to thus interrupt the course of a show, which does not seem yet in the interests of the administration to abandon.[114]

They threatened nothing short of a supply disruption. "Article 4," mentioned here, was instigated by La Harpe's dramatic authors, and so it singles out only *comédiens* and not *auteurs*, which left some ambiguity regarding how far the legislation could extend past the Comédie-Française. Grétry, Marmontel, Le Moyne, and Guillard, hoped to hold the Opéra to the article, and this may be why they were careful to refer to it as a "theater" throughout their memoir. By calling themselves "suppliers," the four embrace a market-based, materialist definition of their work, work that represented tangible "property." And they even threatened to claim the performance rights guaranteed by the January 13 law in order to prove their point. They close the letter characterizing their demand for appropriate compensation as "the first and most sacred" of rights, a clear reference to the sanctity of property set forth in the Declaration of the Rights of Man.

Dalayrac, for his part, saw a danger in such strict equations between musical compositions and market products, although he certainly agreed that composers' rights were sacred. He insisted instead on composers' natural right to their work, discrete from remuneration. After a provincial theater entrepreneur named Jean-Baptiste Flachat criticized the dramatic authors in a pamphlet, they decided to craft a rebuttal comprising five perspectives from among their ranks. They chose Dalayrac to provide a musician's perspective.[115] On the day after Christmas 1791, Dalayrac's "response" was read before the Committee on Public Instruction, an entity established by the Legislative Assembly to reorganize French education. In many ways Dalayrac's response summarized arguments that musicians had long made: composers, who should be considered equal to their librettist peers, often survived on performance revenue alone. Dalayrac emphasized this issue alongside a notable evaluation of music publishing. Contrary to later materialist arguments that purport the birth of copyright protection from an increasingly lucrative print market, Dalayrac explicitly denied the profitability of publication. He identified the problem with printed music as twofold. First, print sales yielded little if any compensation for operas. As Grétry had complained publicly, arrangements and variations made more money from operas than the original composers. There was less demand for full scores, and composers rarely maintained rights to them anyway. Dalayrac's second point was that, once printed, music was treated as public property and performed without authorization from or compensation for the composer. Here again print and performance rights prove maddeningly interdependent and even antagonistic. Dalayrac directly responded to criticisms raised by Flachat, who had argued that once a work was released to the public then the composer should no longer hold rights to performance revenues. Flachat's proposal echoed the January Le Chapelier Law, which stated that once circulating in the public domain a work belonged neither to the author nor to the publisher but to the public.[116]

Dalayrac disagreed and believed that musical compositions represented an inalienable property. To him, the market exchange that passed a score from composer, to engraver, to publisher, to consumer, did not change the moral or natural property rights born during the act of creation. Early in the pamphlet he states, "a work of the mind is the property of its author. Certainly he who, without obligation to anyone for the primary material which serves him, birthed, molded from nothing, should be its proprietor. Nature gave him this property; the law ordained it, reason sanctions it."[117] This is why Dalayrac resisted formalities, the legal procedures necessary to activate property rights. To him this was precisely the distinction between property and privilege; property occurred naturally in the moment of composition, privilege simply granted the right to perform or to print it. The concept drew directly on the work of Sieyes, which ultimately decoupled privilege and power.[118] Dalayrac sought to maintain power over his work even after others had legally acquired the privilege to reproduce it.

Dalayrac specifically responded to a part of Flachat's pamphlet that compared author's rights with technical patents. Flachat had argued, according to Brown, "in logic fully consistent with the prevalent liberalism of 1791—that the commercial sale of a protected work took place when an author sold it." [119] Dalayrac disagreed with the comparison, pointing out that eventually an invention would go on to serve society, what he calls the "general utility." He believed that a musical work did no such thing. "We have no need for my piece," he argued.[120] Perhaps this statement sounds quite shocking to modern ears accustomed to defenses of the fine arts; Dalayrac did not want his works to be considered "useful" because then, as the Declaration of the Rights of Man clearly sets forth, he could be forced to cede rights to his work for the public good. Dalayrac uses the term "utility" only in the most personal manner, musical works were useful to musicians alone because they provided a livelihood.

Unlike Dalayrac, some "authors and publishers of music" realized that property rights could not be granted through "freedom" alone, but only through "an effective means of regulation."[121] More than sixty men signed a petition to the revolutionary government (Figure 3.1) proposing formalities that would assure property rights.[122] Some of the signatories were affiliates of the École Royale de chant and would have been familiar with previous efforts to prevent piracy; at least twenty received appointments at the Paris Conservatory when it formed only four years later.[123] Nearly all of the future Conservatory members who signed the petition had held prerevolutionary Masonic affiliations, particularly with the Loge Olympique. Many already held positions in the orchestras of the Opéra, the Théâtre Feydeau, and the Garde nationale band. These musicians had worked together across Parisian institutions for decades and constituted a professional group that had congealed for over a generation.

Their petition draws directly on rhetoric from the 1789 Declaration of the Rights of Man. "Property being one of the most sacred rights of man," they begin, "the undersigned petitioners believe that it is their duty to inform you, legislators, that there exists among music merchants, a robbery that tends no less than to annihilate the property of merchants, authors, and publishers."[124] Their use of the terms "merchants, authors, and publishers" makes a clear appeal to similar claims and debates that had been raised from members of the book trade. The "brigands" involved in such "thievery" included duplicitous composers who sold "the same manuscript one or more times;" merchants who forged musical editions and sold them in several cosmopolitan centers; "unfaithful copyists who [made] many copies of the same musical work;" engravers who made "many editions of the same manuscript;" and printers who, before providing examples to legal publishers, would send

Signés, Le Jeune, Berton, Guenin, Ott. Vandenbroek, Gasseau, Benoit Pollet, Ragué, Lentz, Dupohnt, L. Jadin, F. Petrini, A. M. Maire, J. H. Schroetter, Bonèsi, Grétry, E. De Lamanière, X. Lefevre, Le Sueur, Fuchs, Wolff, L. Cardon jeune, F. Devienne, Mezger, Gelinek., Blasius, Martini, Steibelt, Rigel, Hostié, Cherubini, Cesar père, Cesar fils, Cauville, M. Gebauer, Mereaux, père, Dezede, Ferd. Mayer, Bisch, Corbelin, Mozin le jeune, Porthaux, Cousineau père et fils, Deshaye, Hausmann, Julien Navoigille, J. B. Mayer, Fodor, Naderman, Gossec, Castel, J. B. Burckhoffer, Blasius l'aîné, Remy, Kreutzer, Ve. Boin, Bailleux, Lévesque, Beche.

FIGURE 3.1 Signatures on the petition "from authors and publishers of music." Courtesy of the Bibliothèque nationale de France.

copies of music to their "correspondents" throughout France and abroad.[125] The petition proposes a series of formalities that "authors of music" would follow to register their compositions' *Thema* with a municipality and obtain a visa before selling or ceding manuscripts.[126] The publishers would then also register the work with a municipality to avoid duplicate printings. Engravers would subsequently require official paperwork from publishers, proving that the author granted rights for the publication. Next, compilers could only alter notes or instrument parts in a score with notarized permission. The law would forbid printers from moving forward with printing without a signed copy from the publishers verifying that these processes had been properly followed. The petitioners also hoped to ban imported counterfeit works and to strictly regulate exportation. Since printing laws in eighteenth-century Europe lacked international harmonization, composers and arrangers exploited loopholes to double dip on publication revenues. Ironically, this petition bears the names of musicians accused of having exploited the nebulous system themselves. The group submitted the petition to the Legislative Assembly along with a sample form including musical staves for *Thema* created by Naderman and a donation to the nation's cause—France had recently declared war on Austria.[127]

A number of the petition signatories earned income more from arranging and publishing than from composing. Minor instrumental composers on the petition, like Michel Joseph Gebauer, Louis Jadin, Xavier Lefèvre, and Benoit François Mozin *le jeune*, could never have hoped to survive on performance revenues like Dalayrac and Grétry. Other signatories, including J. G. Bürckhoffer, Francesco Petrini, François Vincent Corbelin, the Césars, and the Cousineaus, all profited greatly as authorized arrangers of Grétry's wildly popular opera melodies.[128] Even before the Revolution, the violinist and signatory Marie-Alexandre Guénin had opened a small business to publish his own compositions and soon published those of his colleagues, as well. When Georg-Friedrich Fuchs eventually lost his Conservatory job to budgetary cutbacks, he would go on to spend the rest of his life arranging for major music publishers like Imbault, Sieber, and Naderman, the latter among them affixed his name to the petition, too. Jean Gribenski notes that the absences on this petition are equally noteworthy: major publishers including Imbault, Sieber, Boyer, and Leduc, and minor ones, including Durieu, who will return in Chapter 6. "It seems," Gribenski concludes, "that the big publishers did not suffer much from the juridical vacuum: undoubtedly they found themselves more advantaged than inconvenienced in this situation, which allowed all the 'piracy' in authorizing notably discrete, fruitful relations abroad, inaccessible to 'small' publishers."[129] And while a few notable composers signed the petition, namely, Luigi Cherubini, Grétry, François-Joseph Gossec, and Jean-François Lesueur, others did not. Dalayrac, François-Adrien Boïeldieu, Antonio Bartolomeo Bruni, Giuseppe Maria Cambini, Pierre Gaviniés, Hyacinthe Jadin, and Étienne-Nicolas Méhul remain absent from among its signatories.[130]

Some of the petitioners likely sought protection for their pedagogical works and music for domestic audiences; signatories Pierre Lévesque and Jean-Louis Bêche had collaborated to compile *Solfège d'Italie* and harpists Ferdinand Mayer and Louis-Charles Ragué published music for the home. Benoit Pollet eventually became a sheet music dealer exclusively. Other instrument-makers like Dominique Porthaux perhaps anticipated future interests in the case that they expanded from instrument manufacturing to publishing or selling sheet music, a prescient choice, as Chapter 6 will show. As early as 1765, the music publisher Antoine Bailleux had acquired the famous Ballard royal patent and printed foreign works by Stamitz, Haydn, Piccinni, Paisiello, Cimarosa, and Boccherini, to name only a few. He also published the *Journal d'ariettes les plus célèbres compositeurs*, culling famous opera arias for amateurs to enjoy at home.

The petition thus carries some internal contradictions between its argument and its signatories' motivations. Petition signatory Joseph Gelinek, for example, had moved to Vienna sometime between 1789 and 1792. A fortuitous moment to become Viennese, he was acquainted with the entire trinity—Mozart, Haydn, and Beethoven. As a pianist and teacher, Gelinek composed variations and eventually made a lucrative career on piano reductions of Beethoven's First Symphony, variations on the Seventh, and numerous variations based on melodies from popular operas, especially Parisian works by Gluck, Paisiello, Méhul, Cherubini, and Boïeldieu. Even though his arrangements required skill and displayed a charming improvisatory character, the *Allgemeine Musicalische Zeitung* described them as "without any special inner content."[131] Gelinek's work lacked the intangible, original essence that morally constituted property. As a skilled performer, Gelinek was not known for any particular composerly talent, and yet most of his compositions were printed during his lifetime and so he profited from this practice. The dedication to him of a Mozart cadenza came from the publisher Artaria, who likely benefited from Gelinek's entrepreneurial spirit. By the current system, arrangers might plausibly earn more money from well-known melodies than musicians like Grétry and Dalayrac who composed them.

It makes sense, considering the position taken in his speech to the Committee on Public Instruction, that Dalayrac did not sign this petition. It sets forth tangible means by which musicians could assure the preservation and control over their works, yet places the burden of formalities on the composer. As a result, the petition's underlying assumption is that legal rights are granted, not naturally emanating from the act of creation, effectively making them privileges by a different name.

The property that the petition proposed to protect through carefully outlined legal formalities was the composition's *Thema*. This may have been a matter of practicality—far easier to jot down and file a melody than an entire manuscript—but the process would have protected the theme itself as the composer's property, what might be considered the composition's central "idea," in Diderot's sense of the word. Recall Grétry's prerevolutionary complaints to the *Mercure de France* about unauthorized arrangements. Some of the petition's signatories, however, like Gelinek, had profited from other composers' melodies. Arrangements, paraphrases, and variation sets, though commonly accepted and immensely popular genres, remained nevertheless contested.[132]

These genres raised a perplexing legal question that could only be informed by philosophy: to what extent might melodies and harmonies be owned? Authors appealed to authorities like Condorcet or Diderot, philosophers who had weighed in on midcentury debates around the Book Guild's rights. Yet it was midcentury disputes between Jean-Jacques Rousseau and Jean-Philippe Rameau about the primacy of harmony and melody that seemed to haunt revolutionary composers as "expression" came to be understood as an original articulation of the soul rather than as the imitation of exteriorities or the simulation of emotions. Rousseau insisted that melody was the source of musical expression, while Rameau attributed expression to the harmony from which melody derived. Rameau's theories moreover cast sound as a naturally occurring phenomenon; harmony emanated from the preexisting *corps sonore*. According to the Lockean midcentury view of property and Rameau's theories of harmony, no one could ever own music because it already existed in nature as sound, like, as Diderot puts it, a "tree" or a "vine," which humans simply cultivated and extracted. Put differently, according to this logic, music was discovered not created. The proposal to record *Thema* as a legal record obviously had practical, immediate origins in the thematic catalogs of Breitkopf and composers' estates. Philosophically, however, the legal protection of a *Thema* would have located originality—as a legal standard—within melody.

This petition shows that in order to keep music from becoming public property, musical ideas required tangible delineation as a thing that someone could clearly own. Music consequently posed an even more complicated legal case. On the one hand, it needed to be tangible to ascribe private ownership, on the other, it needed to be in some way intangible to avoid complete alienation upon sale. If a composer wanted to maintain rights even after granting performance permissions, some aspect of the music had to remain their natural, inalienable property. Ultimately, it was the vague concept of the composer's expression that could not be alienated.

New legislation soon retracted key advances that the dramatic authors had made in 1791. A law passed on August 30, 1792, in addition to placing the burden of formalities on authors, permitted the free performance of works ten years following publication, regardless of whether the author was still living. This would have dissuaded authors from publishing their work and thus cut off one potential income stream. Three months after the legislation passed, the dramatic authors responded with a petition to the National Assembly, characterizing themselves as patriots: "The men of letters would have blushed to think of their own personal interests and to seek to occupy the Assembly with them for a single second."[133] Their delayed response was, in their words, a "patriotic silence." It also invoked their social identity, according to Brown, as "men of letters," that is, as polite, sociable professionals who did not respond impulsively.[134] Of the thirteen signatories on the letter, including Framery, three were composers: Dalayrac, Grétry, and Champein, the patriot who had brought his case to the Châtelet courts even before the Revolution began.[135] Although they emphasized their identification as "men of letters," they simultaneously embraced patriotism and legal motivations; liberal professionalism and social authority were no longer incompatible with the pursuit of one's rights. If before the Revolution professional legitimacy stemmed from either civility or patriotism, it could now be rooted in both.[136] Champein and Grétry both pioneered this perspective among composers just before the Revolution began, Champein by pursuing his case in court and Grétry in the court of public opinion, as the *Mercure de France* had published. Pierre-Charles-Louise Baudin, a member of the Committee on Public Instruction, agreed with the dramatic authors, and echoing the definition of property set forth by Sieyes, concluded, "Of all properties, the least likely to challenge, that which increasingly could neither injure republican equality, nor overshadow liberty, is without a doubt that of productions of genius."[137]

Composers henceforth began to pursue protection over the fruits of their "genius" more vehemently. One group of composers wrote a letter in direct response to the earlier petition from "authors and publishers of music" that had suggested formalities to regulate music printing, engraving, and publishing (Appendix 1). Musicians who signed both this new letter and the previous petition explicitly retracted their earlier alliance, *"Those undersigned authors whose names are found on the first act mentioned above* declare that they have not taken to this action but by a precipitation of confidence and without considering the next steps; but that it was not until after a careful deliberation that they have herewith signed"[138] (Table 3.1). If they had signed the previous petition in haste without considering its consequences, they had carefully premeditated this letter. The composers claimed that engravers, printers, and publishers enjoyed too many rights, which allowed them, "1.

TABLE 3.1 Composers who authored the letter contra the petition from "authors and publishers of music." Names are listed in the order by which they signed. Asterisks indicate those who signed both the petition and letter.

André-Ernest-Modeste Grétry*
Luigi Cherubini*
André-Frédéric Eler
Henri-Montan Berton*
Adrien Quaisain
Paul Rode
Étienne-Nicolas Méhul
Pierre Gaveaux
Louis-Luc Loiseau de Persuis
Antonio Bartolomeo Bruni
Jean-Paul-Gilles Martini*
Étienne Fay
Charles-Henri Plantade
Louis-Sébastien Lebrun
Louis Jadin*
Nicolas-Marie Dalayrac

To distort, contort, and multiply in every form, and under the author's authorization the works which they have acquired. 2. To engrave and see as their own property all works originally published abroad."[139] The composers argue that these production rights infringed on the composers' "interests and their reputations." The letter characterizes the unrestricted copying and arrangement of musical works as a violence both to the musical works and to the composer. By making "thirty or forty works from one," music publishers constrained "musical genius and the industry that feeds those who cultivate it."[140] Did they intend to refer here to the sale of thirty or forty copies of a single work? Or rather the many arrangements, rearrangements, transcriptions, variations, and parodies extracted from a single musical work? Regardless, their claim is in one sense a materialist one, insisting on compensation for their work in all its iterations.

Yet their letter equally poses an intellectualist stance. The composers assert that "to distort a work in any way is to disfigure it."[141] And here is where the "thirty or forty copies" might be interpreted not simply as prints, but as rearrangements. When the public can no longer distinguish the "originals from the copies," they argued, then the negative reception of the copies affects the composer's reputation, regardless of the original's quality.[142] They considered authorial originality as a necessary criterion for ownership. The composers demanded that concession of rights to a musical work only applied to the work's precise current form. Their request puts a finer point on the registration of themes proposed in the earlier petition by "authors and publishers of music," arguing that publishers, engravers, and printers should only have the right to reproduce the exact version that they receive. Any change would violate property, punishable to the full extent of the law. Logically this would forbid the host of derivate musical genres popular at the time. "Disfigurement" might also occur through performances that did not use an authorized score, as Grétry's previous letter to the *Journal de Paris* had pointed out. These moral, intellectualist claims emphasized the sacredness of musical property as resting specifically within the composer's precise arrangement of notes on the page.[143] The composers moreover emphasize their rights' inalienability. The language found in acts of sales, they argued, "should not and could not be interpreted as a pure and simple guarantee." They conclude the letter by admitting the unlikelihood that their rights would arise naturally without formalities and so demand greater protection before the law.[144]

Clearly this rhetoric articulates a personalist interpretation of music proprietorship. First, it asserts that musical works are the result of "genius" and thus belong inalienably to creators, regardless of sales or political boundaries, and second, that to change any aspect of a musical score is to violate the composer and the composer's property. The underlying assumption of these legal arguments is that musical works exist as discrete works of art—entities outside performance—that should be preserved according to the composer's intentions. Practically speaking, by forbidding publishers from selling any deviation of their original work, composers seemed to seek a larger share of sale profits. They also implicitly demanded more control over the reproduction and circulation of their music. The letter implies that genius is not simply an attribute of the work, rather, the score mediates the composer himself.[145] To change the composer's work therefore violated the very person who created it, not just their property.

Until 1789, the term "inalienability" in France had been associated only with the sovereign, the monarch.[146] The Declaration of the Rights of Man made everyone sovereign over their personal domain. Composers began to draw on a rhetoric of natural rights and sovereignty to argue that their works represented inviolable, sacred property.[147] The clearest way to delineate and control that property was through inscription within a score.

The "Declaration of the Rights of Genius"

It was not until February 1793 that the Committee on Public Instruction finally considered the petition from authors and publishers of music alongside another petition submitted by dramatic authors in September 1792.[148] Although undated, the letter from composers just cited may have in fact been an attempt to clarify their stance upon realizing that the old petition would come under renewed scrutiny. Marie-Joseph Chénier, a librettist who had worked with composer Méhul, was originally tasked with reporting on the petitions. Ultimately Joseph Lakanal presented them to the Convention. Chénier as well as Sieyes receded from government due to political radicalization during the summer of 1793.[149] The Reign of Terror began only a few months later.

Lakanal closed French debates on author's rights for a time when the Legislative Assembly adopted his "Declaration of the Rights of Genius," which passed on July 19–24, 1793.[150] Lakanal defended ownership over creative works as the most natural of property rights, reasoning:

> Of all the forms of property the least susceptible to contest, whose growth cannot harm republican equality, or cast doubt upon liberty, is property in the productions of genius. . . . By what fatality is it necessary that the man of genius, who consecrates his efforts to the instruction of his fellow citizens, should have nothing to promise himself but a sterile glory and should be deprived of his claims to legitimate recompense for his noble labors?[151]

Lakanal sought to correct the pitiable Old Regime circumstance that Grétry would soon bring to light in his own publications.[152] The law's resonance with the original Declaration of the Rights of Man, which guaranteed property rights as inalienable and sacred, unmistakably links this legislation with the Abolition of Privilege, natural rights, and the foundation of modern property rights. The law granted authors, composers, painters, and even draftsmen, the right to the printing and distribution of their work, and these rights transferred to their heirs up to ten years after the creators' death.

While a milestone for artists, this law was a compromise. It prevented the kind of perpetual hereditary privileges critiqued under the Old Regime, the kind that allowed Couperin's descendants to profit from his works long after he had expired. Consequently, the law implied that only the nation could ultimately inherit works of genius.[153] Like the 1791 and 1792 laws before it, the declaration required formalities. Strict regulations demanded that two copies of any printed work remain in the Bibliothèque nationale or Cabinet des Estampes to establish an authoritative collection of legally printed works in France,[154] a practice that, in reality, required some time to take hold. As the legal scholar Jane Ginsburg explains, "conditioning the exercise of copyright upon compliance with formalities undercuts the notion of a right inherent in the author,"[155] in other words, it undercuts the natural rights so vigorously defended by Dalayrac. By the nineteenth century, some Frenchmen even bemoaned the fact that the word "property" had simply replaced the word "privilege."[156] Yet "geniuses" did become the master of their creative "property" according to this law. Among musicians, however, only composers enjoyed this legal definition of "man of genius," and the term "man" excluded women lexically as well as practically.[157] Soon the Napoleonic Civil Code would only further dispossess French women.[158] The Declaration left in its wake some glaring questions: the status of imported and exported music; of arrangements, variation sets, transcriptions, translations, and parodies; and of compositions that predated the law.[159]

The law protecting works of genius presented both material and intellectual challenges for musical production. The Parisian music world was left to implement its new regulation through "trial and error."[160] Composers benefited from Framery's collections agency and received significant remuneration from provincial performances even though 15 percent of revenue collected by the agency went to supporting the commission, 10 percent to Framery as its head, and 5 percent to the provincial correspondents who kept track of performances.[161] Before the Revolution, such performances had amounted to a complete loss. In only two years, Grétry collected the most fees of all authors who worked with the agency, followed closely by Dalayrac.[162] When the laws were finally enforced, composers received more compensation than librettists. The archival record that remains from Framery's agency shows at least seventeen composers who took advantage of its services including Champein and Julie Candeille, who thwarted the masculine conception of composers (Table 3.2).[163] Notably, few composers who sought the agency's aid in collecting performance revenues signed the 1791 petition by "authors and publishers of music." Among the petitions, responses, and letters discussed here, a schism emerged among the dramatic composers who profited primarily from performances, the composer-performers who profited from printed music, the less prolific composers who had previously survived by the dole of the First and Second Estates, and last and certainly least, singers and instrumentalists, who, for all but the most renowned virtuosos, would remain at the mercy of institutions and the public.

The "trial and errors" of the New Regime reveal composers and publishers as the two parties who benefited most from private property rights over music. Music was registered more than any other genre of work in the *dépôt légal* from 1794 through 1796, and from 1797 until 1799 was second only to literature;[164] it exceeded registration of published works in the arts, education, geography, history, law, philosophy, politics, religion, science, and technology. Because no law explicitly addressed arrangements and variation sets, these genres remained lucrative,[165] even as publishers began to note assiduously the works' primary authors in their catalogs.[166] Some variations, like Beethoven's 1790s variation on Grétry's beloved romance "Une fièvre brûlante," represented a welcome homage among peers, not theft.[167] A fine

TABLE 3.2 Composers who collected performance revenues through Framery's agency.

André-Ernest-Modeste Grétry
Nicolas-Marie Dalayrac
Pierre-Alexandre Monsigny
Rodolphe Kreautzer
Nicolas Dezède
Stanislas Champein
François Devienne
Julie Candeille
Pierre Gaveaux
Antonio Bartolomeo Bruni
Étienne Fay
Hyacinthe Jadin
Étienne-Nicolas Méhul
Henri-Montan Berton
Jean-François Lesueur
Luigi Cherubini

line continued to distinguish "brigandage" from flattering imitation. It was primarily publishers, not composers, who brought their cases before the law in the first decade of the nineteenth century to test the limits of the revolutionary legislation.[168] Performers did not have any kind of clear proprietary claims because they did not produce a sufficiently delineated object that could be legally attributed to them. They would continue to receive compensation for performances—a service, not a legally protected product. Composers meanwhile saw potential in the new system. A group of colleagues from the Conservatory founded their own publishing firm. Their publications clearly mark ownership by the composers ("auteur") or editors and note conformance with required legal formalities.[169] The composers cum publishers were notable as stage composers and so likely saw a new income avenue especially for those who had experienced a fallow period in the decade following the Revolution.

The intellectual or epistemological challenges that arose from the "rights of genius" rivaled the law's material complexities. The very notion of genius was poorly defined in France, and the little that was established about the concept had changed by the end of the eighteenth century. Unlike other European and even American traditions, France lacked and would continue to lack a "sustained theoretical scrutiny" of the term.[170] French genius was diverse and discontinuous and yet a declaration of its rights had been set into law.[171] Even the pronoun "it" remains ambiguous here, because "the genius" protected may have rested in the creative work itself or may have been the creator himself (indeed, the third person masculine was always employed in these discourses).[172]

Although originality had already been a defining attribute of genius in eighteenth-century France, it was previously defined, as described earlier, as the ability to see differently what already existed in "nature."[173] This definition further complicates in obvious ways the question of whether composers created music "from nothing," as Dalayrac contended, or simply extracted it from a preexisting *corps sonore* according to the music theories of Rameau. By the time revolutionary debates about musical ownership took place, genius had already transformed in France from something negotiated in the physical world to something completely new put into the world from the soul.[174] This belief, expressed by Diderot though never systematically theorized by him, validated the need to protect creative works as personal property. As Diderot asked, what could be more personal than one's soul? Could another ever purchase it? Earlier in the century, the French had considered genius as self-evident; it required little explanation, what Ann Jefferson describes succinctly as a "you know it when you see it" logic.[175] Or as Catherine Kintzler explains, "Only savants could know what is savant."[176] After Rousseau's discussions of music, genius came to be understood as a quality recognized primarily by other geniuses, and thus requiring some critical explanation.[177] If the law protected genius then it needed to clearly define what kind of works were, in fact, genius.

And indeed such expertise was institutionalized, or perhaps better put, re-institutionalized during the Directory and Consulate governments (1795–1804). The government suppressed academies in 1793 for many of the same reasons that it abolished theater monopolies and guilds. The Paris Conservatory and the National Institute, both addressed extensively in subsequent chapters, were established to promote the advancement of music, the arts, and sciences, not to set strict rules for them as academies had once done. Reviews of scores by the National Institute's music section indicate that these newer understandings of genius began to infiltrate their practices. The Conservatory's method books meticulously identified the composers of musical excerpts included in them. The National Institute codified social distinctions among artisans, artists, and savants by scrutinizing their work through the same values that defined property laws—the presence or absence of genius. The French believed that only through legislation could epistemological practices be protected from political persuasions.[178]

Scores submitted to the National Institute underwent a careful evaluation by those who presumably possessed enough genius or expertise to recognize it in others. When the Prussian composer Johann Friedrich Reichardt submitted compositions in honor of Napoleon, Gossec and Méhul claimed to immediately recognize the composer in the scores because of the "great beauty" found in them. The music, according to them, bore traces of the composer himself.[179] The reason Gossec and Méhul felt a need to verify Reichardt's identity in the scores at all was because the package arrived missing eighty-nine compositions detailed in its accompanying letter. It must have been Reichardt's enemies, they concluded, who caused such a deplorable "infidelity." Their language remarkably echoes the obsession with originality and fidelity described above, and which we will continue to see in Chapter 5. They praised Reichardt as a "savant musician," and determined that his enemies simply disliked that he had "put a demarcation between the Musician Artist, and Artisan Musician."[180]

It is noteworthy that the Institute members retained early eighteenth-century terminology—artisan, artist, and savant—transforming their meaning to conform to new postrevolutionary expectations. Genius had been dissociated by this time from rules, learning, and intellect, in other words, from what was traditionally associated with artists and savants.[181] This was in some ways convenient for musicians who had always struggled to demonstrate these capacities anyway. The French nation became suspicious of tyrannical savants who passed down the rules of arts without practicing them personally. Geniuses established their own rules through practice not learning, and were not expected to articulate them. Part of genius was its mystery. It was left to others to deduce and imitate the rules implied within artworks. Again, musicians were well positioned to take on this role. Gossec and Méhul's appraisal of Reichard as "savant," indicate a change in the term's meaning since earlier in the eighteenth century. No longer an authority who set the rules of an art, savants were endowed with a unique, individual expressive capacity, qualities of "genius." Savants now established rules through examples. No explanation on Reichardt's part was necessary. Méhul and Gossec seem to ascribe the attributes of genius as they were understood in France at the time to Reichardt when they call him a "savant" and "artist" musician.

Members of the National Institute treated scores that had already entered the public domain quite differently.[182] The report on Reichardt contrasted markedly with one on works by the composer Pierre-Joseph Candeille. Candeille had requested a government reward, and his application was sent to the Institute for consideration. Gossec emphasized the public reception of Candeille's operas during the past twenty years rather than any inherent qualities of his music. The operas had earned "goodwill" from "the public."[183] During the pension reforms challenged by Grétry, discussed earlier, Candeille had lost a pension for fifteen years of service to the Opéra. And so Gossec suggested that Candeille receive a national reward for his "talents, his work, and his service."[184] Candeille's right to recognition came not from the quality of what he put into the world, like Reichardt, but from mere work approved of by the nation. While Reichardt was a "savant," Candeille was simply a servant of France. Public recognition was a lesser form of recognition than that of one's peers—a genius to genius kind of thing. This is only one way in which musicians, and specifically composers, like Gossec and Méhul, gained authority in their field.

When the Institute codified its review process in 1804, all works that had already been released to the public would receive only a verbal description of their contents and merit without discussion. Unpublished or unperformed works might instead have a commission assigned to read parts of the work aloud to the *classe*, followed by a formal report. A "faithful copy" was then deposited in the Institute's library.[185] In substance, if a work circulated publicly before reaching the Institute, then it was considered within the public domain, and thus, for the public to decide its quality. This practice was mostly consistent with a reading of the property laws passed in the early 1790s.

Even if the public did not determine genius, they still had a right to inherit it as a collective cultural heritage. A compounding factor for the French, one investigated at length in subsequent chapters, was that individual genius was perceived as intimately tied to collective genius. As Jefferson explains, the genius of France, of its language, or its industry, "was, more often than not, a collective phenomenon linking success or supremacy with the individual character of institutional or abstract entities,"[186] and so individual genius became "a microcosmic replica of the national macrocosm."[187] The symbiosis between individual and national genius complicated any clear delineation between public and private musical property.

For this reason, we must return to Dalayrac's claim that music was not useful to the nation as a technological invention. He realized, being the well-trained Old Regime lawyer that he was, that if music were considered useful then it could be legally confiscated from its creator for the public good, just like any utility or useful knowledge. And formalities rendered music, yet again, a mere privilege. From the law of 1791 regarding performance to the law of 1793 regarding reproduction, composers became a medium for cultural heritage that did not possess his or her creation in perpetuity. They instead contributed to a collective national heritage of genius.[188] When debates arose about property rights over a new Académie française dictionary in 1802, legal arguments cited the 1793 law to cast the French language (and thus any dictionary of it) as a "national property."[189] A similar debate occurred when the Conservatory claimed ownership over publications of patriotic songs.[190] Music publishers immediately identified this practice as far too exclusive. The government funded the Conservatory's subscription publication of revolutionary hymns, and the Conservatory sought to legally prevent publishers from recirculating the works, claiming the compositions as its own exclusive property. Parisian music publishers including Boyer and Imbault disagreed and accused the Conservatory of establishing an unjust monopoly. The publishers argued that civic music was in fact a public property that could be printed and reprinted by anyone. Eventually the government stopped subsidizing the publications and the Conservatory increasingly published instrumental rather than patriotic music.[191] This conflict likely served as the motivation for the group of Conservatory composers who founded their own publishing house.[192]

The goal of legislative actions in 1793 was to create an open commerce of ideas that would balance public and private interest within a free market system.[193] When, consequently, artists' political identities were renegotiated, as the historian Carla Hesse explains, "from a privileged creature of the absolutist police state into a servant of public enlightenment,"[194] works of genius in France had to be awkwardly shared between individual artists, the public, and the people working in musical production.[195] Although intellectual and material concerns informed musicians' arguments, political concerns about where artists and their work would fit into a regenerated France influenced laws and policies. As the remaining chapters will show, the Paris Conservatory, formed in the early years of Revolution and established by 1795, offered one solution to these pressing contradictions by positioning itself as a public utility and institutionalizing the professionalization that musicians had slowly established over the course of the eighteenth century.

The politics undergirding the law did not invalidate its contribution to musicians' professionalization. Brown claims that only upon the founding of Framery's agency could dramatic authors finally be labeled "modern," because they "advocated for . . . material and legal interests," and not simply a privileged social position in the Old Regime hierarchy.[196] Despite the extensive efforts of playwrights from 1777 until 1780, they failed to achieve a "professional" status before the Revolution because they lacked a clear and legitimate social position within the Old Regime privilege structure.[197] Under composers' leadership during the Revolution the former playwrights organization became a "modern authors' agency."[198] Grétry and Dalayrac's activism in dramatic authors' endeavors therefore sheds light equally on musicians' professionalization. During the Revolution, musicians saw an enhancement of legal rights over their work, a defining criterion for professionalization and of modern professional musicianship.

Author's rights were intended to grant composers legal protection over the reproduction of their works in print and in performance, however, the composers discussed in this chapter subtly argued for control over an abstract component of their compositions, as well. The desire to legally register unalterable themes, to restrict derivative genres, and to conform performance to "authorized" scores situates individual musical expression, that is, originality, as a defining characteristic of property. The laws increasingly applied to a tangible entity (the score) while actually protecting the intangible essence of a composer's creation (subjective expression). These laws thus established both the material conditions and terminology later employed in tropes that would become central to the emergence of musical "Romanticism": respect for the "sovereignty" of musical geniuses and their "inviolable" works.

4 | Public Servants

The Revolution presented Parisian musicians with an opportunity to recast their reputations from privileged cosmopolitan artists to public national servants. Early in the Revolution proponents of the visual and plastic arts decried the "servitude" and even "enslavement" that artists had suffered under the Old Regime. Any professional advancements seen by these fields before 1789 were quickly forgotten in favor of a rhetoric connecting the arts with freedom.[1] Some musicians aligned with the military in a logic consistent with revolutionary rhetoric that equated the liberating potential of French arts and armies. Their affiliation ultimately led to the establishment of the Paris Conservatory, an institution that would standardize music as a profession. Its administrators gained a newfound authority in Paris and beyond. By becoming public servants, musicians joined a national agenda to regenerate French society through educational and cultural reform, both of which would henceforth benefit a people rather than a monarch.

This transition to government funding inevitably cast musicians' work as a public property, a compromise that allowed them to institutionalize the professionalization that had been over a century in the making. Contradictions emerged, however, between the motivations of individual musicians like those seeking private property rights in the previous chapter and those who sought collective legal protection, a tension present since Chapter 1's discussion of the legal battles between composer Jean-Baptiste Lully and the musicians' guild. While some musicians including André-Ernest-Modeste Grétry, Étienne-Nicolas Méhul, and Luigi Cherubini, allied with both individual and collective initiatives, others, introduced in the final section of this chapter, struggled to succeed in either. The perception of musicians as public rather than court servants held profound consequences for debates about musical property as France delineated state from civil society and debated the role of the arts in each.

From Pleasing Paris to Serving the Nation

Little is known about the early life of Bernard Sarrette. His adversaries were eager to point out that Sarrette never received musical training, and when the French Revolution began during the summer of 1789, he was likely serving as an accountant for the Garde française, the infantry regiment of the king's household.[2] Sarrette's name appears on two documents from that period, one supporting republican reform and the other supporting the king, a small indication that he was clever, someone who did what was necessary to survive politically.[3]

His earliest known involvement with musicians began the day before the storming of the Bastille, in the Filles-Saint-Thomas district of Paris. It was not necessarily Sarrette's political savvy that helped him to anticipate the patriotic enthusiasm that would take down the infamous prison the following day. To the contrary, the Filles-Saint-Thomas district's army would be known until 1792 as aristocratic, or at the very least moderate and supportive of the king. Some even considered the district counterrevolutionary. Sarrette formed a regiment of 150 soldiers there, including a core group of 45 musicians who would serve under him from that day forward.

Many of these men already knew one another, having been members of the same orchestras and masonic lodges. André Jean Gallet, Jacques Schneitzhoeffer, and Jean-François Veillard, whom we met in Chapter 2, picked up their wind instruments once again, this time not to watch an aristocratic *opéra comique* performance from the sidelines of the lodge La Candeur, but instead to march abreast as musician-soldiers.[4] The three likely moved into the Filles-Saint-Thomas convent with their Garde française comrades. Their housing and pay came from a patchwork of sources including Sarrette's personal accounts, individual Parisian districts' funds, and per diem work dedicated to planning and executing revolutionary festivals. On May 4, 1790, the corps was officially subsumed under the Garde nationale—a citizens' militia hastily formed at the beginning of the Revolution that, despite its name, would ultimately become the army of the city of Paris.[5] This new affiliation entitled the musicians to compensation, clothing, and instruments from the municipal government. During 1791, Jérôme Pétion de Villeneuve, the mayor of Paris (a title created in the wake of the Revolution), attempted to obtain funding to found a school for the musicians. Although Sarrette's band had loyally served Paris during revolutionary festivals and manifestations held from 1789 through 1792—even some that the national government condemned—the municipal government argued that the school was in fact an issue for the National Assembly's general education budget.

From the very earliest days of revolution the founding members of the Conservatory were caught up in changing political tides, especially the political tensions that developed between the municipal Parisian government and the French national government. As Mark Darlow has shown, the municipality and the nation cultivated quite different visions for what music should do in and for society.[6]

Music was not the only art to find itself pulled by competing agendas. Legislators, men of letters, professional artists, and amateurs debated the role that the arts should play in a "regenerated" French society. The essence of their disagreement was nothing less than the relationship between art and freedom. While some felt art's duty was to monumentalize the revolutionary moment, others believed it should continue the distinguished progression it had already begun, just freed from "tyranny."[7]

Most notable among the musicians' municipal services was their performance at a festival held in honor of the Châteauvieux Swiss mercenaries who had died in an antiroyalist internal rebellion in northeastern France.[8] The national government did not support the festival that honored the fallen Swiss soldiers; thus, the Garde nationale musicians' participation in it represented a political position in line with that of the city of Paris, which had always been more radical. Until then, the kind of antiroyalism displayed in the rebellion had been a contested issue. The National Assembly severely punished the Swiss soldiers who participated in the uprising, but French rebels received little or no punishment, an indication of the ambivalence toward antiroyalism early in the Revolution. The Swiss soldiers garnered sympathy mostly among staunch revolutionaries at the time. As the Revolution radicalized, the event was retrospectively recast as patriotic activism. The musicians' collaboration with a festival commemorating this contested rebellion might seem puzzling in light of their affiliation with the ostensibly antirevolutionary Filles-Saint-Thomas district, but it may just as well demonstrate the political savvy or perhaps even the apolitical stance of Sarrette and his music corps. As the national government radicalized, however, revolutionary zeal of the type exhibited at the festival would help the musicians to gain financial support.

Sarrette finally earned approval for a free music school funded by the municipality on June 9, 1792.[9] The school planned to accept 120 sons of national guardsmen as students, indicating an adherence to Old Regime class distinctions in which merit came from lineage rather than talent. Those without musical training would begin between the ages of ten and sixteen, and those with prior musical experience between eighteen and twenty. Prospective students would first sit for an exam; the municipality would supply successful applicants with an instrument, staff paper, and a uniform. The curriculum would include two solfege lessons and three instrument lessons each week. The school aimed to offer musical and military training, to groom participants for public festivals, and to participate in annual public exercises for municipal leadership. The militaristic goals of the school resulted in its concentration on wind instruments, which were easily portable and more audible in outdoor performance settings. By 1792, the music school served both the French nation and the Parisian municipality.

The music corps' military association would have been familiar to many of its participants. By this time, Joseph Bologne, the Chevalier de Saint-Georges, the virtuoso violinist introduced in Chapter 2, had abandoned his musical career altogether to work as a soldier among the French troops. A significant portion of Sarrette's band had been affiliated with masonic lodges, bastions for military culture. Many of the musicians had first come to the brotherhood as Garde française wind players.[10] This military genealogy motivated the school initially to maintain hereditary admissions requirements. The school in many ways resembled other military schools, most founded before 1789, which continued to function during the Revolution despite severe fiscal uncertainty.

But the musician-soldiers were not the only group of musicians seeking financial support for a music school in 1792. The Committee on Public Instruction received a proposal on January 24, 1792, by Jean Joseph Clareton, to establish a music school for individuals with no previous musical training.[11] The school's location, 2 Rue Favart, indicates that Clareton may have intended to affiliate it with the Opéra-Comique and perhaps hoped to join forces with the Théâtre Feydeau in order to create a pipeline of talent into the financially floundering École Royale de chant et de déclamation or the Opéra's singing school.[12] Clareton's proposal argued that "the study of music is part of modern education, and could become a resource for citizens who would like to try their talents in our theatres and concerts. This *bel art* certainly benefits society."[13]

Clareton proposed well-known composers as potential instructors for his school including Grétry and François-Joseph Gossec, as well as musicians already affiliated with major Parisian musical institutions: Jean-Baptiste Rey, director of the Opéra orchestra; Pierre Lahoussaye, former first violin of the Concert Spirituel and one of the two directors of the Théâtre de Monsieur (at this point, called Feydeau); Frédéric Blasius, director of the Comédie-Italienne orchestra; and Giuseppe Puppo, first violin and director of the Théâtre Feydeau orchestra. These musicians shared an interest in improving dramatic music education and crossed significant institutional boundaries, from the Théâtre Feydeau to the Opéra and Comédie-Italienne. Nearly all of these men would soon earn positions at the Conservatory.[14] Their prominence indicates that Clareton's school likely sought to train not only future performers but composers as well.

The two school proposals, one for Sarrette's music corps and the other for Clareton's theater musicians, represent distinct paths that professional musicianship began to follow during the early stages of the Revolution—one supporting the military, the other providing culture. These trajectories followed the two visions for art in a regenerated French society, one a monument to the future and the other a continuation of the past.[15] The paths nevertheless shared missions; first among them, to serve the French public. To achieve this, the schools needed resources that had come from the Crown or the church under the Old Regime. Both initiatives strove to form outstanding performers who would raise the overall quality of musical performances in Paris. Theaters were now decidedly public venues rather than simply luxurious hangouts for the aristocracy and bourgeoisie. Musicians would need to prove their worth in this changing market.

The fact that one request was pursued on the municipal level and the other on the national level is symptomatic of how musicians became entangled in the chaotic education reforms of the early Revolution. As dechristianization intensified, the close ties between clergy and education that had existed for centuries increasingly caused ideological complications. Many musicians trained in churches under the Old Regime. From 1791 until 1792, the period when the two music schools were proposed, the Committee on Public Instruction had been tasked with assessing and planning for new institutions to replace the Old Regime system of schools and universities.[16] Two plans for a new education system, the Talleyrand Plan of 1791 and the Condorcet Plan of 1792, failed to pass through the legislature.[17] The Marquis de Condorcet's plan received critiques as elitist because it separated skilled artisans from learned professionals early in their educations. Condorcet considered music among the "public" professions that needed to be "entrusted to enlightened men."[18] Some proposals for a new education system allowed for national support through the highest levels of specialized training while others only proposed nationalized primary schools, leaving advanced education either to municipalities or to private enterprises.[19] The musicians' appeals to both municipal and national entities during 1792 therefore stemmed at least in part from uncertainty about the emergent education system.

The chaotic state of education was not an isolated phenomenon. The years 1791 and 1792 were a confusing time when the "revolutionary consensus" broke down into increasingly hardline and eventually violent factions.[20] On June 10, 1791, King Louis XVI and his family fled from Paris in an attempt to seek refuge with Queen Marie Antoinette's family in Austria. The king left in his wake incriminating evidence, revealing that he did not in fact support a constitutional monarchy as he had pretended during the previous two years. When the royal family returned to Paris in shame after being recognized at the French border, a crisis ensued as republicans tried to negotiate France's future in the shadow of disingenuous monarchs.[21] In September, Louis XVI reluctantly accepted a constitution, the National Assembly dissolved, and soon the Legislative Assembly formed. But the French would never, neither in this nor in subsequent nineteenth-century revolutions, achieve a sustainable constitutional monarchy. By April 1792, France declared war on Austria to "spread liberty" across Europe and to eradicate what the royal family had hoped would serve as their safe haven. That same month piano maker Tobias Schmidt's guillotine was used for the first time to "humanely" execute enemies of the revolutionary agenda. Even executions had to be enlightened.

With money and property no longer a bar of entry for district-level political organizations in Paris, the city's sections increasingly democratized and radicalized. By July 1792, the Paris sections' resolve to overthrow the monarchy was exacerbated when the Prussians threatened to come to France and end its citizens' antiroyal machinations once and for all. The Prussian threat led the Legislative Assembly to make a detrimental decision: all Parisian citizens were granted the right to bear arms and some were even provided with weapons. It was very possible that they would need to defend the capital from foreign invasion. No longer confident in the Garde nationale's loyalty, the king stationed Swiss guards to protect the Tuileries Palace, where the royal family had been staying since October 1789 when they returned from Versailles at the hands of Parisian women demanding that the monarchs bear witness to the volatile events of the Revolution. In the very early morning hours of August 10, 1792, the tocsins rang throughout Paris, calling its inhabitants to an insurrection that the Jacobin clubs had fueled and planned for months.

The Tuileries Palace was completely ransacked as the royal family huddled in a building across the street. The palace's Swiss guards were slaughtered, their bodies pulled into pieces and scattered throughout the city. The monarchy fell, and the royal family was placed in locations safe from the Parisian masses, a confinement that in reality served as their prison for the short remainder of their lives. Paris and its sections had essentially usurped the French national government. The violence continued to escalate in September, when rumors of Prussia's advance across the French border led *sans-culottes*, the Parisian working classes, to take justice into their own hands. They raided prisons and brutally killed prisoners being held on suspicions of antirevolutionary sentiment. More than half the Parisian prison population—around 1,250 people—were killed in only five days between September 2 and 7, 1792.

When the new National Convention replaced the Legislative Assembly later that month, their first task was to reconcile the French royal family with the constitution. The government seemed to further democratize at this point. The Convention's creation marked the first time that artisans counted among the lawyers, professionals, and property owners serving in the national government, although servants remained excluded. Papers found in the Tuileries Palace on the night of August 10 once again incriminated the king, revealing his true antirevolutionary stance. Ultimately, the Convention decided that it would remain impossible for France to move forward as long as the monarchs lived. After a trial and close vote, Louis XVI became the guillotine's next victim. On January 21, 1793, France committed regicide.

Sarrette's Garde nationale music corps provided service directly to the nation rather than the municipality for the first time later that year, at a festival commemorating the one-year anniversary of the monarchy's fall.[22] One month later, in September 1793, the Reign of Terror, the most violent, radical, and confusing phase of the Revolution, began. In October, Marie Antoinette followed her deceased husband to the guillotine. The Committee on Public Safety, at this point France's de facto executive government, called on twenty-one musicians from Sarrette's Garde nationale to join the nation's western army. The musicians saw the request as an opportunity to appeal to the nation for financial support, and so on November 8, 1793, a representation from the municipal government along with the Garde nationale musicians presented a plan to the National Convention for a National Institute of Music.

Sarrette gave a speech to the Convention during the delegation's presentation. He had a fine political line to tread. With terror as the order of the day, mere suspicion of antirevolutionary sentiments sent French citizens to the guillotine daily. Academies and guilds had already been banned because of the corporate privilege they fostered.[23] The contradictions between the individualism of the laws discussed in the previous chapter and the communal demands of the Terror threatened to derail Sarrette's mission. The proposed National Institute of Music would need to serve the nation through instruction and education without replicating the privileges of now-defunct academies and guilds.[24] Moreover, Sarrette needed to argue that music itself was no longer the privileged, aristocratic entertainment it had been under the Old Regime. His herculean task was to erase music's synonymity with the monarchy and church.

Sarrette drew on two topical issues to make his case: antiacademic sentiment and centralized education. "Public interest," Sarrette began, "intimately tied to that of the arts, requires national protection."[25] His musicians had accompanied French combat and, in the future, pledged to accompany peace. Liberty, equality, and civic duty had prompted his musicians to organize four years earlier, on July 13, 1789. It was not personal interests, he claimed, but patriotic sentiment that had motivated them to organize one day before the fall of the Bastille. Their proposed Institute could "not be considered as an academic assembly, stagnant in its ignorance and presumption, [because] these [were] active artists working without *jalousie* and directed only by a desire to take the knowledge of their art to the nth degree."[26] Academies, Sarrette argued, protected preexisting standards. His musicians, on the contrary, did not blindly accept ancient knowledge; they advanced new musical understandings. Here, he adopted the early-eighteenth-century definition of savants as passive learners to characterize his musicians as their antithesis: artists who actively applied knowledge through skills to productively contribute to society.[27] Their music would not only remain in Paris. The musicians planned to travel to citizens' doorsteps across France, spreading music education throughout the Republic. Thus, responsibility for the Institute could not be passed to the municipal government of Paris, which would risk returning music to its former status as an elite Parisian pastime.

Sarrette's goal to send musicians throughout France not only adhered to a national agenda to "regenerate" France, but also corroborated education plans and cultural agendas that proposed a network of local and national institutions.[28] The revolutionary government hoped to "regenerate" France after the ravishes it suffered during the war by unifying its citizens under a shared language and culture. Regeneration was intimately tied to centralization, a movement ironically begun over a century earlier by Colbert under Louis XIV. The former Talleyrand and Condorcet plans had considered establishing a central Parisian institution where teachers would be trained and then sent throughout the country to ensure uniform, high-quality instruction everywhere in France. Some arts advocates had vehemently argued for access to cultural heritage across France to decenter Paris's long-held monopoly over the arts.[29] While both plans were ultimately abandoned, Sarrette must have known that such a system had been seriously discussed; the Parisian press documented the Committee on Public Instruction's activities during the previous year.

The government's stance toward education continually radicalized, like everything else in 1793. The new Commission on Public Instruction, established in June 1793 with a slight name-change from its predecessor, resulted in the Daunou-Sieyes-Lakanal plan, which provided for universal and free education only at the primary level. Pierre Claude François Daunou felt that advanced education could be left to a free (that is, private) market.[30] This plan, like those before it, was rejected anyway. An anti-intellectual sentiment continued to grip France, casting learned professionals and savants as tyrants, cruel as the now-headless Louis XVI.[31] In this particular revolutionary moment, the musicians could not risk projecting overly academic aims.

A clear delineation between instruction and education emerged in these debates. Instruction imparted knowledge and skills through books and classroom guidance. Education, on the other hand, enhanced the spirit through edifying experiences to develop morality. Upon losing their monarchs (the former center of political life) and their churches (the former centers of education), the French citizenry required a complete reeducation. It was through instruction in reading, writing, and arithmetic that children would acquire basic skills necessary for everyday life, and it was through education at public festivals that adults would learn to become good citizens of the new Republic.[32] According to this perspective, education served a social purpose—the formation of good citizens, a belief that would continue to animate French education throughout the nineteenth century.[33]

The Institute musicians would therefore not only instruct music students throughout France, but also, Sarrette promised, educate "the precious portion of society, who after having engaged in the difficult work of agriculture, will relax and celebrate the virtues and benefits of the Revolution under the tree of liberty."[34] The new Institute would transfer musical pleasures previously monopolized by the Old Regime's First and Second estates to the liberated Third Estate. Sarrette explicitly severed music's affiliation with privileged institutions, where, he claimed, it had been "weakened"—along with the "French soul"—"by its effeminate days in the salons or in the temples." Instead, he promised that "Vast arenas, public plazas [would] henceforth be the concert halls of the free people." "It is in a Republic founded on virtue that liberty reigns," Sarrette proclaimed, "and the reign of liberty is the reign of the fine arts."[35] According to Sarrette, musicians now served the French public and Republic. His position unsurprisingly jibed perfectly with discourses about the new role of the arts in French society, and more specifically with the education reformer Condorcet. Condorcet had criticized the privileged elites like those in Chapter 2 belonging to the Concert de la Loge Olympique, who, according to him, "no longer have taste for the talents of a famous virtuoso if they don't hear it in a concert that they organized." Pushing back against the old privileged system of musical production, Condorcet argued that patrons, "don't need a proprietary privilege to enjoy [the arts]."[36] Condorcet himself had tried to smooth over the same contradictions that Sarrette navigated in his speech. Recall Condorcet's belief that public schools should train only "enlightened men." The same contradictions troubled many visual and plastic artists as they tried to reconcile the cozy noble patronage that had generated great French artworks with the new artistic demands of a democratized France.[37]

However fraught his endeavor may have been, Sarrette's speech promised his band of musicians something in return for their service to the public—institutionalized professionalization. The Institute that he proposed would standardize the techniques, tools, training, and accreditation in music under the authority of their peers. Although in his oration Sarrette rejected the possibility that the Institute would function like an academy, in reality, he simply united and reframed the work accomplished by Old Regime guilds and academies—privileges musicians had never fully enjoyed—within a revolutionary agenda. As Condorcet's thinking laid out, professionalization in a Republic had to proceed in an egalitarian fashion that contributed to instruction and led to independence before the law.[38] These formulations had clear origins in the Old Regime debates about "liberal" and "free" professions discussed in Chapter 1.

An Institution of Their Own

Sarrette's speech was a success. The National Convention approved the formation of the Institute in Paris and asked the Committee on Public Instruction to prepare a plan for its establishment. On the same day, the newly minted "Institute" musicians attended a meeting of the Paris City Council to request a *bonnet rouge* from each council member. As the emblematic hat of republicanism adopted from the liberated slaves of Greece and Rome, the *bonnet rouge* symbolized freedom from tyranny as well as the ideals of antiquity that artists hoped to reanimate in France.[39] Though the hats physically marked the city's recognition of the musicians' patriotism, they also represented an olive branch from Paris as the musicians transitioned from municipal to national service.

The transition did not unfold as smoothly as the Institute musicians had anticipated. The distinction between the Parisian and French governments blurred as Terror raged. The musicians' patronage continued to straddle municipal and national entities as plans for educational institutions were drawn and redrawn, oftentimes simply abandoned as more pressing issues arose daily. This precarious position threatened the musicians not only financially, but also politically, as aesthetic visions between the two levels of government diverged during the Terror's height. The National Convention, mostly Jacobin, still aimed for an "aesthetically challenging form of art," while the government of the city of Paris, radically atheist "Hebertists," promoted simple didactic works that would "educate" audiences.[40] Letters sent by Gossec to a colleague during this period reveal the Institute musicians' anxieties in such a turbulent landscape. He warned Louis Antoine Durieu that the dedicatory epistle included in Durieu's new method book might make the Institute musicians into a "laughing stock" among "republican colleagues," and threatened to "compromise their delicacy."[41] The urgency of Gossec's requests to Durieu indicate that any wrong move could topple the musicians' progress, or worse, topple their heads from their shoulders.

Confusion continued to reign during the first seven months of 1794 as the Committee on Public Safety took drastic measures to rein in the chaotic mess into which the Revolution had devolved. Sarrette was imprisoned from March 25 to May 10, apparently as a result of unsubstantiated claims of antirevolutionary sentiments. His arrest exacerbated the Institute musicians' plight. But when the national government ordered some of the musicians to support the northern French armies, they leveraged the request to expedite their leader's release from prison. At least the increasingly prominent role music played in festivals kept the musicians working. They collaborated closely with the Committee on Public Safety (the de facto executive branch of the national government) to plan the program for a July 14 commemorative concert. Only two weeks after the concert, the National Convention denounced the Committee's outspoken leader, Maximilien Robespierre, as yet another tyrant no better than Louis XVI.

When Robespierre died a dramatic, violent death at the end of July, the Terror came to an end and a conservative political backlash called the Thermidorian Reaction began. This movement, which would last through 1795, inspired a reconsideration of the Terror's policies and eventually gave rise to debates about the necessity of nationally supported music education. Close on the heels of these debates were accusations of cronyism among the Institute's faculty. And so Sarrette drew up a new provisional organization for the Institute. Despite the uncertainty, eighty students received instruction throughout 1794. Although the Institute faculty agreed on a course of action for developing method books on August 29, by November 18, one year after the Convention's commitment to fund the Institute, the Committee on Public Instruction requested an explanation of the musicians' current organization in order to draft a report for the funding allocation that the Committee on Public Safety had already approved. A Commission was created to grapple with various questions that arose regarding the institution, including its process for admitting students and whether similar institutions would be created throughout France. Marie-Joseph Chénier, a poet and politician whose texts had been set by some of the Institute musicians including Méhul, supported his musician comrades and presented the report on behalf of the Committee on Public Instruction and Finance Committee on July 28, 1795.[42] Chénier described the fine arts as "essentially moral" and invoked Orpheus and Amphion to argue that these allegories from antiquity demonstrated "music's very real empire."[43]

On August 3, 1795, the plan was approved with some modifications, the most notable among them was a name change from the National Institute to the Conservatory, "borrowed from the Italian schools, despite the difference in curriculum between the two institutions."[44] Although the new music Conservatory acknowledged its homonymous Italian music institutions, there were more recent revolutionary precedents that it followed. The National Institute of Music was not the only revolutionary institution to take on the title conservatory. In fact, it was one of the last. More than a year prior, the Museum Commission that previously oversaw the creation of the Louvre had been replaced by a "conservatory" of ten men who would "set the standards of competence and patriotism" in the visual arts.[45] Around the same time the Conservatoire des arts et métiers was founded to foster inventions in science and technology. The Institute musicians did not choose to change the name to Conservatory themselves. Daunou, whose education plan was discussed earlier, demanded the change because he wanted the title Institute for what would become the National Institute—the learned society comprising all the arts and sciences in a single institution.[46] It was in fact Durieu's use of the word "Institute" in his method book's dedicatory epistle that had caused Gossec to panic and write his worried letter cited previously. The Conservatory musicians had good reason to distance themselves from their peer institutions in Italy. They were far more eager to align with the peer institutions within France that were also working for the benefit of the nation, and, most importantly, receiving handsome financial support from the government.

The 1795 law forming the Conservatory emphasized both its national affiliation and comprehensive agenda, noting the required service of all faculty members in national festivals through either composition or performance. At the time, the national government continued to promote civic education at festivals, so large sums of money were devoted to any arts, especially music, that would contribute to such events.[47] The school's public library would house principal works on the theory of music as well as an instrument cabinet exhibiting French, foreign, and ancient instruments. Studios for instrument-making and printing housed within the Conservatory would allow music students of both sexes to further assure their subsistence. The Conservatory institutionalized French musical production—from publishing and instrument-building to organology, music theory, and history, taking over the many sectors of musical production that under the Old Regime had been governed by a constellation of privileged individuals and institutions.

The Conservatory would add new professors to its faculty through a jury process and the institution's oversight was assigned to the Committee on Public Instruction until further executive organizations were established. Thirty new professors joined the faculty ranks in November 1795. Musicians who performed with the Garde nationale under Sarrette, as well as those who taught at the École Royale de chant, and many who had been part of the earlier proposal for Clareton's Rue Favart music school were grandfathered into the faculty. Thus, the two distinct paths of professional musicianship that had formed earlier in the Revolution merged (albeit not seamlessly) into a single institution.[48] Composers Méhul, Grétry, Gossec, Cherubini, and Jean-François Lesueur were all named Inspectors and would oversee both teaching and public performances. Ironically, after leading efforts to create the institution for years, Sarrette was at first granted no official role. His colleagues soon rallied around him, however, claiming to need Sarrette's administrative leadership to spare the inspectors distractions from their composing. Indeed, composers took on a greater authority and administrative role in the institution.[49]

Patriotic Servants

Musicians unsure of whether they would find a place in the Conservatory also looked to the government for support when their former livelihoods among the court and church evaporated. As the Terror ended, Marie-Joseph Chénier forcefully defended a new reward set in place by the Committee on Public Instruction intended to support men of letters and artists. "For a long time already," Chénier proclaimed, the government had "destined a sum of three hundred thousand *livres* to laboring men without fortune who cultivate these useful arts that would be called with pride *métiers*."[50] Chénier was criticizing the funds set aside for the crafts and trades, to which we shall return in Chapter 6. He championed the *beaux-arts* as equally useful as the *métiers*. Because "the arts are a national property," he argued, the encouragements given to artists "are a public debt."[51] According to Chénier, and in accordance with discourses about the arts that had gained traction since 1789, the arts constituted an invaluable cultural heritage and its creators required support. His assertions aligned with the at times paradoxical arguments about the deep rapport between freedom and the arts.[52] In Chénier's eyes, artists protected by wealthy patrons alone, as under the Old Regime, were worse than servants; according to him, aristocratic and noble patronage produced artistic "slavery."[53] For this reason, he recognized an imperative for the nation to finance artists. At risk was nothing less than their freedom. In this the nation took over the role of distributing awards and bonuses that in the past had been designated by privileged patrons or institutions; a model that had already transitioned from service- to art-oriented even before the Revolution.[54] The Committee would select recipients of the new reward and publish their names on a list. Following the new initiative's announcement, French citizens submitted requests for the encouragements that Chénier had triumphantly announced. In their bids to make Chénier's list, musicians tried to recast themselves from Old Regime servants to revolutionary patriots even though there was practically speaking little difference between the Old Regime and revolutionary reward systems.

Paris's self-proclaimed role as a new universal capital of European arts was palpable in the first round of reward distributions. Among the first 100 writers, astronomers, historians, naturalists, geometricians, librarians, sculptors, and others who received this national reward, only five among them were musicians, and only one of the musicians was a native Frenchman. Most were Italians, born and trained: the composer and violinist Giuseppe Maria Cambini, the *musico* Antoine Albonèse, mandolin virtuoso Alessandro Mario Antonio Fridzeri, and Felice Bambini, son of Eustache of *Querelle des bouffons* fame. The Abbé d'Haudimont, a renowned cathedral school instructor, was the lone French musician on the list. It is suggestive that D'Haudimont's co-recipients, however few, were predominantly Italian. The support of "foreign" artists might seem contradictory to the nationalist tone of this period. Such dissonances, however, were reconciled through efforts to transport the ideals and arts of Greek antiquity to Paris via Rome.[55]

Personal connections—an Old Regime means of doing business that had come under scrutiny during the Revolution—seemed to remain an effective means of finding a way onto "the list." François Jean Roussel, a blind French musician who hoped that his age and method book would earn him a reward, requested a place on the list immediately after the new law passed.[56] He ultimately failed to make the cut. Conversely, D'Haudimont had been recommended to the Committee by a Citizen Godinot, presumably a friend or former student.[57] And, as discussed later in Chapter 6, D'Haudimont worked closely with composers like Grétry and Gossec to help the government evaluate new education systems like Clareton's. A short note penned by Pierre-Louis Ginguené, a composer and man of letters who became Director of Public Instruction in November 1795, suggested that Bambini earned a place on the reward list at least in part because of his pedigree, noting that he came "from an interesting family."[58] Indeed, many of the reward supplicants had well-known allies submit pleas in their favor rather than requesting a reward for themselves. In this, the Committee seemed to proceed according to Old Regime rules of sociability, quite unlike the legalistic procedures followed by other revolutionary committees. Even more telling, some requests refer to the awards as "pensions," a term that in Chapter 3 Grétry vehemently critiqued for its implicit connotation of a handout from the Second Estate rather than well-earned pay.

Some musicians, fearful of such passé pretensions when they sought unpaid royal pensions, resituated their previous service to the First and Second estates as service to the nation. François Giroust, the last superintendent of music for Louis XVI, requested funding available through the new law.[59] Although he had obtained a position as concierge at the National Palace of Versailles, from the beginning of July 1792 to the end of 1793 he did not have work and subsisted on meager savings to support a wife and eight children. Giroust, an active Freemason, had served the king, moreover, his musical fame came almost exclusively from sacred music. Because he had struggled to pay for his home until taking up this new post, Giroust requested that the aid be converted into housing to keep the roof over his family's head. Giroust, in his modesty, completely avoided discussing his musical achievements, but the General Council of the Commune of Versailles wrote to the committee in his favor to confirm both his "merit" and his "morality" (that is, his fidelity to the nation).[60] The Commune detailed Giroust's musical achievements at length: oratorios of "unrivaled genius," a hymn that emulated Rouget de l'Isle's "La Marseillaise," and a list of all Giroust's revolutionary works, thirty-two in total. They close their letter refashioning Giroust from a court and church musician to "the father of a large family, the citizen thrown into misfortune, the distinguished artist, the republican" who made pecuniary sacrifices in his personal revenue for the sake of the nation. Giroust's "sacrifices" likely aimed to achieve first-class aid (the largest sum available) as laid out in the law establishing the funds.

Like court and church musicians, many dramatic composers (quite unlike Dalayrac or Grétry in the previous chapter) could not survive on performance revenues alone and sorely missed the generous pensions that they had previously received from the monarchy. Among these claims were musicians like Jean-Paul-Gilles Martini. On January 23, 1795, a citizen J. Berlioz wrote to the committee in favor of Martini, citing Martini's major works as an *auteur de musique*: *L'amoureux de 15 ans* (1771), *Droit du seigneur* (1783), and *Sapho* (1794).[61] Berlioz explains that Martini's works did not currently earn enough revenue to sustain the composer's livelihood and the pension promised to Martini by the *liste civile* had failed to materialize. The committees dealing with liquidations should have paid Martini's Old Regime pension in accordance with the laws established for the distribution of national funds. Since the liquidations never delivered, appealing to the aid for artists was likely Martini's next best option. Berlioz cites Martini's misfortune, having been employed by the late king who ostensibly neglected the composer's talent. This was a somewhat inaccurate portrayal designed to corroborate depictions of musicians and artists enslaved at the hands of monarchs. In reality Martini had been a particular favorite composer of Marie Antoinette.[62] In 1788, Louis XVI had named Martini superintendent for music of the king *en survivance*, he would have assumed duties as superintendent upon the retirement or death of the current holder of that position, Giroust.[63] Berlioz assures the committee that Martini is "nonetheless"—that is to say, despite his service to the Crown—a good citizen who remained in "tranquility" throughout the Revolution. Indeed, Martini had fled to Lyon and maintained a low profile until the end of the Terror.[64] Claiming to know Martini for eighteen months, likely since his return from Lyon, Berlioz confirms the composer's honor and expresses his willingness to provide testimonies from other musicians who would support this claim. Martini's misfortune and his talent deserved, according to Berlioz, "encouragement" from the government.[65]

A flurry of musicians requested inclusion in the rewards after their name did not appear on Chénier's initial list. Three days after its presentation, Stanislas Champein—the composer who in the previous chapter brought his case to the Châtelet Court on the eve of Revolution—requested that the Committee on Public Instruction add him.[66] It must have riled Champein that his former artistic collaborator, Albonèse, appeared on the list while his own name was omitted. Champein claimed to have traveled to Rouen for "personal" reasons early in the Revolution and then remained at the behest of its citizens because they enjoyed the compositions he contributed to public festivals. He indexed for the committee the patriotic operas contained in his *portefeuille* that would prove useful to instructing the public in the love of their country. Later that year he would write once again citing his patriotic works, but this time simply to request the barest essentials—string, wood, and candles.[67]

Despite his supplications, André-Jean Rigade, the teacher of reward-recipient Bambini, did not earn a coveted place on the list either.[68] Rigade and his supporter, a Citizen Chapelain, petitioned the Committee on Public Instruction to take into account that the music instructor did not simply teach music according to the training he had received in the Naples Conservatories but that he also considered "music as a science" and accepted only musical systems that granted freedom to genius.[69] This assertion indicates that rhetoric about genius, freedom, and the arts circulated widely by this time, and had reached musicians outside the Conservatory. Musicians seemed to ventriloquize revolutionary rhetoric in any way possible and to explain away extended absences from Paris, the very heart of patriotic sentiment.

The requests submitted by the French cellist and the composer Jean-Baptiste-Aimé Janson *l'aîné* highlighted his participation in festivals, his talents, and his blood sacrificed for the country, even though he had actually served as superintendent of music to the king's brother, future Louis XVIII.[70] Janson's colleagues co-signed a letter in his favor and expressed surprise that he had not yet been granted a national recompense. Below Janson's note, his colleagues express their confidence in his exceptional talents and works, which they claimed were celebrated throughout Europe. They refer to Janson as a composer of works "of a free people," who had sacrificed his fortune for the country, adding social credentials to their patriotic rhetoric: Janson was "an old friend of Gluck and Sacchini." Composers Gossec and Honoré Langlé, organist Nicolas Séjan, and men of letters Jérôme Lalande and Bernard Germain de Lacépède all signed the letter. Thus, Janson boasted supporters including those affiliated with Conservatory, former members of the École Royale de chant, and highly regarded scientists. It bears noting, in light of Chapter 2, that Lalande and Lacépède had been members of the lodge Les Neufs Sœurs with Janson before the Revolution.

Many of the musicians requiring assistance suffered unfortunate collateral damage from the abolition of the First Estate. Organist Nicolas Séjan penned a long, frank, and desperate letter to the committee.[71] With a wife and four children to support, his income as an organist at churches and as professor at the École royale de chant had disappeared. For obvious reasons, organ was not part of the Conservatory's new curriculum. In the letter, Séjan describes his École class as "currently destroyed." Séjan recounts how he was compelled to sell 6,000 *livres* worth of possessions to survive, among them, his beloved pianoforte. He also resorted to borrowing 4,000 *livres* from three good friends. Noting his long career, his large family, and all that he lost to "the events" of the Revolution, Séjan asks that the committee come to the aid of a "citizen artist." Although claiming indigence, Séjan carefully notes recognition by formerly privileged bodies—the École Royale de chant and the Opéra—and though he could not demonstrate any kind of utility to the nation, he claims a patriotic, "citizen" identity. Implicitly the Committee on Public Instruction sought to repair damages from the suppression of the church and academies and so it took seriously the men of letters and artists who had been previously recognized by the Old Regime institutions. The committee members hoped to protect valuable knowledge and its producers from the Terror's anti-intellectualist sentiments. Séjan also explains in his letter that although the Opéra had tried to incorporate his services and he succeeded in obtaining an organ for the theater, he had not yet been compensated for these efforts.[72] Séjan was one of two musicians—both organists—who finally made the next list published in April 1795.[73]

After the April list was presented by Claude François Danou, the Committee on Public Instruction received some requests that focused more on musicians' technical and technological innovations. Jean Joseph Rodolphe, for example, had been placed on the list of artists eligible for aid three times—presumably in late 1794, early 1795, and just before Danou's announcement—and three times found himself inexplicably removed from it.[74] Rodolphe outlines his credentials as the performer who perfected the horn in France and the first composer to write a treatise on harmony that unites the theory and practice of music, appealing to more practical revolutionary agendas discussed further in Chapter 6.[75] He notes that the work was written for the "Institut de musique" on Rue Bergère and claims to have been made director of the institution as a result. He strategically avoids calling the institution by its better-known nomenclature, the École Royale de chant, and fails to mention his early service to the Prince of Conti's orchestra, the Opéra, and the royal chapel. Even earlier in his career Rodolphe had worked as a court musician in Stuttgart. Instead, he appeals to recognition by learned societies—or what was the closest to a learned body that music could boast— and he aligns him with the nascent Conservatory that the Committee on Public Instruction was in the midst of creating. (He would eventually join its faculty briefly in 1798.) Rodolphe also outlines his indigence: at sixty-six years of age, ill and without money, his only son died of an injury sustained in the Vendée wars. Rodolphe's age and family situation index additional aids to which he technically held a right. A law passed in February 1794 granted aid to families of military personnel wounded or killed in service.[76] His emphasis on technological innovation, pedagogical advances, and institutional recognition all situate him to receive aid for artists or for citizens affected by military service. Rodolphe's case illustrates the ambiguity and uncertainty that musicians faced as they attempted to recover from the Revolution. Although vows of patriotism embue their letters, it would be imprudent to derive a cohesive political sentiment from their pleas, which instead seem to haphazardly attempt compliance with vague, overlapping legal standards that entitled individuals to reparations.

Professionalization and Public Patronage

With the abolition of the monarchy, church, academies, and guilds, musicians had no choice but to rely on the public and nation for their livelihood. Those who could not make lucrative careers from performances or publishing, as described in the previous chapter, needed to find other means to survive. The Conservatory initially seemed to offer a reliable haven. Individual appeals to the government were a last resort for those left in the cold outside its walls. Indeed, a frigid bureaucracy and supposed meritocracy soon governed the institution.[77] There were notable exclusions and slights, however; among them, its first female professor of the first class, Hélène de Montgeroult, left the Conservatory claiming health issues only to go on as an acclaimed piano pedagogue for decades to come.[78] The Conservatory congealed into a socially elite male-dominated sphere despite its early lip service to equality.[79]

The establishment of a musician-run Conservatory consummated a professional trajectory that had begun long before the fall of the Bastille. At its founding, the Conservatory was conceived as a central institution overseeing others in the provinces. Although this initiative largely failed, mostly for financial reasons,[80] the intention was to cultivate French music through a system of oversight based in Paris. In the new institution, musicians would set their field's standards by developing techniques, training, tools, and accreditation methods through their own curriculum design and comprehensive faculty-authored method books. The faculty would evaluate their peers and their students through juries. They would even experiment with instrument design and manufacturing. They would house the composition, execution, and even the publication of French music within a single, self-directed institution. They were tasked with no less than the aesthetic progress of French music. After a century of disjointed struggles beginning with Lully and Couperin, a generation of Parisian musicians had finally achieved self-directed, institutionalized professionalization. They were folded into a national cultural and educational agenda that facilitated their transition from serving the monarchy and church to serving the French public, an opportunity that eluded many other artists and craftsmen during the revolutionary decade.[81] Because of their Old Regime associations, many luxury trades were decimated by the Revolution. The same fate threatened musicians, but Sarrette's careful political maneuvering allowed this elite group to extricate itself from associations with former patrons. Their patriotic recasting affected the perception of musicians' work as a public utility, a reality that persisted through the nineteenth century, as Jann Pasler has well elucidated.[82]

They succeeded in part because of the Conservatory's kinship with broader educational and military reforms that had begun during the Old Regime. Prior to the Revolution, there had been a movement in France to establish a national education system that was both standardized and centralized.[83]

A significant step in this effort, in addition to the adoption of uniform instruction through textbooks, was the *aggregation*—exams through which teachers competed for positions across Parisian schools and universities, a practice that would be readopted under Napoleon. Historian Robert Palmer points to the exams as "a step toward the professionalization of teaching."[84] This professional education also included state "financing of art students."[85] Palmer argues that military schools in particular "reflected the rising concern of the government for professional education, as in establishing the schools of mining, engineering, and roads and bridges."[86] And soon both the arts and the military were viewed as conduits to freedom.[87]

The evolution in French military culture during the Revolution is significant in this regard, as its role shifted from serving the king to functioning as the seat of state bureaucracy. This was achieved through the implementation of a merit system and at least the veneer of an apolitical professionalism, which allowed the military to offer stable careers despite the precarious French political climate.[88] Sarrette helped to free his musicians from their representational association with court culture and religious rituals by recasting their work in a similar light.[89] One challenge that the Conservatory faced was military conscription of its students, especially wind players.[90] The institution was founded alongside other Central Schools that brought about a new level of professionalization in French education, including the new Conservatoire des arts et métiers and École polytechnique, both discussed at length in Chapter 6. Parisian musicians no longer served an earthly or heavenly king; their music no longer belonged exclusively to wealthy and noble patrons. Rather, music and musicians enriched the French public. Sarrette's musicians still inhabited Paris, but they now worked for France as self-directed professionals.

The Conservatory musicians did not simply become a propagandistic arm of the revolutionary government as some scholarship would suggest. Rather, they established a new mode of institutionalized professional musical production. Lydia Goehr cites distinct features absent from musical production before 1800: copyright, creative freedom, frequent rehearsals, dependable instrument technology, and a focus on the composition rather than the performance of works.[91] We have already seen in the previous chapter how composers more vigorously pursued copyrights and protection for their intellectual property because of the Revolution. Sarrette's speech and the law forming the Conservatory clearly lay out an institution where musical production including rehearsals, instrument building, and composition would become more deliberate and consistent than it had been under the Old Regime.

Although Jacques Attali viewed the formation of the Paris Conservatory as a moment "possibly unique in history" for the creative freedom it ostensibly provided musicians as they centralized musical production and protected it from bourgeois money,[92] becoming public servants in fact had a costly price: the perception of music as a public property. This view clashed with the individualist perspective propagated by musicians like Nicolas-Marie Dalayrac who, in the previous chapter, emphatically asserted that no one "needed" his music. But France did desperately need music to legitimize its cultural and industrial dominance in Europe and across the globe in the wake of Revolution. The French nation began to conscript every public good available toward the projection of a successful and stable image. The next two chapters show music taken up into this late revolutionary imperial agenda as a form of cultural heritage and national industry.

5 | Cultural Heritage: Music as Work of Art

As the revolutionary decade waned in 1799, Bernard Sarrette, director of the Paris Conservatory, wrote to Napoleon Bonaparte's brother Lucien, who was serving as French Minister of the Interior.[1] With construction on the Conservatory's library scheduled to begin soon, Sarrette asked whether Lucien might obtain three artworks for the new building: a marble copy of a statue, the Apollo Belvedere, and two busts, one of Orpheus, the other of Amphion. Sarrette specified that the commissioned sculptor should design "an explanatory emblem" to appear in bas-relief beneath each bust. The figures were not simply decorative; they represented particular mythical characters that Sarrette wanted clearly announced to the Conservatory's visitors.

The Apollo Belvedere's mythic and cultural symbolism required little explanation at the time. Apollo, as the god of music, held obvious significance for musicians, but the Belvedere statue had acquired other well-known layers of meaning over the course of the eighteenth century, especially during the Revolution. In 1764, the archaeologist Johann Joachim Winckelmann authoritatively dubbed the statue "the highest ideal of art among all the works of antiquity."[2] Napoleon later brought the statue to Paris from Rome, during his 1796 Italian campaigns. At the time of Sarrette's request, the Louvre exhibited the Belvedere not only as "the highest ideal of art" but also as an icon of France's European domination—material proof that republican antiquity had been resurrected and reanimated on the banks of the Seine. By the turn of the nineteenth century, the Belvedere became such a ubiquitous marker of Europe's great artistic heritage that the French writer Stendhal critiqued the United States' infant culture by asking, "Can one find anywhere in that so prosperous and rich America a single copy, in marble, of the Apollo Belvedere?"[3] The statue's aesthetic and political import were inextricably connected in the French imagination. As this chapter shows, the pristine universality attributed to ancient artworks like the Belvedere found application in musical compositions, as well.

Lucien would have found it unremarkable and perhaps even pleasing that Sarrette requested busts of Orpheus and Amphion. Revolutionary discourses drew widely on Greek antiquity to reimagine the nation. According to mythology, Orpheus's lyre seduced nature while Amphion's constituted civilization. Their instruments generated rather than ornamented society. Both of and above the everyday, Orpheus and Amphion's music was at once prelapsarian and civic, transcendent and ordinary, correlations that would soon pose an impossible contradiction to what Lydia Goehr calls the "separability principle," which severed the fine arts from the everyday around 1800.[4] At the time, musicians employed Orphic discourse, as Vanessa Agnew has shown, "to carve out their intellectual turf and to insist on their own specialist knowledge,"[5] precisely the task Sarrette set out to achieve for musicians in the new Paris Conservatory. A Neoplatonic, utilitarian view of music as social did not yet diminish its aesthetic power. Musicians could still simultaneously embody the roles of what Agnew terms "poetic metaphysicists" and "rational empiricists."[6] The Revolution projected its own unique complexities onto artists, who in the wake of political turmoil faced a mandate to retell French history and regenerate French society through art.[7] Like the Belvedere, Orpheus, and Amphion, the new Conservatory's mission was simultaneously political and artistic.[8]

By the late 1790s, Conservatory members followed in the wake of French military victories across Europe to collect musical "masterpieces" that would contribute to a universal history of European art over which Paris would preside as capital. They hoped to author a new music history that would erase previous representational connotations from compositions in order to preserve them for instructional and artistic purposes. Administrators nostalgically imagined a future in which their creations of genius would hang in museums alongside Rubens and Titians. As Edouard Pommier frames it, "The genius of the arts moved toward the future contemplating the past."[9] The musicologist Katharine Ellis asserts that to understand the revival of early music in nineteenth-century France, one must begin with this "idea of the museum spirit" during the Revolution.[10] Sarrette set out to acquire musical works to fill what he called a "museum," not an "imaginary museum of musical works" like the one theorized by Goehr, but a real brick-and-mortar musical monument to France's universal cultural heritage. Fueled by budding French nationalism and imperialism,[11] the Conservatory adopted a future-oriented, object-centered discourse.

Property rested at the very heart of this transformation in professional musical production and epistemic practice. As Conservatory faculty joined national educational and cultural agendas, they worked with other artists, savants, and bureaucrats to distribute property among new or reformed institutions. This process brought musical scores and instruments into a preestablished evaluation system based on both the fine arts and scientific instruments. As these historical actors sought a language to articulate musical value, they concomitantly negotiated who held the right to make expert judgements about music. Once again claims to musical property, in this case as cultural heritage, proved foundational to the interdependent transitions that I have already begun to trace: from servitude to professionalism, from cosmopolitanism to nationalism, and, here, from social practice to work of art.

Music and the Fine Arts under the Revolution

The material resources that the government provided to the Conservatory primarily came from *biens nationaux*, or, national property, which the government confiscated from the Catholic church and the noble *émigrés*. Church property was nationalized early in the Revolution, in November 1789, and by 1790 any religious organization not dedicated to charity or education was dissolved. That July, the Civil Constitution of the Clergy subordinated priests to the nation. Those who refused to take an oath of loyalty (called refractory, and later, nonjuring priests) were forced to hide or to flee in order to avoid certain persecution. In 1792, the government began to seize property from noble *émigré* households, where extensive libraries and art collections were abandoned as the occupants fled carrying only the clothes on their backs. The revolutionary government considered the *émigrés* as traitorous deserters. Underneath the seizures lay a conviction that the First and Second Estates' cultural property had in reality belonged to the nation all along. And so the national domain was initially created in order to be emptied into private, more deserving hands.[12]

Confiscated art posed an immediate contradiction to revolutionary ideals. On the one hand, the arts seemed to have somehow heralded or ushered in the political Revolution. Like the Ancient Greeks (or so the French believed), revolutionaries saw a "consubstantial line between art and freedom."[13] On the other hand, the symbols of oppression that prerevolutionary artworks contained "injured the gaze" of a freed people, particularly the now-free artists who until 1789 had lived under "servitude," or what some even described as "enslavement."[14] Claude-Maurice Talleyrand, a clergyman who served in the National Assembly and promoted public education plans, went as far as claiming that before the Revolution the arts had been "prostituted to tyrants."[15] According to him, the arts were in fact "common property."[16] Interested parties brought their suggestions to the National Assembly about how to handle the monuments to feudalism and slavery that stood throughout France. Their ideas for ameliorating this situation varied: transport the monuments to museums or "restore" the monuments to conform with new democratic values. And so ironically from very early in the Revolution a concern for the history of the arts and their potential for the future was immediately bound up in the iconoclasm spreading throughout the nation.[17]

In the volatile revolutionary atmosphere, artists and experts collaborated to protect the quickly accumulating *biens nationaux*. The Monuments Commission inventoried, appraised, and facilitated transport of newly acquired national property to depots established throughout Paris. Official paperwork from the committee consistently described its objective as the "research and conservation of monuments relative to the letters, sciences, and arts." The endeavor was a massive logistical undertaking, one for which the participants were overwhelmingly unprepared. Reams of reports describe artworks made of porcelain, marble, and bronze, tactical maps, military treatises, microscopes, hydraulic machines, paintings by Titian and Raphael, travelogues, and more.[18] Although Rousseau's *Dictionnaire de musique* appears among the inventories from this period, music was not explicitly included at first among the divisions that the commission devised: printed books, manuscripts, charters, and seals; antique and modern medals; inscribed stone and inscriptions; machines and other objects relating to the mechanical arts and sciences; natural history; and ancient, modern, European, and foreign costumes. Within a few years, the commission's objects of interest specified and expanded to "monuments of antiquity, painting, sculpture, physics, machines, music, and literature."[19] These exhaustive and exhausting lists bear witness to a frantic attempt to account for cultural heritage through scrupulous, objective auditing.

Academy members evaluated confiscated objects related to their specialties and developed strict appraisal parameters for those that did not fit preexisting academic standards. For example, the commission created a system to evaluate hunting, reliquary, and other metal works, objects not traditionally scrutinized in Colbert's academy system.[20] To be conserved, an object in this category first needed to equal or surpass the value of its constituent materials. Certain other attributes immediately qualified an object for preservation: creation after 1300, beauty, "instruction on history and the epochs of art," or "details interesting for art," history, morals, and manners. Even if a work did not merit preservation, any inscription or legend that would be of interest to history, art, or both, was to be detached and preserved. History increasingly provided the justification for keeping aesthetically uninteresting artworks. Thus, the commission appraised "monuments" through material and cultural criteria, ideally seeking "objects" that were "highly estimated and highly esteemed," put differently, expensive and admirable.[21] As early as 1790, the management of artistic heritage brought artworks into the rewriting of French history; "a history of art," according to Edouard Pommier, "that did not yet exist."[22]

Part of this process required artists and academicians to translate objects' worth from ritual to aesthetic value. A painting of Jesus Christ with Martha and Mary became "highly estimated" and "highly estimable" not for its biblical or theological significance, but for its creator, its use of color, its representation of a particular school of painting, or its historical origins. As ecclesiastical property became government property, it was expunged of its religious connotations and instead acquired aesthetic, historical, and pedagogical worth.[23] Accordingly, among the commission's reports, artworks began to earn classification according to "schools," an approach soon taken up by the founders of the Louvre and advocated by the painter Jean-Baptiste-Pierre Lebrun.[24] The concept was considered quite modern compared to the Old Regime approach to exhibition, which prioritized mixed schools. In one report on the contents of an *émigré* household, the commissioners categorized paintings by the Italian, Flemish and Dutch, and French schools.[25]

Detailed documentation of confiscated property notes each object's title, creator, quality, and dimensions, from microscopes to Da Vincis. Eventually reports mapped the commissioners' path as they appraised each building, room by room, and described in minute detail every object they encountered—its situation, its material, its color, weight, and height, all measurable attributes were considered. When necessary, they tried to convey their findings in drawings (Figure 5.1). The reports offer a vivid even eerie reenactment of ambling through each opulent, deserted, "formerly royal" residence.[26]

The commission soon realized that musical scores and instruments made up a significant portion of the clergy and nobility's property. It consequently established a separate depot on Rue Bergère in buildings formerly belonging to the king's household entertainments to house confiscated musical objects, just as discrete depots across Paris contained plastic and visual artworks, scientific and mechanical instruments, and printed books and manuscripts. Musicians were not yet included in the commission's work, and it required lobbying on the part of the (then) National Institute of Music faculty to earn representation in the confiscation agenda.[27]

When, as recounted in the previous chapter, the Revolution radicalized in August 1792, Jean Roland, then Minister of the Interior, sought not only to reclaim property from the church and nobility but also to protect national monuments from iconoclasm. The government's ambivalent stance toward Old Regime artworks had seemingly granted permission to destroy them. In addition to the many lives lost, the violent night of August 10 saw mass destruction of art and architecture throughout the Tuileries Palace and central Paris. Even as a staunch revolutionary, Roland was horrified by the defacement that he had witnessed. And it was a certain class of people—"barbarians"— who were described as having committed such acts. He thus sought to establish a national library (the Bibliothèque nationale), a museum (the Louvre),

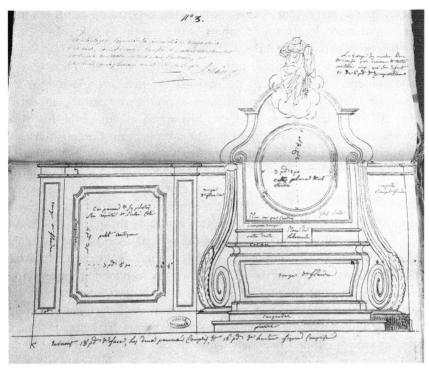

FIGURE 5.1 Detailed drawings depict artworks confiscated from formerly royal households inventoried by the Monuments Commission. Courtesy of the Archives nationales de France, Pierrefitte-sur-Seine.

and an archive (the Archives nationales), where precious vessels of cultural heritage and public education would be protected for future generations.[28]

The revolutionary government abolished academies, universities, and corporations in August 1793. Paradoxically some artists supported the suppression of academies in favor of "freedom" even as academy members were helping them to rescue artworks from iconoclasts. The Temporary Arts Commission was formed at this time to inventory objects found within these new sources of national property. Preservation and conservation became ever more urgent and challenging. Legislation was passed to divest artworks of their "royal attributes" and any other signs of feudalism.[29] A law from October 9 declared, "all signs of royalty or feudalism must be suppressed on printed books, manuscripts, bindings, and prints or engravings in all libraries but particularly in the National Library."[30] The mandate came only days before Marie Antoinette's execution. At this volatile point in the Revolution, a *fleur de lis* or a noble crest threatened to topple the precarious Republic. An anti-intellectual spirit bred disdain for the former academies and any art that conjured Old Regime privilege. A decree passed on October 24, however, quickly "put an end to official iconoclasm and consecrated the museum's role as a neutralization location for symbols,"[31] making the French people "sole proprietors" of national artworks.[32]

Members from the National Institute of Music—still yet to take on the name Conservatory—petitioned the national government on December 17 to request scores and instruments housed within the depots of confiscated property.[33] Florence Gétreau interprets this action as part of the Institute musicians' attempts to earn a more prominent role in the Commission's activities.[34] The next day, the Temporary Arts Commission officially replaced the Monuments Commission.[35] Despite its revised name, the new commission retained the approach and organization of its predecessor, seeking "but to continue and to perfect" the work the Monuments Commission had already begun.[36] Music earned a designated place alongside antiquities and geography underneath "bibliography," one of five general divisions that included natural history, physics, mechanics, and painting.[37] Soon the Committee on Public Instruction published guidelines for conducting inventories, and when even more distinct divisions were established, music earned its very own (Table 5.1).[38] These delineations reveal the French state actively arranging and rearranging the epistemology of the arts, letters, and sciences based on each discipline's materials and methods.

This epistemological reorganization occurred in relation to time as France attempted to craft a new history and future rooted in "freedom."[39] As Pommier explains, "France was becoming the inheritor of its own culture, and its grandeur would be inscribed at once in the perspective of regeneration and in that of history."[40] Music's categorization with antiquities and geography

TABLE 5.1 Divisions established by the Temporary Arts Commission.

Natural History (Minerology, Zoology, and Botany)
Physics
Chemistry
Anatomy, Medicine, and Surgery
Mechanics, Arts and Crafts
Geography and Marine
Fortifications, military genius
Antiquity
Literary Depots
Painting and Culture
Architecture
Music
Bridges and Roads

indicate its role in this liberating project. Bibliography closely aligned music with literature, casting it as a textual medium that could be organized and preserved in libraries. The composers who sought property rights as *auteurs* in Chapter 3 clearly drew on such associations. Antiquities acquired enormous cultural weight, as noted previously, when France sought to reincarnate ancient Greece's "consubstantiality" between art and freedom.[41] While music of ancient Greece of course had not survived, a musical equivalent was found in the pristine polyphony of the sixteenth century and the unbreakable rules of counterpoint codified by the eighteenth century and fossilized in sacred music. As both texts preserving musical knowledge and objects serving as models, musical scores and instruments would establish a history of style through objects much like the paintings in the newly opened Louvre.[42] Geography's place in this trivium looked instead toward the future; it eventually came to represent, according to Thomas Richards, "the queen of all imperial sciences" when it was instrumentalized in nineteenth-century colonial endeavors.[43] And so music was situated alongside texts and plastic artworks, as well as scientific instruments and methods. The former projected a long history of imperial power, the latter would constitute it. Indeed, by 1794 the cohesion of the arts, power, and the military became a matter of policy.[44] To describe this as mere propaganda would be woefully simplistic.

Once Conservatory administrators joined the Temporary Arts Commission, they began to objectify musical works in accordance with parameters created for the fine arts—a correlation that Goehr identifies as crucial to the emergence of a work-concept, the idea that musical compositions exist as discrete works of art.[45] By early 1794 Sarrette was listed alongside Antoine-Barthelemy Bruni as music representatives on the Commission.[46] Sarrette soon resigned, however, as he took on the time-consuming role as Director of the National Institute of Music. The Institute administrators asked the Committee on Public Instruction to appoint musicians to inventory the instruments put at their disposal. To make their case for representation, they noted recent ill-informed sales and compared the confiscated musical instruments to works of art. "The goal of this request was to prevent expensive instruments from being sold for nothing, which has happened many times," they complained, "Ruckers harpsichords, which are what Rubens are to painting, were exhibited to be sold with old tapestries, old furniture."[47] They brought this concern at precisely the moment when the government forbade the sale of French artworks to foreign entities without authorization.[48] In March the Commission officially put the music depots at the Institute's disposal, and by May it granted the Rue Bergère depot to the Institute outright.[49]

Bruni was chosen to serve as "conservator" of the music depot at Rue Bergère, and in August 1795 was promoted to "commissioner" on the Temporary Arts Commission, where he would undertake its tripartite mission—preservation, conservation, and restoration. As an Italian violinist who had performed at the Concert Spirituel, played in the Comédie-Italienne orchestra, and briefly directed the Théâtre Feydeau orchestra, Bruni had also composed duos, trios, and quartets for strings and authored method books for both the violin and viola. He even took advantage of Framery's collections agency for composers discussed in Chapter 3. He went on to conduct the Opéra-Comique orchestra from 1795 until 1801 before returning to Italy. In January 1795, Frédéric Rousseau, a cellist from the Opéra and former member of the Loge Olympique orchestra, joined him to focus on inventorying manuscripts, which Bruni had allowed to lag in favor of instruments.[50]

Bruni's duty was to preserve and conserve the musical objects by providing a stable storage environment, cleaning, and maintenance. In doing so, he explicitly adopted an agenda from his counterparts in the visual and plastic arts, which had first been established by the Monuments Commission. Consequently, the physical state of all objects had to be meticulously recorded as they were removed from their original location, upon receipt at the depots, or when distributed to new owners. The guidelines for inventorying confiscated cultural property emphasized that old instruments were to be preserved for the sake of "art history" while modern instruments deserved preservation if they "offered a high degree of perfection."[51] Like artifacts and instruments from the other arts and sciences, history and technological perfection were of the utmost importance. Henceforth only instruments "with no character of perfection or age" would be sold.[52] Bruni's meticulous instrument catalogs indicate that he tried to follow these guidelines carefully (Figure 5.2).[53]

Technique became a critical component of working with these musical materials.[54] While Bruni's duty could have been overseen by any nonmusician, the Commission tried to appoint artists and experts who possessed knowledge of "materials" and "schools," and who could thus not only recognize the value of artworks but also go about restoring them authentically. Bruni's extensive knowledge would allow him, for example, to notice pages missing from a score, to identify the possible composers of unattributed works, or to restring a violin. Such care restored musical objects to their proper state in the same way that new techniques were being developed to restore the color or clarity of deteriorated artworks acquired by the Louvre.[55] A form of music professionalism emerged, which applied extensive technical and stylistic knowledge to critical evaluation and restoration.

The Commission tasked the National Institute of Music with choosing the music depot's *gardiens* or custodians.[56] Unlike the conservator, who served in an administrative and advisory capacity overseeing the depot, the custodians would manage the building's daily workings and oversee tasks such as accepting cartons of scores and crates of instruments, and ensuring that the objects were physically safe from elements like water, air, and fire. They were explicitly dedicated to assuring preservation through a safe and stable storage

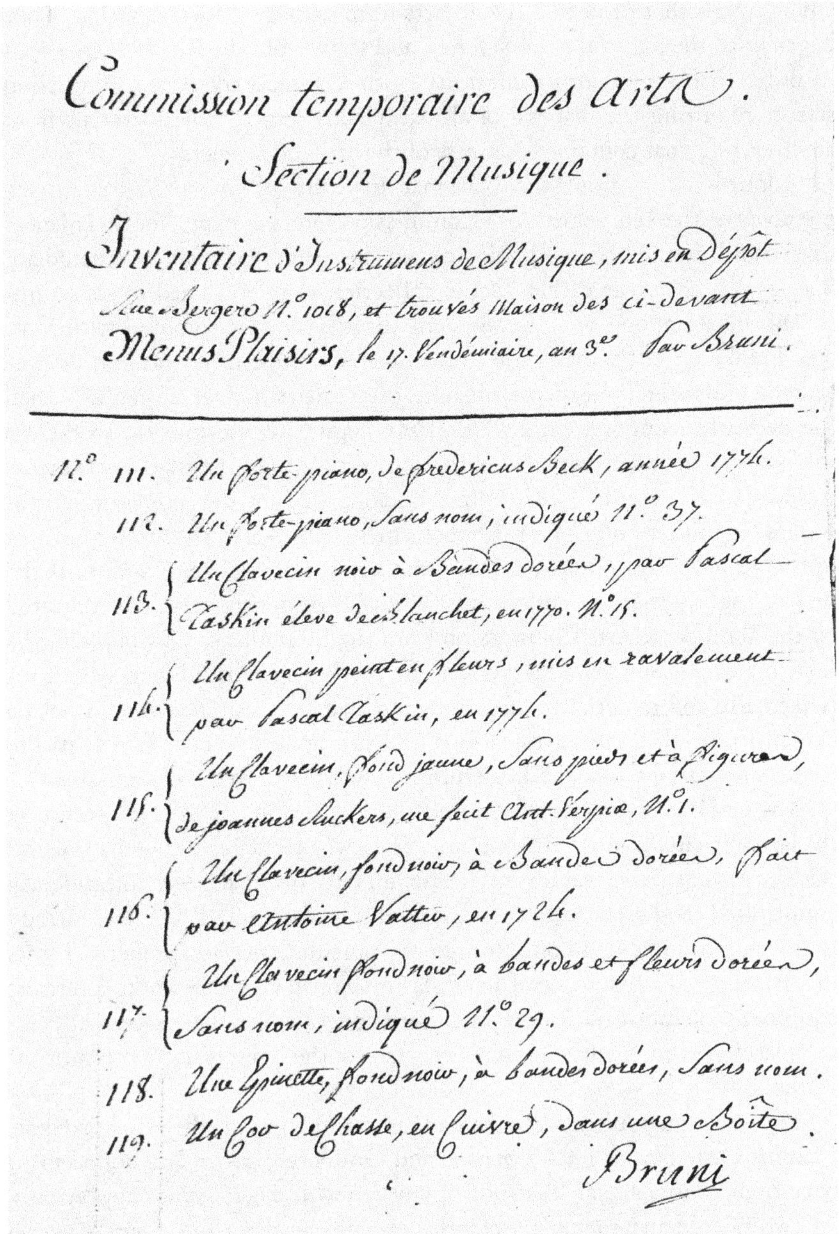

Commission temporaire des arts.
Section de Musique.

Inventaire d'Instrumens de Musique, mis en Dépôt Rue Bergere N.° 1018, et trouvés Maison des ci-devant Menus Plaisirs, le 17. Vendémiaire, an 3.° Par Bruni.

N.° 111. Un forte-piano, de fredericus Beck, année 1774.

112. Un forte-piano, Sans nom, indiqué N.° 37.

113. { Un Clavecin noir à Bandes dorées, par Pascal Taskin éleve de Blanchet, en 1770. N.° 15.

114. { Un Clavecin peint en fleurs, mis en ravalement par Pascal Taskin, en 1774.

115. { Un Clavecin, fond jaune, Sans pieds et à figures, de joannes Auckers, une petit Cart. Sergiæ, N.° 1.

116. { Un Clavecin, fond noir, à Bandes dorées, fait par antoine Vatter, en 1724.

117. { Un Clavecin fond noir, à bandes et fleurs dorées, Sans nom, indiqué N.° 29.

118. Une Epinette, fond noir, à bandes dorées, Sans nom.

119. Un Cor de Chasse, en Cuivre, dans une Boîte.

Bruni

FIGURE 5.2 Bruni maintained meticulous instrument inventories for the Rue Bergère depot. Courtesy of the Archives nationales de France, Pierrefitte-sur-Seine.

environment that protected the objects from damage or deterioration. They began with the removal of horses, hay, and straw from the Rue Bergère depot in order to bring it into conformity with a Temporary Arts Commission statute requiring the disposal of all extraneous combustible materials from any building that contained "objects of the arts and sciences."[57]

Administrators from the National Institute of Music together with members of the Temporary Arts Commission foresaw many "inconveniences that could result" from appointing an Institute musician as custodian. Specifically, they feared that "if the collection were entrusted to some musician, to a composer who, under some disguises, or by some substitutions, could make or partly make [the collection] his property to ward off his ungrateful muses at the expense of some great men's flowers of genius," then the deceitful composer might "multiply copies [of the musical works] to infinity."[58] The letter emphasized that protecting the scores and instruments was absolutely essential "for the public good . . . for the interest of art, as well as for those who inspire the famous men who created the masterpieces of music . . . to conserve intact, to keep from any attack, exchange, and waste the precious scores that the nation must enjoy."[59] Adopting the goals inherited by the Temporary Arts Commission from the Monuments Commission, the Institute musicians shared a concern for protecting musical works both intellectually and materially. After agreeing that the custodian should not be chosen from "the class of musicians," in the same letter, certain Institute faculty including Gossec and Cherubini vowed fealty to the commission.[60]

The Institute musicians embraced the mission to conserve and preserve the authenticity of musical "monuments." Two attributes imbued a musical work with authentic value: its creator and its originality. If imprudently "multiplied" and circulated, then the work's worth diluted. We have already heard this argument among composers pursuing private property rights in Chapter 3. The violence of iconoclasm against visual artworks found its equivalent in music when creators were concealed or their scores altered. Inviolability and fidelity became central to the preservations of musical works.[61]

The two men ultimately named as custodians of the music depot, Citizens Castellant as *garde provisoire* and Guilbert as *portier*, do not seem to have been musicians, at least not of any renown. Their names appear only on two documents that list expenditures for the daily functioning of the depot such as candles, paper, and basic supplies.[62] It seems that the Institute and Commission agreed that nonmusicians needed to guard the musical "art objects" because only a musician would know the scores and instruments' worth, and thus, which pieces might be profitable to pass off as one's own.

Perhaps counterintuitively, the National Institute of Music and Commission both supported a view that the conservators who inventoried, appraised, and guarded the science and art objects should not necessarily be the highest regarded practitioners in their field. In fact, in setting forth parameters for Commission membership, the organization used music as an illustrative example for what it sought in a conservator like Bruni:

> In the sciences and arts, there are two principle objectives to consider: on one side genius, the talent that gives birth to the masterpieces, and on the other the wisdom and erudition that contemplates and compares them. The two are not always exclusive, but rarely are they found united within the same individual. It is the works of genius and the arts that we are charged with researching and assembling from all sides. To inventory and care for the canvases, to assemble the instruments or pieces of music, without a doubt requires knowledge of them; but such knowledge is absolutely independent from the genius that produced them. We could even argue that there is no necessary relationship between the transcendent talent of the latter, and the very ordinary works of the enlightened conservator. The Commission must have enlightened artists without a doubt; but, above all, they must be able to dedicate almost all their time, and it is after having been assured that the designated members could usefully serve public things, that [the Commission] recommended them to the Committee on Public Instruction.[63]

The Commission therefore articulated a significant and wide-reaching maxim about the nature of genius and savants. The Commission felt that "genius" did not have time to dedicate to administrative tasks. As Goehr asserts, "What seemed to matter most to [Romantic] composers was their freedom from worldly demands."[64] In effect, the Commission distinguished the "genius" creators of art from those who were able to recognize and explain it. The distinction between those who made art and those who evaluated it transformed the early eighteenth-century concept of "savants." Because rules were now to be found within the works of art themselves, savants were more in the business of exegesis than rule setting, and some even questioned whether the arts had rules any longer.[65]

The music depot's conservator, Bruni, was neither a member of the National Institute of Music nor of its later iteration as the Conservatory. He did not choose the materials for preservation, but simply tended to whatever he received at the depot. For this reason, Bruni resigned from his position as soon as the depots were transferred to the Conservatory in September of 1796.[66] In an opera Bruni would publish in 1799, the opening air's lyrics seem to echo his position on the Commission: "the most learned often displeases those who know art."[67] In this he contrasts the savants concerned with theoretical rules ("the most learned") and the artists like himself ("those who know art"). Bruni represented a new kind of professional musician. The enlightened conservator, not the fiery genius or frigid savant, could rationally inventory, appraise, and preserve great musical artworks. This was a matter of knowledge, technical skill, and above all, management, and all of these constituted a change in epistemic practice.

The Conservatory's "Museum" of Musical Works

The Thermidorian Reaction, a conservative response following the Terror, caused some logistical setbacks for the Conservatory yet also engendered more serious considerations about how to protect national treasures. In 1795, the same year that the Conservatory was legally founded, 850,828 *francs* were allocated to the "preservation of national monuments," of which 516,692 went to the Temporary Arts Commission. Once again, musical scores were considered among the nation's monuments worthy of preservation. Articles X and XI of the August 3, 1795, law establishing the Conservatory created the institution's library. Initially, the library collection was to be gathered by a commission of Conservatory faculty named by the Committee on Public Instruction including Méhul, Lesueur, Rodolphe Kreutzer, and others.[68] Sarrette traveled to Versailles with Cherubini and Charles-Simon Catel to choose confiscated scores and instruments for their collection, and he continued to request materials from various revolutionary depots.[69] While they gathered both printed and manuscript scores, they were most concerned with obtaining works that had not yet been published, perhaps with an eye toward profitable material for the Conservatory's publishing house. The Rue Bergère depot was soon absorbed into the new library. The Conservatory's first librarian, whose term was short-lived, took up the position around the time of the school's official opening on October 22, 1796.[70]

Sarrette gave a speech to honor the occasion. In it, he highlighted the Conservatory's plan to remedy educational challenges faced by French musicians before the Revolution.[71] He emphasized the deficiencies in the study of composition under the Old Regime, asserting that in the past composers had lacked models for their work. He claimed that Old Regime pedagogical texts had not only failed to provide the basic principles of theory, performance, and composition, but also ignored the relationship between music and the sciences.[72] He criticized the lack of centralized standards for composition, which poetry, painting, and architecture enjoyed in the form of academies. Without institutional quality control, he implied, composers could agree neither on their professional standards nor on their collective aspirations for the art. Sarrette promised that the new Conservatory would surmount these past challenges through a holistic curriculum. All of Sarrette's goals worked toward professionalization by seeking to standardize techniques, assessment, and accreditation in music. The Conservatory would regulate musical production.

It would also provide a context where composers could cultivate genius. Sarrette drew on a distinctively French understanding of genius as collective.[73] While genius in Europe would soon come to be associated with institutional independence, individuality, and subjectivity, the Conservatory's bipartite political and artistic mission made this collective perspective a more natural argument. Sarrette planned for the library to serve as a pillar of professionalization because its vast collection of instruments and "masterpieces" from all times and nations would offer models just as the Louvre displayed artworks for students to study and sketch. The curriculum aimed to improve students' compositional skills, and eventually to improve French music more generally. The harmony treatise ultimately adopted by the Conservatory also promulgated a prescriptive approach to composition.[74]

Sarrette characterized the Conservatory library as a museum of European musical objects created by "the masters."[75] His explanation of the ideology behind the future collection echoed nearly verbatim the arguments that had been made by those in the visual and plastic arts:

> Alongside the famous museums that the genius of liberty formed for the progress of the sciences and the arts and their prosperity in the Republic, the friends of national glory will see elevated that of music, too: this new institution, in rescuing from oblivion the masterworks of all schools, will offer the unique exhibition of the sublime riches of this art, and will show to history its progressive march; everything great that the genius of music produced will be performed by the Conservatory in its exercises, whether these works had been created for worship, whether they were written in different languages or a new taste entirely removed from the theatre. It is thus that enlightened Europe, will appreciate the results of this school, and will acknowledge it with impartiality a place that it will occupy alongside those of Germany and Italy.[76]

His speech provides emblematic examples of how "genius" was not simply an individual attribute, but one of an entire nation, France's "genius of liberty" and "genius of music."[77] Sarrette takes his rationalization for the collection directly from the Commission's stated goals: to conserve works by "rescuing," aestheticizing, and classifying them according to "schools," so that France could compete with its European peers. Conservation, preservation, and restoration served as the very heart of the Arts Commission's, and now the Conservatory's agenda.

Sarrette's speech raises a number of phenomena that Goehr identifies as central to the process by which musical compositions, conceived as artworks, began to dictate musical practice around 1800: an institutionalized account of music history's progression;[78] the exhibition of works not simply through objectified scores but also through consistent performances;[79] and finally, a separation of musical works from their social contexts—music "in service to nothing but itself."[80] The distinction in France, however, was the intentionality with which the Conservatory set about establishing these practices. Rather than functioning under the shadow of a past tradition, Sarrette set out to consciously build a tradition and canon for the future that would acquire weight through institutional force.

These objectives were achieved in part by drawing on music's recent affinity with the visual and plastic arts. Sarrette translated the Commission's language on "schools" to music. As mentioned previously, Lebrun and those associated with the recently formed Louvre had begun to advocate a new, "modern" approach to exhibiting art by school, rather than mixing works from diverse time periods and geographic locations within single galleries, an approach deemed "Old Regime."[81] The art Conservatory implemented "simplicity, method, and rigorous selection" to its works, which under the Old Regime had been dictated by "flattery, superstition, and debauchery."[82] Similarly, as Sarrette set forth in his 1796 speech, the music Conservatory sought to collect musical works that were deemed beautiful and instructive regardless of their origins. This approach served a dual function, one practical and the other ideological. Practically, chronological organization by school facilitated comparison and classification. Ideologically, it elevated musical works above their ritual or social function ("superstition" and "debauchery"), so that they might be understood instead as works of fine art, ostensibly relieved of their heavy cultural baggage. Moreover, it served to imbue music's progress with a "naturalness," by exhibiting it in a manner similar to the scientific cabinets established in other revolutionary institutions like the Jardins des Plantes. Through this approach, Lully's works, for example, might be respected as French masterpieces of dramatic music rather than relics of Louis XIV's despotism. This organization scheme depoliticized and renaturalized the works. The overall effect was a universalizing of musical compositions. Music seemed well-suited to adapt to the revolutionary ideology that had evolved from one of national heritage to universal heritage.[83] Music had already been characterized by a cosmopolitan exchange throughout the eighteenth century and many French were tired of the national genre, the *tragédie lyrique*, long before the Revolution began.

Florence Gétreau points to Sarrette's speech as evidence of a new diptych in French education at the end of the Revolution, constituted by books and objects, libraries and museums.[84] Condorcet and Lakanal's educational vision, discussed in the previous chapter, emphasized the exhibition of objects. Indeed, the arguments for Old Regime artworks' preservation was in part their didactic value. The Conservatory's library and museum followed this broader mandate.[85] For Sarrette, scores represented not only textual vehicles of knowledge but also objective models for study. Catherine Massip identifies two principles at the heart of Sarrette's vision for the library: timelessness and internationalism.[86] These ideologies—books and objects, libraries and museums, timelessness and internationalism—were all cultivated first by the Monuments and Temporary Arts Commissions. Sarrette adopted the Commission's preexisting rhetoric and doctrines surrounding the fine arts as he established the Conservatory. His assimilation of this language may have had practical intentions—to elevate music to the status of the other arts in order to obtain government funding—but the consequences were nevertheless profound. Musical works transformed into objects of art, conserved and preserved at the center of the Conservatory's workings in order to dictate future performance repertoire and compositional practices.

In his subsequent depot requests for the Conservatory, Sarrette continued to employ the commissions' frameworks, focusing on the material conditions of masterpieces and the aestheticization of religious or political works. Soon after receiving approval to collect music from the Enfants de la Patrie literary depot, Sarrette was also invited to choose musical works from the literary depots in Paris and Versailles.[87] According to the system established years prior by the Monuments Commission, Minister of the Interior François de Neufchâteau asked Sarrette to provide the titles, condition, and location of the musical works that he desired so that they could be sent by the depots' conservators. The minister continually emphasized the imperative to record the music's material conditions. Sarrette followed Neufchâteau's instructions, providing a detailed list of works that he hoped to acquire from the Cordeliers depot (see Table 5.2). In addition to the musical works he desired, he also listed literary works, including works for the theater by Corneille, Molière, "the Greeks," and other "masters," as well as poetry, "religious ceremonies and costumes of all people," and a dictionary. Neufchâteau quickly approved the request, and Sarrette soon gained access from the minister to works from the Capuchins Honoré et Rue Antoine depots, as well.[88]

The rhetoric of timeless, universal masterpieces was in tension with the nationalist aesthetic vision held by some of Sarrette's colleagues, particularly the composer and Conservatory inspector Lesueur, who hoped to return overlooked, mature French composers to the first stage of Paris—the Opéra. A similar sentiment was shared by visual artists who felt that France should look to its own past rather than Greece and Rome's for inspiration.[89] While Sarrette focused on the acquisition of objects for future composers to study, Lesueur hoped instead to gather experts who could teach young French composers a holistic approach to composition through drama, gesture, and declamation. In light of the Conservatory agenda advanced by Sarrette, Lesueur's perspective seemed increasingly dated.[90]

Lesueur expressed to the Conservatory librarian Langlé a desire to establish a distinctively French school of music.[91] Worried that French musical "genius" was yet to be "illuminated," he hoped that a music school "whose

TABLE 5.2 Musical works requested by Sarrette from the Cordeliers depot on November 17, 1798, noting that "many bundles of old music [were] not inventoried."

Title	Volumes	Composer
18 Italian operas	44	Hasse
Italian opera	3	Saller [Salieri?]
French as well as Italian operas	206	"Different authors"
Italian airs	114	"Different authors"
18 bundles of music*		"Different authors"

excellence could rival the foreign" ones would solve this crisis. Although Lesueur accepted that the French would take inspiration from foreign institutions, he insisted this only be with a goal of improving the French school, which should not be built on foreign practices and tastes. Unlike Sarrette, Lesueur took a more protectionist, almost Colbertist, stance, demanding that "foreign genius should not find a place in our Conservatory but to be surrounded by efforts to overcome it."[92] Like Rousseau before him, Lesueur presents an ambivalent argument that music should be simultaneously a unifying universal art and a mark of national difference. He acknowledged a European republic of fine arts, but maintained a deep commitment to French exceptionalism. He used a metaphor to emphasize his point: rather than adding a new column to the musical structure already built by foreign schools, an entirely new structure should be built in France, one as big as or bigger than its neighbors'. Lesueur saw no reason why France, which had been deemed for centuries by historians both at home and abroad as the best in all other arts, could not be the best at music, too. The reason for the current lag in French music, he concluded, stemmed from the lack of a proper school. Here, at least, he and Sarrette agreed.

His reference to a "school" meant more than an institution like the Conservatory. Lesueur hoped to build a new national music curriculum, and consequently a distinctive national style. He employed the term much as it had been used by visual and plastic artists during the revolutionary decade. Like Sarrette in his speech for the Conservatory opening, Lesueur blamed the lack of a proper school on the "old government," particularly in comparison to foreign regimes. (Both Lesueur and Sarrette likely had European courts such as Stuttgart, Mannheim, Berlin, and Vienna in mind.) Under such poor patronage, Lesueur felt no surprise that other nations had surpassed the French in music over the course of the eighteenth century. Lesueur assured Langlé that this could be resolved through the Conservatory. "Our Conservatory is French, let our goal be but to perfect the French school," he determined.[93]

Lesueur's nationalist anxieties were likely fueled by the massive influx of Italian music into the Conservatory. While Lesueur still clung to the hope that French opera would be restored to its former glory, Sarrette moved forward to establish a new, and, to use Massip's words, "timeless," "international" collection of works, a future canon, based on objectified musical works that would contribute to France's musical superiority. Sarrette's requests from domestic depots of *biens nationaux* overwhelmingly focused on Italian vocal music, a genre that had during the previous two years become a fixation for the Conservatory's library collection, and not only because Italians had dominated the European musical landscape throughout the eighteenth century. Despite Lesueur's misgivings, an imperial logic transformed Italian masterpieces into French cultural property. Museums, Pommier explains, had "become universal thanks to the victories of soldiers of the Republic." These institutions recast cultural objects into art objects by "display[ing them as] consecrated models."[94] And indeed Sarrette often referred to the Conservatory's new library as a "museum" of universal musical masterworks.

The Museum's Imperial Agenda

The ownership that France claimed over property that had once belonged to privileged individuals and institutions soon extended to the cultural property of all humanity.[95] When the French military began to spread the Revolution across Europe, or put more directly, to impose revolutionary ideologies, it started with Austria. But the collection of artworks as "universal heritage" started in earnest during the height of Terror, when the Temporary Arts Commission advised the French army as it confiscated artworks from Belgium.[96] An imperialistic discourse imbued French acquisitions of cultural property and couched the agenda within a rhetoric of liberation. The French justified the confiscation of cultural property from "enemy countries" through claims to the progress of the arts or by simply arguing that a great work of art could not possibly be on foreign territory while resting in France. Luc Barbier, after accompanying the convoy back to Paris from Belgium "justified the confiscation of great artworks" to the National Convention, stating that the works had arrived "in the country of the arts and their presiding genius, in the country of liberty and equality in the French Republic." As Europe's new center of the arts, Paris was their proper home.[97] France would not only "liberate" Europeans, it would "liberate" European art.

A series of treaties legally granted France the rights to foreign artworks. An armistice signed with the Duke of Parma on May 9, 1796, required that Italian artworks be surrendered.[98] The subsequent Treaty of Tolentino, signed in February 1797, granted the French access to manuscripts from the Vatican, as well. The French representatives conquered Italian works first in Milan, then in Bologna, Mantua, San Salvatore, Monza, Rome, Modenz, Padua, Verona, Venice, and by 1799, in Turin.[99]

Under French occupation, the "formerly royal" palace in Turin immediately became a Palace of the Sciences and Arts, where Piedmontese scientists and artists were required to submit the very best regional works for display and to exhibit the objects in a manner instructive to foreigners who sought to expeditiously learn about local agricultural and industrial production. While the journal that the French founded at the new institution would be bilingual, all students studying at the school conducted their exams, the *concours*, in French.[100] Military domination meant cultural domination, as well as appropriation. As art historian Herman Lebovics has explained, "By taking possession of the historically multilayered—culturally wrapped—art of the past, France validated its aesthetic-political universalism."[101] Music participated in this universalizing agenda.

Some artists tried to warn the French government early on about the perils of this new imperialistic cultural campaign, particularly when it came to removing Roman artifacts. It was one thing to confiscate French cultural property from the former First and Second Estates for the purposes of public instruction, as these properties already belonged to France on moral grounds; it was quite another endeavor, they argued, to pilfer artworks from their native soil. A group of visual artists petitioned the government asking "whether it is useful to France, [and] whether it is advantageous to artists in general, to displace monuments of antiquity from Rome, and the masterpieces of painting and sculpture that compose the galleries and museums of this capital of the arts."[102] While the French government would carefully employ the expertise of such artists and savants on these missions, it rarely paused to question the justice of its actions. And so French "heroes" began returning to Paris with the "masterpieces" that they had "conquered" on "enemy" soil.[103]

The Conservatory inspector Cherubini heard about Napoleon's success in Bologna and immediately took action. He wrote to the Director of Public Instruction, Louis-Marie de la Révellière-Lepeaux, asking "whether it would be possible that, like painting, music profit from the success of his armies."[104] Cherubini knew precisely what he wanted from the Italian town where he had studied as a young apprentice, he requested, "a collection of works by Giovanni Battista Martini, together the most precious collection of works dealing with this art." He even specified the location of the collection he sought in the convent of St. Francis. He also requested another collection by Giacomo Antonio Perti located in Bologna's St. Petronio chapel. To support his request, Cherubini reminded the director that the Conservatory was in the process of forming a library and suggested that the "enemy's contributions" were "too important to be neglected." He submitted the letter through his friend, Pierre-Louis Ginguené, an *"amateur* of the truly beautiful." But Ginguené was much more than this; he was a true friend of musicians. He had helped the Conservatory musicians in the past in his capacity as member of the Committee on Public Instruction, and as an author and music aficionado, he had been a member of the masonic lodge Les Neufs Sœurs during the 1780s, eventually going on to co-author the music volume of the *Encyclopédie méthodique* (1791) with Nicolas-Étienne Framery, who had founded the agency to facilitate composers' collections of performance revenues back in Chapter 3. In response to Cherubini's request, the Minister of the Interior, who oversaw the Committee on Public Instruction, soon drafted a letter to General Napoleon Bonaparte. Riddled with deletions and substitutions, he complimented "the most precious harvest" that Bonaparte was gathering "for the arts" in Italy. After reminding the general about the new music school and its library, he asked Napoleon to seek out the Martini works requested by Cherubini. A year later Napoleon assured the Conservatory's inspectors that he would take "the greatest pains to ensure that [their] wishes are fulfilled and to enrich the Conservatory with material that it might lack."[105]

And so began the Conservatory's own imperial mission. From 1796 to 1801, while the French government methodically negotiated its rights to Italian cultural property, the Conservatory violin professor Rodolphe Kreutzer made a successful concert tour, including stops in Italy, Austria, Germany, and the Netherlands.[106] Kreutzer, who had been named to the library commission by the Committee on Public Instruction in 1795, enjoyed a considerable performing career as a virtuoso violinist even during the waning years of the Revolution. It was not, however, only individual fame that Kreutzer sought when he took his act on the road under the Directory government. He also took on the role of "Commissioner in Rome for the provision of music from Italy for the library of the new Conservatory in Paris."[107] Kreutzer played a crucial role in identifying and obtaining music from the massive Italian collections that the various armistices and treaties had guaranteed to the French.

Kreutzer's task was not an easy one. Two of his associates in Rome, Giovachino Caribaldi and Luigi de Rossi, struggled with dubious Italian copyists who constantly tried to conceal the best manuscripts from the French commissioners. Caribaldi complained that "however much has been collected in Rome up to now, both from the Vatican archives and the papal Chapel, by no means have all the best manuscripts for the basic study of music been included."[108] Caribaldi wrote to his friend Bernardo Mengozzi, a singing professor at the Conservatory, asking for the French to send an official license testifying to Caribaldi's superior music-copying skills so that future manuscript work would not be stolen away by a less meticulous and decidedly disingenuous copyist named Vincenzo Freddi.[109] Caribaldi and De Rossi, in separate letters, referenced Freddi's sloppy penmanship and wide spacing, which sought to maximize profit without much concern for musical details; the copies were paid for by the page.

Caribaldi monitored the musical genres copied in Rome and Naples, and noted those that he felt were still missing from the collections destined for France. He was concerned that "church music by good composers of the past" (Table 5.3) had not been sufficiently considered by the commission.[110] To be fair, the commission had merely followed the Conservatory's original order, which focused on *opera serie* and *opera buffe*.[111] Caribaldi pledged to continue suggesting the newest and best dialogue operas. This was all in fact part of Caribaldi's larger professional agenda to use Mengozzi's influence to earn a position directing *opéra comique* in Paris. Caribaldi had sung as a tenor in Paris in 1778, and Mengozzi, in addition to his Conservatory position, had recently seen more than a dozen of his own operas performed in the smaller theatres that had opened in Paris since the Le Chapelier Law went into effect. Caribaldi desperately wanted to return to Paris. Mengozzi was his ticket.

As a professional "dealer in music manuscripts,"[112] De Rossi, who worked with Caribaldi on the French acquisitions, boasted genuine authority on the

TABLE 5.3 Composers of "religious music" suggested by De Rossi to Kreutzer on August 30, 1798. Original orthography maintained.

Composers as Transcribed by De Rossi
Landi
Sanpaolo
Sartori
Lottini
Pitoni
Animuccia
Liberati
Benevoli
De Marla
Canicciari
Raimondi
Tinazzoli
De Rossi
Arcade
Feo
Melani
Jasquino
Brummel

issue of music copying. De Rossi wrote to Kreutzer nearly a year after the above exchanges hoping to finally receive payment for his previous work.[113] Knowing that Kreutzer might still be on tour (he was), De Rossi addressed the letter to Kreutzer's superior at the Conservatory, Sarrette. De Rossi needed more funds to pay for manuscripts already copied and to continue copying for the French in Rome. Yet again, Sarrette was made aware of Italians trying to hide manuscripts. De Rossi warned, "I must tell you that from the [papal] Chapel . . . you have not even received the best music, because the singers who provided it to you did not give you the material most necessary for study—that is, the material concerned with technical skills."[114] Moreover, the chapel musicians who had copied previous manuscripts had overcharged Sarrette. De Rossi guaranteed quality manuscripts copied by "two professional musicians," Giuseppe Censi and Filippo Ciciliani, the second, "a man still capable of writing in the style of Palestrina."[115] To provide evidence of Ciciliani's Palestrinian skills, De Rossi directed Sarrette to manuscripts already sent to Paris that had been copied by the singer.

But De Rossi had even more to offer Sarrette. His entrepreneurial flair shines through the letter as he opportunistically confided, "I have found in other more restricted archives a quantity of music of still greater quality."[116] This music would fulfill the requests that the Commissioners had initially brought to Rome "at the time of the Armistice."[117] De Rossi promised Sarrette precisely what the Conservatory director had hoped for, "With this select material, your library will be unique, the only one of its kind in the world."[118]

De Rossi kept a list of the scores that the Paris Conservatory received from Rome and Naples and those obtained by the first Commission to Rome, which contained, as Caribaldi had noted, many *opera serie* and *opera buffe* composed by what he referred to as "classical composers."[119] He attached the lists to his letters (see Tables 5.4a and b).[120] He added that he also had access to "many other pieces of music by excellent composers of the past but which are anonymous," reiterating that "they are recognized as very good by our best musicians and could be acquired for a moderate sum."[121] Like the Monuments and Temporary Arts Commissions, Caribaldi knew that the crucial component of his mission was to secure for the Conservatory the most respected works by the most prestigious composers. And perhaps these works that he pointed out were overlooked for precisely this reason: without a famous composer's name attached to them, scores were not as valuable. In order to maintain the integrity of the works, they had to be carefully copied by experts who possessed the relevant stylistic knowledge to render them accurately, like Ciciliani who had mastered "writing in the style of Palestrina." Such understanding was crucial to constituting the prescriptive models needed by Conservatory students to develop technical skills

TABLE 5.4A List provided by De Rossi to Kreutzer and Sarrette of composers initially sought by the commission "of which a part has already been sent and all the rest that can be found will follow." Original orthography maintained.

Palestrina	Sala
Bonifacio Graziani	Antonio Cifra
Jommelli	Carlo Agostini
Gio. M. Nanino	Giu. Ant. Bernabei
Pietro Valentini	Leonardo Vinci
Frescobaldi	Pergolesi
Terradellas	Galuppi
Venosa	Claudio Merulo
Mazzocchi	Andrea Gabrielli
Borghi and other composers of Cap. of Loreto	Benedetto Marcelli
Il P. Martini	Zarlino
Francesco Foggia	Sarti
Paolo Colonna	Sacchini
Costanzo Porta	Monte Veroe
Giovanni Navarro	Ant. Goti
Cristoforo Morales	Lusarchi
Bonifacio Pasquale	Luca Marenzio
Leonardo Leo	Stradello
Francesco Durante	Stefani
Scarlatti	Trajetta
Porpora	Valtotti
Hasse	Tartini
Caffaro	Fioroni
De Majo	Ceri and Caccini

in composition, particularly counterpoint, and they could also be performed merely for their intrinsic aesthetic value.

The "masters" that Caribaldi and De Rossi collected later became canonized in Goehr's nineteenth- and twentieth-century imaginary museum of musical works. Tables 5.4a and b show at least two dozen composers who still maintain places in standard narratives taught in the music history classroom.[122] Palestrina and Bach remain the models for courses in counterpoint. They were already part of the musical works gathered by the Conservatory to regulate, in the future, compositional practices in the institution.

"The objects of science and art gathered in Italy" entered Paris in triumph during the Festival of Liberty. The splendid event showcased everything from lions to grains to Titians. Among the riches were musical scores

TABLE 5.4B De Rossi's "Catalogue of opera scores." Original orthography maintained.

Anfossi	Oralandini
Astaritta	Paisiello
Bach	Pergolesi
Bernasconi	Perillo
Cimarosa	Piccini
Galuppi, called Burranello	Rust
Gluk	Sacchini
Gazaniga	Salieri
Guglielmi	Scolari
Jommelli	Sarti
Latilla	Scarlatti
Lucchesi	Trajetta
Majo	"and other celebrated composers"
Mortellari	

and instruments. Music continued to bridge the letters, arts, and sciences. Conservatory musicians marched in the cortege situated within the division of sciences and arts and alongside "books, manuscripts, and medals," not the fine arts, where the painters, sculptors, and architects marched. As the nine muses entered on opulent floats, the goddesses of music sat alongside the muses of epic poetry and astronomy. Minister of the Interior Neufchâteau had to assuage growing discontent around the pillaging of cultural property from other nations,[123] and so in his speech at the festival he manipulated a vast historical chronology to justify this redistribution of property. Neufchâteau welcomed the artworks into France where, he said, they had finally come home. Because art was the product of liberty, created by artists enslaved to tyrants, Neufchâteau reasoned, the objects were in fact always destined for "free," meaning French, soil. Da Vinci, Michelangelo, all of the visionary artists of the past had in fact created their masterworks for Paris. The following month Neufchâteau wrote to Sarrette inviting him to choose from the recently "returned" Italian musical works deposited at the Bibliothèque nationale.

"The Edifice Is Rising"

After success in Italy, the French military turned its attention to the east, and began to extend through Dusseldorf in 1797, Mannheim in 1798, Bavaria and Nuremberg in 1800, Munich in 1801, and throughout the Rhine territories by 1802.[124] Score requests from the Conservatory followed closely behind the French troops and alongside the other artists and scientists who were commissioned to confiscate cultural property from lands conquered by France. The Conservatory library budget, approved in August 1799, allotted 2,400 *francs* for "copies of music for the establishment of the library."[125]

Around the same time that Sarrette asked the new French Minister of the Interior, Lucien Bonaparte, for statues and busts to decorate the Conservatory library, he sent another request pleading for Lucien to exert all his power to obtain Latin, Italian, and German scores from the duchies of Württemberg and Bavaria, which Sarrette hoped, "would be useful to our museum."[126] Throughout his requests and correspondences, Sarrette consistently interchanged the terms "museum" and "library." Indeed, the branch of the Minister of the Interior's office that handled the Conservatory requests was called the Office of Museums, Libraries, and Conservatories, and after all, the Conservatory planned to house both a library and an instrument museum. "Munich and Stuttgart hold a large quantity of works of which the publication is indispensable for facilitating the progress of musical arts," Sarrette explained in his request to Lucien.[127] Three weeks later, Sarrette forwarded a more specific request, clarifying the previous inquiry.[128] He asked for Jommelli operas held in the library of the Duke of Württemberg, Frederick II, whom Napoleon would soon crown Frederick I, King of Württemberg. A hastily transcribed list attached to the letter notes the operas that Sarrette hoped to obtain from the duchy. Table 5.5 shows the titles requested by Sarrette, along with the genre, librettist, and premiere locations and dates of each work.[129]

Jommelli's operas represented some of the first examples of integrated operatic works that demanded complete control by the composer and precise execution and compliance from the performers—two ideals at the heart of the Conservatory's curricular vision. On a tangible level, Jommelli's Stuttgart operas seemed to offer a model of instrumental and specifically wind composition that Sarrette hoped to develop in the new curriculum. The operas also ideologically resonated with Conservatory goals. Far from the production-oriented patchwork that operas had sometimes been during the eighteenth century, Jommelli's Stuttgart operas demonstrated that vocal works could become artistic masterpieces requiring exceptional performance skills from musicians and dancers, all as a result of the composer's complete control over musical production.[130] In fact, when François-Marie Neveu, a visual artist who served as a French commissioner in Bavaria, set forth his vision for the perfect "reunion of the arts," he identified opera as the perfect example.[131]

The library budget did not last very long. By the end of August 1800, Sarrette forwarded a letter from Neveu to Adrien Duquesnoy, who worked

TABLE 5.5 Niccolò Jommelli operas requested by Sarrette from the Stuttgart library.

Title	Genre	Librettist	Location	Premiere Date
La clemenza di Tito (v.2)	opera seria	Metastasio	Stuttgart	30 August 1753
			Ludwigsburg, Schloss	6 January 1765
Catone in Utica	opera seria	Metastasio	Stuttgart	30 August 1754
Pelope	opera seria	Verazi	Stuttgart	30 August 1754
Enea nel Lazio	opera seria	Verazi	Stuttgart	30 August 1755
Artaserse (v.2)	opera seria	Metastasio	Stuttgart	30 August 1756
Ezio (v.3)	opera seria	Metastasio	Stuttgart	11 February 1758
L'asilo d'amore	serenata/theatre piece	Metastasio	Stuttgart	11 February 1758
Nitteti	opera seria	Metastasio	Stuttgart	11 February 1759
Endimione, ovvero Il trionfo d'Amore	pastorale	after Metastasio	Stuttgart	spring 1759
Alessandro nell'Indie (v.2)	opera seria	Metastasio	Stuttgart	11 February 1760
L'olimpiade	opera seria	Metastasio	Stuttgart	11 February 1761
Semiramide riconosciuta (v.3)	opera seria	Metastasio	Stuttgart	11 February 1762
Didone abbandonata (v.3)	opera seria	Metastasio	Stuttgart	11 February 1763
La pastorella illustre	pastorale	Tagliazucchi	Stuttgart	4 November 1763
Demofoonte (v.3)	opera seria	Metastasio	Stuttgart	11 February 1764
Vologeso	opera seria	Verazi after Zeno	Ludwigsburg, Scholss	11 February 1766
Il matrimonio per concorso	opera buffa	Martinelli	Ludwigsburg, Schloss	4 November 1766
Il cacciatore deluso	dramma serio-comico	Martinelli	Tübingen	4 November 1767
La schiava liberata	dramma serio-comico	Martinelli	Ludwigsburg, Schloss	18 December 1768

in the Ministry of the Interior's office.[132] Neveu had offered to gather scores for Sarrette during his mission in Bavaria, but asked whether Sarrette might provide Conservatory resources that could be exchanged in return. Funding had run out, and so simply paying for the copies was not possible. The French did not enjoy the same unrestricted access to cultural property in Bavaria that the treaties of Parma and Tolentino had granted them in Italy. Sarrette responded to Neveu's request with regret, "The Conservatory has nothing but old French works that would not be well received I think."[133] As an expert in drawing, Neveu needed more guidance about the kinds of scores that he should seek. Sarrette, a nonmusician himself, explained his position, "I could but respond to him to gather what is good . . . what has an established reputation."[134] Referring to the detailed list of Jommelli operas that he had requested from Stuttgart, Sarrette emphasized that the Conservatory still had none of the works held by the Munich court library. Sarrette's best advice to Neveu was to focus attention on "the masterpieces by the great masters."[135]

The challenges that Sarrette faced as he tried to explain the Conservatory's repertoire needs to Neveu stemmed from the emergent moment in which he worked. The problem was not that Sarrette and Neveu did not have musical training; Neveu just needed names and titles. The difficulty came from the fact that, although there seemed to be a general agreement about a small group of renowned composers and works, the "great" musical works were not yet agreed on, despite Sarrette's vague insinuation to the contrary.[136] This is precisely what Edouard Pommier identifies in the case of the visual arts, where administrators insisted on managing artworks through a history that had not yet been written.[137]

In September, Sarrette sent more requests for scores from the Munich court library to General Victor Abel Dessalles, a member of the French military working in the region.[138] This time, Sarrette had more funding to provide to his emissaries and he also benefited from the presence of a musician and composer, Peter von Winter, *kapellmeister* of the Munich court, who could help the French convoy select repertoire.[139] Among the works purchased in Munich for the Conservatory were compositions by Sacchini, Albrechtsberger, Handel, di Lasso, and most notably, Mozart's Requiem (see Table 5.6).[140] In arguing that these works contributed to the progress of music, Sarrette was both situating them within an institutionalized understanding of music history and discussing medieval and Renaissance music anachronistically, both key features of Goehr's regulative work-concept.[141]

Sarrette's pursuits in German lands coincided with continued progress in Italy. Kreutzer, back in Milan by the fall of 1801, detailed his recent acquisitions for the Conservatory: "elementary works" in Turin and scores by Sarti and Anfossi in Milan. The violinist spent two days in the Milan Cathedral, where, after sorting through one hundred manuscripts and haggling with Cathedral administrators, he obtained all that he wanted. He left "very pleased with what [he] had done."[142] But if his success were to continue in Italy, he needed more funds from the French Minister of the Interior (now Jean-Antoine Chaptal) to meet him at his next site of conquest—Naples. Even without funds, Kreutzer promised that he would continue the Conservatory's agenda by putting an advance on his own credit, although he

TABLE 5.6 Inventory of music and books sent from Munich to the Conservatory. Original orthography maintained.

Composer	Genre	Title
Andrea Bernasconi	"Grand Operas" (opera seria)	*Temistocle*
		Adriàno in Siria
		Artaserse
		L'Olimpiade
		La Clemenza di Titto
		Demetrio
		La Betulia liberata
Tommaso Traetta		*Siroe*
Pietro Pompeo Sales		*Antigone*
		Achille
Antonio Sacchini		*Scipione*
Pietro Torri		*Orfeo et Euridice*
		Zenobia
Gailelmi		*Endimione*
Andrea Bernasconi	"Musique d'Eglise"	Confitebor
		Miserere
		Stabat mater
Giuseppe Antonio Bernabei		Ave Maria
		Stabat mater
Giovanni Porta		De profundi
		Miserere
Johann Caspar Kerll		2 Masses
Orlando di Lasso		Chorus populi
Saenftl		2 Motets
Justin Heinrich Knecht		Preludes & Fugues
George Frideric Handel		Fugues
George Pasterwiz		Fugues
Johann George Albrechtsberger		Fugues
Johann Peter Kellner		Fugues
Stecheo		Fugues
Josef Seger		Fugues
Joseph Aloys Schmittbauer		Fugues for organ
Olbers		Fugues
Volkmar		Fugues
Johann Ernst Rembt		Fugues
"old masters"		Fugues

(*Continued*)

Table 5.6 (Continued)

Composer	Genre	Title
Mozart		Requiem
Franz Anton Dimmler	Concertos	2 for 2 hunting horns
		4 for clarinet
		2 for oboe
		4 for flute
		1 for bassoon
		1 for harpsichord
	Sextet	for clarinet, violin, viola, 2 horns, and bass
	Quartet	for clarinet, violin, viola, and bass
	Quintet	for clarinet, violin, bassoon, viola, and bass
	Sonatas	6 for guitar, violin, and bass
	German operettes	
Francesco Antonio Vallotti	"most famous works"	

admitted that doing this would "embarrass [him] a little."[143] Kreutzer asked that Sarrette not share this offer with Chaptal, since it might cause the government to delay sending its own funds.

Money from the Minister of the Interior did not meet Kreutzer when he arrived in Naples, nor did any letters from Sarrette. Kreutzer nevertheless reported back on his recent work in Rome, where he had taken "precise details of the music remaining in the Académie de France . . . in order to send it to Paris with the other art objects."[144] François Cacault, minister plenipotentiary in Rome from March 1801 until 1803, told Kreutzer that he believed the Neapolitans had absconded with the music that had been copied in Rome along with "many other objects such as statues."[145] Léon Dufourny, an architect who was serving as a French commissioner in Naples, assured Kreutzer that he would demand reimbursement for the cost of the Roman copies if the Italians did not return the stolen manuscripts. Dufourny had not yet begun to gather the Conservatory's music requests in Naples, and so Kreutzer planned to work with him to obtain the works as expediently as possible. Still seeking funds that he had already requested from Milan, Kreutzer told Sarrette to send his future posts to Florence. He wanted to complete his work for the Conservatory, not only out of a sense of duty but also because he was "getting very bored" in Italy.[146]

Kreutzer's letter had crossed in the mail with one from Sarrette, in which Sarrette expressed satisfaction with Kreutzer's accomplishments. In his next letter, Kreutzer had the unpleasant task of informing Sarrette that the missing Roman manuscripts were indeed irrecoverable. Fortunately, Kreutzer had already begun to make up the loss by obtaining works that the Conservatory requested from Naples. Dufourny, with no experience in music, had been duped by the trickery of Italian music copyists before Kreutzer's arrival. "You have no idea of the roguery of the copyists in this country," Kreutzer complained to Sarrette, "they change the titles of works [and] skip whole scenes." The French envoys, like the Temporary Arts Commission before them, did not simply desire authenticity in musical works; at the very least, they wanted opera plots to make sense. Fortunately for Sarrette, Kreutzer and his fellow French composer Nicolò Isouard had intervened in Naples before it was too late.[147] Dufourny and Kreutzer had also taken it upon themselves to write directly to Chaptal, informing the minister that they were taking letters of credit against his funds to pay for the Neapolitan music. This time, they weren't asking. Kreutzer and Isouard likely had personal motivations that explain their flexibility in financing when the government did not come through. In 1802 they would found a publishing house with Cherubini, Méhul, Rode, and Boïeldieu.[148]

Kreutzer set his sights on Venice and Bologna next. He planned to acquire English horns and music for them in Venice, as well as more general elementary works on music. His focus on smaller wind instruments makes sense in light of the fact that many *émigrés* brought portable instruments with them when they fled France, and thus, few English horns were left in the depots back home.[149] He promised Sarrette that despite the depleting funds, he would continue to take advantage of the recent peace agreements. He believed it was "the right moment to render to the arts their full splendor."[150] Kreutzer directed Sarrette to send further funds to meet him in Venice. Kreutzer's Naples acquisitions would be headed to Paris on a ship with Dufourny's other "art objects."

But Kreutzer began to worry that he might lose his position as violinist at the Opéra because of his extended leave from Paris. Since positions at the Opéra were at this point government jobs, it was the Minister of the Interior who had granted Kreutzer two months leave from the position, a period that had been flagrantly surpassed. "I hope that, having regard to the new commissions that I have carried out, he will not find it out of order if I am not back in Paris at the fixed time."[151] From Kreutzer's perspective, he had continued to do important work for the French government in Italy, even if he was not playing his violin back home at the Opéra. He asked Sarrette to "act as [his] intermediary" on the matter.[152] Eventually, Kreutzer took it upon himself to return to Paris and to demand funds from the minister for his ambassadorship in Italy. Kreutzer left his wife, Adélaïde-Charlotte Foucard, and his friend and colleague Isouard to continue collecting and copying in Italy.

Madame Kreutzer wrote to Sarrette in December 1801 from Florence. Her husband had not made it to Paris, but was in Lyon, where he heard the minister would be passing through.[153] Without funds from Kreutzer, Sarrette, or the Minister of the Interior, Mme. Kreutzer and Isouard had moved forward with taking letters of credit in the minister's name to fund the cases of music sent by Dufourny with the other "art objects" from Naples. She feared losing credit in Italy and begged Sarrette to ensure that they receive some kind of confirmation from Paris about the credit they had taken.[154]

In the new year, 1802, Kreutzer arrived back in Paris, and Mme. Kreutzer received an encouraging letter from the Minister of the Interior that allotted her 4,000 *livres* to continue her work (her costs had already risen to 5,000 *livres*). This mattered little, since Dufourny, the French official charged with overseeing the commission on the arts in Italy, had already authorized her to draw on the minister's funds without limit anyway. In Mme. Kreutzer's calculation, the total cost of the Conservatory's original requests from Italy would have amounted to at least 40,000 *livres*. Only 15,000 had been officially allotted. Despite the confusion and difficulty surrounding funding, and particularly because the case from Rome had been lost in transit, she persisted. She implored Sarrette to find the funds to support the mission she had taken over from her husband.

Mme. Kreutzer reminded Sarrette of a recent missive he had sent to her, "the edifice is rising," he reported of the library, "and [it] must be filled."[155] The first stone for the Conservatory library had been laid only months earlier, and Sarrette urgently needed masterpieces to fill his "museum," to display a history that had never been told and project a future that promised glory for France.

Cultural Property and Artworks for the Future

France's imperial agenda from 1796 to 1802 must be situated within a longer historical trajectory. The country's first colonial flourish occurred during the two centuries leading up to the Revolution, however, during the eighteenth century France experienced painful losses like Quebec in its global empire. Revolutionary ideals destabilized France's position in colonies, particularly Saint-Domingue. The colonial empire's economic profitability lingered in recent memory, and so diverting attention from internal revolutionary strife to external conquest made sense from a policy standpoint.[156] Yet by 1798, when Napoleon left for Egypt, France was not actually in control of its empire, primarily because its military strength continued to dilute in campaigns throughout Europe. Thus, the campaigns might be considered a compensatory strategy, an attempt to build an imperial culture in anticipation of actual success, which would indeed eventually occur during France's second colonial flourish from the mid-nineteenth- to the twentieth centuries.[157]

The theft of cultural property from across Europe allowed France to attach its fantasies of domination and superiority to tangible objects—material proof of a vibrant empire that did not yet exist in reality. Recall from the previous chapter how Chénier, when speaking to the French legislature on behalf of the Conservatory, had argued that the allegories of Orpheus and Amphion (the two busts that Sarrette requested for the Conservatory) demonstrated music's "real empire." Music's alignment with geography among the Temporary Arts Commission's divisions indicated as much. And indeed an imperial discourse imbued the French "repatriation" of confiscated foreign artworks.[158] The seeds of music's role in French national, imperial, and colonial agendas were planted during the Revolution.[159]

Government support entitled the Conservatory to national property, a privilege that had enormous ramifications. As property was redistributed, music came under a preexisting system for evaluating the fine arts, a system fixated on the materiality of art objects born of "genius." Goehr claims that music "first sought its independence by becoming like something else that was or seemed already to be emancipated. Music allied itself to the fine arts, notably the plastic arts of painting and sculpture, arts that had found some (if not complete) independence during the eighteenth century."[160] Music in fact did nothing on its own. Rather, historical actors like the bureaucrats depicted in this chapter began to evaluate music according to criteria established for the plastic arts, and they did so for a reason—to manage vast holdings of cultural property. They objectified and aestheticized compositions, consequently aligning music with the other fine arts.

As the social and ritual connotations were stripped away from scores, composers were elevated above those with expert knowledge in music. Sarrette became director of the Conservatory precisely because composers claimed to require unmolested time and space to create their work, time that Sarrette, as a nonmusician bureaucrat, did not need. Similarly, Bruni was chosen to inventory instruments and manuscripts because he had sufficient expertise, but did not require the kind of time demanded of composers. This new perspective might partially explain why no one seemed to question the fact that Grétry, though named as a Conservatory inspector from the very beginning, never participated in the institution's governance or its regular functioning. In 1799, Méhul wrote in a preface to his opera *Ariodant* that composers should begin to publish explanations of their works so that their scores could be better judged and contribute to "laying the foundations of an edifice which will rise from age to age, and which will attest to [composers'] glory in future centuries."[161]

Contrary to Goehr's claim that as "a temporal and performance art," music "could not be preserved in physical form or placed in a museum like other works of fine art," Sarrette set out to do precisely that.[162] The scores gathered for the Conservatory's library (or, as Sarrette often referred to it, the Conservatory's "museum") were to authoritatively model "schools" of composition established by "great" composers. The Conservatory's future-oriented, object-centered approach to musical scores included sacred, popular, instrumental, and vocal music. Although Lesueur wanted to move forward in founding a French school of composition through expertise in declamation, libretto authorship, and gesture, Sarrette committed the Conservatory to a national agenda to monumentalize and universalize great works from diverse times, places, and genres. These works would serve as pedagogical tools for performers and composers, they would facilitate "progress" in music when printed and circulated by the Conservatory publishing house (or the private publishing firm founded by its faculty members!), and would offer test cases to improve instrument technologies. Regular concerts would also exhibit the scores for their aesthetic value—art for art's sake. The musical scores collected by the Conservatory during the Directory and Consulate governments were artworks placed in a museum for the future. The work-concept as it was conceived around 1800 was a project as much about the future as about the past; and it emerged in many ways from the material exigencies of standardizing professional musical production in the Conservatory during the French Revolution. As professional musicians became autonomous authorities in their own institution, music also began to emerge as an autonomous art form. This process formed lasting epistemic practices, which centered composers and their universalized works.

6 | National Industry: Music as a "Useful" Art and Science

Scientists and engineers in revolutionary France feared that political fervor distracted from what should be the nation's highest priority—internationally competitive industry. The French chemist Jean Henri Hassenfratz, a founding member of the École polytechnique and a physics and chemistry professor at the School of Mines, warned his compatriots to:

> take care that while we occupy ourselves with the organization of festivals our neighbors are not organizing their industry and destroying our manufactures and commerce. It is not by festivals that the English had come to have a great preponderance in the political balance of Europe. It is not by festivals that the United States of America are becoming a flourishing people.[1]

All the festivals in the world could not save France from its dire wartime economy. The Directory government (1795–1799) eventually turned to industry as a means to recover from revolution, an agenda that would continue under the Consulate (1799–1804) and Empire (1804–1815).

Property laws affected industrial initiatives from early in the Revolution. The French government needed to negotiate ownership over technological and technical innovations in order to spur economic revitalization. Like the contradictions at the heart of the Le Chapelier Laws and the "Declaration of the Rights of Genius" discussed in Chapter 3, legislators sought to balance delicately the public's access to useful information with incentives that might encourage inventors to share their work. A report on behalf of the Committee on Agriculture and Commerce in favor of inventors' property rights suggested, "Nature [had] done everything for [France], but [the

From *Servant to Savant*. Rebecca Dowd Geoffroy-Schwinden, Oxford University Press. © Oxford University Press 2022.
DOI: 10.1093/oso/9780197511510.003.0007

French had] not helped nature."[2] In other words, although France had always possessed the requisite natural resources and workforce, Old Regime laws had excluded too many subjects from the inventive enterprises that might put them to profitable use.

A series of laws were established in 1791 to protect inventors' property and therefore to encourage innovation in France. As we have seen in previous chapters, a similar care for individual rights guided the laws that abolished guilds and academies, deregulated theaters, and protected "works of genius." But the new property regime prohibited individuals from owning public goods such as the infrastructure necessary to industrial advancement.[3] Recall from the Introduction how the piano maker Tobias Schmidt was required to hand over his "useful" guillotine to the government. Industrialization thus required a continual negotiation among the owners who held the rights to raw materials, the inventors who created techniques for extracting them or designed new tools, the engineers who implemented inventors' designs, the laborers who executed industrial processes, and the government ultimately responsible for directing processed goods and utilities toward the public. This chapter illuminates a third form of property that music took on during the Revolution, as a national industry, which extracted then processed natural resources such as air, wood, and metal.[4]

According to the historian Thomas Le Roux, claims to public utility provided a political medium through which individuals could join the profitable economic community born of the Revolution.[5] Jann Pasler has shown that French citizens in First Republic France considered music as a public utility in both its social and political capacities.[6] The natural and moral sciences were by no means mutually exclusive in revolutionary France. To the contrary, they were co-constitutive.[7] People working in the Parisian music world thus aspired to industrial and economic utility, too, particularly through innovation. The government bodies established to review technological and technical inventions received proposals for musical instruments and methods alongside designs for all manner of industrial machines.

Citizens like Hassenfratz who rejected political education in favor of economic revitalization threatened to derail the important advances that professional musicians had made through the foundation of the Conservatory as described in Chapters 4 and 5. This chapter examines how the Conservatory faculty capitalized on music's affinities with applied sciences like engineering, mining, and surgery, to align themselves with the nation's new industrial agenda when their original political mission receded during the late 1790s. While musicians' contribution to national industry in some ways complemented their role in building cultural heritage (Chapters 4 and 5), it posed a challenge to musicians who argued for inalienable, individual legal rights to their work (Chapter 3). As music entwined with technical education, technological innovation, and scientific experimentation, it joined a national domain of public goods that individuals could not possess. The Conservatory identified means of regulating this sector through its newfound capacity as the heart of music training and accreditation. Another crucial aspect of music professionalization, the standardization of the tools and techniques, therefore arose in relation to revolutionary proprietary debates.

From the revolutionary government's earliest invention evaluations between 1791 to 1795, committees favored musical mechanisms like instruments because they promised to advance the "useful" arts more readily than the pedagogical methods relegated to the mere "pleasurable" arts. Decisions about financial support for the "useful" arts rested with a set of interconnected revolutionary organizations until they transitioned in 1795 into more stable, lasting advisory institutions like the National Institute. Conservatory inspectors embedded themselves into a number of these networks, where they at times resisted industrial initiatives that might hurt professional musicians for the sake of national profit, providing a level of protection that Old Regime musicians had never enjoyed. The Conservatory meanwhile refined its curriculum by imbuing its new method books with the applied agenda that animated other science-based educational institutions like the École polytechnique. The mechanization favored by property laws, the profitability of musical products, and the applied nature of national curricula, are brought together at the end of this chapter to inform a new reading of the Conservatory's method books as a conscious attempt to contribute to the French industrial agenda. The method books mediated competing revolutionary perspectives on music as a form of property and helped to secure for the Conservatory a monopoly over professional musical production in nineteenth-century France—in effect, a new corporate privilege, the kind of privilege that had been ostensibly abolished on August 4, 1789.

Music, the Useful Arts, and Mechanical Invention

A set of laws passed in 1791 established a legal process for inventors to claim their ideas and inventions as personal property. The turgidly titled "Law on useful discoveries and means to assure property to those recognized as their authors," passed on January 7 and was refined on May 25 and September 12 of the same year. It changed the French legal system from one that recognized useful inventions through royal privileges to one that automatically distributed patents, called *brevets*.[8] The title of this new inventors' law recognizing "authors" of "useful discoveries," harkens back to the debates about composers' rights discussed in Chapter 3. Indeed, inventors who agitated for the new law wanted their property to stem from natural rights rather than formalities, a claim some composers like Nicolas-Marie Dalayrac had vigorously defended. If property rights were naturally born through the very act of creation, they argued, then no formalities should be necessary to activate them. Until 1791, the Board of Commerce had relied on experts from the Academy of Sciences to evaluate inventions and submit privilege recommendations to the king and Parlement.[9] Such a legal privilege would then exclude others from making the same product. Critiques against the inconsistency and nepotism of the Old Regime system intensified during the Revolution.[10] The new 1791 laws automatically granted a five, ten, or fifteen-year exclusivity to inventors who properly completed an application and paid a fee to the government, leaving its utility to be judged by the public.[11] It nevertheless still required formalities. The law also established an alternative system to encourage the immediate release of inventions into the public domain. Rather than pay for a patent, inventors could submit their work to the government to be considered for a reward or bonus.[12] This new system placed a burden on inventors to predict whether their invention would garner more money in public circulation than from the maximum government reward. Regardless, the law inherently favored inventors who already had some financial means; like the Old Regime printing privileges discussed in Chapter 1, patents required a fee. Each invention could legally receive only one type of government compensation, either a patent or a reward.

The 1791 invention laws established the Advisory Board for Arts and Trades to provide the Minister of the Interior with nonlegally binding recommendations on inventors' applications for rewards. During its initial five-year existence, the Board awarded support to a variety of inventions, processes, and perfections, from floating bridges and mechanical beds, to new veterinary remedies, the introduction of rhubarb into France, and even overall contributions to the military arts and fashion.[13] Its goal was to enliven "the most useful arts and commerce."[14] The Board was populated by a cohort of French citizens committed to "economic and technical progress rather than training for membership in a future form of society."[15] In other words, they did not find patriotic and moral education, as defined in Chapter 4, quite as important as a practical instruction. Among this cohort was Hassenfratz, as well as many faculty members from the Lycée des Arts, an institution that offered public lectures primarily in the sciences. The Lycée proposed on its menu of science courses lectures in harmony, given by none other than the Conservatory's future librarian, the music theorist Honoré Langlé (see Figure 6.1).[16] There were numerous connections to be found among the Conservatory and the Board, Langlé was not the only one among them.

The 1791 laws offered two major classifications of rewards shown on the right-hand page of Figure 6.2. Those of the "first class" required sacrifice as well as innovation, those of the "second class" simply contributed something deemed "new" by the Board.[17] An inventors' age was also taken into consideration during review. A third class of rewards provided bonuses to

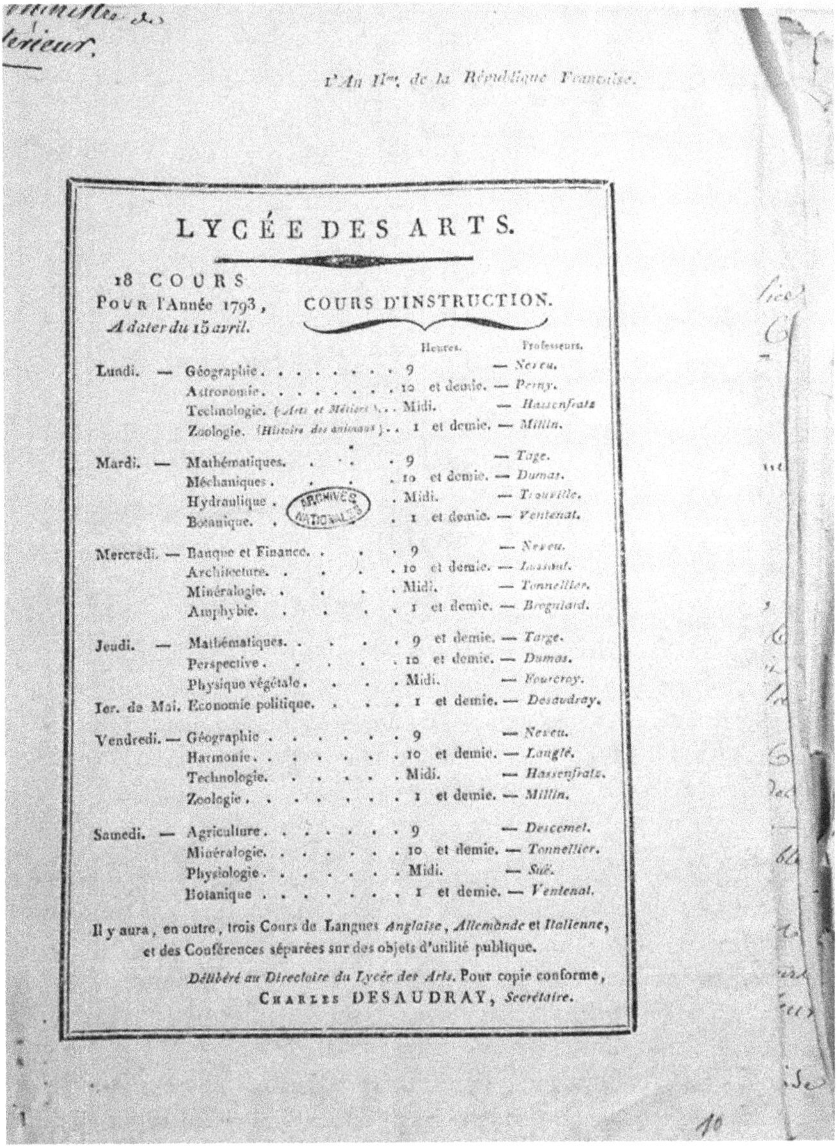

LYCÉE DES ARTS.

18 COURS
POUR l'Année 1793,
A dater du 15 avril.

COURS D'INSTRUCTION.

		Heures.	Professeurs.
Lundi. —	Géographie	9	— *Neveu.*
	Astronomie	10 et demie.	— *Perny.*
	Technologie. (*Arts et Métiers*)	Midi.	— *Hassenfratz*
	Zoologie. (*Histoire des animaux*)	1 et demie.	— *Millin.*
Mardi. —	Mathématiques.	9	— *Tage.*
	Méchaniques	10 et demie.	— *Dumas.*
	Hydraulique	Midi.	— *Trouville.*
	Botanique.	1 et demie.	— *Ventenat.*
Mercredi. —	Banque et Finance.	9	— *Neveu.*
	Architecture.	10 et demie.	— *Lussaud.*
	Minéralogie.	Midi.	— *Tonnellier.*
	Amphybie.	1 et demie.	— *Brogniard.*
Jeudi. —	Mathématiques.	9 et demie.	— *Targe.*
	Perspective	10 et demie.	— *Dumas.*
	Physique végétale	Midi.	— *Fourcroy.*
Ier. de Mai.	Economie politique.	1 et demie.	— *Desaudray.*
Vendredi. —	Géographie	9	— *Neveu.*
	Harmonie	10 et demie.	— *Langlé.*
	Technologie.	Midi.	— *Hassenfratz.*
	Zoologie	1 et demie.	— *Millin.*
Samedi. —	Agriculture	9	— *Descemet.*
	Minéralogie.	10 et demie.	— *Tonnellier.*
	Physiologie	Midi.	— *Sué.*
	Botanique	1 et demie.	— *Ventenat.*

Il y aura, en outre, trois Cours de Langues *Anglaise*, *Allemande* et *Italienne*, et des Conférences séparées sur des objets d'utilité publique.

Délibéré au Directoire du Lycée des Arts. Pour copie conforme,
CHARLES DESAUDRAY, *Secrétaire.*

FIGURE 6.1 In this Lycée des Arts course schedule from 1793, alongside future Conservatory librarian Honoré Langlé, who taught harmony there, is Hassenfratz, lecturing in technology, and François-Marie Neveu, who worked to secure scores from Bavaria for the Conservatory's library, lecturing in geography. Courtesy of the Archives nationales de France, Pierrefitte-sur-Seine.

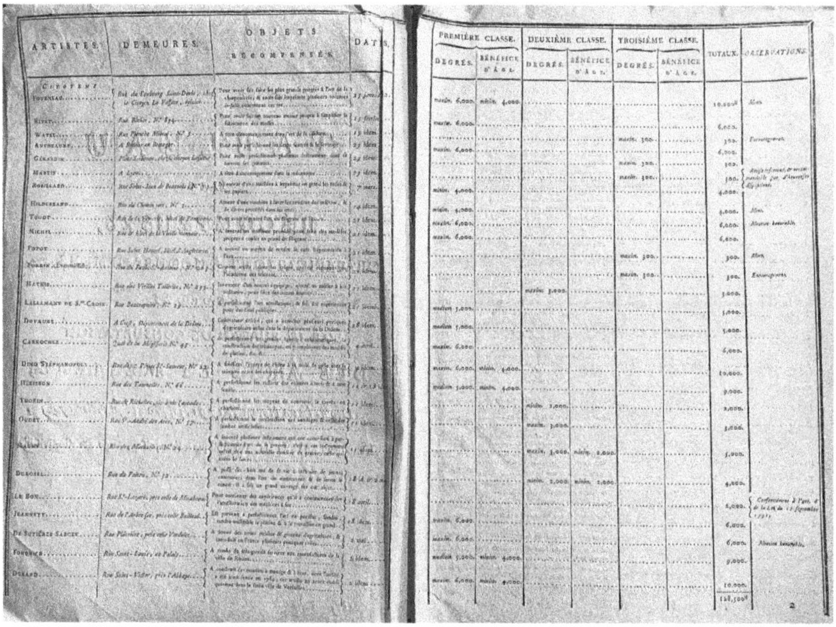

FIGURE 6.2 The Table of Rewards granted by the Bureau de Consultation des arts et métiers from November 1791 to January 1793 shows on the right-hand page the minimum, medium, and maximum awards for inventions of the first, second, and third class. Courtesy of the Archives nationales de France, Pierrefitte-sur-Seine.

"indigent" innovators. The Revolution would soon ravage many industries, and the reward system seemed to get ahead of this problem. The classes were further divided into minimum, medium, and maximum rewards, which pertained to the "merit of the objects" themselves, as determined by the Board's reports. Figure 6.2, a Board reward table from 1791 to 1793, includes from left to right the artist's name, address, "object rewarded," date, and the three classes of rewards, followed by the total reward and extra notes. As the Board persisted under many different guises during the 1790s and into the nineteenth century, it increasingly preferred "limited claims restricted to individual machines and objects," to "principles or ideas."[18] It therefore prioritized instruments that would make industrial production more efficient, more technically perfect, and most importantly, more profitable. Even from this early stage, the Board held mechanical inventions in higher esteem than methods. This preference proved particularly true when it came to music. As we have seen in Chapters 3 and 5, the more precisely individuals could delimit musical property into objective terms, the more likely they were to enjoy the laws and regulations protecting property.

From the very first musical invention rewarded by the Board, its members were fascinated by instruments that mechanized music-making. Of the approximately 100 innovations that received the Board's recognition between 1791 and 1793, only two were musical inventions: *rhythmomètres* (protometronomes) created by a horologer, M. Dubos, and "a new method to give music lessons to a large number of students at once," created by Jean Joseph Clareton.[19] The Board's report on Dubos's *rhythmomètre* predicts the instrument's utility in musical training and performance. They determined that it would engrain a sense of tempo in students, ensure that their variations in musical meter served expression without succumbing to caprice, and, eventually, the instrument might even regulate the erratic tempo of the Opéra orchestra.[20] A brief digression in the report considers whether such a tool might also offer a means to measure the relationship among civilization, national morals, and movement, however, this musing, more reminiscent of the Committee on Public Instruction's reports, is quickly set aside to address more practical issues like the precise mechanical innovations that contributed to Dubos's success and how the instrument evolved from earlier attempts to create a *chronomètre* or *metromètre*. (The Board settled on *rhythmomètre* as the ideal term for the instrument.) Barring slight improvements that remained to be achieved, Dubos's instrument greatly impressed the Board, especially because, unlike its predecessors, it was portable and thus readily available to musicians.

The Board's response to Clareton's application reveals how a practical industrial agenda focused on machines and profit conflicted with more ideological aspirations to promote a greater social good through music, a perspective championed by the Committee on Public Instruction. We already encountered Clareton in Chapter 4, when he applied for funding from the national government to establish a music school on Rue Favart. His school had opened by the time that he applied to the Board for a monetary reward; he had "invented" a new method to teach music to many students at once through the use of simple tools of his own invention, which included large writing boards and rudimentary percussion instruments.[21] Children sang scales together while learning notation from the board and tapping time on simple instruments. Clareton then added string accompaniment to assure accurate pitch. By performing and sight reading simultaneously, Clareton's students embodied music theory skills. Composers André-Ernest-Modeste Grétry, François-Joseph Gossec, and a well-respected cathedral school director, the Abbé d'Haudimont, championed Clareton's method over individual lessons in their report for the Board, claiming that this approach promised to "someday naturalize music among" the French.[22] The three men likely had in mind the effective Bohemian music education system exemplified by wind players who had settled in Paris during the late eighteenth century or the Neapolitan conservatories where the performers and composers who dominated cosmopolitan Europe had trained. Grétry, Gossec, and D'Haudimont's report explicitly noted the need to replace the defunct cathedral schools, which had been another casualty of the Revolution. The Board suggested Clareton receive a "medium second class" reward, which would have amounted to 2,000 *livres*.[23] According to the law, the second class of rewards was reserved for inventors who had created something new through little sacrifice. Clareton's teaching method earned a medium rating for merit.

But the Board's suggestions for Dubos and Clareton's rewards were precisely that—recommendations that the French government (at the time, the provisionary Executive Council) could choose to heed or, in the case of Clareton, to disregard. Then Minister of the Interior, Dominique Joseph Garat, held the final say in reward distribution. He wholly rejected Clareton's application despite the Board's approval, as well as another music application submitted by Anselme Montu for a harmonic violin. To appeal Garat's decision, Clareton and Montu joined forces with a Greek doctor named Dimo Stephanopoli, who was refused a reward for importing into France a new herb with known medicinal benefits. Together, the three petitioned the National Convention to overturn Garat's decisions. Stephanopoli and Clareton cited specific precedents for their rewards. Earlier in the year rewards had been granted for the importation of rhubarb cultures and for a new mechanism to teach children reading and writing. They argued, moreover, that Montu's violin should have been considered in "commercial and material terms, and not musical ones."[24]

The Convention forwarded their petition to the Committee on Public Instruction and requested that Garat draft an explanation for his decisions; he immediately conceded the full reward to Montu citing the "September 12th" law on inventors' rights. From then onward, this law, the final version of the inventors' property rights laws passed during 1791, would be consistently cited as the standard by which all aid applications were measured. The Executive Council explained its error in their evaluation of Montu's harmonic violin, having "at first viewed [Montu's] invention as uniquely relating to the pleasurable arts, and that under these terms it would have seemed not to be eligible for national rewards for discoveries and inventions in the useful arts, or the arts and trades."[25] Because Montu's invention was in the field of instrument building, Garat clarified, it legally contributed to "an essential branch of industry and commerce," a useful art.

The council's opinion on Clareton's case remained suspended. His discovery, from their reading of the law, fell under the pleasurable not useful arts. They suggested that he apply instead to other kinds of rewards.[26] The Council failed to consider that the encouragements it suggested to Clareton were for visual and plastic artists, not musicians. The Executive Council also rejected Stephonopoli's appeal. He and Clareton's cases convinced Garat that more specific laws needed to be set in place to outline eligibility for national rewards for inventors.

When the National Convention took the case up again after the exchange between Garat, his Executive Council, and the Committee on Public Instruction, it began by revisiting the legal definition of the useful arts, "all the arts from which society could draw advantages and that serve to grow national industry,"[27] including agriculture. On these terms, they concurred with Garat's finding that Montu's harmonic violin clearly contributed to national industry. The Convention overturned the Executive Council's other rulings, however, and granted Montu's co-petitioners, Clareton and Stephonopoli, national rewards, although not in the amounts suggested by the Board. Stephonopoli, they determined, promised to contribute to the field of medicine—clearly useful. And because another inventor had already received a reward earlier in the year for inventing a mechanism to teach students reading and writing, they agreed that Clareton deserved a reward based on this precedent. Clareton only received a maximum third class or "indigent" reward of 300 *livres*, which was to be held against any future rewards he might receive. In essence it was an incentive to produce a more useful "object."[28] As a point of comparison, Dubos's reward for the *rhythmomètre* was of the first class, Clareton's, the third. Dubos received 9,000 of a possible 10,000 *livres* maximum reward for his tempo-keeping instruments. Clareton only received 300 *livres* to cover the costs associated with developing tools to enhance his new teaching method.

The case of Clareton and Montu legally defined music's utility through strict application of the law on inventors' property rights. Montu was more successful because his invention was an object and not an idea.[29] He had combined string and keyboard instruments in a new and novel way, and the Board's report on it, like others the committee produced, describes the mechanisms of the new instrument at length, even citing the *Encyclopédie Méthodique* to prove the instrument's distinction from other bowed spinets. In later applications to the Board, Clareton changed tactics and emphasized the mechanisms that he created to enhance teaching rather than the teaching method itself.

Eventually the Board embraced its duty to evaluate musical applications. The same week that the National Convention vindicated Clareton and Montu's innovations, the Board bestowed a maximum first-class reward to Jean Jacques Schnell and Christian Tschirziki for an invention that seemed to take Montu's invention a step further. Their *anémocorde* combined string, keyboard, and wind instruments. In his reward application, Schnell cleverly wove the government's anxiety about foreign industrial competition into his appeal, threatening that if he could not enjoy profit from his instrument in France, then he would be "obligated" to introduce it in other countries.[30] The Board suggested that Schnell and Tschirziki receive 10,000 *livres*, likely hoping that the *anémocorde* would eventually attract substantial foreign revenue to France. Its members had clearly taken the recent debates about their realm of authority into consideration. In the report they explicitly accepted a responsibility to evaluate "all mechanical means that tend to simplify or perfect the pleasurable arts."[31]

The Board found it difficult to judge applications in the field of music because such proposals rested at the intersection of craftsmanship, science, and the pleasurable arts. When in doubt, they simply resorted to the language of the 1791 laws. Gabriel Antoine de Lorthe proposed building a new musical instrument, referred to throughout the Board's reports as a *dodétracorde*, by which he hoped to liberate keyboard instruments from "imperious" temperament. He planned to accomplish this feat with the addition of only a single string. When reviewing De Lorthe's request for funding to construct the instrument, the Board tried to strictly confine itself to the parameters set forth in the "law of September 12th."[32] The commissioners who reviewed De Lorthe's proposal admitted a host of anxieties about his request including their own ability to evaluate such a project, its basis in theory rather than practice, and a lack of plans or models demonstrating the probability that De Lorthe could successfully build the instrument.[33] The committee agreed, however, that his findings were scientific, and thus fell clearly within their purview. De Lorthe's work, they determined, was rooted in physics, geometry, and the works of "Descartes, Leibnitz . . . [and] D'Alembert."[34] Reports note that De Lorthe had properly completed the necessary paperwork, but did not provide a model for his instrument. Such visual plans were eventually required by the Board (see Figure 6.3).[35] Indeed, formalities permeated the reward process, and logistics were scrutinized as much as, if not more than, the quality of inventions.

Although the Board members strictly held applicants to the protocols set forth in the law of September 12, they did not always hold themselves to the same standards. On numerous occasions the Board affirmed the quality of De Lorthe's project, yet ultimately denied his requests for aid because he did not provide designs, and therefore, the machine's probable advantages could not be verified.[36] They never actually adhered to the mandate that the public rather than the government should determine an invention's use and value. The Board considered another criterion that did not technically fall within its legal domain when it took issue with the primacy of De Lorthe's invention. One report notes a publication by Antoine Surmaine de Missery, *Théorie acoustico-musicale* (1793), which, like De Lorthe, suggested adding a new note to the scale in order to do away with temperament. The report affirms that De Lorthe seemed to have reached this conclusion before Surmaine de Missery, and consequently, because De Lorthe seemed to have primacy as well as the support of other research, the commissioners suggested that he receive half the requested sum up front and the other half upon completion of the

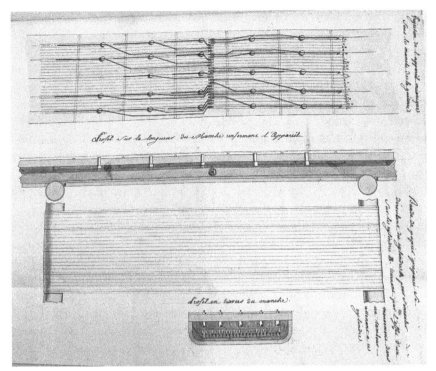

FIGURE 6.3 The Bureau eventually required designs in its applications. This guitar, invented by a M. Racicourt, would notate music during performance. Courtesy of the Conservatoire nationale des arts et métiers, Archives historique, Saint-Denis, P 288.

instrument. The Law of September 12 did not actually grant the Board with the authority to determine primacy of invention. De Lorthe insisted on receiving the sum in full. While the Board acknowledged that he had already expended "research," "pains," and "care"—all criteria explicitly required by the law—without "plans, models, or proportions," they could not offer him the maximum reward, which, according to their reading of the legislation, was reserved only for completed machines. He received a 1,500 *livres* "indemnity" for his efforts, but not the 6,000 *livres* he requested to finance the construction of his proposed instrument.

The musical inventions that received the Board's highest recognition promised to make musical production more efficient, just as other tools proposed to the Board aspired to improve the extraction and processing of natural resources. Inventors offered mechanical means to regulate musicians' bodies, standardize instrument construction, achieve uniform rhythm, pitch, and timbre, and notate during performance. The natural resources air, wood, and metal were quite easy to come by, but transforming them into

NATIONAL INDUSTRY: MUSIC AS A "USEFUL" ART AND SCIENCE | 175 music required perfectly trained bodies manipulating advanced instrument technologies. It was here, as we shall see later, that the Conservatory would find a place in the revolutionary industrial agenda.

The Board was not the only government agency concerned with musical instrument technology. An array of committees and commissions, rarely made up of musicians, devoted time to evaluating organs. One such bureaucrat was Claude-Pierre Molard. He boasted a technical background that practically minded revolutionaries like Hassenfratz appreciated. Agriculture, manufacturing, and political economy had always interested Molard. During the 1780s he trained in drawing and fortifications, in essence, a kind of military engineering, and he went on to work on mechanics in the Vaucanson studio of automata fame. Molard collaborated with Hassenfratz in the field of metallurgy and studied silk and cotton processing under the guidance of English mechanics. By 1793, Molard's diverse experiences in science, industry, and manufacturing made him a logical choice for the Arts et Métiers section of the Temporary Arts Commission as it evaluated scientific "objects" confiscated from the defunct academies and *émigré* households. As an engineering marvel of the eighteenth century, organs counted among such objects.[37] In the Temporary Arts Commission's files, a report on Parisian organs appears not among those related to other confiscated musical instruments discussed in the previous chapter, but rather between descriptions of hydraulic and splitting machines useful for industrial production, and among diverse "inventories, memoirs, and reports concerning machines relating to arts and crafts."[38] A group of organists and organ builders met under Molard's supervision as the "Mechanical, Physical, and Music" section of the Temporary Arts Commission to deliberate "on the utility of organs," and then to draft a policy recommendation on organs for the Committee on Public Instruction.[39]

The section presented a variety of reasons that Parisian arrondissements cited for saving organs in their communities from the craftsmanship and quality of the instruments themselves, to their monetary value or utility at public festivals. In his capacity as a representative on the Arts et Métiers section of the Commission, Molard wrote, "The utility of the conservation of organs . . . can be considered from diverse points of view."[40] He and his interlocutors seemed to anticipate the turn music's utility would take from political instrument to industrial product as Terror faded and economic revitalization gained urgency. But even at the height of the Terror, commercial, industrial, and political arguments were used in tandem to support the conservation of organs. Organist Pierre Jobert, for example, provided a detailed report on the organ at the Abby of Salival and deemed it a "masterpiece" likely built by the famed French builder Nicolas Dupont.[41] In his report, Jobert praises everything from the organ's carpentry to its tuning and ability to hold air. Noting the recent fall in organ prices, Jobert suggested transferring the organ into the municipality's protection until it could be sold for an appropriate (high) price, since organs valuable both for mechanical and harmonic reasons were selling far below their actual monetary value. The commission shared Jobert's concern that organs sold so cheaply, a complaint that we heard surface in the previous chapter among the Conservatory musicians who also worked with the Temporary Arts Commission.[42] Everyone agreed that organs were a distinctively French industry that the nation could not afford to lose. The report emphasizes one primary justification for saving the instruments: "the art of organ building has been since the invention of these instruments a branch of commerce and industry that is advantageous to the Republic to conserve."[43]

In the report to the Committee on Public Instruction, Molard connects music's dual character as a craft and art to recast musicianship more broadly as an industrious labor that attracted foreign regard (and investment) to France. He describes the organ as an ideal tool; as the "premier of all instruments," it provided a place "where the talent of the artist constructor" could "open new routes to the performing musician's genius."[44] It was through instruments that craftsmanship and artistry in both performance and composition met. The organ inspired artistic genius, Molard explained, because of its varied sonic capabilities; it offered the "advantage[s] of an orchestra," because of its ability to produce and accompany many voices and instruments.[45] The instrument's unique "effects" encouraged composers and performers alike to develop "celebrity" musical abilities like those of Couperin and Charpentier, who paved the "path for those who distinguish themselves today."[46] Thus, he situated the instrument in a distinctively French history. If organs were not conserved, then musicians would be deprived of a crucial "resource" through which to cultivate French "genius."[47] The report also justifies the conservation of organs as testaments to the French perfection of "the art of organ building."[48] Molard calls the instruments "monuments of industry" capable of attracting "foreign curiosity."[49] As monuments of industry, organs, like the scores and instruments discussed in the previous chapter, would serve as models for future craftsmen and artists alike, useful for training a new generation of French citizens who would continue a profitable tradition and industry.

Yet Molard's report did not completely abandon the idea of organs as instruments of political culture useful for public festivals. Molard and his commission may have genuinely held this belief, yet the report's balance between industry, culture, and politics also indicates that they knew quite well their intended audience, the Committee on Public Instruction, and Marie-Joseph Chénier, who we met in Chapter 4 as he promoted the founding of the Conservatory and forcefully defended rewards for men of letters and artists rather than craftsmen. Molard, perhaps bending to Chénier's prejudices, notes music in his report as a universal component of popular festivals throughout history from the ancient Greeks to contemporary "savages."[50] Moreover, for smaller provincial festivals, Molard suggested, organs provided a cheap alternative to the massive musical forces required for Parisian festivals. The report concludes with this more political argument, that organs accompany "civic songs."[51] That is, if in the past they accompanied liturgical services, they now accompanied secular festivals. Like Bernard Sarrette in his speeches in favor of the Conservatory, Molard jettisoned music's previous associations with the First Estate. His report demonstrates the interdependency of cultural heritage and national industry in France's evolving post-Terror agenda.

The more practically minded Committee on Finance lacked reverence for instrumental marvels and mandated the sale of organs for national revenue on March 6, 1795, an imperative that conflicted with the National Convention's instruction to preserve all musical instruments that were "good, precious, old, or rare."[52] In response to two conflicting government directives, an influx of requests for exemption from the Committee on Finance's decision arrived to the Committee on Public Instruction, which proceeded to pass the appeals to the Temporary Arts Commission in its capacity as evaluator of all arts and sciences instruments confiscated as national property.[53] Because church property sold during the Revolution had on occasion been used not for its intended purpose but as a source for scarce raw materials, petitioners worried that organs would be taken apart for their constituent materials such as wood and metal, and consequently sold below the price they would yield if preserved as musical instruments.[54] The price of organs remained a consistent point of concern even for those who hoped to conserve the instruments.

As a result of the mandated sale, organs figured into a wider national conversation about the technologies useful to France's industrial efforts. Officials working for two new executive commissions dedicated to French industrial development—the Commission for Agriculture, Arts, and Manufactures, and the Commission for Weapons, Powders, and Mining—facilitated exemption requests for provincial organs. The agricultural and mining officials suggested that the organs could provide a variety of "public utilities"[55] and "utility for the arts."[56] They yielded to musicians' expertise to determine whether organs in their respective districts merited conservation based on their value. Value remained broadly defined and always in terms of "utility." Although some petitioners focused on the organs' significance as architectural or sculptural artworks (multiple petitions suggest that local organs be saved for museums),[57] most often they praised the instruments' mechanical attributes. The requests valuated organs primarily in terms of the foreign investment they might attract. One petition suggests saving the organs to sell to the Italians and Spanish, who, officials claimed, lacked organs comparable to those made in France.[58] The government official Jacque Cambry noted in one correspondence that, in his understanding, the British even kept organs in their tea salons. Although he worried that the French would surely miss out on such a luxury should they be hastily dispossessed of their organs, he nevertheless took care to identify a potential market for the instruments.[59] Facing what seemed to be a genuinely painful process of prioritizing cultural products, officials like Molard across agriculture, mining, and industry, continued to see both practical and pleasurable reasons to preserve organs.

Government aid requests for musical inventions became increasingly complicated as committees disappeared, merged, and reemerged. Christoph Chiquelier, an elderly man who formerly served as the king's instrument keeper, began requesting recognition from the Board in June 1795 for three keyboard instruments that he had invented.[60] A prospectus on Chiquelier's instruments highlights their technological innovation. He claimed to have tempered them justly so that string genres like the *symphonie concertante* and string quartet could be performed "more faithfully" on them. He also created a mechanism that would immediately transcribe anything played on the keyboard, effectively eliminating the inconvenience of transcribing during composition.[61] The Board offered the aged luthier 300 *livres* to tide him over until commissioners could arrange an inspection of the instruments. He lived in Versailles, apparently a great inconvenience for the Board. As late as 1796, colleagues at the Lycée des arts petitioned the government on Chiquelier's behalf.[62] As Chiquelier awaited a response from the Board regarding his inventions, he remained absent from the list of artists receiving pensions and awards from the government. In the meantime, the Board's duties were transferred to the new National Institute, a transition discussed further in what follows, and Chiquelier's allies asked that the government bring his still-desperate need to yet another entity for evaluation. Chiquelier's ordeal is but one example of how the pursuit of rewards for musical inventions proved maddeningly complicated during the Revolution, a consequence of new policies and laws in flux.

From 1791 to 1795, a growing number of individuals and organizations promoted a national agenda that prioritized mechanical musical inventions because they promised to "grow national industry." Although "utility" was not a legal criterion for the Board's judgment, it nevertheless remained the dominant criterion employed across these industrial conversations. Invention and preservation were moreover two sides of the same coin. The government needed to encourage innovation through individual property rights and rewards to advance industrial growth while also preserving past innovations as models for future inventors to follow. In this the industrial agenda precisely mirrored the cultural one described in the previous chapter. By the logic of the public domain, publicly available technologies were likely to inspire innovation. Officials hoped that new instruments would improve the efficiency of musical production and continue a long French history of craftsmanship and artistry, attracting foreign spending in the process. This focus on the nation and public, however, held the potential to sacrifice the good of musicians for the good of music, as the violinist Louis-Antoine Travenol complained back in Chapter 1.

Interlude: A Method in the Madness

Authors of music methods turned to the Committee on Public Instruction to seek rewards, since the Board and Executive government deemed their work, as we saw in the case of Clareton, more "pleasurable" than "useful." Like Chiquelier, Louis Antoine Durieu became increasingly frustrated in his attempts to receive government support for a method he had authored. Then, as now, he enjoyed little notoriety. Nevertheless, as a violin teacher formerly affiliated with the Concert Spirituel and Concert des Amateurs, a music merchant, and the editor of a collection of Italian ariettes, he seemed to have effectively navigated the Old Regime privilege system described in Chapters 1 and 2.[63] The Revolution proved far more trying for him. Although Durieu authored and published at least two method books during this period, the *Nouvelle méthode de musique vocale* and *Méthode de violon*, he began to slip between the institutional fissures that the political upheaval had opened.[64] Durieu takes the title "author, professor, and publisher" of music in his letters to the Committee on Public Instruction, situating himself as a pedagogue and entrepreneur.

The first of Durieu's series of letters to the Committee begs for justice.[65] Durieu sent his *Nouvelle méthode de musique vocale* to the National Convention. The Convention forwarded the publication on to a subcommittee of the Committee on Public Instruction, the Committee on Elementary Books, which replied to Durieu that music did not fall under its jurisdiction. "What should I do?" he asked with palpable exasperation. Durieu had authored the first section of the method book, a general introduction to basic music theory, and Joseph Agus, whom Durieu refers to in the letters as a "famous" composer, had composed the second section consisting of solfege and harmony lessons. In a follow-up letter Durieu demanded a response regarding his *Méthode élémentaire de musique*; he was teaching for free at three schools and needed recognition—a polite word for "money"—for his "sacrifices."[66]

One month later, on July 16, 1795, Durieu's co-author Agus, and composers discussed in Chapter 4—François Giroust, Jean-Baptiste-Aimé Janson *l'aîné*, and Jean Joseph Rodolphe—all received first class awards of 3,000 *livres* from the Committee on Public Instruction.[67] These were rewards set in place to counteract what Chénier felt was an overrepresentation of "useful" artists receiving government rewards based on the Board's recommendations. Two days later, two beloved Old Regime composers, Jean-Paul-Gilles Martini and Pierre-Alexandre Monsigny were awarded second class awards of 2,000 *livres*.[68] It must have irritated Durieu to see Agus on the list. Indeed, years later Durieu would reveal publicly to his colleagues the complete indignation he felt.

Durieu had submitted documentation supporting his own case only weeks before the Committee announced these awards.[69] His documents contain the testimonies of many soon-to-be Conservatory faculty members including Langlé, Marie-Alexandre Guénin, Jean-Jacques Nochez, Jean-François Méon, and one of the Rigels (the letter is unclear whether father or son), as well as musicians who had been officially assigned to review Durieu's method book for the Committee: Luigi Cherubini, Étienne-Nicolas Méhul, Jean-François Lesueur, and Gossec, all Conservatory inspectors. Their testimonies praise Agus's section of the method book as perfect. Durieu's section they agreed, though quite clear and good, required a bit more "development." Durieu asked permission from the president of the Committee, Pierre-Louis Ginguené, to present analyses of his work to the Committee.[70] Ginguené, seemingly exhausted by the exchange, asked the Committee simply to grant Durieu's method approbation (without financial reward), which was duly sent two days before another set of awards was announced on July 16. Durieu's battle, it seems, was far too small for a committee in the midst of rebuilding an entire national education system.

The last letter from Durieu, sent only days after the reward announcement, stated rather glibly that while he appreciated the Committee's latest letter of approval, he was "waiting for something other than compliments." What he would have liked, he suggested, were "government awards and bonuses."[71] The following day the Committee granted Durieu a second-class reward.[72] The gesture silenced him for a time as his colleagues at the Conservatory made plans for method books of their own.

Mechanical Innovations: Useful to Whom?

A law on public instruction founded the National Institute in October 1795, only months after the music Conservatory's establishment. In the National Institute, the greatest French minds would collaborate across disciplines to perfect the French arts and sciences, bringing together within a single institution the expertise that under the Old Regime had been distributed across separate academies. According to the Institute's initial three sections—the physical sciences and mathematics, moral and political sciences, and literature and the fine arts—music was situated in the latter alongside grammar, ancient languages, poetry, antiquities, monuments, painting, sculpture, and architecture, the fields with which we saw music aligned in Chapter 4. The Conservatory inspectors and composers Méhul, Gossec, and Grétry ran the subdivision for Music and Declamation in the National Institute alongside three *comédiens* (actors and playwrights). Rather than reincarnate an idealized version of the Old Regime academies, the National Institute strove to embody a new postrevolutionary intellectual vision. The Directory government instructed the Institute members during their first session that, "public utility was the goal which should tend all their works."[73] The Institute was not to fancy itself a new-and-improved academy, but rather a comprehensive institution dedicated to utility, the publication of useful discoveries, and the perfection of the arts and sciences. In reality, it somewhat awkwardly combined functions previously divided among Academies, the Board, and the Committee on Public Instruction.

Although the Marquis de Condorcet, an Enlightenment philosopher and mathematician, had died in prison under the Terror in 1794, the Institute's formation owed much to his influential thinking. The evolution of his personal beliefs from the Old Regime to the Revolution encapsulate the institutionalized knowledge production he helped to implement in France.[74] Early in his career, Condorcet focused on theoretical mathematics, purporting the long-term utility of theory and immediate utility of practice. Over the course of his work, however, Condorcet began to emphasize the interdependence of theory and practice. By the time he proposed his education plan discussed in Chapter 4, he considered the sciences as a necessary basis for education in eighteenth-century "arts," from the military, to engineering, to medicine. He saw progress in the arts and sciences as symbiotic; theories became practically applicable while practical skills yielded abstract theories.[75] He considered artisans, those who applied the sciences, not as mere implementers but as inventors.[76] In Condorect's vision, the new Institute had a role to play in the tools and techniques developed to advance French industry. This was not, of course, an entirely new idea in France. Under the Old Regime, the monarchy had nurtured technological advances for its mercantile ambitions and the Academy of Sciences had provided the Board of Commerce with evaluations. Yet public utility and national profit rather than monarchical glory and wealth underpinned this new academic vision. Music, previously divided along institutional lines between the Academy of Sciences and Académie Royale de musique, finally unified within the Institute as it did in the Conservatory. With the exception of a few prerevolutionary efforts to interweave music theory and practice, it was not until the Revolution, in the context of national educational initiatives, where such a large-scale endeavor to marry music's theories with its practices finally took root.[77]

The Conservatory inspectors' role as Institute members granted them a place of authority in the nation's new industrial agenda. When the government dissolved the original Board in 1796, the National Institute took over the review of applications submitted by inventors for government rewards and bonuses. A new version of the Board continued to review patent applications separately, although it occasionally requested input from the National Institute's first division for physical sciences.[78] Recall the difference between rewards and patents; rewards allowed for an immediate release of an invention into the public domain while a patent cost a fee and protected the inventor's property for a specified duration of time. The Institute's mandate to advance "public utility" directly conflicted with the 1791 laws that forbade any consideration of "utility" as a basis for rewards, because, according to the law, utility could not be anticipated before an object or method's release to the public. Nevertheless, as we saw in previous sections, utility had long been a standard of measures for reward reviewers. Authors, inventors, and the Minister of the Interior began to submit methods and inventions to the National Institute for review.

The review process was straightforward enough. After an initial presentation of the method or instrument during a general session, the *classe* of Institute members would choose a delegate or delegates from among themselves to review the submission and to write a report on it. Upon the report's completion, one of the selected delegates would read some or all of it to the *classe*. If the report was submitted by the Minister of the Interior, the Institute usually made a recommendation regarding whether the applicant should receive a monetary reward. If submitted directly by the creator, the applicant usually sought the Institute's approval for their work or relevant designs and samples to be deposited in the Institute library, a sign of prestige and public regard. The Conservatory's inspectors who served as members of the Institute *classe*, especially Gossec and Méhul, regularly participated in these review processes.

The Institute's reviews offered an alternative to the formalities of the patent and printing rights systems established from 1791 to 1793. Indeed, it continued the Board and Committee on Public Instruction's missions to encourage direct release of useful knowledge into the public domain through rewards-based incentives. But the copy deposited in the Institute's library might also prevent others from claiming priority on an idea or invention in the future. "Priority" was a legal term denoting status as an innovation's original creator. At the time, whoever registered an invention held the rights to it, regardless of priority. The successor to the Board, which granted patents, required only the payment of fees and submission of appropriate paperwork, not proof of priority. An application included a description of the invention, perfection, or importation (an innovation originating outside France), along with designs or samples (See Figure 6.3). A law passed in 1800 required all patent documentation to note explicitly that the receipt of a patent indicated neither priority nor merit.[79] Exacting descriptions and images in patent applications no longer served as means of evaluation as they had in the Board from 1791 to 1795; they simply documented the precise object or process protected. A patent holder was required to submit a new application with each "perfection" made. For this reason, the Érard brothers received four separate patents on harps from 1798 through 1809 because each individual application protected a specific improvement to the instrument's construction.[80]

Unlike patents, the National Institute acknowledged both the merit of and priority on inventions. Perhaps authors and inventors submitted their work to the National Institute library precisely because the law remained unsettled and they anticipated such documentation with a government entity might prove useful in future legal cases. The 1791 and 1793 property laws were yet to be ironed out along juridical lines. Cases brought in 1803, however, sought to claim priority on processes patented by others; in other words, inventors claiming priority began to complain that someone else patented their creation. Laws remained vague regarding what kinds of evidence might be considered in such cases and which judicial or administrative body even held the right to revoke patents. The law carefully defined patents as a right to property, not as property per se—precisely what privileges had been.

Like the Academy of Sciences before it, the Institute's approval carried social value as well. Many methods submitted by musicians to the Institute were simply accepted, without report, accompanied by a formulaic response: "Ordered that appreciation will be made to the author and the work will be deposited at the library."[81] The cellist Janson, who received a national reward in July 1795 for his public service, later received recognition from the Institute for his method book.[82] Méhul's evaluation of Janson's method focused exclusively on the quality of its examples and explanations. He concluded that the method would certainly become requisite study materials for Janson's "successors."[83] Méhul's evaluation was not to determine whether Janson merited a national reward, but simply to obtain the Institute's approval and placement in its library. The approbation from a learned body would help its sales, just as, back in Chapter 1, the Academy of Science's recognition under the Old Regime helped authors seeking privileges. The interdependence of legal and social advantages in rights over property persisted within revolutionary institutions long after privilege had been ostensibly abolished.

The Institute continued to evaluate instruments and musical inventions for their utility and commercial promise as its predecessor the Board had done. When a Citizen Baud submitted silk strings to the National Institute, Gossec reported that there had been attempts to infringe on Baud's ideas, however, because of the "mediocrity of his fortune," Baud could not afford a patent to protect his work.[84] Baud only sought the Institute's verification that he was indeed the first to manufacture strings in this manner, a confirmation that, at the very least, would serve as proof that he held priority on the production process.[85] Although the box of strings was deposited with the Sciences section of the Institute as a sealed submission, intended for a later patent approval, Baud never seems to have pursued the process.[86] He would have been ineligible to do so according to the 1791 law anyway, because inventors were prohibited from applying for both a patent and a reward. A detailed inspection of the strings by Gossec, Méhul, and members of the Conservatory determined that they were indeed useful to percussive string instruments like pianos, harps, and lutes, though less so for bowed string instruments because of tuning difficulties. Gossec determined that Baud had "rights to public recognition, and merited encouragement."[87] The ultimate reason, however, for Baud's success under Institute review was utilitarian: the method provided musicians a more "economic" option for strings and promised France "an interesting new branch of commerce."[88]

The Conservatory inspectors seemed to prefer inventions that made musical production more affordable; to them, utility and commercial viability as well as cost-effectiveness mattered. When an Institute commission including Gossec and Méhul reviewed a new music printing method, it concluded, "The general object to consider at the moment and that which should principally occupy the commission's attention, is the resulting utility of employing the process."[89] Nicolas-Étienne Framery, in a different review, similarly noted "commercial advantages" of a new printing process.[90]

The inventions economically advantageous to professional musicians thus began to come into tension with those that advanced the French industrial agenda; musicians sought affordable technology while the nation hoped to draw revenue from higher prices. When considering another new music printing method proposed by Citizen Grassal, Méhul identified a pressing problem. Prices of engravings had risen because of the high cost of materials and labor. Despite the desire by "savants, artists, speculators . . . musicians, and amateurs" to switch to movable type printing for economic reasons, "Economist Publishers," as Méhul called them, had no incentive to improve methods and lower prices, particularly because the high quality of music engravings were preferred despite the existence of cheaper, lower-quality printing options.[91] He named the culprits specifically in his report: François-Henri Ollivier, Jean-Louis Duplat, and Antoine Bouvier.[92] All three had paid for and received patents on printing methods, the kinds of patents that Baud could not afford.

The printing proposal before them seemed to offer a solution, but property rights hindered Méhul and his co-commissioners from making a final judgment. The machines submitted by Grassal indeed seemed to offer remedies to Méhul's music printing crisis, but without experiments on their usage and comparisons with the mechanisms employed by other printers, it was impossible to fully support the proposal under review. Méhul asked whether other printers would, "not have the right to oppose the publicizing of their products?" were they to be scrutinized by the Institute. "Would they even want to make them known to your Commission?" he wondered, "And if by chance one of your comrades would know them, could he speak of them without exposing them to infringement on the right of property?"[93]

With this, Méhul identified a conundrum of inventors' property rights: if Grassal's colleagues exposed their methods and machines to scrutiny and all were compared in front of the Institute, their intellectual property would be vulnerable to theft. Yet Méhul saw potential in Grassal's method, suggesting that the government provide funds to support his continued work on his printing machines and processes, which promised a great utility to the music industry's consumers—cheaper scores.

Méhul directly addressed the tension between public goods and personal property in musical production. The new method would be "good" for musical production, but to achieve it would require infringement on private property and profit. Méhul pointed out this paradoxical task of simultaneously growing cultural heritage and national industry under the new French property regime that considered individual rights as sacred.

The Conservatory inspectors had found a place to voice their concerns in increasingly powerful institutions dedicated to industrial advancement, providing a means to challenge those in the world of printing, publishing, and instrument-building who at times frustrated working musicians. Beginning in 1798, national Industrial Exhibitions were held in Paris to showcase the French products that contributed to innovation in fields ranging from agriculture to mining, ceramics, and beyond.[94] Familiar faces in the world of instrument evaluation populated the exhibition music juries: Molard who had served on the Temporary Arts Commission and served as director of the new Conservatoire des arts et métiers, members of the National Institute and the newest iteration of the Board, and Conservatory director Bernard Sarrette.[95] Instruments and scores increasingly counted among the products displayed at the events. It was crucial that exhibitors "emphasize the latest invention patents" to earn prizes.[96] In these early years, jurors frequently evaluated musical instruments for their "commercial and industrial success," Malou Haine argues, rather than for "real artistic or technological quality."[97] When evaluating the newest Cousineau harp, for example, the jury noted that its perfections would "contribute greatly to assuring France the exclusive possession of a branch of commerce that becomes every day more important."[98] Many of the exhibition's musical inventors had already obtained *brevets* from the government when they entered the competition, including Ollivier and Bouvier, the "Economist Publishers" ridiculed by Méhul. The piano maker Tobias Schmidt had finally obtained patents for his work and advertised the accomplishment, "par brevet d'invention," at the exhibitions (Figure 6.4).[99] After years of pursuing patents, Schmidt had finally succeeded. The government granted around twenty-five patents to music-related objects from 1798 until 1810. Recipients came from among inventors and instrument builders, the best known included Érard, Cousineau, and Pleyel. It is worth noting that these were also the publishers who benefited from the property laws established in Chapter 3. In 1806, four men holding patents

FIGURE 6.4 An advertisement for Tobias Schmidt's booth at the Exposition of French Industrial Products in 1806 notes that he holds a *brevet d'invention* or invention patent. That year he exhibited the piano-harmonica. Courtesy of the Conservatoire nationale des arts et métiers, Archives historique, Saint-Denis, P 293.

for musical inventions received rewards from the industrial exposition jury. Unsurprisingly, those who could afford patents could also afford to participate in expositions. Booths and other related exhibit expenses posed a significant cost to inventors.[100] Méhul likely had such advantages in mind when he critiqued "Economist Publishers" in his National Institute report. Much like Old Regime privileges, those who could afford to pay the formalities were more likely to succeed in protecting their work as property and consequently to earn more revenue from their products in return.

As concerns for economic and commercial utility colored musical evaluations by the Institute, a glaring question emerged: useful to whom? For the French nation, instruments and scores contributed to public utility when they drew higher prices. For professional musicians, affordable access to the newest tools and techniques proved far more useful. When the Institute was reorganized under Napoleon in 1803, the fine arts were separated out into their own fourth section and the *comédiens* and "declamation" removed from the music section. Music finally earned its own unique place among the other fine arts, independent of dramatic forms, an autonomous realm of knowledge production. Yet music faced challenges as an autonomously "progressing" art when its materials—staff paper, scores, and instruments—were increasingly subordinated to commercial considerations. It would be impossible for musicians to make a decent living if the tools of their profession became prohibitively expensive. Professional musical production and musical products' contribution to national industry needed to harmonize. And Bernard Sarrette's Conservatory was already hard at work on a desirable solution.

The Conservatory's Design for a "Romantic Machine"

While Sarrette established the Conservatory's library and museum, as discussed in the previous chapter, his mission shifted. When the Conservatory inspectors justified their requests for government funding in 1796, they had continued to wager the institution's utility on contributions to cultural heritage and the revolutionary political agenda. But by then the tides had already begun to change; the Terror bred disillusionment with zealous patriotism and left a desire for stability in its wake. As if heeding Hassenfratz's quote that opened this chapter, the didactic festivals that Conservatory musicians were legally bound to support attracted skepticism and were soon eliminated altogether.

When Sarrette appeared before the government to justify his institution once again in 1801, this time in the face of debilitating budget cuts, he changed strategies and chose to promote the Conservatory's industrial rather than only its cultural or political utility.[101] Sarrette presented his plan to the legislature's Committee on Public Instruction, admitting that, "In the past, French commerce did not profit from musical objects; the products from this part of national industry were null for the taxman."[102] Taking a page from Hassenfratz's playbook, Sarrette blamed foreign competitors. Under the Old Regime, Sarrette argued, musicians from abroad had circulated through Paris, awed audiences, and returned home with their pay, all while French musicians relied on quality instruments from outside French borders—English pianos, German horns, and Italian violins. Sarrette identified German wind instruments, in particular, as having stolen an "important branch of industry" and "means of existence from a large part of the [French] population."[103] He nevertheless felt encouraged by recent improvements in the French instrument industry: "Our pianos are now sought throughout Europe; their price has risen from 1,000 to 2,400 *francs*; the price of our horns, preferred for their finish over those from Germany, have risen to 300 *francs*, our luthiers make violins the quality of which has caused the ordinary price to rise to 400 *francs*."[104] Whatever concerns Méhul expressed to the National Institute about high prices in music printing, Sarrette embraced them, knowing that higher prices prompted legislators to imagine hefty government coffers, which might translate into funding for his school's budget. After all, the same legislators had been convinced to save organs based on the revenue they might generate from foreign investment. Sarrette even suggested a tax on quality music engraving and printing. "Can the art that contributes the most to procuring such resources to the government," Sarrette asked, "hope to obtain the means necessary to its conservation?"[105]

To keep the meager government support that remained for the Conservatory, Sarrette needed to demonstrate its contributions to the national industrial agenda, an agenda in which other schools were already actively participating. Recall from Chapter 4 how, following the chaotic Terror, the Committee on Public Instruction set new educational institutions in place to standardize fields and efficiently train professionals who would support France's economic revitalization. In 1794 and 1795 alone the School of Health, the School of Mines, the École polytechnique, and the Conservatoire des arts et métiers were founded alongside the music Conservatory. The schools' first task was to arrive at a professional consensus in theoretical knowledge to form the basis for their respective training.[106] Their mission was to teach students how to apply such knowledge practically for commercial and economic gain.[107] Students in health, for example, would study anatomy and chemistry, while engineers would study geometry and physics. Military training in fortifications and topography required the study of "descriptive geometry,"[108] so that students learned to conceptualize both the man-made structures and the terrains that they would encounter in real-life scenarios on the battlefield. The institutions would then design and evaluate instruments and methods particular to their fields, providing professionals with a practical means to implement their scientifically based theoretical knowledge. Military education provided the model for this practical, science-based education system implemented in 1795 to improve French industry. The military, like the other fields that adopted state-sponsored education as a result of the Revolution, professionalized during the Directory government, particularly through the establishment of schools.[109] By the end of the Revolution, state-educated professionals were elevated over those who had been privately educated.[110] The Conservatory quite palpably aligned itself with this broader scientific and educational mission by the late 1790s.

The correlations between the Conservatory and the military is already well-trodden territory,[111] but an extended comparison between music and mining further illustrates these scientific and professional connections. The French mining agency had originated in a prerevolutionary school founded in 1783, which came under the direction of the Minister of the Interior during the Revolution, when engineering was officially situated "at the intersection of the public good and professional practice."[112] Although earlier attempts to codify mining knowledge had occurred before the Revolution, the act that created the schools of public service on October 22, 1795, "marked a turning point" in the field, argues Isabelle Laboulais, "because it specified recruiting conditions and established a training program for mining engineers."[113] The École polytechnique, where mining students acquired their theoretical training, sought to link the knowledge it produced with "commercial exploitation."[114] And its efforts to visualize France's mineralogical resources through the tables, display cabinets, and maps in its collection of machines and its library represented not simply an encyclopedic effort following in Enlightenment epistemologies, Laboulais contends, but a bureaucratic effort, as well.[115] Mining definitively professionalized as a result of the Revolution, and ultimately, engineers advised on "everything from extraction to commercialization,"[116] serving the public good "by helping to extract its resources."[117]

Both in its institutional evolution and its role in national industrial agendas, the Conservatory shared remarkably similar professionalization and bureaucratization with mining. Like the first mining school, the École Royale de chant opened its doors just before the Revolution, in 1784, when, as we saw in Chapters 2 and 3, music was increasingly considered a public good. The Conservatory's foundation represented a definitive step toward institutionalizing uniform training in the theory and practice of music, which had previously been decentralized primarily in cathedral schools and master-student lessons. Although the Conservatory was not established explicitly as a "school of service," like the other schools founded in October 1795 (see Table 6.1), its original inception as a branch of the military put it in service to the nation, as we saw in Chapter 4. Moreover, the Conservatory was involved in commercialization, as shown earlier, through the evaluations that its inspectors provided both to the National Institute and to the Industrial Exhibitions. Sarrette's library and museum described in the previous chapter shared similarities with those of the mining school, too. And in many ways the Conservatory's mission, like that of the School of Mines, was a bureaucratic endeavor.[118] The Conservatory shared a final affinity with its engineering counterpart; it developed a knowledge base that allowed its students to enter the world prepared to extract, process, and

TABLE 6.1 Schools established by the "Loi du 30 vendémiaire, an IV [October 22, 1795], concernant les écoles de services publics."

École polytechnique (Polytechnic School)
Écoles d'artillerie (Artillery School)
École des ingénieurs militaires (School of Military Engineers)
École des ponts et chaussées (School of Bridges and Roads)
École des mines (School of Mines)
École des géographes (School of Geography)
École des ingénieurs de vaisseaux (School of Shipping Engineers)
École de navigation (School of Navigation)
École de marine (Maritime School)

transform natural resources (in the case of musicians, air, wood, and metal) into a commercially viable industry. This brings us to one of the primary means by which the Conservatory would achieve this training—its method books (Table 6.2).

The Conservatory's method books have earned a bewildering array of labels: early Romantic, un-Romantic, disciplinary, propagandistic, nationalistic, and sensationist. Many of these readings presume either a mid-1790s political sentiment (an initiative that had been largely lost by the time the methods were compiled) or an Enlightenment epistemology, which had in fact receded or at the very least muddied in the revolutionary waters. These remarkably varied interpretations belie precisely what the method book authors set out to achieve—a compromise among the competing practical

TABLE 6.2 Method books authored by Conservatory faculty according to the "Décision relative à la rédaction des méthodes d'enseignement musical; 12 fructidor an II [August 29, 1794]."

Agus, Joseph et al. *Principes élémentaires de musique; arrêtés par les membres du Conservatoire, pour servir à l'étude dans cet établissement, suivis de solfèges.* 2 vols. Paris: Imprimerie du Conservatoire de musique, an VIII [1799–1800].

Agus, Joseph, et al. *Solfèges pour servir à l'étude dans le Conservatoire de musique* (deuxième partie), Paris: Imprimerie du Conservatoire de musique, an X [1801].

Catel, Charles-Simon. *Traité d'harmonie: adopté par le Conservatoire pour servir à l'étude dans cet établissement.* Paris: Imprimerie du Conservatoire de musique, an X [1801–1802].

Duvernoy, Frédéric-Nicolas. *Méthode pour le cor suivie de duo et de trio pour cet instrument.* Paris: Imprimerie du Conservatoire de musique, [1802].

Lefèvre, Jean-Xavier. *Méthode de clarinette: adoptée par le Conservatoire pour servir à l'étude dans cet établissement.* Paris: Imprimerie du Conservatoire de musique, an XI [1802–1803].

Ozi, Étienne. *Nouvelle méthode de basson: adoptée par le Conservatoire pour servir à l'étude dans cet établissement.* Paris: Imprimerie du Conservatoire, an XI [1803].

Baillot, Pierre, Pierre Rode, and Rodolphe Kreutzer. *Méthode de violon: adoptée par le Conservatoire pour servir à l'étude dans cet établissement.* Paris: Magasin de musique [du Conservatoire] Faubourg Poissionniere, [1803].

Mengozzi, Bernardo, et al. *Méthode de chant du Conservatoire de musique: contenant les principes du chant, des exercices pour la voix, des solfèges tirés des meilleurs ouvrages anciens et modernes et des airs dans tous les mouvemens et les différens caractères.* Paris: Imprimerie du Conservatoire de musique, an XII [1803–1804].

Baillot, Pierre, Jean-Henri Levasseur, Charles-Simon Catel, and Charles-Nicolas Baudiot. *Méthode de violoncelle et de basse d'accompagnement: adoptée pour servir à l'étude dans cet établissement.* Paris: Imprimerie du Conservatoire Impérial de Musique, [1804].

Hugot, Antoine, and Johann Georg Wunderlich. *Méthode de flûte du Conservatoire: adoptée pour servir à l'étude dans cet établissement.* Paris: Imprimerie du Conservatoire, an XII [1804].

Adam, Louis. *Méthode de piano du Conservatoire: adoptée pour servir à l'enseignement dans cet établissement.* Paris: Imprimerie du Conservatoire, an XIII [1805].

Domnich, Heinrich. *Méthode de premier et de second cor: adoptée pour servir à l'étude dans cet établissement.* Paris: Imprimerie du Conservatoire Impérial de Musique, [1807].

and intellectual pressures placed on the Conservatory during the Directory and Consulate governments. The very adaptability of the method books to such diverse scholarly analyses reveals a stunning accomplishment. The varied evaluations are not easily attributed to the fact that each book concerns a different instrument since, as we shall see, the methods were deeply intertextual and interdependent, clearly conceived as a whole. The practical industrial and scientific agendas identified in this chapter are yet to be carefully scrutinized as an influential context for these methods.[119] These agendas put into relief the multivalent work that the method books were intended to achieve at a moment when the Conservatory's future remained devastatingly uncertain.

Four significant industrial factors inflected the method books' authorship.[120] First, as shown previously, the governmental bodies that regulated industrial innovation had cast music methods as less "useful" in comparison to the art's machines, tools, and instruments. This partially explains the method books' preoccupation with *mécanisme* and instrument technology. Second, the Conservatory needed to at least appear to contribute to the French industrial agenda in order to pursue financial support like other science-based professional and service schools; it had already experienced budget cuts as a result of its waning political utility and its faculty were paid far less than their counterparts at, for example, the École polytechnique.[121] The methods recommend the newest instruments, provide excerpts composed by the most famed composers, and cite one another copiously. Thus, they prompted readers to acquire more musical products in the form of method books, scores, and instruments, spurring sales that the nation desperately wanted. Third, the knowledgeable use of instruments had become associated since the mid-eighteenth century with professional status. If the Conservatory leaned too far into the industrial agenda, then they threatened to undo their elevation as artists since the 1770s. The methods develop theoretical knowledge and technical expertise symbiotically in a manner similar to other well-respected professionals in the sciences. Finally, around 1800, the Conservatory began to attract criticism for "cronyism" and for monopolizing Parisian musical production.[122] Its members had to tread carefully along proprietary lines, securing influence while appearing dispassionate, disinterested even, in any collective gain or exclusivity. The method books provided a seemingly objective means to achieve this end because they were cloaked in a bureaucratic and apolitical veneer propagated by all of the new national schools, and especially by the military.

I hesitate to attach rigid epistemological or ideological labels to the method books, not only because they are so clearly a product of practical circumstance but also because they appeared during a fitful transition from Enlightenment sensationism to Romantic idealism. They are, however, certainly predicated on a deep reciprocity between mechanical innovation and innate human capacity. With a few notable exceptions discussed below, the methods sought to form musicians into a single orchestral context.[123] And so together they resemble, even herald the "romantic machines" described by the historian John Tresch. Although some elements of the method books like fingering charts, prescriptions for bodily control, and expression through gestures and tempi, are remnants of Enlightenment music methods, all of the Conservatory methods also include discussions of expression that transcend Enlightenment era linguistic taxonomies,[124] defining it instead as an innate, subjective quality brought forth by the performer, the composer, and even by the musical work itself.[125] To call the books sensationist would ignore their idealist and nativist inclinations, which had been already nascent in mid-eighteenth-century French sensationist theory.[126] Any rigid label of the methods disserves their idiosyncrasies. It is more urgent to situate them in a specific historical context rather than an epistemological one; the books' authors were likely only familiar with such epistemologies in passing. They did, however, explicitly concern themselves with preserving hard-won professional advances that came under threat in the twilight of Revolution.

The method books provided the design for a living "romantic machine" that the Conservatory would clearly own, its orchestra. Like the Romantic machines in 1820s and 1830s Paris illuminated by Tresch, the method book authors depicted musical instruments that, "drew forth invisible powers, converted them, and put them to use."[127] Obsession with mechanical objects in early nineteenth-century Paris did not efface labor,[128] rather, romantic machines were "imbued with the aesthetics and the affects of the organic, the vital, and even the transcendent."[129] The Conservatory methods above all set out to form perfectly trained musicians. In this sense, they cultivated bodies in a manner similar to the later "Romantic anatomies" described by musicologist James Q. Davies.[130] Musical instruments in the method books, like subsequent scientific instruments, were "extensions of human senses and intentionality."[131] Deirdre Loughridge contends that, "notions of extending the senses and mastering invisible forces increasingly came to supplement or supplant"[132] eighteenth-century mimetic and representational aesthetics. The methods reveal a pivotal moment in the transition shown by both Tresch and Loughridge. By communing mechanical capabilities with human anatomies, romantic machines also forged new relationships to the earth, what Tresch calls a "second nature."[133] As Napoleonic armies reaped "harvests" of musical scores alongside plant and animal specimens from foreign environments, the French required new ways to process these musical resources. And so this approach served to naturalize musical production—further distancing it from its courtly, decadent Old Regime reputation—and to exploit technological advances.

Conservatory students began their studies with the two method books on elementary music principles, which they were required to understand "perfectly before beginning to study an instrument."[134] A lack of theoretical knowledge could ultimately lead to serious performance errors, the books warned. Jean-Xavier Lefèvre's admonition in the clarinet method epitomizes those found throughout the books, "The artist . . . should be a good reader and should know harmony," Lefèvre suggests, "since instead of adding to the charm of a piece of music, he would destroy the effect by inappropriately introducing defective notes that would have no relation with the harmony."[135] The method books rely on harmonic logic to explain performance and ornamentation choices.[136] The author of the second horn treatise, Heinrich Domnich, is even more emphatic in this prescription:

> Musical organization is thus here the first required condition; and the student who has received it from nature should, before placing lips on a mouthpiece, have acquired through solfege exercises the habit of comparing sounds, measuring intervals, to know the intonations . . . this preliminary study is the most useful of all.[137]

And so students needed to orient themselves in sonic space before picking up an instrument.[138] The first two methods are distinctly geometric in nature, a feature of French music theory treatises as far back as Jean-Philippe Rameau, and before him, Marin Marsenne. The method begins by defining sound as, "air set in motion by the impact of two bodies," which upon "reaching the organ of hearing produces sensation." Unlike noise, sound was "rational or appreciable."[139] "Nature" organized sound into an "immense chain" arranged from low to high pitches.[140] Music was defined simply as the "art of combining sounds."[141] The *Principes élémentaires* goes on to introduce, as its title suggests, the most basic elements of music like notation, solfege syllables, clefs, intervals, scales, key relationships, et cetera.[142] Figure 6.5 provides an example of the kinds of diagrams and explanations typical of the *Principes élémentaires*, in this case, the generation of accidentals through motion by fifth, presented as an ascending and descending ladder, isolated from a keyboard, instrument, or even a staff.[143] In his evaluation of the Conservatory's method books for the National Institute, Framery described the *Principes élémentaires* as useful to students "who through practice would like to join the notions of theory and reason."[144] Like the military engineer's descriptive geometry, the *Principes élémentaires* situated students in theoretical space first.

Along with Charles-Simon Catel's *Traité d'harmonie*, the *Principes élémentaires* provided students with the theory to navigate any musical terrain they might encounter. Catel's harmony treatise has been accurately summarized as simple, practical, and uniform. It left behind the convoluted music theoretical treatises scrutinized by the Academy of Sciences under the Old Regime in favor of explaining music theory—as Framery described the *Principes élémentaires*—for musicians. Méhul, likely with Catel in mind, noted in a report to the National Institute that musicians had recently adapted

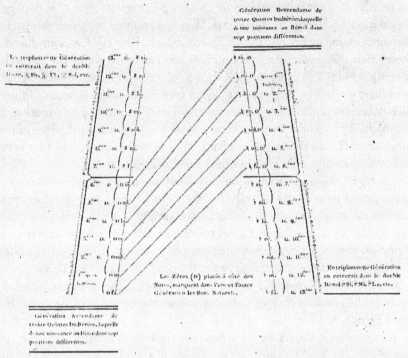

FIGURE 6.5 The diagrams in the first two method books present the basic theories of music geometrically as sound in space rather than in relation to any particular instrument or praxis.

scientific theories through practical considerations. "Geometry wanted to submit music to its laws, physics reclaimed it in favor of its own," Méhul said, "but practitioners unable to work in either physics or in geometry, sensed the necessity to break scientific chains, and arrived by long trials and

NATIONAL INDUSTRY: MUSIC AS A "USEFUL" ART AND SCIENCE | 195 numerous observations, to create for themselves independent rules, taking for the base of their system, the approbation or disapprobation of the ear."[145] Catel's treatise rejected Rameau's system of fundamental bass in favor of a far simpler concept comprising only two types of chords, those that required preparation and those that did not. Catel accounted for everything else through passing or prolongation.[146] According to Framery, Catel improved a theory that was previously "incompatible with an art in which the ear is the sovereign judge."[147] Here, as in Chapter 3, musicians claim "sovereignty" over their work. The method introduced counterpoint fundamentals immediately because rather than being concerned with an implied bass motion, it emphasized movement between consonances and dissonances. The flexibility inherent in Catel's theory meant that it could provide background for composition while also presenting a broad analytic language.

Catel's theory could account for just about any music. Rameau's theory of fundamental bass, on the contrary, had frequently identified "errors" in other composers' works, especially Italians. Not simply a political ploy to cultivate a national musical style, Catel's treatise accommodated a great variety of European common practice music at the precise moment when trunks filled with Italian and German music were flooding back to the Conservatory's library from the Napoleonic campaigns. It reflected the irony identified already in the previous chapter—that by universalizing art, art "naturally" became French. Students thus needed to learn how to "process" any music they might encounter. Catel's theory could "convert" foreign music and "put [it] to use,"[148] like Tresch's romantic machines, just as the agricultural and industrial methods developed in France or imported from other countries could process natural resources like seeds, livestock, and soil. The method books prepared students, as Domnich puts it, "to give [the student] an idea of [the difficulties] that could be encountered,"[149] a descriptive music theory equivalent to the military engineers' descriptive geometry. Unlike artisans of the early eighteenth century, professional musicians trained at the Conservatory would be able to articulate the rules underlying their praxis.

Like their peers in mining and surgery, Conservatory students later applied their theoretical knowledge to instruments, developing the techniques that, in the field, would prove crucial to productivity.[150] All of the Conservatory instrument methods begin with a discussion of mechanism (*mécanisme*), in other words, physical properties and processes of performance. Domnich prescribes directly that, "a cold calculation should precede all expression."[151] The flute, clarinet, and bassoon methods include detailed images of the instruments, identifying their parts, how to hold them, and the proper fingering for each note (see Figures 6.6.a and 6.6.b). The bassoon and horn methods also include images of reeds and mouthpieces (See Figure 6.7). Exercises first familiarize the student with the instrument's "mechanism" before moving on to scales.[152] Then, the methods progress into drill-like exercises practiced

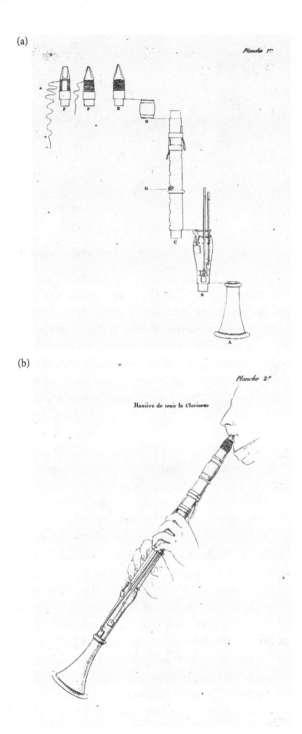

FIGURE 6.6 a and b. The Conservatory's wind and brass methods provide detailed depictions of the instruments and fingering charts. The clarinet method also shows how the instrument interfaces with the body, emphasizing the necessary role of a musician's expertise in the production of music.

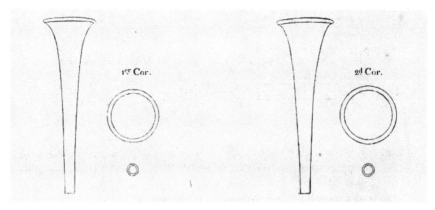

FIGURE 6.7 The horn method represents the instrument's mouthpiece to scale.

slowly at first, gradually increasing the speed, but never sacrificing precision.[153] Only after the students had learned music's basic principles, mastered harmony, and gained perfect control of their instrument's mechanism would they then move forward into expressive dimensions of performance like ornamentation and dynamics. The goal of these drills was to prepare the music student, like the engineering or military student, for any situation they may encounter in their field.[154] This hypothetical scenario would require the students to transcend mechanistic capabilities and to draw on their own creative or intuitive capacities.

Instrument technology preoccupies the first section of each method book, where the authors address the history of the instrument's progress, its persistent challenges, and how the human body could overcome or enhance its capabilities. The words *bornes* and *borné* (limits and limited) appear frequently throughout the texts, demarcating the physical capacities and boundaries of the romantic machine, one component at a time. Through these tools, the authors also delimit musicians' field of knowledge. Lefèvre concedes in his clarinet method, "It is for physicists to demonstrate the cause that, in wind instruments, produces the sound by the action of air on itself, I should not consider here its formation but in relation to the instrument mechanism for which I write."[155] Antoine Hugot and Johann Georg Wunderlich's flute method published the following year reprints Lefèvre's disclaimer verbatim.[156] The violin method cites a M. Charles's *Cours d'acoustique* for students interested in reading a detailed explanation about the physics of sound.[157] Domnich offers a more extensive footnote on the matter, acknowledging that his acoustic description of the horn's sound is "under developed," and suggesting a more classic text, a 1762 memoir written for the Academy of Sciences by Daniel Bernouilli, as well as the more recent *Traité élémentaire de physique*, by the mineralogist René Just Haüy.[158]

It is telling that the Conservatory published a horn method first, because the horn had long posed a technical and technological challenge to the French. Throughout the Revolution, musicians affiliated with the Conservatory (and before that, with the National Guard) consistently voiced a desire for improved horn manufacturing. Horn techniques were so hotly debated and quickly advanced during this period that a new Conservatory method had to be authored for the horn only five years after the first one by Frédéric Duvernoy appeared in 1802 (see Table 6.2). Heinrich Domnich's 1807 *Méthode de premier et de second cor* implies that Duvernoy's method was one of many failed attempts to improve horn technique. Duvernoy comes down in history as having promoted the *genre mixte*, a method in which hornists played primarily in the instrument's middle register in order to avoid the more difficult upper and lower ends of its range.[159] Although Duvernoy does not actually advocate this approach in his method, and in fact, explicitly suggests that students specialize in first or second horn, Domnich nevertheless accuses Duvernoy of having promoted the *genre mixte*. Transpositions attempted through this practice could cause an "inversion of the harmony... that would make no more honor to the author as to the pleasure of the listener."[160] Domnich thus subordinated performance to the composer and the listener, a priority that most of the method books emphasize.

All of the Conservatory method books present material histories of the instruments, some, like the violin and flute, trace mythic, even ancient origins. The authors then elucidate stylistic genres through such technological genealogies. Domnich, for example, begins his method with the horn's long technological history and implicates the instrument's physical capabilities in the musical genres composed for it. Only after "numerous" experiments with different materials could hornists settle on the perfect sound for the instrument,[161] yet composers still could not "leverage" it because they were unsure whether what they wrote could be executed in reality.[162] Hornists eventually realized that their techniques had only exacerbated the instrument's problems. And so the specialization in the high or low register based on the performer's embouchure represented a major technical intervention. Efforts to further improve the horn's sound involved wooden mutes and cotton plugs inspired by oboes. Hornist Anton Joseph Hampel is credited as the "genius" who brought about a "revolution" in horn technique when he "invented" hand-stopping to play the chromatic scale, consequently codifying the position in which performers held the instrument.[163] The invention of a slide horn inspired by trombone technology further advanced the instrument's capabilities by avoiding inconvenient crooks. The Conservatory had long promised the French government that it would perfect horn technology, and so it comes as no surprise that Domnich carefully interlaced Parisian musicians into this history, most notably Conservatory professors Gossec and Rodolphe.

The methods claimed that instruments' individual characters emanated from their sound and technology, which in turn constituted musical genres appropriate to the instrument. The cellist was advised to avoid inappropriate genres.[164] Each instrument provided a unique element to the orchestra and instrumental timbre itself provided a powerful means of expression.[165] Louis Adam, like the other method book authors, insists on the unique quality of each instrument's sound; so he admits, "There are certain violin traits that cannot be rendered on the piano as they are written."[166] Domnich described this in detail in the horn method, how the "serious and melancholy" quality of a low *si* on the horn cast a "darker shade" over a sad melody and a "religious character" to a harsh one. A high *ut*, to the contrary, "seemed to give a fast performance even more movement and life."[167] Flautists were to develop the instrument's naturally "sweet" sound.[168] The cello had been perfected and could not be changed "without risking making them lose their great advantage that consists in an admirable simplicity, capable of all means of expression."[169] The method books identify "genius" then, as manifesting through the manipulation of these materials, a connection that calls to mind Molard's defense of organs as marvels of engineering that provided a tool for cultivating French genius. This material emphasis renders the method books as more than guides for executing superficial "pleasurable art," they instead focus on the art's "useful" tools and the techniques that constituted music.

The method books served as a kind of advertisement for the advanced instrument technology that Sarrette had assured the government was bringing more money than ever into France. They identify technological flaws in each instrument, as much for the benefit of performers, who needed to compensate, as for composers, who needed to understand the limitations of the orchestra's component parts. The clarinet had sounds that were "ugly," "out of tune," "too high," or "too low," all "imperfections" to be "corrected."[170] The trill exercises in both the clarinet and bassoon methods indicate notes that sounded "bad" or were "impractical."[171] Ornamentation on the piano is described as a remedy for the instrument's inability to extend the vibration of a note easily achievable on a wind or string instrument.[172] The methods encourage students to choose advanced technology like the four-keyed flute.[173] The piano method offers guidance on how to evaluate a good instrument, estimating how long each note should resonate when the key is depressed.[174] Adam also carefully reviews the piano's pedal mechanisms, admitting that the notation for pedal performance had not yet caught up to instrument technology.[175] String instruments, all method authors agree, especially the violin, had already reached technological perfection.

An emphasis on instruments alone, however, would have threatened musicians with a classification as mere artisans performing rote physical tasks. Musicians had long been alienated from scientific enquiry. But technical mastery of instruments had more recently come to represent a kind of professionalization.[176] When scientists hoped to gain insight into the effects of music on living beings in 1798, they drew on the expertise of Conservatory musicians, who staged a concert in the Jardins des Plantes for two elephants, Hans and Marguerite.[177] At its most tangible, the performance was a scientific experiment.[178] The account published in the *Décade philosophique* conveyed its rigorous empirical method. The orchestra was at first placed outside the elephants' sight, just behind a hatch adjacent to their enclosure, and later, within their line of sight. The musicians cycled through a variety of genres, keys, and solo instruments, to test the animals' reactions to varied stimuli. The solo clarinet from the overture of Dalayrac's *Nina* piqued the interest of the male elephant (perhaps this was evidence of its superiority over Paisiello's version of the opera!). Both elephants were surprisingly immune to the hunting horn, which "would have had a greater impression," the *Décade* author speculated, "if it had been presented earlier" in the performance.[179] The musicians repeated the patriotic anthem "Ça ira" four times, in the keys of D and F and in various orchestrations. The musicians entered the experiment, "armed, not with scalpels and torture instruments, but with oboes, flutes and violins."[180] And so here, instruments are cast as tools of expertise capable of contributing to scientific inquiry. The musicians thus probed bodies for knowledge without harming them, a "living demonstration" never "seen in the anatomical theatres," where doctors dissected corpses lacking the vitality that might illuminate biological processes.[181] "I believe," the *Décade* author wrote, "that it is more reasonable, and above all more humane, to study the motives and the functions of life in life itself, than to go seeking them in death, or in the convulsions of a dying animal."[182] Musicians were now equated with surgeons—experts who applied knowledge, through instruments, to living bodies—a comparison that contrasted starkly with those made between the two professions only a few decades prior.

Surgery had only recently earned a reputation in France as "the most useful of medical sciences," when during the mid-eighteenth century the practical application of theory came to be viewed as the most valuable use of knowledge.[183] Surgery was considered to surpass the utility of more theoretical medicine because it immediately helped living beings.[184] When at mid-century critics emphasized the artisanal nature of surgery because it employed only manual skills,[185] surgeons retorted that they were not at all like violinists. Their response cast performing musicians as mere artisans, oblivious to the rules of their trade. As expertise increasingly emanated from a combination of theory and practice, it was also associated with the application of knowledge to instruments.[186] Instruments were keys to knowledge production in the sciences when manipulated by appropriate techniques. Surgeons distinguished themselves as "artists," because their work required a complex set of "anatomical, pathological, and clinical knowledge"[187] to guide their use of instruments. And so when around 1800 musicians appeared in scientific experiments applying their instruments to living bodies to advance scientific knowledge, they had come a long way, indeed, as professionals. The Conservatory method books capitalized on this privileging of instruments as conduits to professional knowledge and expertise, while also satisfying the national industrial agenda that saw technology and tools as a vital aspect of economic revitalization.

Where the method books transition from mechanistic to expressive elements of performance, like dynamics and ornamentation, they rely on metaphors internal to the orchestra, prescribing technique through an exclusively musical logic, a significant change from the nonmusical metaphors that had been employed to describe music-making in eighteenth-century France. Because the other methods rely so heavily on Bernardo Mengozzi's *Méthode de chant*, the orchestra itself takes on a distinctively human quality. For ornamentation, every book refers back to Mengozzi's vocal method, oftentimes reproducing his ornamentation section in its entirety. The flute method instructs flautists to study the singing method for phrasing.[188] The bassoon method republishes Mengozzi's breathing instructions, as well, "since we sing with the bassoon as with the voice."[189] Only the singing and bassoon methods include a section on instrument maintenance, in the voice method this involves some level of physiognomy and health, the bassoon method provides instructions for proper cleaning and making reeds. Authors of the cello method praise the instrument's timbre as having the quality of a human voice.[190]

Internal metaphors and comparisons permeate the method books, depicting the orchestra as a unified, autonomous, and organic whole. Instruments are used to illuminate one another's mechanisms and expressive capabilities. Domnich critiqued the *genre mixte* horn technique by pointing out how absurd it would have sounded if string players performed only in the middle register of their instruments.[191] Lefèvre explains the column of air in a clarinet by comparing it to the strings of a violin.[192] Both the flute and clarinet methods describe the tongue as the "bow of wind instruments."[193] Horn players were particularly encouraged to learn another instrument, preferably a string instrument, in order to properly train their ears, and all students were urged to familiarize themselves with the piano as a tool for theory.[194] The violin above all serves as the most frequent point of comparison; likely because it was not only familiar to most students, but also technologically "perfected"—a status to which the other instruments aspired.

The instruments extended the capabilities of the musicians' minds and bodies. The method books order lessons by key, with major modes grouped alongside relative minors, so that students could train their ears.[195] Lefèvre suggests that the clarinetist should "subordinate" their breathing "to the musical rhythm."[196] The well-formed lips that nature granted flautists were only, "the first means for obtaining beautiful sounds," "work produce[d] the rest."[197] Duvernoy's horn method encouraged performers to allow their ears to guide their performance, and a deep coordination between the hands, lips, and ears was required.[198] Domnich's horn method requires that players cultivate "powerful physical means, a perfectly organized ear, much warmth and aplomb."[199] The methods strove toward a human ideal, thus their constant reference to the singing method—this was not simply imitation. The horn, although the most challenging instrument technologically and technically, appears as perhaps the least mechanical instrument of all, because it could not depend on mere fingering or the rote digital repetition that in the mid-eighteenth century had relegated performers to the status of mere artisans. The horn method suggests that the performer begin by imagining the sound they are about to produce before attempting to execute it.[200] Baillot attributes rhythm and meter to "the movement of blood," and so it would be impossible to regulate mathematically with a *chronomètre*.[201] The Conservatory method books depict a vital system in which each component listened, breathed, moved, and even imagined relationally.

Ultimately, the method books strove to transcend mechanisms and materials, what the violin method calls "the material of expression,"[202] to achieve a more abstract "expression," an emotional, intangible articulation of the soul.[203] Conservatory director Sarrette condemned performers who were "but brilliant machines" or produced "purely mechanical work."[204] Domnich introduces musical excerpts early in his method "to develop in the student musical feeling and to avoid the distaste that could result from too uniform a study."[205] In fact, the violin method explicitly sought to replace "mechanism" with "feeling," and for the student to "make forgotten the means he uses to move."[206] The piano method alone concludes with "style," distinguishing the mechanics of style (the ability to execute music from certain time periods and composers properly) from the expression of style (the articulation of subjectivity through performance).[207]

If the violin represented the romantic machine's ideal component, then the piano served as its ideal interface[208] (see Figure 6.8). And so it is perhaps unsurprising that Adam's piano method refers frequently to other instruments. Whereas the introductory images in the other methods depict fingering, instrument parts, and posture guidance, the piano method immediately relates the keyboard not to the human body but to other instruments.[209] The piano method guides composers as much as it guides pianists. "One of the greatest advantages that we draw from the piano-forte," Adam proclaims, "is the power to execute the music of all the other instruments, and to take account of all the parts that enter into the harmony."[210] He confesses the, "great *jouissance*," he feels upon realizing the possibility of replacing "with a single instrument, an entire orchestra."[211] Adam emphasizes the piano's utility above its capacity as a solo instrument; suggesting its use for accompaniment, for

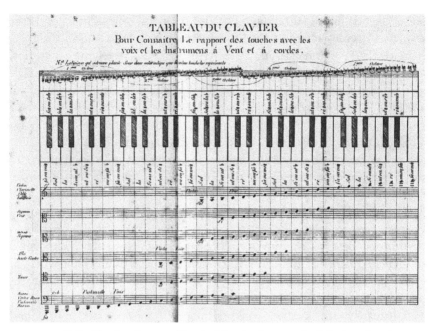

FIGURE 6.8 The first image of Louis Adam's piano method depicts the piano as a tool for the composer and an interface for the orchestra.

the study of harmony and theory, or for the composer to test out his works and "account for all the parts that would form his orchestra."[212] Framery described Adams's approach as "cool headed" and "logical."[213]

The methods subordinate music to the composer and his keyboard, fulfilling a dream that Couperin had imagined over a century earlier. It was, after all, a commission of composers assigned to supervise the books' production. The violin method demanded that performers "faithfully translate all the composer's intensions." Domnich's horn method insisted that the student "impose on himself the law of strictly rendering articulations as they are indicated."[214] And although they warned against becoming mere "copyists"[215]—plagiarism was, by now, a *faux pas*, even in performance!—Baillot, like the composers in Chapter 3 who petitioned the revolutionary government, critiqued musical performances that "distort[ed]" the "productions of genius."[216] Indeed, the method books seem to be a model of citation practice, noting the source of every excerpt.

The "genius of performance" was in "making pass into the soul of the listener the feeling that the composer had in his."[217] The performer was a conduit. The communion of the listener and composer's souls through the performer as medium represented the supreme transcendence from mechanism to expression. When achieved, the violin, for example, was "no longer an instrument," Baillot claimed, but "a sonorous soul."[218] "Each composer possesses a seal," Baillot explains, "that he imprints on all his works, a style that is his own, that holds to his manner of feeling."[219] Sarrette suggests in prefatory material to the piano method that only the study of "good music" by "the masters" could facilitate a transition from mechanism to expression.[220] And so the cultural agenda of the library and museum described in the previous chapter emerges in the method books via mechanical, scientific means.

The method books harmonize the cultural and industrial agendas that faced the Conservatory around 1800, and more generally, that pulled music in two directions as a kind of national, public property. It would be too easy, and incorrect, to cast the method books—so influential throughout nineteenth century Europe—as simply another element of political propaganda aimed to establish a distinctively French musical style (much to Lesueur's chagrin). The methods extol the music of Haydn, Mozart, Gluck, and other foreign composers.[221] The violin method encourages students to study their neighbors' music for "new sources of knowledge" and then to "return to enrich [one's own] country." "Welcome the foreign," it recommends, "with the sentiment of fraternity." [222] Becoming an accomplished French performer did not preclude appreciation of other nations' achievements, and *"Voilà"* the "metaphysics" of music, the violin method resolves.[223]

The Conservatory did not intend only to create a unique musical style, it sought to imperialize Europe's. No wonder, then, that Framery championed the Italian-ness of the singing method.[224] Science-based industry offered one clear path toward this Napoleonic agenda. Perhaps the English had "improved" the piano, but Adam celebrates that "The French could boast of having brought it to its high degree of perfection."[225] The Conservatory supported French competition with British innovation and industry, while also advancing the imperial cultural agenda described in the previous chapter. Sarrette could claim the advancement of instrument technology and its contribution to France's industrial and commercial success because the Conservatory enjoyed a powerful say in what constituted progress, particularly through its representation in the National Institute and Industrial Expositions.[226]

The Conservatory effectively reconciled, even exploited these revolutionary cultural and industrial agendas to attain a new form of corporate privilege, long after such privileges had been abolished in favor of individual rights. As part of a set of cultural and educational institutions dedicated to training French professionals, the method books contributed to an economic goal. Yet they also represented something more: a monopoly, precisely the advantage that inventors' property laws were designed to prevent. Although revolutionary legislators set the 1791 laws on intellectual property in place to avoid the nepotism of Old Regime privileges, by 1796 the main arbiter of methods—the National Institute—was deeply enmeshed with the Conservatory inspectors who ran its music section. The Conservatory held significant influence over which instruments and methods would circulate to the general public, a power that intersected (some might even say an interest that conflicted) with its own initiative to create a uniform system of music methods for France. When the National Institute received a significant musical submission for review, they forwarded it directly to the Conservatory, which the Institute considered the "natural judge of all that concerns the theory and practice of the art."[227] With three of the Conservatory's own inspectors, Gossec, Méhul, and Grétry, running the music section of the Institute, it is hard to imagine how the Conservatory's own set of method books could have failed review at the National Institute.

The Conservatory fulfilled a dual mission, one utilitarian, the other, idealistic; it both trained future musicians and guided the progress of the art itself.[228] With the Institute's approbation, the Conservatory could rely on its standardized method to dominate the industry. When Framery gave his report on the Conservatory's method books to the Institute, he concluded that the books "would suffice to demonstrate the utility" of the Conservatory and to "silence its detractors." [229]

Postlude: A "Detractor" Breaks His "Silence"

From around 1800 to 1803, a series of pamphlets criticizing the Conservatory's dominance, especially Sarrette, emboldened Durieu, the violinist who had desperately sought rewards for his method book, to go public with his frustrations. In a pamphlet, he urged the Conservatory to remember that while it may possess talent, talent still existed outside its walls. As a lone violinist taking recourse against a powerful institution through a pamphlet, his case strikingly resembles that of Travenol recounted in Chapter 1. Durieu reprinted his communications with the Committee on Public Instruction described above alongside letters he apparently exchanged with Gossec from 1789 to 1792. Durieu raised a disturbing accusation in his publication—that the Conservatory had pirated parts of the *Principes élémentaires* from his own method. Durieu claimed that Gossec had dealt in "the vile trade of plagiarism."[230]

The claim gained little traction in part because, from its very inception, the Conservatory considered the musical works it acquired as national property unless otherwise noted; Baillot's violin method was the only Conservatory method book to indicate on its title page that it remained the property of its editors.[231] The legal question, of course, would have been simply whether Gossec acquired Durieu's work through the proper formalities. (It seemed, from the reprinted letters, that he had not.) Durieu committed a telling slippage in his pamphlet, however, conflating what belonged to the nation, to the Conservatory, and to individuals. "I admit," he conceded, "that Agus's works are indeed Sarrette's property."[232] Sarrette had apparently purchased Agus's solfege exercises, as Durieu puts it, in *"bon assignats."* Did that make the method the property of the nation, of the Conservatory, or of Sarrette personally? To Durieu, and to many others, the legality of the question hardly mattered. The nation, the Conservatory, and its members were now as one. "It is very strange, not to say indecent," Durieu concluded, "that the Conservatory dares to assume the *privilège* of deciding the talents and the fate of those who possess them. . . But from where," he asks, exasperated, "comes this thirst to reign?"

Conclusion: Privilege by Any Other Name

Music under the Old Regime was quite literally privileged in both a historical and contemporary sense of the word. Because musical production required permission, legally or socially advantaged groups enjoyed greater access to music, a reality made clear in Chapter 1. Bernard Sarrette referred to this particular state of affairs when he recalled music's "effeminate" days before the Revolution, when it circulated primarily across leisurely, elite spaces like salons, churches, and even Masonic lodges. Lodges, however, as shown in Chapter 2, pursued an Enlightenment project to ostensibly deprivilege music along with the other arts and sciences according to the tenets of secular humanism. This exclusive but publicly minded group of men and women hoped to enrich culture apart from monarchical sovereignty in order to improve society as a whole.

A wider audience indeed gained access to music along with the emergence of modern democracies. (And I state this with no intention of championing music's "power" nor its universality.) Sarrette drew on a widespread revolutionary rhetoric about the freedom of art when he promised that the Conservatory would circulate music throughout France as a medium for citizens' edification (see Chapter 4). He also, espoused the Revolution's mission to construct a new art world with Paris at its center (see Chapter 5). These two missions stemmed from codependent ideologies to cultivate "good" music for the purposes of both art and leisure in a postrevolutionary, regenerated French society.[1] Music would occupy workers in their leisure time, a social practice soon adopted in the form of workers' choirs throughout industrialized Europe. And it would also be monumentalized as "masterpieces" of "genius," a practice adopted in concert halls across nineteenth-century Europe and the United States, and soon the world over. This twin endeavor demanded the cultivation of music among a select group of knowledgeable experts and practitioners secured in their authority through a reliable infrastructure of laws, policies, and institutions. This restricted echelon of production extended to publishers and instrument builders who enjoyed access to these new legal mechanisms.

While the revolutionary rhetoric of music as a universal, educational tool seemed to continue Enlightenment projects concerned with public utility and social good, the protectionism of academies lurked behind this patriotic veneer. Musicians understandably wanted to maintain the professionalization that they had so painstakingly established. Their institutionalized status as artists, savants, and even geniuses within the Conservatory, the National Institute, and other bureaucratic bodies, reinforced their authority. Men credentialed in performance and composition would curate music before it ever reached listeners. They would prune and process the art behind the Conservatory's walls and then, after sending their work through regulative bodies such as the Advisory Board for Arts and Trades or the National Institute, music would circulate to the public along with clear instructions (method books) and profitable tools (instruments). In return for the nation's support, the Conservatory would provide a legitimatizing cultural heritage and contribute to a lucrative commercial industry, both intended to rival foreign competitors. Such regulation was not limited to music. In France, sectors like agriculture or wine, for example, were submitted to a system of production designed to ensure consistency and quality. And so it was not long before the Conservatory's increasing dominance attracted accusations of cronyism. We see in Chapter 6 that Louis Antoine Durieu charged the Conservatory musicians with an even worse offense—taking "privileges." Similar complaints about the Conservatory would persist into the early twentieth century among the likes of Claude Debussy and Maurice Ravel; the Conservatory seemed to own French music.

It was not simply commodification that took place when music became an objective form of property during the Revolution. A modern property regime, like capitalism, required a certain ethics in order to take root. Proprietorship served as a seemingly just bedrock for a socio-political structure rooted in possession. The most fundamental suffrage required property. Without it, personhood ceased and slipped into the violent realm of servitude and slavery. Even as property masquerades as an equalizing force in foundation documents of the modern West, as Nicolas-Marie Dalayrac proclaimed in his speech in Chapter 3, there was nothing "natural" about the expensive formalities required to obtain and maintain it. These proprietary mechanisms correlate to persistent legacies—the privilege registers from Chapter 1 and manuscripts collected by the Conservatory in Chapter 4 contain many of the lasting names of music history. Even though the monarchy and church returned to power in France after the Revolution, property remained a defining feature of the nation's civil code that endures to this day. Property, according to French anarchist Pierre Proudhon, was simply privilege by a different name; by the mid-nineteenth century, he described it "as a power of exclusion" and "invasion."[2]

The modern property regime excludes and imperializes through seemingly neutral means. It simply required the delineation and objectification of music as a legal entity. Modern professional musicianship crystallized within a system of possession at the service of liberal individuals who naturalized their supremacy by using property to replace a *passé* Old Regime term— *privilège*. The French Revolution created a property infrastructure favorable to composers, their works, and the nation, all three of which were centered in the nineteenth-century discourses and practices later folded into music historiography. Most importantly, revolutionaries constructed lasting institutions that would perpetuate these values. By legally privileging composers (Chapter 3), revising the social meaning of scores (Chapter 5), authoring a comprehensive set of training methods to dominate the field (Chapter 6), and establishing a national regulative infrastructure for music (Chapters 3 through 6), France adopted an exclusive model of musical production that soon imperialized the professional and epistemic practices of European, and eventually, global "Classical" music.[3]

APPENDIX

Undated letter from composers about property rights, altering the position put forth in an earlier petition. From BHVP, MS 772, fol. 1, doc. 6. Original orthography and diacritics retained.

Les compositeurs ci dessous dénommés, ayant été convoquer pour délibérer sur une acte signé par quelques uns de leurs collégues et par lequel ceux ci reconnaitroient aux marchands de musique le double droit:

1. De denaturer, décomposer et multiplier sous toutes les formes, et sous l'autorisation des auteurs les ouvrages dont ils ont fait l'acquisition.
2. De graver et débiter, comme leurs propriétés tous les ouvrages originairement publiés à l'étranger.

Les Signataires déclarent, quant au premier article, qu'ils le regardent comme attentatoire à leurs intérêts et à leur réputation.

à leurs intérêts, parce que cette faculté de dénaturer, décomposer leurs productions et de présenter au public le même œuvres sous une multitude de formes différents, ne serait autre que celle de faire trente ou quarante ouvrages d'un seul : faculté que ne pourraient exercer les éditeurs sans restreindre dans les Bourses les plus étroites et le Génie musical, et l'industrie qui alimente ceux qui le cultivent.

à leurs réputations, parce que dénaturer un ouvrage quelconque c'est le Défigurer : parce que l'opinion publique égaré par les accessoires dont ces métamorphoser sont accompagnées ne peut plus distinguer les originaux des Copies informes quils produisent et finit pour imputer à la négligence en à la sterilité des auteurs l'altération et la répétition fatigante de leurs idées dont rependant les imitateurs sont tous responsables.

Parcqu'enfin ce droit de métamorphoser à volonté les productions musicales serait une arme cruelle dont la malveillance et la cupidité pourraient incessant abuser contre les auteurs en séquestraient leurs originaux pour ne mettre en évidence que des [?] de mauvaiser copies et des caricatures de leurs ouvrages.

En conséquence les signataires déclarent pour ce qui les concerne soit collectivement soit individuellement.

1. Que lorsquils cèdent un œuvre de musique, ils n'entendent céder que la forme actuelle sont laquelle cet œuvre est rédigé, et quils tiennent pour abusif tout changement qu'on lui serait subir sans leurs participation et à moins d'une stipulation précise motivée dans l'acte de vente.
2. Que ces mots, <u>en toute propriété</u>, qui se trouvent ordinairement dans ces actes de vents ne doivent et ni peuvent être interpréter que comme une garantie pure et simple, accordée à l'acquérent contre les usurpations possibles du vendeur ; garantie que la raison et l'équité disent devon être réciproque.

Quant au droit prétendu par les marchands de musique sur les ouvrages venant de l'étranger :

Sans approfondir la nature de ce Droit qui n'est autre que celui de représailles exploitée au détriment des auteurs de tous les pays, les signataires pensent qu'au moins ne peut il s'éxercer, qil en l'absence de tout propriété naturelle ou légale, et que la présence de pareilles propriétés assénait radicalement aux yeux de la délicatesse, de la justice et du bon sens toute autre prétention quelconque.

Ceux des auteurs soussignés dont les noms se trouvent dans le premier acte ci dessus mentionné déclarent ne s'être préter à cette démarche que par precipitation de confiance et sans en prevoir les suittes ; mais que ce n'est qu'après une mûre délibération qu'ils ont revêtu la présente de leurs signatures. Grétry, Cherubini, Eler, Berton, Quaisain, P. Rode, Méhul, Gaveaux, Persuis, Bruni, Martini, Fay, Plantade, Lebrun, H. Jadin, Dalayrac

NOTES

Preface

1. George Lipsitz, *The Possessive Investment in Whiteness: How White People Profit from Identity Politics*, Twentieth Anniversary Edition (Philadelphia: Temple University Press, 2018), viii.

Introduction

1. *Loi relative aux découvertes utiles et aux moyens d'en assurer la propriété à ceux qui seront reconnus en être les auteurs*, January 7, 1791.

2. David Wills, *Killing Times: The Temporal Technology of the Death Penalty* (New York: Fordham University Press, 2019), 68.

3. Tobias Schmidt, "Adresse au Comité d'Agriculture et de Commerce de l'Assemblée nationale de France," January 3, 1791, F-Pan F[17] 1136.

4. Translation in Laure Murat, *The Man Who Thought He Was Napoleon: Toward a Political History of Madness* (Chicago: University of Chicago Press, 2015), 30.

5. For an overview of the "around 1800" discourse, see Emily Dolan, "Introduction," *The Orchestral Revolution: Haydn and the Technologies of Timbre* (Cambridge: Cambridge University Press, 2012); and for one origin of this scholarly conversation, see Lydia Goehr, *The Imaginary Museum of Musical Works: An Essay in the Philosophy of Music* (1992; repr., New York: Oxford University Press, 2007).

6. On the separation of public from private property, see Rafe Blaufarb, *The Great Demarcation: The French Revolution and the Invention of Modern Property* (New York: Oxford University Press, 2016), 119–47.

7. Jeff Horn, "The Privilege of Liberty: Challenging the Society of Orders," *Proceedings of the Western Society for French History* 35 (2007): 171.

8. *Le dictionnaire de l'Académie française*, Vol. 2 (1694), accessed through the ARTFL Project *Dictionnaires d'autrefois* October 11, 2019. "Faculté accordée à un particulier, ou à une Communauté de faire quelque chose à l'exclusion de tous autres."

9. *Le dictionnaire de l'Académie française*, Vol. 2 (1694). "Se dit aussi de toutes sortes de droits, de prérogatives, d'avantages attachez aux charges, aux emplois, aux conditions, aux estats, &c."

10. Jeff Horn shows the many economic opportunities afforded by privilege in the eighteenth century. *Economic Development in Early Modern France: The Privilege of Liberty, 1650–1820* (Cambridge: Cambridge University Press, 2015).

11. Blaufarb, *The Great Demarcation*, 7.

12. *Le dictionnaire de l'Académie française*, Vol. 2 (1694). "Le droit, le titre par lequel une chose appartient en propre à quelqu'un."

13. Blaufarb, *The Great Demarcation*, 4.

14. *Le dictionnaire de l'Académie française* (1762), accessed through the ARTFL *Dictionnaires d'autrefois* October 11, 2019. "Le propriétaire d' une maison peut expulser le locataire, en vertu du privilège des Bourgeois." "Bourgeois," a term that signals a social category, was in eighteenth-century Paris legally defined by residency and taxes. David Garrioch, *The Making of Revolutionary Paris* (Berkeley: University of California Press, 2002), 103.

15. Blaufarb, *The Great Demarcation*, 63. Blaufarb offers a much more nuanced explanation of this process, simplified here for practical, disciplinary reasons.

16. *Dictionnaire critique de la langue Française* (1789), accessed through the ARTFL *Dictionnaires d'autrefois* October 11, 2019. "PRIVILÉGIÉ, qui a un privilège. Marchand *privilégié*: persone *privilégiée* (n°. 1°.) Créancier *privilégié* (n°. 4°.) Il est *privilégié* dans cette maison (n°. 6°.)"

17. *Le dictionnaire de l'Académie française* (1798), accessed through the ARTFL *Dictionnaires d'autrefois* October 11, 2019. "Privilege, signifie aussi quelquefois la liberté qu'on a, ou qu'on se donne de faire des choses que d'autres n'oseroient faire."

18. Michael P. Fitzsimmons, *The Night the Old Regime Ended: August 4, 1789, and the French Revolution* (University Park: Pennsylvania State University, 2002), and Blaufarb, *The Great Demarcation*.

19. Michael P. Fitzsimmons, *The Place of Words: The Académie Française and Its Dictionary during an Age of Revolution* (Oxford: Oxford University Press, 2019), 130.

20. Blaufarb, *The Great Demarcation*, xiii.

21. On collective aristocratic patronage, see David Hennebelle, *De Lully à Mozart: Aristocratie, musique et musiciens à Paris (XVIIe–XVIIIe siècles)* (Seyssel: Champ Vallon, 2009).

22. Howard S. Becker, *Art Worlds*, 25th Anniversary Edition (1982; repr., Berkeley: University of California Press, 2008).

23. Toby Gelfand, *Professionalizing Modern Medicine: Paris Surgeons and Medical Science and Institutions in the Eighteenth Century* (Westport, CT: Greenwood Press, 1980); Antoine Picon, *L'invention de l'ingénieur moderne: L'École des ponts et chaussées, 1747–1851* (Paris: Presses de l'École Nationale des Ponts et Chaussées, 1992); Harrison C. and Cynthia A. White, *Canvases and Careers: Institutional Change in the French Painting World* (1965; repr., Chicago: University of Chicago Press, 1993); Rafe Blaufarb, *The French Army, 1750–1820: Careers, Talent, Merit* (Manchester: Manchester University Press, 2002); Gregory S. Brown, A *Field of Honor: Writers, Court Culture, and Public Theatre in French Literary Life from Racine to Revolution* (New York: Columbia University Press, 2002); Pierre Baron, "Dental Practice in Paris," in *Dental Practice in Europe at the End of the Eighteenth*

Century, ed. Christine Hillam, Clio Medical Series (Amsterdam and New York: Rodopi, 2003), 113–62; Jonathan Simon, *Chemistry, Pharmacy, and Revolution in France, 1777–1809* (Burlington, VT: Ashgate, 2005); Gregory S. Brown, *Literary Sociability and Literary Property in France, 1775–1793: Beaumarchais, the Société des Auteurs Dramatiques, and the Comédie Française* (Aldershot, England: Ashgate, 2006); Sean Takats, *The Expert Cook in Enlightenment France* (Baltimore: Johns Hopkins University Press, 2011); Colin Jones, "Chapter 3: Cometh the Dentist," in *The Smile Revolution in Eighteenth-Century Paris* (Oxford: Oxford University Press, 2014).

24. See, for example, William Weber, ed., *The Musician as Entrepreneur, 1700–1914: Managers, Charlatans, and Idealists* (Bloomington: Indiana University Press, 2004), and Walter Salmen, ed., *The Social Status of the Professional Musician from the Middle Ages to the 19th Century*, Sociology of Music, no. 1 (New York: Pendragon Press, 1983).

25. On "epistemic" practices in studies of expertise, see Ann Laura Stoler, *Along the Archival Grain: Epistemic Anxieties and Colonial Common Sense* (Princeton, NJ: Princeton University Press, 2009), 38.

26. See, for example, Glenda Goodman, *Cultivated by Hand: Amateur Musicians in the Early American Republic*, New Cultural History of Music Series (New York: Oxford University Press, 2020).

27. Bonnie Smith, *The Gender of History: Men, Women, and Historical Practice* (Cambridge and London: Harvard University Press, 1998).

28. Paola Bertucci, *Artisanal Enlightenment: Science and the Mechanical Arts in Old Regime France* (New Haven: Yale University Press, 2017).

29. Bruno Belhoste, *Paris Savant: Capital of Science in the Age of Enlightenment*, trans. Susan Emanuel (New York: Oxford University Press, 2018).

30. Fitzsimmons, *The Night the Old Regime Ended*.

31. Timothy Tackett, *Becoming a Revolutionary: The Deputies of the French National Assembly and the Emergence of a Revolutionary Culture (1789–1790)* (University Park: Pennsylvania State University Press, 1996).

32. Despite the common orthography of the name Sieyes including a grave accent on the second *e* ("Sieyès"), he most commonly spelled his name unaccented. For a detailed historical survey of the orthography, see William H. Sewell, *A Rhetoric of Bourgeois Revolution: The Abbé Sieyes and "What Is the Third Estate?"* (Durham and London: Duke University Press, 1994), 2n2. Sewell's orthography is adopted throughout this book.

33. Sewell, *A Rhetoric of Bourgeois Revolution*, 41.

34. Olivia Bloechl, *Opera and the Political Imaginary in Old Regime France* (Chicago: University of Chicago Press, 2017), 203.

35. Tackett, *Becoming a Revolutionary*, 169–75.

36. Blaufarb, *The Great Demarcation*, 48–52; William Doyle, *The Oxford History of the French Revolution*, 2nd edition (Oxford: Oxford University Press, 2002), 116–18; and Fitzsimmons, *The Night the Old Regime Ended*.

37. Blaufarb, *The Great Demarcation*, xiv. Blaufarb "[carefully distinguishes] between the tenurial system of property-*holding* that prevailed before 1789 and the ideal of property-*ownership* that triumphed thereafter."

38. Historians disagree regarding how and the extent to which privileges were transferrable. Blaufarb specifies that, "Since they usually adhered to individuals, privileges could not be sold, inherited, or used as collateral for loans like real estate. In a sense, they

were personal property in public power" (*The Great Demarcation*, 53). Gail Bossenga, however, argues that the "commodification of privileges" over the course of the eighteenth century rendered privileges into "marketable . . . 'things' that could be transferred, possessed, owned, and sold." See Bossenga's "Estates, Orders, and Corps," in *The Oxford Handbook of the Ancien Régime*, ed. William Doyle (New York: Oxford University Press, 2012), 152. It is certainly true that they could be leased or subcontracted, as I discuss in the case of music in Chapter 1.

39. Blaufarb, *The Great Demarcation*, 52–3: "Privileges conveyed a bewildering variety of capacities, powers, rights, prerogatives, exemptions, and functions. Because of this, they operated like private property in public power associated with *seigneuries* and venal office. . . . By abolishing them, the revolutionaries were removing public power from the most personal property of all—the individual self. Even though it is not technically correct to consider privilege as a form of property, it resembled privately held public power very closely."

40. "Declaration of the Rights of Man," *The Avalon Project: Documents in Law, History and Diplomacy* (New Haven, CT: Lillian Goldman Law Library, 2008), accessed January 28, 2019, http://avalon.law.yale.edu/18th_century/rightsof.asp.

41. Blaufarb, *The Great Demarcation*, 145.

42. The French took a law-centered approach to preservation while the Americans created a rights-centered system. Dan Edelstein, *On the Spirit of Rights* (Chicago: University of Chicago Press, 2019), 2–4, 95–6, 103, and 185–6.

43. On French music culture as representational of the monarchy's power, see T. C. W. Blanning, *The Culture of Power and the Power of Culture: Old Regime Europe, 1660–1789* (Oxford: Oxford University Press, 2002); and Richard Taruskin, *Music in the Seventeenth and Eighteenth Centuries*, in *Oxford History of Western Music* (Oxford: Oxford University Press, 2005), 3:86.

44. Roger Chartier, *The Cultural Origins of the French Revolution*, trans. Lydia G. Cochrane (Durham, NC: Duke University Press, 1991), xiii.

45. Aulard even wrote a manual to teach the French how to be French citizens: *Élements d'instruction civique; suivies des résumés et questionnaires* (Paris: Edouard Cornely, 1902).

46. See "Michel Brenet [(Antoinette Christine) Marie Bobillier]," *Grove Music Online*.

47. Jann Pasler, *Composing the Citizen: Music as Public Utility in Third Republic France* (Berkeley: University of California Press, 2009).

48. Constant Pierre, *Le magasin de musique à l'usage des fêtes nationales et du Conservatoire* (Paris: Fischbacher, 1895); *Bernard Sarrette et les origines du Conservatoire national de musique et de déclamation* (Paris: Delalain frères, 1895); *Musique des fêtes et cérémonies de la Révolution française; œuvres de Gossec, Cherubini, Lesueur, Méhul, Catel, etc.* (Paris: Imprimerie Nationale, 1899); *Le Conservatoire national de musique et de déclamation: documents historiques et administratifs* (Paris: Imprimerie Nationale, 1900); and *Les hymnes et chansons de la Révolution: aperçu général et catalogue avec notices historiques, analytiques et bibliographiques* (Paris: Imprimerie Nationale, 1904).

49. Chartier, *Cultural Origins of the French Revolution*, xiv.

50. Chartier, *Cultural Origins of the French Revolution*, xv.

51. Chartier, *Cultural Origins of the French Revolution*, xvi.

52. Paul Hanson, *Contesting the French Revolution* (Chester, UK, and Malden, MA: Wiley-Blackwell, 2009), 7. See Furet's *Interpreting the French Revolution*, trans. Elborg Forster (Cambridge: Cambridge University Press, 1981).

53. I am grateful to Rafe Blaufarb for pointing out this inconsistency. See François Furet, *Marx and the French Revolution*, trans. Deborah Kan Furet (Chicago: University of Chicago Press, 1988).

54. Lynn Hunt, *Politics, Culture, and Class*, 20th Anniversary Edition (1984; repr., Berkeley: University of California Press, 2004).

55. On the genealogy of recent cultural approaches to the Revolution, see Sophia Rosenfeld, "The French Revolution in Cultural History," *Journal of Social History* 52, no. 3 (2019): 555–65.

56. Edited volumes that proliferated during the bicentennial of the Revolution in 1989 reveal that music certainly contributed to the budding political culture of the Revolution, even if it contributed less so to the repertoires that typically interest music historians. Jean-Rémy Julien and Jean-Claude Klein, *Orphée phrygien: les musiques de la Révolution* (Paris: Éditions du May, 1989); Jean-Rémy Julien and Jean Mongrédien, *Le tambour et la harpe: œuvres, pratiques et manifestations musicales sous la Révolution, 1788–1800* (Paris: Éditions du May, 1991); and Malcom Boyd, *Music and the French Revolution* (Cambridge and New York: Cambridge University Press, 1992).

57. Laura Mason, *Singing the French Revolution* (Ithaca: Cornell University Press, 1996).

58. James H. Johnson, *Listening in Paris: A Cultural History* (Berkeley: University of California Press, 1995).

59. Carl Dahlhaus, *Die Musik des 18. Jahrhunderts* (Laaber: Laaber-Verlag, 1985), 365.

60. See Julia Doe's nuanced summation of this correction in *The Comedians of the King: Opéra Comique and the Bourbon Monarchy on the Eve of Revolution* (Chicago: University of Chicago Press, 2021), 159–96.

61. Michael Fend, "The Problem of the French Revolution in Music Historiography and History," in *Musicology and Sister Disciplines: Past, Present, Future: Proceedings of the 16th International Congress of the International Musicological Society, London, 1997*, ed. D. C. Greer, J. King, and I. Rumbold (New York: Oxford University Press, 2000), 239–50.

62. For examples, see, Jacques Attali, *Noise: The Political Economy of Music*, trans. Brian Massumi, Theory and History of Literature 16 (1985; repr., Minneapolis and London: University of Minnesota Press, 2003); Larry Shiner, *The Invention of Art: A Cultural History* (Chicago: University of Chicago Press, 2001); and Tim Blanning, *The Triumph of Music: The Rise of Composers, Musicians, and Their Art* (Cambridge, MA: Belknap Press of Harvard University Press, 2008).

63. The reference to "Frenchified trash" is attributed to Joseph Haydn, see H. C. Robbins Landon, *The Collected Correspondence and London Notebooks of Joseph Haydn* (London: Barrie and Rockliff, 1959), 197. Although Haydn was referring specifically to the overt use of imitative aesthetics, the simplicity and volume of French music from the 1790s took on a negative aesthetic reputation during the nineteenth century.

64. Notably, Matthew Gelbart, *The Invention of Folk Music and Art Music: Emerging Categories from Ossian to Wagner* (Cambridge: Cambridge University Press, 2007); David Gramit, *Cultivating Music: The Aspirations, Interests, and Limits of German Musical Culture, 1770–1848* (Berkeley: University of California Press, 2002); and Tia DeNora, *Beethoven*

and the Construction of Genius: Musical Politics in Vienna, 1792–1803 (Berkeley: University of California Press, 1997).

65. Loren Kajikawa, "The Possessive Investment in Classical Music: Confronting Legacies of White Supremacy in U.S. Schools and Departments of Music," in *Seeing Race Again: Countering Colorblindness across the Disciplines*, ed. Kimberlé Williams Crenshaw, et al. (Berkeley: University of California Press, 2019), 155–74.

66. For one strand of this turn, see James Q. Davies, *Romantic Anatomies of Performance* (Berkeley: University of California Press, 2014), 6.

67. Goehr, *The Imaginary Museum of Musical Works*, 176–204 and 205–42.

68. On composer- and work-centered production, see Michael Talbot, "The Work-Concept and Composer-Centredness," in *The Musical Work: Reality or Invention?*, ed. Michael Talbot, Liverpool Music Symposium I (Liverpool: Liverpool University Press, 2000), 168–86.

69. An example of this overstatement of political intentions in opera repertory can be found in Emmet Kennedy, et al. *Theatre, Opera, and Audiences in Revolution Paris: Analysis and Repertory* (Westport, CT: Greenwood Press, 1996).

70. In addition to Doe, *Comedians of the King*, see M. Elizabeth C. Bartlet, *Étienne-Nicolas Méhul and Opera: Source and Archival Studies of Lyric Theatre during the French Revolution, Consulate, and Empire* (Heilbronn, Germany: Edition Lucie Galland, 1999); David Charlton, *Grétry and the Growth of Opéra-comique* (Cambridge: Cambridge University Press, 1986) and *Opera in the Age of Rousseau*, Cambridge Studies in Opera (Cambridge: Cambridge University Press, 2013); Victoria Johnson, *Backstage at the Revolution: How the Royal Paris Opera Survived the End of the Old Regime* (Chicago: University of Chicago Press, 2008); Solveig Serre, *L'opéra de Paris (1749–1790): politique culturelle au temps des Lumières* (Paris: CNRS Éditions, 2011); and Mark Darlow, *Staging the French Revolution: Cultural Politics and the Paris Opéra, 1789–1794*, New Cultural History of Music Series (New York: Oxford University Press, 2012).

71. Julia Doe, "Two Hunters, A Milkmaid, and the French 'Revolutionary' Canon," *Eighteenth-Century Music* 15, no. 2 (2018): 177–205.

72. Doe, "Epilogue: The Foundation of a 'People's' Art," in *Comedians of the King*, 197–216.

73. This is particularly true of the work of Patrick Taïeb, "Le Concert des Amateurs de la rue de Cléry en l'an VIII (1799–1800), ou la resurgence d'un établissement 'dont la France s'onorait avant la Révolution,'" in *Les sociétés de musique en Europe, 1700–1920: structures, pratiques musicales et sociabilité*, ed. Hans Erich Bödeker and Patrice Veit (Berlin: Berliner Wissenschafts-Verlag, 2005); "L'exploitation commerciale du concert public en l'an V (1797): l'exemple de Charles Barnabé Sageret," *Organisateurs et organisations du concert en Europe (1700–1920)*, ed. Hans Erich Bödeker, Patrice Veit, and Michael Werner (Berlin: Berliner Wissenschafts-Verlag, 2006); and "Suzette au concert Feydeau (1797) ou la vertu déconcertée," *Le concert et son public: mutations de la vie musicale en Europe de 1780 à 1914 (France, Allemagne, Angleterre)*, ed. Hans Erich Bödeker, Patrice Veit, and Michael Werner (Paris: Éditions de la maison des sciences de l'homme, 2002), 403–25; and Alexandre Dratwicki, *Un nouveau commerce de la virtuosité: émancipation et métamorphoses de la musique concertante au sein des institutions musicales parisiennes (1780–1830)* (Lyon: Symétrie, 2006).

74. Cited here throughout Chapters 4 through 6.

75. Jean Mongrédien, *La musique en France des lumières au romantisme (1789–1830)* (Paris: Flammarion, 1986).

76. On *archivistique* and the ways that French archives were both a means of accounting and managing as well as dictating future practices, see Pauline Lemaigre-Gaffier, *Administrer les menus plaisirs du roi: la cour, l'état et les spectacles dans la France des Lumières* (Céyzerieu: Champ Vallon, 2016), 157–82.

77. Michel De Certeau explained harshly, "The label 'research' cannot be applied to a study that purely and simply adopts former classifications, which sticks to the limits posed, for example, by series H in the National Archives, and which therefore does not define its own field of study." *The Writing of History*, trans. Tom Conley (New York: Columbia University Press, 1988), 74–5.

78. Rebecca Dowd Geoffroy-Schwinden, "Music, Copyright, and Intellectual Property during the French Revolution: A Newly Discovered Letter from André-Ernest-Modeste Grétry," *Transposition* [Online], 7 (2018), online since September 15, 2018, connection on November 15, 2019. http://journals.openedition.org/transposition/2057; doi: 10.4000/transposition.2057.

79. William H. Sewell Jr., "Connecting Capitalism to the French Revolution: The Parisian Promenade and the Origins of Civic Equality in Eighteenth-Century France," *Critical Historical Studies* 1, no. 1 (Spring 2014): 5–46.

80. Rebecca Spang, *Stuff and Money in the Time of the French Revolution* (Cambridge, MA: Harvard University Press, 2015).

81. Katie L. Jarvis, "Exacting Change: Money, Market Women, and the Crumbling Corporate World in the French Revolution," *Journal of Social History* 51, no. 4 (Summer 2018): 839, and *Politics in the Marketplace: Work, Gender, and Citizenship in Revolutionary France* (New York: Oxford University Press, 2019).

82. Blaufarb, *The Great Demarcation*.

83. Paul Cheney, Review of *The Great Demarcation*, *History: Reviews of New Books* 45, no. 3 (May 2017): 71.

84. Edelstein, *On the Spirit of Rights*, 76 and 79.

85. Carla Hesse, *Publishing and Cultural Politics in Revolutionary Paris, 1789–1810*, Studies on the History and Society of Culture 12 (Berkeley: University of California Press, 1991).

86. Katie Scott, *Becoming Property: Art, Theory, and Law in Early Modern France* (New Haven: Yale University Press, 2018), 35 and 16.

87. This quote is from Spang's title, *Stuff and Money in the Time of the French Revolution*.

88. Edelstein shows a spike in usage of "natural rights" in France from the 1750s to the 1780s and credits this increase to the spread of physiocratic ideas, particularly in salons, *On the Spirit of Rights*, 61–85.

89. Kenneth Loiselle, *Brotherly Love: Freemasonry and Male Friendship in Enlightenment France* (Ithaca: Cornell University Press, 2014).

90. A number of scholars consider the Revolution a kind of triumphant turning point for music and musicians. For examples, see Attali, *Noise*; Shiner, *The Invention of Art*; and Blanning, *The Triumph of Music*.

91. Here I draw directly on Jonathan Sterne's approach of, "offering a history of the *possibility* of" a phenomenon. In this case, "Romanticism." *The Audible Past: Cultural Origins of Sound Reproduction* (Durham, NC: Duke University Press, 2003).

Chapter 1

1. "Jean-Baptiste Lulli fils rend plainte contre l'imprimeur Ballard," F-Pan Y.12,335, trans. in Graham Sadler and Caroline Wood, eds., *French Baroque Opera: A Reader*, 2nd edition (Oxon and New York: Routledge, 2017), 9. The opening anecdote here comes from this document.

2. *Proserpine* was a *tragédie en musique*, the five-act genre of French opera that Lully cultivated in France at the end of the seventeenth century.

3. On Jean-Baptiste Lully's ennoblement in 1681, see Jérôme La Gorce, *Jean-Baptiste Lully* (Paris: Fayard, 2002), 260, and 284–5. See also, James P. Fairleigh, "Lully as Secrétaire du Roi," *Bach* 15, no. 4 (1984): 16–22. It is important to emphasize for readers familiar with the hierarchy of court positions that Lully became a *conseiller-secrétaire du roi*, not a *secrétaire du roi*.

4. The imprint was called a *paraphe*. L. de la Laurencie, "Une convention commerciale: entre Lully, Quinault et Ballard en 1680," *Bulletin de la Société française de musicologie* 2, no. 9 (July 1921): 176–82.

5. Michael Kwass, *Privilege and the Politics of Taxation in Eighteenth-Century France: Liberté, Égalité, Fiscalité* (Cambridge: Cambridge University Press, 2000).

6. Jeff Horn, *Economic Development in Early Modern France: The Privilege of Liberty, 1650–1820*, Cambridge Studies in Economic History (Cambridge: Cambridge University Press, 2015).

7. Gail Bossenga, *The Politics of Privilege: Old Regime and Revolution in Lille* (Cambridge: Cambridge University Press, 1991).

8. Gail Bossenga provides a concise explanation of social privilege in "Chapter 9: Estates, Orders and Corps," in *The Oxford Handbook of the Ancien Régime*, ed. William Doyle (New York: Oxford University Press, 2012), 141–67.

9. See Michael P. Fitzsimmons, "Privilege and the Polity in France, 1786–1791," *American Historical Review* 92, no. 2 (April 1987): 270. Fitzsimmons does not subscribe to a constitutional view but surveys it. Horn refers to it more directly as "the constitutional basis of the early modern state" (3). For caution against this position, see Julian Swann, "Parlements and Provincial Estates," in *The Oxford Handbook of the Ancien Régime*, ed. William Doyle (New York: Oxford University Press, 2012), 98.

10. To say these positions were "inherited" would be legalistically incorrect, as they had to be arranged, for example, as *en survivance* positions to which one ascended only after the death of a predecessor. Contemporaries would nevertheless sometimes refer to such positions as "inherited." Privileges differed from strictly seigneurial rights in this sense.

11. On the cost and arrangement of musicians' positions at court during this period, see Marcelle Benoit, *Versailles et les musiciens du roi: étude institutionnelle et sociale, 1661–1733*, and *Musiques de cour: chapelle, chambre, écurie*, La vie musicale en France sous les rois Bourbons 19 and 20 (Paris: Éditions A. et J. Picard, 1971).

12. La Gorce, *Jean-Baptiste Lully*, 246.

13. I draw on Patricia Ranum's use of "belong" because it indexes both the original verb used in contemporaneous sources and also emphasizes its implication that musicians were a kind of noble property. Patricia Ranum, "Lully Plays Deaf: Rereading the Evidence on His Privilege," *Lully Studies*, ed. John Jajdu Heyer (Cambridge: Cambridge University Press, 2000), 17–18, 20–1.

14. Alain Viala, *Naissance de l'écrivain: sociologie de la littérature à l'âge classique* (Paris: Les éditions de minuit, 1985), 51–4.

15. Ranum, "Lully Plays Deaf," 17–18, 20–1.

16. David Hennebelle, *De Lully à Mozart: aristocratie, musique et musiciens à Paris (XVIIe–XVIIIe siècles)* (Seysell: Champ Vallon, 2009), 35.

17. Hilton L. Root, *The Fountain of Privilege: Political Foundations of Markets in Old Regime France and England* (Berkeley: University of California Press, 1994), 161.

18. Root, *The Fountain of Privilege*.

19. Carla Hesse, *Publishing and Cultural Politics in Revolutionary Paris, 1789–1810*, Studies on the History and Society of Culture 12 (Berkeley: University of California Press, 1991), 7–20, see especially Figure 1.

20. On networks resulting from the privilege system, see Bossenga, "Estates, Orders, and Corps," 155.

21. Primary sources on the legal-social divisions among professional musicians in seventeenth and eighteenth-century Paris are compiled in *Documents du Minutier Central concernant l'histoire de la musique (1600–1650)*, ed. Madeleine Jurgens, 2 vols. (Paris: S. E. V. P. E. N., 1967, and Paris: La Documentation Française, 1974); *Musiciens de Paris 1535–1792*, ed. Yolande de Brossard (Paris: J. Picard, 1965); and *Documents du Minutier Central concernant l'histoire de l'art (1700–1750)*, ed. Marielle Rambaud, 2 vols. (Paris: S. E. V. P. E. N., 1964).

22. Toby Gelfand, *Professionalizing Modern Medicine: Paris Surgeons and Medical Science and Institutions in the Eighteenth Century* (Westport, CT: Greenwood Press, 1980); Antoine Picon, *L'invention de l'ingénieur moderne: l'École des ponts et chaussées, 1747–1851* (Paris: Presses de l'École Nationale des Ponts et Chaussées, 1992); Rafe Blaufarb, *The French Army, 1750–1820: Careers, Talent, Merit* (Manchester: Manchester University Press, 2002); Pierre Baron, "Dental Practice in Paris," in *Dental Practice in Europe at the End of the Eighteenth Century*, ed. Christine Hillam, Studies in the History of Medicine and Health 7 (Amsterdam: Rodopi, 2003), 113–62; Jonathan Simon, *Chemistry, Pharmacy, and Revolution in France, 1777–1809* (Burlington, VT: Ashgate, 2005); and Colin Jones, "Cometh the Dentist," *The Smile Revolution in Eighteenth-Century Paris* (Oxford: Oxford University Press, 2014).

23. Paola Bertucci, *Artisanal Enlightenment: Science and the Mechanical Arts in Old Regime France* (New Haven: Yale University Press, 2017), 34. "'Savant' and 'artisan' were categories that my historical actors employed, often to articulate epistemological claims about the superior nature of their own working practice. In other words, 'savant' in this book is an ethnographic category, not an epistemic one."

24. Betucci, *Artisanal Enlightenment*, 4–5.

25. Luc Charles-Dominique, *Les ménétriers français sous l'ancien régime* (Paris: Klincksieck, 1994), 242.

26. Charles-Dominique, *Les ménétriers français*, 253–4.

27. See Horn, *Economic Development in Early Modern France*.

28. Victoria Johnson, *Backstage at the Revolution: How the Royal Paris Opera Survived the End of the Old Regime* (Chicago: University of Chicago Press, 2008), 108.

29. Johnson, *Backstage at the Opera*, 105.

30. Johnson, *Backstage at the Opera*, 114–18.

31. The *ménétriers* employed royal descriptors for its leaders until the end of the seventeenth century.

32. Johnson, *Backstage at the Opera*, 91.

33. Ranum, "Lully Plays Deaf," 22. La Gorce offers a clear explanation of this competition in *Jean-Baptiste Lully*, 173–240.

34. Ranum, "Lully Plays Deaf," 23. Although Lully convinced Perrin to turn over the privilege in return for enough money to secure the poet's release from prison and to repay his debts, the privilege did not truly belong to Lully until Perrin's was legally revoked because it was a *privilège octroyé*—royally bestowed. See La Gorce, *Jean-Baptiste Lully*, 180.

35. Mark Darlow, *Staging the French Revolution: Cultural Politics and the Paris Opéra, 1789–1794*, New Cultural History of Music Series (New York: Oxford University Press, 2012), 37. For a detailed history of the Opéra's privilege and its challengers, see also, Johnson, *Backstage at the Revolution*; Solveig Serre, *L'opéra de Paris (1749–1790): politique culturelle au temps des Lumières* (Paris: CNRS Éditions, 2011); and Julia Doe, *The Comedians of the King:* Opéra Comique *and the Bourbon Monarchy on the Eve of Revolution* (Chicago: University of Chicago Press, 2021).

36. A *lettre patente* was thus the opposite of a *lettre de cachet*, the sealed monarchical orders that became so bitterly despised for their secretive nature.

37. A privilege for a marionette theater was nevertheless revoked in 1677 because it infringed on Lully's privilege. Marcell Benoit, ed., *Les événements musicaux sous le règne de Louis XIV: chronologie* (Paris: Picard, 2004), 151.

38. Johnson, *Backstage at the Opera*, 132–5.

39. Ranum, "Lully Plays Deaf," 24.

40. On Lully's selective enforcement of his privileges, see Ranum, "Lully Plays Deaf." It could be argued that the performances in the D'Orléans household were private and therefore did not in fact legally conflict with Lully's privileges.

41. Ranum, "Lully Plays Deaf," 25.

42. See Bernhard Bernard, "Recherches sur l'histoire de la corporation des ménétriers, ou joueurs d'instruments, de la ville de Paris. Troisième période," in *Bibliothèque de l'école des chartes* (1844), 5:277–8.

43. Charles-Dominique, *Les ménétriers français*, 263. Charles-Dominique offers the most recent nuanced historical account and interpretation of the musicians' guild system through the eighteenth century, and so this is the main source for the proceeding discussion of the *ménétriers* unless otherwise specified.

44. See Horn, *Economic Development in Early Modern France.*

45. See for example Benoit, *Les événements musicaux.* In nearly all of the transactions noted there we find court or church-affiliated musicians securing permissions from the Crown far more frequently than guild musicians.

46. Florence Gétreau elaborates on Dumanoir's argument regarding the relationship between dancers and violinists in "Guillaume de Limoges et François Couperin ou comment enseigner la musique hors le Ménestrandise parisienne," in *Musik—Raum—Akkord—Bild: Festschrift zum 65. Geburtstag von Dorothea Gaumann*, ed. Antonio Baldassarre, et al. (Bern: Peter Lang, 2012), 166.

47. Charles-Dominique, *Les ménétriers français*, 265.

48. Charles-Dominique, *Les ménétriers français*, 265.

49. Charles-Dominique, *Les ménétriers français*, 227–32.

50. Charles-Dominique, *Les ménétriers français*, 233.

51. Charles-Dominique, *Les ménétriers français*, 268. John C. O'Neal, *The Authority of Experience: Sensationist Theory and the French Enlightenment* (University Park: Pennsylvania State University Press, 1996).

52. Charles-Dominique, *Les ménétriers français*, 236.

53. Quoted in Gétreau, "Guillaume de Limoges et François Couperin," 168. "la dextérité du corps . . . renferment dans l'esprit."

54. On surgeons, see Gefland, *Professionalizing Modern Medicine*.

55. See Benoit, *Les événements musicaux*, 330.

56. Because the word *métier* has a distinctive character in French poorly represented in English translation as a craft or trade, I maintain it in French here. Charles-Dominique, *Les ménétriers français*, 266.

57. Gétreau, "Guillaume de Limoges et François Couperin," 169.

58. Gétreau, "Guillaume de Limoges et François Couperin," 169. "Et leur anoblissement en 1696 est une consécration certaine dans cette bataille pour la liberté artistique."

59. This argument draws on William H. Sewell Jr.'s that the later Abolition of Privilege in fact disenfranchised French laborers whose corporate affiliation was the only real property that they owned. See *Work and Revolution in France: The Language of Labor from the Old Regime to 1848* (Cambridge: Cambridge University Press, 1980).

60. Gétreau, "Guillaume de Limoges et François Couperin," 169.

61. Charles-Dominique, *Les ménétriers français*, 252.

62. Georgia Cowart, *The Origins of Modern Musical Criticism: French and Italian Music 1600–1750* (Ann Arbor: University of Michigan Research Press, 1981), 67–8.

63. Olivier Baumont, "Les fastes de la grande et ancienne Mxnxstrxndxsx," CD, disc 6, *Couperin: Pièces de Clavecin*, Erato 825646417667 (October 26, 2010).

64. Gétreau, "Guillaume de Limoges et François Couperin," 170–1.

65. Robert A. Green, *The Hurdy-Gurdy in Eighteenth-Century France* (Bloomington: Indiana University Press, 1995), 1.

66. Gétreau also notes this in "Guillaume de Limoges et François Couperin," 172.

67. Gétreau "Guillaume de Limoges et François Couperin," 168. Charles-Dominique argues that harmonists "refused to accept the *lettres de maîtrise*" precisely to resist association with an oral musical tradition (267), because in the seventeenth century "L'harmonie apparaît comme l'esthétique de la raison, de la modération, de la connaissance, de la sagesse" (232–3).

68. Charles-Dominique, *Les ménétriers français*, 236.

69. Bertucci, *Artisanal Enlightenment*, 3 and 118.

70. Bertucci, *Artisanal Enlightenment*, 22–3.

71. Dan Edelstein, *The Enlightenment: A Genealogy* (Chicago: University of Chicago Press, 2010), 33. Edelstein explains, "By the early eighteenth century social usefulness had become a standard by which to determine the value of all things."

72. Denis Diderot and Jean le Rond D'Alembert, "Discours préliminaire des Éditeurs," in *Encyclopédie, ou dictionnaire raisonné des sciences, des arts et des métiers, etc.*, ed. Denis Diderot and Jean le Rond d'Alembert (University of Chicago: ARTFL Encyclopédie Project [Autumn 2017 edition], ed. by Robert Morrissey and Glenn Roe, http://encyclopedie.uchicago.edu/).

73. Jann Pasler, *Composing the Citizen: Music as Public Utility in Third Republic France* (Berkeley: University of California Press, 2009).

74. Bertucci, *Artisanal Enlightenment*; and Eric H. Ash, in "Introduction: Expertise and the Early Modern Nation State," *Osiris* 25, no. 1 (2010): 1–24, address the commercial and imperial motivations behind expertise in early modern France, while Edelstein's *Genealogy* explains the social and intellectual concerns that underpinned these socioeconomic phenomena: "Identifying social improvement as the benchmark for national glory expressed instead a wish that the new science serve to transform human conduct, beliefs, and relations" (35).

75. Stephen Rose, *Musical Authorship from Schütz to Bach* (Cambridge: Cambridge University Press, 2019), 126–40.

76. Katie Scott, *Becoming Property: Art, Theory, and Law in Early Modern France* (New Haven, CT: Yale University Press, 2018), 53.

77. Michel Brenet [Marie Bobillier], "La librairie musicale en France de 1653 à 1790, d'après les Registres de privilèges," *Sammelbände der Internationalen Musikgesellschaft* 8, no. 3 (1907): 408.

78. Hesse, *Publishing and Cultural Politics*, 40.

79. Hesse provides a detailed breakdown of the kinds of privileges available in *Printing and Cultural Politics*, 11–12.

80. This was even more the case in German principalities, where after 1650, "composers rarely applied for printing privileges." Stephen Rose, *Musical Authorship from Schütz to Bach*, 148.

81. Brenet, "La librairie musicale en France," 416. For the process to obtain and register a publishing privilege see Hesse, *Printing and Cultural Politics*, 7–20.

82. Brenet, "La librairie musicale en France," 411.

83. Anik Devriès-Lesure, *L'édition musicale dans la presse parisienne au XVIIIe siècle: catalogue des announces*, Science de la musique (Paris: CNRS Éditions, 2005), xi.

84. Jean Gribenski, "Un métier difficile: éditeur de musique à Paris sous la Révolution," in *Le tambour et la harpe: œuvres, pratiques et manifestations musicales sous la Révolution, 1788–1800*, ed. Jean-Rémy Julien et Jean Mongrédien (Paris: Éditions du May, 1991), 21.

85. For examples, see Devriès-Lesure, *L'édition musicale dans la presse parisienne*. This practice extended outside of France; see Steven Zohn, "Telemann in the Marketplace: The Composer as Self-Publisher," *Journal of the American Musicological Society* 58, no. 2 (Summer 2005): 275–356.

86. Rose also argues that music engraving offered composers more "control." *Musical Authorship from Schütz to Bach*, 150.

87. Reprinted in Devriès-Lesure, *L'édition musicale dans la presse parisienne*, xxi. "Le Sieur Lanzetti . . . averti le public que les deuxième et troisième œuvres de sonates pour le violoncelle qu'on a fait graver à Paris sous son nom et à son insu, sont pleins des fautes."

88. Scott, *Becoming Property*, 32–3.

89. Jacques Champion de Chambonnières, *Pièces de clavecin, livre 1* (Paris: Chez Jollain, 1670). "Je devois donner volontairement ce que l'on m'otoit avec violence et . . . mettre au jour moy méme ce que d'autres y avoient desja mis a demy pour moy."

90. Rose, *Musical Authorship from Schütz to Bach*, 148. In the case of France, Gribenski notes that privileges prevented counterfeiting in theory; however, it remains difficult to

determine today, based on the extant sources (and it was certainly unclear to those in the Parisian music world then) the extent to which privilege actually hindered music piracy. Gribenski, "Un métier difficile," 21–2.

91. This conclusion is based on music in the printer's register from 1653 to 1790 reprinted in Brenet, "La librairie musicale en France."

92. Hesse, *Publishing and Cultural Politics*, 123. Again, the term "inherit" here reveals a confusion between legal practice and perception. Families were required to fulfill the formalities of renewing privileges that their predecessors held.

93. Brenet, "La librairie musicale en France," 424n1.

94. Devriès-Lesure, *L'édition musicale dans la presse parisienne*, xiv.

95. Anita Breckbill and Carole Goebes, "Music Circulating Libraries in France: An Overview and Preliminary List," *Music Library Association Notes* 63, no. 4 (June 2007): 764–8.

96. On LeClerc and the international music-printing market, see Sarah Adams, "International Dissemination of Printed Music during the Second Half of the Eighteenth Century," in *The Dissemination of Music: Studies in the History of Music Publishing*, ed. Hans Lenneberg (Amsterdam: Gordon and Breach, 1994), 25–9.

97. Brenet, "La librairie musicale en France," 453–4.

98. Devriès-Lesure, *L'édition musicale dans la presse parisienne*, x.

99. This is not to imply that Gossec was not concerned with ownership over his works. He presented himself at the Châtelet court to retrieve his compositions from the estate of aristocratic orchestra patron La Pouplinière. See Hennebelle, *De Lully à Mozart*, 215.

100. Gribenski, "Un métier difficile," 22, based on Brenet.

101. Brenet, "La librairie musicale en France," 411.

102. Albert Cohen, *Music in the French Royal Academy of Sciences: A Study in the Evolution of Musical Thought* (Princeton, NJ: Princeton University Press, 1981), 43. For a succinct discussion and useful citations on the instrument builders' guild, see John N. Hunt, "Jurors of the Guild of Musical Instrument Makers of Paris," *The Galpin Society Journal* 51 (July 1998): 110–13.

103. Cohen, *Music in the French Royal Academy of Sciences*, 49.

104. Cohen, *Music in the French Royal Academy of Sciences*, 83–4.

105. Cohen, *Music in the French Royal Academy of Sciences*, 101.

106. Brenet, "La librairie musicale en France," 430. "approuvé par MM. De l'Académie des Sciences le 5 juin dernier, lesquels ils ont approuvé estre sans comparaison plus facile, plus court et plus seur à apprendre et à mettre en pratique que tous ceux qui l'ont précédé."

107. Cohen, *Music in the French Royal Academy of Sciences*, 76; and Devriès-Lesure, *L'édition musicale dans la presse parisienne*, x. On Paris as the music-printing capital compared to other European centers, see Adam, "International Dissemination."

108. Jeff Horn shows this to be the case in other sectors of production in *Economic Development in Early Modern France*.

109. Devriès-Lesure, *L'édition musicale dans la presse parisienne*, xi.

110. Here I extend David Hennebelle's use of the term "dilution," which he uses to describe the collective music patronage of orchestras in mid- to late-eighteenth-century Paris. See David Hennebelle, "Un paysage musical de Paris en 1785: les tablettes de

renommée des musiciens," *Société française d'histoire urbaine* 26, no. 3 (2009): 93, and *De Lully à Mozart*, 127–57.

111. Root, *The Fountain of Privilege*.

112. I put public in quotation marks here to signal the scholarly debate about whether it should truly be considered as such given the price for entry and audience demographics.

113. Michèle Root-Bernstein, *Boulevard Theater and Revolution Eighteenth-Century Paris* (Ann Arbor: University Microfilms International, 1984), 24.

114. David Charlton, *Opera in the Age of Rousseau: Music, Confrontation, Realism* (Cambridge: Cambridge University Press, 2012), 3. In context, Charlton is discussing the Opéra along with the Comédie-Française and Théatre-Italienne. His statement is amended slightly here to focus on the Opéra in particular.

115. Beverly Wilcox, "The Music Libraries of the Concert Spirituel: Canons, Repertoires, and Bricolage in Eighteenth-Century Paris" (PhD diss., University of California—Davis, 2013), 40.

116. Wilcox, "The Music Libraries of the Concert Spirituel," 32. My discussion of the Concert Spirituel is based on Wilcox's meticulous dissertation, particularly "Chapter 2: The Entrepreneurs." For a more detailed overview of the workings of the Concert Spirituel's privileges, consult Wilcox. Given the choice, the concert's own entrepreneurs would have preferred to deal directly with the king (42).

117. Jean-Benjamin de La Borde, *Essai sur la musique ancienne et moderne*, reprinted and translated in Sadler and Wood, *French Baroque Opera*, 4.

118. Benoit, *Musiques de cour*, 438.

119. Quoted and translated in Johnson, *Backstage at the Opera*, 149.

120. Root-Bernstein, *Boulevard Theatre and Revolution*, 17–18.

121. Wilcox, "The Music Libraries of the Concert Spirituel," 69.

122. Louis-Antoine Travenol, *Nouveau catéchisme des Francs-Maçons, concernant tous les mystères de la Maçonnerie* ("Jerusalem," 1748). The "*privilège*" on the pamphlet is not the customary "du Roi," but "du Roi Salomon." Thus, Travenol was already subtly critiquing or at least poking fun at the system.

123. G. Charles Walton, *Policing Public Opinion in the French Revolution: The Culture of Calumny and the Problem of Free Speech* (Oxford: Oxford University Press, 2009), 48–9.

124. Bossenga, "Estates, Orders, and Corps," 155. See also, Fitzsimmons, "Privilege and the Polity."

125. Louis-Antoine Travenol, *Les entrepreneurs entrepris, ou complainte d'un musicien opprimé par ses camarades, adressée aux protecteurs et aux protectrices des sciences et des Beaux arts* (Paris: S. Jorry, 1758). I am grateful to Beverly Wilcox for bringing this pamphlet to my attention.

126. Travenol, *Les entrepreneurs entrepris*, 25. "Vous m'avez mis dans le cas, Monsieur, d'avoir tout le tems de solliciter des Procès."

127. Travenol, *Les entrepreneurs entrepris*, 22–3. "Je ne suis pas, comme lui, homme de Cour . . . Je parle & j'écris comme je pense surtout à mes Camarades."

128. Louis Mannory, the attorney who had represented Travenol against Voltaire, may have provided editorial assistance on this pamphlet.

129. Travenol, *Les entrepreneurs entrepris,* 3. "Aux protecteurs et aux protectrices des sciences & des Beaux Arts."

130. Emily H. Green, *Dedicating Music, 1785–1850*, Eastman Studies in Music (Woodbridge, UK, and Rochester, NY: Boydell and Brewer and University of Rochester Press, 2019), 50.

131. Green, *Dedicating Music*, 89.

132. Travenol, *Les entrepreneurs entrepris*, 3. "Je me vois exilé de la Cour D'Apollon."

133. Travenol, *Les entrepreneurs entrepris*, 9. "Nous sommes tous Enfans du Divin Apollon. / La Noblesse entre nous est donc, sans doute, égale; / Et la Basse, suivant la Régle Musicale, / Doit prendre & ménager avec affection / Les intérêts du Violon."

134. Cary R. Alburn, "Corpus Juris Civilis: A Historical Romance," *American Bar Association Journal* 562 (1959): 640.

135. He took a similar approach to demanding pay from the Opéra, see "Observations du sieur Travenol, pensionnaire de l'Académie royale de musique, sur les frivoles motifs du refus que fait le sieur Joliveau, caissier de ladite Académie, de lui payer sa pension, adressées à Mgr le Cte de S. Florentin, ministre et secrétaire d'État" (Paris: Didot, 1761).

136. Travenol, *Les entrepreneurs entrepris*, 15.

137. Travenol, *Les entrepreneurs entrepris*, 18.

138. Travenol, *Les entrepreneurs entrepris*, 19–20. "qu'il n'étoit pas juste . . . celui qui avoit occupé ma place ne me valoit pas."

139. Travenol, *Les entrepreneurs entrepris*, 20. "Les raisonnemens du Sieur Mondonville ne sont pas aussi séduisans que ses Motets."

140. Travenol, *Les entrepreneurs entrepris*, 33. "vous n'étiez nullement en droit d'exiger le payement de la Quinzaine, puisque vous n'aviez point servi, & qu'il est de régle de tous les tems; qu'on ne peut envoyer un autre Sujet à sa Place."

141. Travenol, *Les entrepreneurs entrepris*, 35. "Je ne suis pas le seul à qui vous avez accordé plusieurs fois ce privilège."

142. Root-Bernstein, *Boulevard Theater and Revolution*, 47.

143. Travenol, *Les entrepreneurs entrepris*, 36. "La Justice ordinaire ne fauroit les y contraindre."

144. Travenol, *Les entrepreneurs entrepris*, 39–40. "Ces Législateurs de ces deux Spectacles ont pour principe, à l'exemple des anciens Romains, de sacrifier le bien particulier des Musiciens, au bien général de la Musique, ou, pour mieux dire, à leur propres intérêts . . . j'ai cru devoir publier l'injustice, & l'inhumanité de ces petits Tyrans du Parnasse."

145. Neal Zaslaw, "Jean-Pierre Guignon," *Grove Music Online*.

146. This paragraph is based on Charles-Dominique, *Les ménétriers français*, 269–74.

147. *Recueil d'Édit, arrêt du conseil du roi, lettres-patentes, mémoires, et arrêts du Parlement, &c. En faveur des Musiciens du Royaume* (Paris: Ballard, 1774), i.

148. *Recueil*, i. "de les mettre à portée de s'instruire des loix qui assûrent l'honneur & la liberté de l'Art Musical, sont les motifs qui ont donné lieu à l'impression de ce Recueil."

149. For a similar discussion about contested definitions of a "liberal" art, see Charlotte Guichard, "Arts libéraux et arts libres à Paris au XVIIIe siècle: peintres et sculpteurs entre corporation et Académie royale," *Revue d'histoire moderne et contemporaine* 49, no. 3 (2002): 54–68. See, too, Horn, *Economic Development in Early Modern France*.

150. *Recueil*, ii. "puisqu'elle leur procure les moyens de se défendre, si, contre toute attente, il arrivoit que la Communauté de Saint-Julien voulût attaquer de nouveau la liberté de leur Profession."

151. David Hennebelle, "Un paysage musical de Paris en 1785," 93, and *De Lully à Mozart*, 127–57.

152. François Joseph Gossec, *Messe des morts* (Paris: Chez Henry, 1780). "Votre zèle soutenir longtems encore une institution si avantageuse pour les professeurs des encouragemens que vous leur donnés, le plus puissant, je ne crains pas de le dire, est la noble distinction avec laquelle vous les traités, elever l'ame des artistes. C'est travailler à l'agrandissement des arts: voilà ce que n'ont jamais senti ceux qui usurpent le titre de protecteurs, plus soigneux de l'acheter, que de le meriter" (n.p.).

153. Green, *Dedicating Music*, 79.

154. Liana Vardi, *The Physiocrats and the World of the Enlightenment* (New York: Cambridge University Press, 2012).

155. Dan Edelstein, *On the Spirit of Rights* (Chicago: University of Chicago Press, 2019), 185.

156. On the expansion of physiocracy to the political realm see Edelstein, *On the Spirit of Rights*, 81. This is not to say that everyone followed physiocratic tenets as they were originally laid out by Quesnay, but that engagement with physiocratic ideas changed the political landscape (85).

157. On guilds, Lorraine Daston and Peter Galison, *Objectivity* (New York: Zone Books; Cambridge, MA: Distributed by the MIT Press, 2007), 96.

158. Although there were aspects of tax law that technically defined bourgeois professionals, the term was employed more widely and with less specificity in everyday discourse, as shown here in the case of the Academy musicians. See David Garrioch, *The Making of Revolutionary Paris* (Berkeley: University of California Press, 2002), 103.

159. Simon, *Chemistry, Pharmacy, and Revolution*, 46. Simon explains, "The scientific status of pharmacy and particularly its use of chemistry (understood as the art of analysis in pharmacy) was deployed in order both to stress the public utility of the art and to [demonstrate] the value of the expertise resident in the body of pharmacists."

160. Brown, *Literary Sociability*, 23.

161. Brown, *Literary Sociability*, 40.

162. For a succinct overview of literature on prerevolutionary patriotism, see John Shovlin, *The Political Economy of Virtue: Luxury, Patriotism, and the Origins of the French Revolution* (Ithaca and New York: Cornell University Press, 2006), especially p. 5. Shovlin also reveals alternative views to physiocratic conceptions of the political economy from the 1750s to 1780s.

163. Gregory S. Brown, "Le Fuel de Méricourt and the *Journal des Théâtres*: Theatre Criticism and the Politics of Culture in Pre-Revolutionary France," *French History* 9, no. 1 (March 1995): 1–26. For a nuanced discussion of "patriot" discourse in relation to the Opéra, see also, Darlow, *Staging the French Revolution*, 22–43.

164. Brown, *Literary Sociability*, 27–34.

165. Brown, *Literary Sociability*, 18.

166. Hesse, *Publishing and Cultural Politics*, 42.

167. Carla Hesse, "Enlightenment Epistemology and the Laws of Authorship in Revolutionary France, 1777–93," *Representations* 30 (Spring 1990): 109–37.

168. *Édit du roi concernant le corps de la musique du roi* (Versailles, 1782).

169. *Édit du roi concernant le corps de la musique du roi*, 3.

170. Darlow, *Staging the French Revolution*, 40–2.

171. Root, *The Fountain of Privilege*, 5–10.

172. Root-Bernstein, *Boulevard Theatre and Revolution*, 28.

173. Horn, *Economic Development in Early Modern France*, 1–3. Horn's explanation of these industrial exceptions complement those noted by Root-Bernstein in *Boulevard Theatre and Revolution*.

174. Root-Bernstein, *Boulevard Theatre and Revolution*, 29.

175. See Mark Darlow, "L'effritement du privilège théâtral les débats de 1789–1790," in *L'Opéra de Paris, La Comédie-Française, et L'Opéra-Comique: approches comparées (1669–2010)*, ed. Sabine Chaouche, Denis Herlin, and Solveig Serre, Études et rencontres 38 (Paris: Publications de l'École Nationale des Chartres, 2012), 66.

176. Root-Bernstein, *Boulevard Theatre and Revolution*, 31.

177. Alexandre Dratwicki, *Un nouveau commerce de la virtuosité: émancipation et métamorphoses de la musique concertante au sein des institutions musicales parisiennes (1780–1830)* (Lyon, France: Symétrie, 2006), 54–5.

178. Doe, *The Comedians of the King*, 117–22.

179. Gribenski, "Un métier difficile," 22; based on Brenet. In *Musical Authorship from Schütz to Bach*, Rose notes a similar decline in German privilege registers during the first half of the eighteenth century, when music began to circulate there primarily via manuscripts.

180. "On a là, en tout cas, l'un des nombreux symptômes de l'affaiblissement de la monarchie à la fin du règne de Louis XV et pendant celui de Louis XVI : d'un côté, la protection du pouvoir royal paraît en général inutile ; d'un autre côté, la 'fraude au privilège' (c'est-à-dire l'utilisation frauduleuse du signe A. P. D. R.), si elle semble au contraire traduire une certaine confiance dans le pouvoir royal, montre en même temps qu'il est quotidiennement bafoué." Gribenski, "Un métier difficile," 22.

181. *Tablettes de renommée des musiciens, auteurs, compositeurs, virtuoses, amateurs et maitres de musique vocale et instrumentale* (Paris: Calleau, 1785).

182. *Tablettes royales de renommée ou almanach général d'indication des négocians, artistes célèbres et fabricans des six corps, arts et métiers . . . de Paris et autres villes du royaume* (Paris, 1773), n.p.

183. Root, *Fountain of Privilege*, 10.

184. Hennebelle, "Un paysage musical de Paris," 104.

185. Hennebelle, "Un paysage musical de Paris," 93.

186. Hennebelle, "Un paysage musical de Paris," 102–3.

187. Hennebelle, "Un paysage musical de Paris," 110. "Les *Tablettes* façonnent un nouveau visage de la dignité musicienne, où la singularité l'emporte sur l'anonymat, où les compositeurs et interprètes à succès de la scène lyrique n'éclipsent pas les maîtres de la musique instrumentale, ni même les musiciens d'orchestre."

188. Hennebelle, "Un paysage musical de Paris," 96.

189. Hennebelle, "Un paysage musical de Paris," 96.

190. Johnson, *Backstage at the Opéra*, 179.

191. Constant Pierre, *Le Conservatoire national de musique et de déclamation: documents historiques et administratifs* (Paris: Imprimerie nationale, 1900), 14.

192. Constant Pierre, *Le Conservatoire national de musique*, 13. In fact, Piccinni was approached to teach singing at the school, although he at first declined the position in order to focus on composing.

193. R. R. Palmer, *The Improvement of Humanity: Education and the French Revolution* (Princeton: Princeton University Press, 1985), 64–8.

194. Michel Noiray, "L'Ecole royale de chant (1784–1795): crise musicale, crise institutionnelle," in *Musical Education in Europe (1770–1914): Compositional, Institutional, and Political Challenges*, ed. by Michael Fend and Michel Noiray (Berlin: Berliner-Wissenschafts Verlag, 2005): 1:59–61.

195. Noiray, "L'Ecole royale de chant," 71.

196. Noiray, "L'Ecole royale de chant," 73.

197. Noiray, "L'Ecole royale de chant," 57.

198. Garrioch, *The Making of Revolutionary Paris*, 273.

199. Scott, *Becoming Property*, 28.

Chapter 2

1. André-Ernest-Modeste Grétry, *De la vérité, ce que nous fûmes, ce que nous sommes, ce que nous devrions être* (Paris: Chez Ch. Pougens, 1801), 2:4. "Sous l'ancien régime, les artistes étoient humiliés par le peu de considération dont ils jouissoient, non pas comme artistes, mais comme hommes."

2. "J'ai vu naître et s'effectuer une révolution parmi les artistes musiciens, qui a précédé de peu la grande révolution politique." Grétry, *De la vérité*, 2:6.

3. "Quelque scènes de ce genre eurent lieu dans différens endroits." Grétry, *De la vérité*, 2:9.

4. "Il seroit bien plus dégradant pour votre noblesse, lui dit le musicien, si vous m'obligez, M. le marquis, à vous donner une correction roturière." Grétry, *De la vérité*, 2:8.

5. "*Privilège*, signifie aussi quelquefois la liberté qu'on a, ou qu'on se donne de faire des choses que d'autres n'oseroient faire. *Il a le privilège de faire & de dire dans cette maison tout ce qu'il luy plaist. C'est un homme qui a des privilèges que d'autres n'ont pas*," *Le dictionnaire de l'Académie française*, Vol. 2 (1694), accessed through the ARTFL Project *Dictionnaires d'autrefois* October 11, 2019.

6. John Leigh, *Touché: The Duel in Literature* (Cambridge, MA: Harvard University Press, 2015), 1.

7. Leigh, *Touché*, 1.

8. George Armstrong Kelly, "Duelling in Eighteenth-Century France: Archaeology, Rationale, Implications," *The Eighteenth Century* 21, no. 3 (1980): 244 and 254. In feudal society, dueling had prevented widespread bloodshed by allowing two nobles to rectify *injures* without involving other parties and devolving into war. But after Louis XIV abolished the practice, it declined in France and continued to do so under Louis XVI. Enlightened individuals generally looked down on dueling as brutish, and it became more common among the bourgeoisie.

9. Leigh, *Touché*, 11.

10. "Social harmony" is best encapsulated in Rousseau's correlation between music and politics. See Robert Wokler, *Rousseau on Society, Politics, Music and Language: An Historical Interpretation of His Early Writings* (New York: Garland Publishing, 1987) and Julia Simon, *Rousseau among the Moderns: Music, Aesthetics, Politics* (University Park: Pennsylvania State University Press, 2013). On the strict hierarchies within lodges, see Jean-Luc Quoy-Bodin, *L'armée et la franc-maçonnerie au déclin de la monarchie sous la Révolution et l'Empire* (Paris: Economica, Edic, 1987).

11. David Stevenson, *The Origins of Freemasonry* (Cambridge: Cambridge University Press, 1998), 5–9.

12. A French translation of the *Constitutions* was published in 1736, and a German translation appeared in 1741.

13. Gérard Gefen, *Les musiciens et la franc-maçonnerie* (Paris: Fayard, 1993), 11.

14. Pierre-François Pinaud, *Les musiciens francs-maçons, au temps de Louis XVI de Paris à Versailles: histoire et dictionnaire biographique* (Paris: Éditions Véga, 2009), 17.

15. The Apollo Society for the Lovers of Music and Architecture, which opened in London in 1725, exemplifies the conceptual resonance between the two arts within masonic ideology. See Gefen, *Les musiciens et la franc-maçonnerie*, 32; and Andrew Pink, "A Music Club for Freemasons: Philo-musicae et architecturae societas Apollini, London, 1725–1727," *Early Music* 38, no. 4 (November 2010): 523–36.

16. On the first Parisian lodge and for a succinct summary of the early years of Freemasonry in Paris, see Alain Le Bihan, "Les premiers pas (1725–1771)," in *Histoire des Francs-maçons en France*, ed. Daniel Ligou (Toulouse: Editions Privat, 1987), 30.

17. R. William Weisberger, "Benjamin Franklin: A Masonic Enlightener in Paris," *Pennsylvania History* 53, no. 3 (July 1986): 166.

18. Roger Dachez, *Histoire de la franc-maçonnerie française* (Paris: PUF, 2003), 79.

19. Jürgen Habermas, *The Structural Transformation of the Public Sphere: An Inquiry into a Category of Bourgeois Society*, trans. Thomas Burger (Cambridge, MA: MIT Press, 1991 [1962]) and Antoine Lilti, *Le monde des salons: sociabilité et mondanité à Paris au XVIIIe siècle* (Paris: Fayard, 2005).

20. William H. Sewell Jr., "Connecting Capitalism to the French Revolution: The Parisian Promenade and the Origins of Civic Equality in Eighteenth-Century France," *Critical Historical Studies* 1, no. 1 (Spring 2014): 5–46.

21. Colin Jones, *The Smile Revolution in Eighteenth-Century Paris* (Oxford: Oxford University Press, 2014), 93.

22. Antoine Lilti, "The Kingdom of Politesse: Salons and the Republic of Letters in Eighteenth-Century Paris," *Republic of Letters: A Journal for the Study of Knowledge, Politics, and the Arts* 1, no. 2 (2009): 1–9.

23. This is addressed briefly in musicological scholarship in Melanie Lowe, "Difference and Enlightenment in Haydn's Instrumental Music," *Rethinking Difference in Music Scholarship*, ed. Olivia Bloechl, Melanie Lowe, and Jeffrey Kallberg (Cambridge: Cambridge University Press, 2015), 136n11.

24. On the republican political culture of lodges, see Margaret C. Jacob, *Living the Enlightenment: Freemasonry and Politics in Eighteenth-Century Europe* (Oxford: Oxford University Press, 1991); and Kenneth Loiselle, *Brotherly Love: Freemasonry and Male Friendship in Enlightenment France* (Ithaca: Cornell University Press, 2014). On the tensions within lodge democracy, see Jacob, *Living the Enlightenment*, 203–214.

25. Habermas, *Structural Transformation of the Public Sphere*, 35; Roger Chartier, *The Cultural Origins of the French Revolution*, trans. Lydia G. Cochrane (Durham, NC: Duke University Press, 1991), 162–8; Dena Goodman, *The Republic of Letters: A Cultural History of the French Enlightenment* (Ithaca: Cornell University Press, 1994), 253–9; Pierre-Yves Beaurepaire, *L'espace des francs-maçons: une sociabilité européenne au XVIIIe siècle* (Rennes: Presses Universitaires de Rennes, 2003); and Loiselle, *Brotherly Love*.

26. In *Brotherly Love*, Loiselle explains how the creation of women's lodges in Paris originated in part due to accusations of homosexuality in masonic lodges.

27. Mark Darlow, *Dissonance in the Republic of Letters: The Querelle des Gluckistes et des Piccinnistes* (London: Modern Humanities Research Association and Maney, 2013), 141–7. Darlow discusses the two terms in the context of the Querelle des Gluckistes et Piccinnistes and translates their original salon context to the pamphlet wars. See also Antoine Lilti, *Le monde des salons*, especially chapter 4, "L'espace mondain." It is appropriate to extend the application of these terms to lodges where the arts, especially music, were a keen interest of its members; lodge and salon sociability shared many sensibilities.

28. Statistics on Masonry are calculated from tables in Jacques Brengues, Monique Mosser, and Daniel Roche, "Le monde maçonnique des Lumières," in *Histoire des francs-maçons en France*, ed. Daniel Ligou (Toulouse: Editions Privat, 1987), 105. In an apocryphal letter from Marie Antoinette to her sister Marie-Christine, on February 27, 1781, the queen is said to have claimed that it seemed everyone in Paris had become a Mason. In her official correspondences, there are no extant letters from that year. *Marie-Antoinette Correspondance (1770–1793)*, ed. Evelyne Lever (Paris: Tallandier Éditions, 2005), 399.

29. One notable exception during the early eighteenth century was the lodge Coustos-Villeroy, which inducted four musicians as brothers: Jacques-Christophe Naudot (c. 1690–1762), the best flutist of the time, who composed in the Italian style; Jean-Pierre Guignon (1702–1774), the virtuoso violinist from the Chapelle and Chambre du Roi discussed in the previous chapter; Pierre Jélyote (1713–1797), a tenor/contratenor who premiered many Rameau roles; and Louis-Nicolas Clérambault (1676–1749), an organist. Gefen, *Les musiciens et la franc-maçonnerie*, 40.

30. Pierre-Yves Beaurepaire emphasizes that Masonic lodges had roots in "craft guilds and confraternities." See "Sociability," in *The Oxford Handbook of the Ancien Régime*, ed. William Doyle (New York: Oxford University Press, 2012), 374–6.

31. While the Grand Orient leadership was made up of 10 percent clergy, 48 percent nobles, and 42 percent Third Estate, Parisian Masonry overall was 3.9 percent clergy, 22.5 percent nobility, and 73.6 percent Third Estate. Ligou, "Le Grand Orient de France (1771–1789)," and Brengues et al., "Le monde maçonnique," *Histoire des francs-maçons en France*, 76, 105.

32. Ligou, "Le Grand Orient de France (1771–1789)," *Histoires des francs-maçons en France*, 76.

33. The account of social practices and the statistical data in this paragraph are drawn from Brengues et al., "Le monde maçonnique," 114–16.

34. Jacob, *Living the Enlightenment*, 186.

35. Jacob, *Living the Enlightenment*, 185. Jacob was able to reconstruct the Strasbourg lodge quarrels because its archive has remained largely intact, an unusual advantage in Masonic studies.

36. Jacob, *Living the Enlightenment*, 186.

37. Brengues et al., "Le monde maçonnique," 115.

38. Rebecca Dowd Geoffroy-Schwinden, "Politics, the French Revolution, and Performance: Parisian Musicians as an Emergent Professional Class, 1749–1802" (PhD diss., Duke University, 2015), Appendix 1, and 85–90.

39. Pinaud, *Les musiciens francs-maçons*; Roger Cotte, *La musique maçonnique et ses musiciens* (Braine le Comte: Éditions du Baucen, 1975); and Pierre Chevallier, *Histoire*

de Saint Jean d'Écosse du Contrat Social Mère Loge Écossaise de France à l'orient de Paris (Paris: Éditions Ivoire-Clair, 2002), 285. Pinaud systematically built on the work of Cotte to identify the names, biographies, and masonic affiliations of Parisian musicians. Gerard Gefen's research emphasizes the aesthetic and symbolic ramifications of musician-masons in *Les musiciens et la franc-maçonnerie*; and "La franc-maçonnerie, vecteur du classicisme," in *Journée d'étude Hyacinthe Jadin et le classicisme européen*, ed. Denis Le Touzé and Gérard Streletski (Lyon: Université Louis-Lumière Lyon 2, Départment de musique et de musicologie, 2001), 90–100.

40. Colin Jones provides a convincing critique of the term's ambiguity in "Bourgeois Revolution Revivified: 1789 and Social Change," in ed. Colin Lucas, *Rewriting the French Revolution* (Oxford: Clarendon Press, 1991), 69–118.

41. "Demande de Constitution," F-Pn, Baylot, FM2-97, doc. 1.

42. "Tableau des F. F. qui composent la Respectable Loge St. Jean sous le titre distinctif de La Réunion des Arts," Paris, 1776, F-Pn, Baylot, FM2-97, doc. 65.

43. "Tableau des F. F. qui composent la Respectable Loge St. Jean sous le titre distinctif de La Réunion des Arts," Paris, 1776, F-Pn, Baylot, FM2-97, doc. 65; "Tableau des F. F. qui composent la respectable Loge Saint Jean sous le titre distinctif de La Réunion des Arts," Paris, 1777, F-Pn, Baylot, FM2-97, doc. 66; and "Tableau des membres qui composent la L. St. Jean sous le titre distinctif de la Réunion des Arts," Paris, 1778, F-Pn, Baylot, FM2-97, doc. 67. Musicians' institutional affiliations from Pinaud, "Dictionnaire biographique," *Les musiciens francs-maçons*.

44. "Décision de la chambre de Paris, du 6 d'août 1777," F-Pn, Baylot, FM2-97, doc. 4.

45. "Décision de la chambre de Paris, du 6 d'août 1777," F-Pn, Baylot, FM2-97, doc. 4.

46. "Décision de la chambre de Paris, du 6 d'août 1777," F-Pn, Baylot, FM2-97, doc. 4.

47. For explanation of the Grand Orient chambers and council, see Ligou, "Le Grand Orient de France (1771–1789)," *Histoire des Francs-maçons en France*, 77–82.

48. Devillière is noted on the 1778 and 1779 tableaux as "associé libre et notre député."

49. "Nouvelle demande," June 23, 1778, F-Pn, Baylot, FM2-97, doc. 7.

50. "Nouvelle demande," June 23, 1778, F-Pn, Baylot, FM2-97, doc. 7.

51. Gefen, "La Franc-maçonnerie vecteur du classicisme," 97.

52. "Tableau des F. F. qui composent la Respectable Loge St. Jean sous le titre distinctif de La Réunion des Arts," Paris, 1777, F-Pn, Baylot, FM2-97, doc. 66.

53. "Tableau des F. F. qui composent la Respectable Loge St. Jean sous le titre distinctif de La Réunion des Arts," Paris, 1778, F-Pn, Baylot, FM2-97, doc. 67.

54. The lodge existed from 1775 until 1783. Dates from Alain Le Bihan, *Francs-maçons parisiens du Grand Orient de France (fin du XVIIIe siecle)* (Paris: Bibliothèque nationale, 1966), 13.

55. The 1778 and 1779 banquets are described in two documents: "La L. d'adoption dirigé par les officiers de la L. régulières de la Candeur, tenant ses travaux à Paris," Paris, May 15, 1778, F-Pn, Baylot, FM2-58bis, dos. 1, doc. 44–49; and "Seconde Esquisse des Travail d'adoption, dirigés par les officiers de la loge de la Candeur," Paris, May 15, 1779, F-Pn, Baylot, FM2-58bis, dos. 1, doc. 73–77.

56. Julia I. Doe, "Marie Antoinette et la musique: Habsburg Patronage and French Operatic Culture (1770–89)," *Studies in Eighteenth-Century Culture* 46 (2017): 81–94; Rebecca Dowd Geoffroy-Schwinden, "A Lady-in-Waiting's Account of Marie Antoinette's Musical Politics: Women, Music, and the French Revolution," *Women and Music: A Journal of Gender and Culture* 21 (2017): 72–100; and Julia Doe, *The Comedians of the King: Opéra Comique and the Bourbon Monarchy on the Eve of Revolution* (Chicago: University of Chicago Press, 2021), 123–58.

57. Tomaso Giovanni Albinoni probably composed this particular melody.

58. "Tableau des frères qui composent la Loge S. Jean sous le titre distinctif de La Candeur," Paris, 1776, F-Pn, Baylot, FM2-58bis, dos. 1, doc. 57; and "Tableau des Frères composans la Loge régulière de S. Jean de La Candeur," Paris, 1777, F-Pn, Baylot, FM2-58bis, dos. 1, doc. 65.

59. The historian Pierre Chevallier also interprets the placement of names on masonic membership tables as indicative of brothers' statuses within a lodge. See, for example, Chevallier, *Histoire de Saint Jean d'Écosse du Contrat Social*, 285, on the musician Étienne Floquet's position as *architecte de musique* in the lodge Saint Jean d'Écosse du Contrat Social.

60. The musicians were Nicolas Bonnaire, Louis Bruand, Jacques Falcoz, André Jean Gallet, Jean Christophe Koch, François Antoine Lix (cadet), Jean-Michel Lix (aîné), Joseph Philippe Louis (cadet), Jacques Schneitzhoffer, and Louis Zémédé Serveta. On positions in the Gardes françaises, see Pinaud, "Dictionnaire biographique," *Les musiciens francs-maçons*.

61. Pinaud, *Les musiciens francs-maçons*, 21. See also, "harmonie (ii)," *Grove Music Online*.

62. André-Ernest-Modeste Grétry, *L'ami de la maison* (Paris: Houbaut, 1772).

63. "À deposer dans le même étui après qu'ils avoient joué leur sonate." Grétry, *De la verité*, 2:7.

64. Pinaud, *Les musiciens francs-maçons*, 33; and Tableaux from F-Pn, Baylot, FM2-97, docs. 65–7. Although musicians were fundamental to the foundation of La Réunion des Arts, the lodge did not remain a haven for them. The most famous musician to join the lodge after its founding was undoubtedly the composer François-Joseph Gossec, who appears on the 1781 table. Only six other musicians in addition to Gossec joined the lodge after its 1778 installation. A single founding member—Devaux—remained on its tables through 1785, and throughout the remainder of the 1780s, musicians' membership in La Réunion des Arts steadily declined. By 1787, no musicians appear on its tables at all.

65. David Hennebelle, *De Lully à Mozart: aristocratie, musique et musiciens à Paris (XVIIe– XVIIIe siècles)* (Seysell: Champ Vallon, 2009), 142.

66. Cotte, *La musique maçonnique et ses musiciens*, 202. Antoine Lilti emphasizes the problematic polysemy of the term *société* in late eighteenth-century Paris, although Cotte provides a useful definition of how the term was typically employed in lodges. In the case of concerts, it seemed to adhere to the definition of a group "in the search for pleasure or amusement." Antoine Lilti, *The World of Salons: Sociability and Worldliness in Eighteenth-Century Paris*, trans. Lydia G. Cochrane (New York: Oxford University Press, 2015), 27–9.

67. Pinaud distinguishes "musical" and "non-musical" lodges based on the reputation (or lack thereof) of their *harmonie* and the number of musicians affiliated (28). My own research corroborates his designations.

68. Pinaud, *Les musiciens francs-maçons*, 28 and 54.

69. Le Bihan, *Francs-maçons parisiens* 12. These statistics are from 1771–1792.

70. *Procès-verbaux de l'Académie des Beaux-Arts* identifies *aggrégé* as a new category created by a 1777 ordonnance for the Académie Royale de Peinture et Sculpture (XXXIII).

71. Pinaud, *Les musiciens francs-maçons*, 27.

72. *Philalèthes, Loge les Amis-Réunis, circulaire* (Paris, 1784), F-Pn, Baylot, FM2-33. Founded by Charles-Pierre-Paul Savalette de Langes, Les Amis Réunis constituted a unique masonic legacy because of its dedication to a branch of philosophical or mystical Freemasonry called the Philalèthes—lovers (or seekers) of truth. The secrets revealed on initiation into each of its many ranks earned the lodge a reputation in masonic historiography as an occult academy. Indeed, its founders hoped to bring together experts from diverse fields to establish a perfected "science of Masonry."

73. Charles Porset, *Les Philalèthes et les convents de Paris: une politique de la folie* (Paris: Honoré Champion Éditeur, 1996).

74. Pinaud, *Les musiciens francs-maçons*, 182.

75. Saint-Jean d'Écosse existed from 1776 until 1791.

76. Chevallier, *Histoire de Saint Jean d'Écosse du Contrat Social*, 271. Recruitment was focused in 1781 and 1782.

77. He took on the position on December 27, 1779, and so it was perhaps Floquet's efforts that influenced the intensive 1781–1782 musician recruitment.

78. Chevallier, *Histoire de Saint Jean d'Écosse du Contrat Social*, 279–80.

79. Chevallier, *Histoire de Saint Jean d'Écosse du Contrat Social*, 273.

80. Chevallier, *Histoire de Saint Jean d'Écosse du Contrat Social*, 280.

81. Grétry, *De la verité*, 2:7.

82. Jean Kriff with Charles Porset, "Saint-Georges," in Charles Porset and Cécile Révauger, *Le monde maçonnique des lumières (Europe-Amériques & Colonies): dictionnaire prosopographique* (Paris: Honoré Champion Éditeur, 2013), 2445.

83. Claims about Saint-Georges's role in these negotiations are not confirmed by known documentation. See Daniel Heartz, *Music in European Capitals: The Galant Style 1720–1780* (New York: W. W. Norton, 2003), 680–5.

84. *Liste des membres qui composent la Société Olympique: avec leurs qualités et demeures pour l'année 1786*, BHVP, Imprimé no. 14,718. *Annuaire-tableau de la Société Olympique pour 1788*, F-Pn, I Baylot FM 153. Olympique received its first constitution from the Mère Loge Écossaise on November 27, 1779. The Grand Orient renewed the constitution on December 18, 1782. Le Bihan, *Francs-maçons parisiens*, 17.

85. Although it had existed in some form or another since 1779, the Loge Olympique de la Parfaite Estime was officially established through the Grand Lodge on March 22, 1783.

86. "L'origine & la nature essentielle de la Loge & Société Olympique est absolument maçonnique. . . . Son objet principal & intéressant pour le plus grand nombre des Maçons qui se sont réunis pour la former, & de ceux qui s'y font associés depuis, est l'établissement *d'un bon Concert* qui puisse, à quelques égards, replacer la perte du Concert des Amateurs," *Réglemens de la Loge et Société Olympique* (Paris: n.d., c. 1788), 5–6. The *réglemens* were approved on the second Monday of November 1784, and confirmed on January 7, 1785. They were reviewed, corrected, and sent for printing on December 12, 1785. The extant copy represents those same bylaws, further considered and corrected based on "four years

of experience" (11). Since this copy of the *réglemens* specifically refers to 1788, four years since the original approval of the bylaws in 1784, 1788 is the likely publication year.

87. Warwick Lister, "The First Performance of Haydn's 'Paris' Symphonies," *Eighteenth-Century Music* 1, no. 2 (September 2004): 289–300.

88. Beverly Wilcox, "The Music Libraries of the Paris Concert Spirituel: A Commerce in Masterworks (1734–1778)," *Revue de musicologie* 98, no. 2 (2012): 363–403.

89. One *livre* could purchase a modest meal, a cheap wig cost about 10 *livres*, and a good seat at the Opéra might cost two *livres*. One needed at least 3,000 to 4,000 *livres* annual income for a comfortable lifestyle and about 15,000 for an elegant one. A workingman in Paris probably made around 300 to 500 *livres* per year, while a professor at the Sorbonne might earn 1,900. From P. N. Furbank, *Diderot: A Critical Biography* (New York: A. A. Knopf, 1992), 474–5, cited in Leonore Loft, *Passion, Politics, and Philosophy: Rediscovering J.-P. Brissot* (London: Greenwood Press, 2002), 163.

90. *Liste des membres qui composent la Société Olympique*, 8.

91. Chevallier claims that the free associates in Le Contrat Social were "extras" who were engaged like servants to perform when orchestra members were not available. See Chevallier, *Histoire de Saint Jean d'Écosse du Contrat Social*, 285. However, the prestigious reputation of free associates in many lodges and the benefits they received as brothers, particularly as the positions are outlined in Olympique, indicate that in some lodges they were held in higher regard than the orchestra members.

92. Emily H. Green agrees that the "geniality . . . morality and class" of composers increasingly mattered to music consumers during this period. *Dedicating Music, 1785–1850*, Eastman Studies in Music (Woodbridge, UK, and Rochester, NY: Boydell and Brewer and University of Rochester Press, 2019), 116.

93. Lister, "First Performance of Haydn's 'Paris' Symphonies," 290.

94. Jacques Marquet de Montbreton de Norvins, *Souvenirs d'un historien de Napoléon* (Paris: Furne et cie., 1827), 159. It is possible, too, that Viotti only conducted when he starred as a virtuoso at performances. He is listed on the 1788 membership table.

95. *Réglemens de la Loge et Société Olympique* (Paris: n.d., c. 1788), 15.

96. Three musicians were subscribing members, and at least 73 professional musicians participated in 1786; that number rose to 86 in 1788. But in 1788, 78 of these 86 professional musicians were either orchestra or chorus members.

97. *Liste des membres qui composent la Société Olympique; annuaire-tableau de la Société Olympique pour 1788*.

98. Norvins, *Souvenirs d'un historien de Napoléon*, 159.

99. The Concert des Amateurs was funded by members' subscriptions, which covered the cost of maintaining the orchestra and occasionally hiring virtuoso performers. Mathilde de Garidel-Thoron, "Le Concert des Amateurs à l'Hôtel de Soubise au XVIIIème siecle" (Master's Thesis, Université de Paris-Sorbonne—Paris (IV), 1979), 23 and 70.

100. Paola Bertucci, *Artisanal Enlightenment: Science and the Mechanical Arts in Old Regime France* (New Haven: Yale University Press, 2017), 9.

101. See Gerardo Tocchini, "Massoneria, cultura della rappresentazione e mecenatismo musicale nel Settecento," *Studi Storici* 41, no. 2 (Spring 2000): 471–531.

102. John Shovlin, *The Political Economy of Virtue: Luxury, Patriotism, and the Origins of the French Revolution* (Ithaca and New York: Cornell University Press, 2006); Alain

Viala, *Naissance de l'écrivain: sociologie de la littérature à l'âge classique* (Paris: Les éditions de minuit, 1985), 51–4; and Hennebelle, *De Lully à Mozart*.

103. Sewell, "Connecting Capitalism to the French Revolution."

104. "Bel orchestre vraiment, dont une partie y paraissait en habit brodé, en manchettes à dentelles, l'épée au côté et le chapeau à plumet sur les banquettes!" Norvins, *Souvenirs d'un historien de Napoléon*, 159.

105. This began in the Concert des Amateurs, which set the significant precedent for the Société Olympique. Hennebelle also notes this change in *Lully à Mozart*, 167–8.

106. Jean-Luc Quoy-Bodin, "L'orchestre de la Société Olympique en 1786," *Revue de Musicologie* 7, no. 1 (1984): 95–107.

107. Beverly Jerold, "Mystery in Paris, the German Connection, and More: The Bérard-Blanchet Controversy Revisited," *Eighteenth-Century Music* 2, no. 1 (2005): 93.

108. David Hennebelle, "Nobles, musique et musiciens à Paris à la fin de l'Ancien Régime: les transformations d'un patronage séculaire (1760–1780)," *Revue de Musicologie* 87, no. 2 (2001): 395–418.

109. *Édit du roi, concernant le corps de la musique du roi* (Versailles 1782).

110. Pinaud, *Les musiciens francs-maçons*, 93–103.

111. Tocchini also views the treatment of music in lodges like Le Contrat Social and Olympique as representing an older patronage model. See "Massoneria, cultura della rappresentazione e mecenatismo."

112. See M. Bassi, "Lettre adressée à la Société Olympique de Paris, à l'occasion de l'Opéra Bouffon Italien de Versailles" (Paris, 1787). The letter begins, "Permettez moi, Messieurs & Mesdames, de porter au Tribunal le plus compétente que je connaisse dans la Capitale, un discussion qui eut lieu entre un Amateur de musique & moi."

113. Maria Rika Maniates, "'Sonate, que me veux-tu?' the Enigma of French Musical Aesthetics in the Eighteenth Century," *Current Musicology* 9 (January 1969): 117–41; John Neubauer, The *Emancipation of Music from Language: Departures from Mimesis in Eighteenth-Century Aesthetics* (New Haven: Yale University Press, 1986); and Alexandre Dratwicki, *Un nouveau commerce de la virtuosité: émancipation et métamorphoses de la musique concertante au sein des institutions musicales parisiennes (1780–1830)* (Lyon: Symétrie, 2005).

114. Chevallier, *Histoire de Saint Jean d'Écosse du Contrat Social*, 280.

115. "Tableau des frères qui composent La R. L. de Saint Jean sous le titre distinctif de l'accord parfait sous Diane," c. May–July 1789, Paris, F-Pn, Baylot, FM2-31, f. 1.

116. "Tableau alphabetique des frères qui composent la loge de saint Charles de la parfait harmonie a l'orient de Paris," 1778, and "Tableau de la Loge St. Jean sous le titre distinctif de St. Charles du Triomphe de la parfait harmonie," January 1780, Paris, F-Pn, Baylot, FM2-102.

117. "Luigi Cherubini, compositeur de musique," November 29, 1784, Paris, F-Pn, Baylot, FM2-104, f. 14.

118. Harrison C. and Cynthia A. White, *Canvases and Careers: Institutional Change in the French Painting World* (1965; repr., Chicago: University of Chicago Press, 1993); Toby Gelfand, *Professionalizing Modern Medicine: Paris Surgeons and Medical Science and Institutions in the Eighteenth Century* (Westport, CT: Greenwood Press, 1980); Antoine Picon, *L'invention de l'ingénieur moderne: L'École des ponts et chaussées, 1747–1851* (Paris: Presses de l'École Nationale des Ponts et Chaussées, 1992); Rafe Blaufarb, *The French Army,*

1750–1820: Careers, Talent, Merit (Manchester: Manchester University Press, 2002); Pierre Baron, "Dental Practice in Paris," in *Dental Practice in Europe at the End of the Eighteenth Century*, Willcome Series in the History of Medicine, ed. Christine Hillam (Rodopi: Brill, 2003); and Gregory S. Brown, *A Field of Honor: Writers, Court Culture and Public Theater in French Literary Life from Racine to the Revolution* (New York: Columbia University Press, 2005).

119. "Discours du F. Oudet," April 13, 1783, Paris, F-Pn, Baylot, FM2-100 bis, dos. 1, f. 32. Although the lodge Saint-Charles du Triomphe de la Parfaite Harmonie never received a constitution from the Grand Lodge, it functioned as a lodge from at least 1778 until 1789, and from 1782 on received official recognition under the name Saint-Alexandre d'Écosse by the mother Scottish Rite lodge. Le Bihan, *Francs-maçons parisien*, 18 and 28. After Saint-Charles became Saint-Alexandre, six musicians continued to participate in the lodge from 1782 to 1789. They joined Saint-Alexandre in 1782 and 1783, were sometimes listed discretely as the *harmonie*, and all lived in the same location—the Hôtel de Choiseul. They may have been recruited from the same household orchestra, and thus may not have circulated within the lodge socially. Because Saint-Alexandre was a Scottish lodge, its *harmonies* probably served to project legitimacy.

120. On secular humanitarianism in Enlightenment France, see Catherine Duprat, *"Pour l'amour de l'humanité": le temps des philanthropes ; la philanthropie parisienne des Lumières à la monarchie de Juillet*, preface by Maurice Agulhon, vol. 1 (Paris: Éditions du Comité des Travaux historiques et scientifiques, 1993).

121. Gelfand, *Professionalizing Modern Medicine*; and Baron "Dental Practice in Paris."

122. Gelfand, *Professionalizing Modern Medicine*, 75.

123. Gelfand, *Professionalizing Modern Medicine*, 11.

124. As a young man he had been mentored by Rameau. He later performed as a violinist in the Concert des Amateurs under the direction of Gossec and Saint-Georges, and he also subscribed to the Loge Olympique concerts (though he did not perform in its orchestra). In addition to his publications on musical aesthetics, Chabanon authored the libretto to Gossec's *Sabinus* (1773) and composed sonatas for the harpsichord, pianoforte, and violin. *Trois sonates pour clavecin ou forte piano avec accompagnement de violon* (Paris, n.d.), and *Sonate pour le clavecin ou le piano-forte* (Paris, 1785).

125. Michael-Paul-Guy de Chabanon, *De la musique considérée en elle-même et dans ses rapports avec la parole, les langues, la poésie et le théâtre* (Paris: Chez Pissot, 1785), see esp. 21–24; *Observations sur la musique* (Paris: Chez Pissot, 1779).

126. Johann Adam Hiller, trans., *Über die Musik und deren Wirkungen* (Leipzig: Friedrich Gotthold Jacobäer und Sohn, 1781). I am grateful to Robert Michael Anderson for sharing this with me in his unpublished paper, "Musical Instinct as Sensation and Expressive Genius: On Musical Autonomy in Hiller's Translation of Chabanon's *Über die Musik und deren Wirkungen*."

127. Chabanon's membership in the lodge is indicated in *Liste des membres qui composent la Société Olympique*; and *Annuaire-tableau de la Société Olympique pour 1788*.

128. Ligou, *Histoires des francs-maçons en France*, 15. On the culture of guilds and corporations, see William H. Sewell Jr., *Work and Revolution in France: The Language of Labor from the Old Regime to 1848* (Cambridge: Cambridge University Press, 1980).

129. Chabanon, *De la musique*, 24.

130. "Hors ceux qui, toute leur vie, on exécuté de la Musique, il est peu d'hommes en état de subir l'épreuve que nous proposons," Chabanon, *De la musique*, 390.

131. Luc Charles-Dominique, *Les ménétriers français sous l'ancien régime* (Paris: Klincksieck, 1994), 279. Charles-Dominique uses the term "savant" to refer to the lyric tradition of composer-keyboardists who dominated social spaces compared to guild-like musicians who participated in civic or popular performances.

132. This group included Nicolas-Étienne Framery, also an Olympique free associate, and Marie Alexandre Guénin, a highly regarded composer and violinist. Claude Role, *Marie-Alexandre Guénin* (Maubeuge: Édition Les Amis du Livre, 2003).

133. Pinaud, *Les musiciens francs-maçons*, 33.

134. "Fête Académique, donnée par la Société connue sous le nom des Neuf Sœurs, Le 26 mai Waux-hall de la Foire Saint-Germain," Paris, F-Pn, FM2-89, dos. 1, doc. 1; and "Fête Académique, donné, par extraordinaire, à l'occasion de la paix, par la L. des Neuf-Sœurs, Conjointement avec l'Ex. V. F. Franklin," Paris, F-Pn, Baylot, FM2-89, dos. 1, doc. 3.

135. R. William Weisberger deemphasizes musicians' role in the lodge of the Nine Sisters in "Parisian Masonry, the Lodge of the Nine Sisters, and the French Enlightenment," *Heredom* 10 (2002): 155–202.

136. Blaufarb, *The French Army*.

137. *Éloge funèbre du T. R. F. Dalayrac* (Paris: L'imprimerie d' A. Égron, 1810), 9. F-Pn, Baylot, FM2-148.

138. Weisberger, "Benjamin Franklin," 175.

139. Weisberger, "Parisian Masonry," 170.

140. "C'était pour la première fois qu'une institution basée sur l'égalité semblait attaquer elle-même, en apparence, ce principe qui dirigea les premiers homme sur la terre, en n'admettant qu'une classe de citoyens, c'est-à-dire, ceux qui professeraient une des sciences, un des arts relatifs à l'un des attributs des filles de Jupiter et de Mnémozime," *Éloge funèbre*, 9.

141. Bernard Harrison, *Haydn: The Paris Symphonies*, Cambridge Music Handbooks (Cambridge: Cambridge University Press, 1998).

142. Neubauer, *Emancipation of Music from Language*; and Mark Evan Bonds, *Wordless Rhetoric: Musical Form and the Metaphor of Oration* (Cambridge, MA: Harvard University Press, 1991). Charles-Dominique makes a similar argument about composers and keyboardists' status in *Les ménétriers français*.

143. James H. Johnson, *Listening in Paris: A Cultural History* (Berkeley: University of California Press, 1995).

144. Pinaud, *Les musiciens francs-maçons*, 93–103; and Chevallier, *Histoire de Saint Jean d'Écosse du Contrat Social*, 286–7.

145. Méhul is listed as a subscribing member in the 1786 table, but by 1788 he was a free associate. *Liste des membres qui composent la Société Olympique*; *Annuaire-tableau de la Société Olympique pour 1788*.

146. Brown, *Field of Honor*; Blaufarb, *The French Army*; Gelfand, *Professionalizing Modern Medicine*; Picon, *L'invention de l'ingénieur moderne*; White, *Canvases and Careers*; Baron, "Dental Practice in Paris."

147. In *Brotherly Love*, Loiselle demonstrates how Freemasonry cultivated both ritualized and unritualized friendships among men, simultaneously fostering "private

venues of sociability" while also providing "a powerful apprenticeship in classical republicanism" (253). This "politicization of the private prefigured the revolutionary concern from 1789 onward to create a morally regenerated citizenry that would anchor the new nation and leave behind the decadence of the Old Regime" (248) as, privately, Freemasons relied on one another as outlets for personal or professional dissatisfaction.

148. Brengues et al., "Le monde maçonnique des lumières," 97–98. "Au même titre que les institutions de culture—collèges, académies, salons, sociétés littéraires, savants, agricoles—les loges sont porteuses d'un idéal culturel unificateur et éducatif ou la société civile se dessine dans sa modernité, à la fois indépendante et liée au pouvoir qui l'observe—comme dans un autre registre les académiciens, les francs-maçons œuvrent au dessein d'un absolutisme éclairé pour l'unification du royaume et l'intégration de la 'Nation.'"

149. Lilti emphasizes the "semi-public" nature of gatherings called *société*. *The World of Salons*, 7 and 25.

150. Pinaud, *Les musiciens francs-maçons*, 193. "Tableau des F. F. qui composent la Respectable Loge St. Jean sous le titre distinctif de La Réunion des Arts," Paris, 1776, F-Pn, Baylot, FM2-97, doc. 65; "Tableau des F. F. qui composent la respectable Loge Saint Jean sous le titre distinctif de La Réunion des Arts," Paris, 1777, F-Pn, Baylot, FM2-97, doc. 66; and "Tableau des membres qui composent la L. St. Jean sous le titre distinctif de la Réunion des Arts," Paris, 1778, F-Pn, Baylot, FM2-97, doc. 67.

151. Chevallier, *Histoire de Saint Jean d'Écosse du Contrat Social*, 280.

152. Quoted in Chevallier, *Histoire de Saint Jean d'Écosse du Contrat Social*, 284–5.

153. Grétry, *De la vérité*, 2:8. "Je n'ai pas voulu vous tuer, mais seulement vous donner une petite leçon d'harmonie sociale dont vous aviez grand besoin."

154. Leigh explains, "In fact, the duel appeals more to the Enlightenment, even as it irks the thinkers of this age, because it is scrupulous, rule bound, equitable, and above all, temperate" (10).

Chapter 3

1. Jacques Brengues, Monique Mosser, and Daniel Roche, "Le monde maçonnique des Lumières," in *Histoire des francs-maçons en France*, ed. Daniel Ligou (Toulouse: Editions Privat, 1987), 125.

2. The French did not employ the specific term "copyright," so it is used here only in Anglo-American contexts where the term does in fact date back to the eighteenth century. In the French context, I use the phrase "printing rights" to distinguish types of *droit d'auteur*. See Benedict Atkinson and Brian Fitzgerald, *A Short History of Copyright: The Genie of Information* (Cham: Springer, 2014).

3. "Music Copyright in Late Eighteenth and Early Nineteenth-Century Britain," in *Research Handbook on the History of Copyright Law*, ed. Isabella Alexander and H. Tomás Gómez-Arostegui (Cheltenham, UK and Northampton, MA: Edward Elgar Publishing, Inc., 2016), 139–58; on Bach and Abel, specifically, see Ann van Allen-Russell, "'For Instruments Not Intended:' The Second J.C. Bach Lawsuit," *Music and Letters* 83, no. 1 (2002): 3–29.

4. Glenda Goodman, *Cultivated by Hand: Amateur Musicians in the Early American Republic*, New Cultural History of Music Series (New York: Oxford University Press, 2020), 43–4.

5. See Laurent Guillio, "Legal Aspects," in *Music Publishing in Europe 1600–1900: Concepts and Issues Bibliography*, ed. Rudolph Rasch (Berlin: Berliner Wissenschafts-Verlag, 2005); and Nancy A. Mace, "Haydn and the London Music Sellers: Forster v. Longman & Broderip," *Music and Letters* 77, no. 4 (November 1996): 527–41.

6. Carla Hesse, *Publishing and Cultural Politics in Revolutionary Paris, 1789–1810*, Studies on the History and Society of Culture 12 (Berkeley: University of California Press, 1991), 42.

7. Stephen Rose also notes that proprietary rights conflicted with a privilege system. Stephen Rose, *Musical Authorship from Schütz to Bach* (Cambridge: Cambridge University Press, 2019), 150.

8. Rose, *Musical Authorship from Schütz to Bach*, 117.

9. Michael W. Carroll, "The Struggle for Music Copyright," *Florida Law Review* 57, no. 4 (September 2005): 914.

10. Peter Tschmuck, "Eighteenth-Century Vienna," in *Copyright in the Cultural Industries*, ed. Ruth Towse (Cheltenham, UK, and Northampton, MA: Edward Elgar Publishing, 2002), 218.

11. Martin Kretschmer and Friedemann Kawohl, "The History and Philosophy of Copyright," in *Music and Copyright*, 2nd edition, ed. Simon Frith and Lee Marshall (New York: Routledge, 2004), 31.

12. As Emily H. Green puts it, "composers navigated complex careers in these years [1785–1850] as more people—filling more types of roles—sought ways to profit from copying, printing, and distributing their music." *Dedicating Music 1785–1850*, Eastman Studies in Music (Woodbridge, UK, and Rochester, NY: Boydell and Brewer and University of Rochester Press, 2019), 32.

13. Rose has similarly cited changing economic conditions as one factor among many, both moral and material, in musicians' claims to intellectual authority over their compositions. *Musical Authorship from Schütz to Bach*, 12–13.

14. Rose also points out that music privileges in early modern German lands "reveal underlying ideas about musical authorship, including the balance between individual recognition and social obligations." *Musical Authorship from Schütz to Bach*, 136. As he explains it, princes had a legitimate right to "resist the notion of sharing music for the common good. As feudal overlords, princes had a proprietorial claim over their servants including musicians," 123.

15. Rose, *Musical Authorship from Schütz to Bach*, 214.

16. Mark Darlow has shown how the writers associated with playwright Pierre Beaumarchais drew on "current legislation" during the Revolution "to legitimate their claims" (40) in "Beaumarchais, Framery, and the Society of Dramatic Authors," in *Beaumarchais: homme de lettres, homme de société*, ed. Philip Robinson, French Studies of the Eighteenth and Nineteenth Century (Oxford: Peter Lang, 2000), 39–55.

17. Jann Pasler, *Composing the Citizen: Music as Public Utility in Third Republic France* (Berkeley: University of California Press, 2009), 53–93.

18. Gregory S. Brown, "Intermission: Beaumarchais and the *Société des Auteurs Dramatiques*," *A Field of Honor: Writers, Court Culture, and Public Theatre in French Literary Life from Racine to Revolution* (New York: Columbia University Press, 2002), 195–208.

19. Carla Hesse, "Enlightenment Epistemology and the Laws of Authorship in Revolutionary France, 1777–93," *Representations* 30 (Spring 1990): 109–37.

20. Constant Pierre, *Le Conservatoire national de musique et de déclamation documents historiques et administratifs* (Paris: Imprimerie nationale, 1900), 15.

21. Furthermore, "author" tends to be applied more frequently to composers who wrote for the stage and church, that is, vocal music, rather than instrumental music.

22. *Mercure de France*, April 9, 1785. "Nous avons souvent l'occasion de parler contre tous ces arrangemens de musique, faits sans la participation de l'Auteur, véritable brigandage, dont les artistes, & souvent même le Public, sont également dupes. M. Grétry vient aussi de s'en plaindre publiquement. Il est à désirer qu'à force de réclamations, il s'établisse un nouvel ordre qui mette en sûreté la propriété des Auteurs. Nous croyons que le plus sûr moyen est que les Auteurs se chargent eux-mêmes à l'avenir de ces arrangemens, qui mériteront alors aux yeux du Public un entière préférence" (48–9).

23. André-Ernest-Modeste Grétry, *De la vérité, ce que nous fûmes, ce que nous sommes, ce que nous devrions être* (Paris: Chez Ch. Pougens, 1801), 2:1–6.

24. Constant Pierre, *Le Conservatoire national de musique*, 22.

25. Jean Gribenski provides a detailed summary of this September 15, 1786, arrêt, "Un métier difficile: éditeur de musique sous la Révolution," in *Le tambour et la harpe: œuvres, pratiques et manifestations musicales sous la Révolution*, ed. Jean-Rémy Julien and Jean Mongrédien (Paris: Éditions du May, 1991), 22–3.

26. Jacques Attali notes that Lully was denied the right to print and profit from his works, but that in 1749 when the Ballard press failed to acquire "a general privilege for music engraving," publishers' power over composers was slightly weakened. As shown in Chapter 1, this is a bit of a misunderstanding both of Lully's printing agreements with Ballard and the circumstances around the breakup of the Ballard family monopoly. Attali also assumes that legislation around author's rights automatically applied to composers at midcentury. *Noise: The Political Economy of Music*, trans. Brian Massumi, Theory and History of Literature 16 (1985; repr. Minneapolis and London: University of Minnesota Press, 2003), 54.

27. André-Ernest-Modeste Grétry, *La correspondance générale de Grétry, augmentée de nombreux documents relatifs à la vie et aux œuvres du compositeur liégeois*, ed. Georges de Froidcourt (Brussels: Brépols, 1962), 125n1.

28. Gribenski, "Un métier difficile," 23.

29. Froidcourt, *La correspondance générale de Grétry*, 135.

30. Froidcourt, *La correspondance générale de Grétry*, 135–43.

31. Gribenski, "Un métier difficile," 23, and n. 10.

32. Gribenski, "Un métier difficile," 23, and n. 9.

33. Brown, *Literary Sociability*, 27–34. See also, Brown, "'*Politesse Perdu*': The Patriot Playwright between Court and Public," in *A Field of Honor*, 121–5.

34. Ironically, Champein had created his most successful composition, *La mélomanie*, from a preexisting play. I am grateful to Julia Doe for alerting me to this rich coincidence.

35. Stanislas Champein, *Les amours de Bayard* (1786), Gallica, https://gallica.bnf.fr/ark:/12148/btv1b8447319g, accessed May 6, 2019.

36. Because the reports were managed by a variety of administrating bodies, they are found throughout the Archives nationales series Y1899–1906. Georges Wildenstein, ed.,

Rapports d'experts, 1712–1791, procès-verbaux d'expertise d'œuvres d'art extraits du fonds du Châtelet, aux Archives Nationales (Paris: Les Beaux-Arts, Édition d'études et de documents, 1921), VII.

37. Wildenstein, *Rapports d'experts*, VII.

38. The variations in how this process took place would be too numerous to recount here, but are outlined in Wildenstein, *Rapports d'experts*, VII–III.

39. Wildenstein, *Rapports d'experts*, IX.

40. Wildenstein, *Rapports d'experts*, IX–X. Wildenstein explains, "Il s'agissait d'établir si cet artiste devait être considéré comme un maître-graveur sur métaux—et par conséquent assujetti aux lois de la maîtrise—ou comme un artiste graveur—et ainsi entièrement libre—ces rapports donnent d'utiles indications sur la différence des deux états."

41. These are the examples given by Wildenstein (XI) and are cases that are not actually included in his publication, but that exist in the F-Pan series.

42. Wildenstein, *Rapports d'experts*, 119.

43. Wildenstein, *Rapports d'experts*, 21–2. "ressemble un peu à celuy d'un vase un peu feslé . . . une harmonie un peu sourde . . . fort bonnes."

44. Wildenstein, *Rapports d'experts*, 146–7. The report reproduced in Wildenstein is located in F-Pan, Y 1906. "des droits d'auteur redevables à [Stanislas] Champein, [compositeur de musique], pour la partition d'une comédie musicale."

45. Although it would require more extensive research, this may be one of the earliest instances of a composer in France drawing on "author's rights" in a legal context.

46. Wildenstein, *Rapports d'experts*, 147. "la fixation et l'estimation de cet ouvrage."

47. Wildenstein, *Rapports d'experts*, 148. "chants, pantomimes, ballets, ouverture, qu'entracte et chœurs."

48. Wildenstein, *Rapports d'experts*, 148. "considérant la musique par son propre mérite, par le prix du travail qu'elle a dû coûter, par les beautés qui s'y trouvent et enfin par le succès et les applaudissements qu'elle a eus et qu'elle aura, je dois l'estimer d'une manière noble et juste et relativement au profit qu'elle a dû produire à l'auteur des paroles. "

49. *Règlement pour les comédiens français ordinaires du roi* (Paris: Ballard, 1781), 47.

50. Brown, "*Droits d'auteur* and *Approbation* as Cultural Capital: Literary Property, Censorship, and Legitimacy at the Comédie Française, 1760–1780," in *A Field of Honor*, 209–65.

51. Wildenstein, *Rapports d'experts*, 148.

52. Hesse, *Publishing and Cultural Politics*, 101n65, offers an extensive bibliography on authorial originality as a claim to property rights.

53. Denis Diderot, "Lettre historique et politique adressée à un magistrat sur le commerce de la librairie," quoted and translated in Hesse, *Publishing and Politics*, 100.

54. Quoted and translated in Hesse, *Publishing and Politics*, 100.

55. Jane C. Ginsburg, "A Tale of Two Copyrights: Literary Property in Revolutionary France and America," reprinted in *Intellectual Property Law and History*, ed. Steven Wilf (Ashgate, 2012), 36. Ginsburg identifies a "Lockean principle," by which, "a property right arises out of one's labors."

56. Hesse, *Publishing and Cultural Politics*, 104.

57. Quoted and translated in Hesse, *Publishing and Cultural Politics*, 100.

58. Ann Jefferson, *Genius in France: An Idea and Its Uses* (Princeton, NJ: Princeton University Press, 2015), 34.

59. Brown, *Literary Sociability*, 116–17.

60. Brown, *Literary Sociability*, 122.

61. Brown, *Literary Sociability*, 124–6.

62. Darlow, "Beaumarchais," 44.

63. Brown, *Literary Sociability*, 143.

64. On national, collective genius in France, see Jefferson, *Genius in France*, 45–61.

65. Rafe Blaufarb, *The Great Demarcation: The French Revolution and the Invention of Modern Property* (Oxford: Oxford University Press, 2016), 10.

66. Blaufarb, *The Great Demarcation*, 145.

67. Hesse, *Publishing and Cultural Politics*, 120–1. Hesse makes this point clear throughout the entire book.

68. Hesse, *Publishing and Cultural Politics*, 201.

69. Brown, *Literary Sociability*, 127.

70. Mark Darlow, *Nicolas-Étienne Framery and Lyric Theatre in Eighteenth-Century France*, Studies on Voltaire and the Eighteenth Century (Oxford: Voltaire Foundation, 2003), 276.

71. Brown, *Literary Sociability*, 131. Brown notes the inaccuracy of sharp distinctions made by some scholars between the American Revolution's public-centered rights and the French Revolutions author-centered rights. See p. 137–8 and n. 48. This reading is supported by Ginsberg's "A Tale of Two Copyrights."

72. Brown, *Literary Sociability*, 135.

73. Rebecca Dowd Geoffroy-Schwinden, "Music, Copyright, and Intellectual Property: A Newly Discovered Letter from André-Ernest-Modeste Grétry," Le prix de la musique, *Transposition. Musique et Sciences Sociales* 7 (2018): 3.

74. Sewell, *A Rhetoric of Bourgeois Revolution*, 14–15.

75. Sewell, *A Rhetoric of Bourgeois Revolution*, 15–16.

76. Sewell, *A Rhetoric of Bourgeois Revolution*, 41.

77. Sewell highlights Sieyes's astute articulation of representative government, which applies Rousseau's conception of the social contract to representative government within an economy based on the division of labor, 77–80.

78. "Honorables membres formant Le Comité pour la liberté de la presse," undated, F-Pan, AP^{284} 8, dos. 1. The petition is from the group of dramatic authors, including Grétry, Dalayrac, and Lemierre, who were part of La Harpe's reincarnation of Beaumarchais's *société*.

79. Sewell, *A Rhetoric of Bourgeois Revolution*, 283.

80. "Musiciens, comme associés de talens avec les Gens de lettres dans la composition des ouvrages destinés aux Théâtres lyriques, et en communauté de travaux, d'intrêts, et de droits avec eux, sollicitent auprès de l'assemblée nationale la même protection pour leur proprieté et la même part aux benefice de leurs opéra sur les Théâtres de Province," in "Honorables membres formant Le Comité pour la liberté de la presse," undated, F-Pan, AP^{284} 8, dos. 1.

81. Letter from Grétry to Sieyes, dated October 16, 1790, F-Pan, AP^{284} 8, dos. 4. For full transcription, see Geoffroy-Schwinden, "A Newly Discovered Letter."

82. R. J. Arnold, *Grétry's Operas and the French Public from the Old Regime to the Restoration*, Ashgate Interdisciplinary Studies in Opera (Farnham and Burlington, VT: Ashgate Publishing Limited, 2016), 112.

83. Sieyes, quoted in Sewell, *A Rhetoric of Bourgeois Revolution*, 73. In his postrevolutionary text, *De la verité*, Grétry derides the servitude that artists endured "as men" at the hands of nobles under the Old Regime. See Arnold, *Grétry's Operas and the French Public*, 112.

84. Letter from Grétry to Sieyes, dated October 16, 1790, F-Pan, AP[284] 8, dos. 4. Michael McClellan offers a clear chronology of La Harpe's petitioning and its implications for intellectual property in "The Italian Menace: Opera Buffa in Revolutionary France," *Eighteenth-Century Music* 1, no. 2 (2004): 252–7.

85. Letter from Grétry to Sieyes, dated October 16, 1790, F-Pan, AP[284] 8, dos. 4.

86. Jean-François de La Harpe, *Adresse des auteurs dramatiques à l'Assemblée nationale, prononcé par M. de la Harpe, dans la séance du mardi soir 24 août {1790}*, n.p., n.d.; and *Discours sur la liberté du théâtre prononcé par M. de la Harpe le 17 décembre 1790 à la Société des amis de la Constitution* (Paris: Imprimerie nationale, 1790).

87. For background on these arguments, and on dramatic authors' struggle for intellectual property rights, see Brown, *Literary Sociability*. For a more specific perspective on Dalayrac's role in these debates, see Françoise Karro, "Le musicien et le librettiste dans la nation: propriété et défense du créateur par Nicolas Dalayrac et Michel Sedaine," in *Études sur le XVIIIe siècle: fêtes et musiques révolutionnaires: Grétry et Gossec*, ed. Roland Mortier and Hervé Hasquin (Bruxelles: Éditions de l'Université de Bruxelles, 1990), 17:9–52; and Michael E. McClellan, "Battling over the Lyric Muse: Expressions of Revolution and Counterrevolution at the Théâtre Feydeau, 1789–1801" (PhD diss., UNC–Chapel Hill, 1994); and "The Italian Menace."

88. Letter from Grétry to Sieyes, dated October 16, 1790, F-Pan, AP[284] 8, dos. 4.

89. McClellean, "The Italian Menace," 257–61.

90. See Brown, *Literary Sociability*, and Karro, "Le musicien et le librettiste dans la nation," n. 3.

91. See Brown, *Literary Sociability*, 149.

92. François Fétis, *Biographie Universelle* (Paris: Fermin Dido Frères, 1837) 2:246.

93. See McClellan, "The Italian Menace."

94. Letter from Grétry to Beaumarchais, dated August 18, 1791, in Froidcourt, *La correspondance générale de Grétry*, 158–9.

95. Jefferson, *Genius in France*, 25.

96. McClellan, "The Italian Menace," 259.

97. Letter from Grétry to the *Journal de Paris*, dated January 1, 1791, in Froidcourt, *La correspondance générale de Grétry*, 155. "L'espoir qu'il existera bientôt des lois qui feront respecter la propriété des artistes, me font supporter avec patience cette dernier injustice."

98. Ginsburg, "A Tale of Two Copyrights," 42.

99. Darlow, *Framery*, 279.

100. Michel Thiollière, "IV. Les débats révolutionnaires: Droits d'auteur et domaine public," in *Projet de loi relatif au droit d'auteur et aux droits voisins dans la société de l'information*, rapport n° 308, 2005–2006, fait au nom de la commission des affaires culturelles, déposé le 12 avril 2006, http://www.senat.fr/rap/l05-308/l05-3084.html, accessed December 2, 2014.

101. Quoted in Ginsburg, "A Tale of Two Copyrights," 43.

102. Brown, *Literary Sociability*, 137. According to Brown, "Le Chapelier linked personal expression, national patrimony, and the Abolition of Privilege—three distinct issues in the debates over 'liberty of theatres'—into a single endorsement, not of the rights but of the moral authority of *gens de lettres*."

103. Jacques Boncompain, "Dalayrac, fortune d'une œuvre: du droit d'auteur aux droits d'auteur," in *Nicolas Dalayrac: musicien murétain, homme des lumières*, ed. François Karro-Pélisson (Muret: Société Nicolas Dalayrac, 1991), 55.

104. Darlow, *Framery*, 281–2.

105. The June Le Chapelier was the conclusion to a series of decisions that ended French guilds. See Michael P. Fitzsimmons, "The National Assembly and the Abolition of Guilds in France," *The Historical Journal* 39, no. 1 (March 1996): 133–54.

106. McClellan, "Battling the Lyric Muse," 68–78.

107. See Mark Darlow, *Staging the French Revolution: Cultural Politics and the Paris Opéra, 1789–1794*, New Cultural History of Music Series (New York: Oxford University Press, 2012), 63–182, on the bureaucratic negotiations involved in Opéra repertory decisions from 1789 to 1794. Darlow has illuminated in great detail the political negotiations that underpinned the Opéra's administration and repertory from 1789 to 1794, as well as its relation to free trade thinking and property rights, and so I address it only in a cursory manner here.

108. Darlow, *Staging the French Revolution*, 126.

109. Darlow, *Staging the French Revolution*, 101.

110. Darlow, *Staging the French Revolution*, 78–79.

111. As David Hennebelle's work shows, the aristocracy had for some time transitioned to a collective patronage model anyway. David Hennebelle, *De Lully à Mozart: aristocratie, musique et musiciens à Paris (XVIIe–XVIIIe siècles)* (Seyssel: Champ Vallon, 2009), 127–51.

112. Letter from Grétry to Beaumarchais, dated August 18, 1791, in Froidcourt, *La correspondance générale de Grétry*, 158–9.

113. Mémoire from Grétry, Marmontel, Guillard, and Le Moyne, sent to M. Jurieu, August 22, 1791, F-Pan, F^{17} 1288, doc. 4. "Le traitement annuel que le gouvernement s'est engagé à faire aux auteurs d'un nombre indiquée d'ouvrages pour le théâtre de l'opéra a été très improprement appelé *pension*" (emphasis original).

114. Mémoire from Grétry, Marmontel, Guillard, and Le Moyne, sent to M. Jurieu, August 22, 1791, F-Pan, F^{17} 1288, doc. 4.

> Cependant la loi relative aux pensions est d'autant moins applicable aux auteurs que par l'article 4. Du décret du 13 janvier qui les concerne, L'assemblée déclare expressément que les actes ou marchés conclu entre les auteurs et les administrations de spectacle seront éxécutés. C'est précisément le cas où se trouvent les auteurs. C'est l'exécution d'un marché qu'ils demandent. Ils réclament le prix d'un vent qu'ils ont faite. Ils supplient donc Monsieur le Ministre de l'Intérieur qui vient d'ordonner le payement d'anciennes fournitures faites les années precédents pour le service de l'opera de vouloir bien les faire comprendre, au moins comme fournisseurs, pour tout ce qui leur ont du d'arriéré jusqu'au moin de Juillet 1791. Ce titre de fournisseurs dont ils s'appuient est vrai dans une telle rigueur que l'opera n'auront pu et un pourroit encore se soutenir 15. Jours sans leurs ouvrages. Les décrets même de l'assemblés au sujet de ce genre de propriétés leur donne le droit de s'opposer à la représentation de leurs ouvrages et d'interrompe ainsi les cours d'un spectacle qu'il ne paroit pas encore de l'intérêt de l'administration d'abandonner.

Puisqu'on veut bien reconnoitre les dépenses accessoires de ce théâtre, ils ne pensent pas demander une chose injuste en presant qu'on veuille bien l'occuper de leur créance qui est, sans aucune difficulté, le première et la plus sacrée.

115. Brown, *Literary Sociability*, 152.

116. Quoted in Ginsburg, "A Tale of Two Copyrights," 43.

117. Dalayrac, *Réponse de M. Dalairac à MM. les directeurs de spectacles, réclamans contre deux décrets de l'Assemblée nationale* (n.p.), read before the Committee on Public Instruction December 26, 1791, 2–3. "Un ouvrage d'esprit est la propriété de son auteur. Certainement celui qui, sans avoir obligation à personne de la matière première dont il s'est servi, a enfanté, a tiré du néant un ouvrage d'esprit, doit être le propriétaire. La nature lui donné cette propriété; la loi l'a décretée, la raison la sanctionne."

118. Blaufarb, *The Great Demarcation*, 10.

119. Brown, *Literary Sociability*, 147.

120. Dalayrac, *Réponse*, 7. "On a pas besoin de mon pièce."

121. Gribenski, "Un métier difficile," 23. "S'il s'agissait aussi pour eux d'obtenir un droit de propriété, ce ne pouvait être grâce à la liberté (celle-ci était, nous l'avons vu, Presque totale sous l'Ancien Régime, même après 1786), mais au contraire au moyen d'une réglementation efficace."

122. *Pétition adressée à l'Assemblée nationale par les auteurs et éditeurs de musique* (Paris: Laurens, aîné, s.d.).

The dating of this petition has been the source of some confusion. Karro dates it to 1791 in "Le musicien et le librettiste." The Petition is addressed to the National Assembly, which existed from July 1789 until September 30, 1791, when the Legislative Assembly replaced it. The petition addresses "legislateurs," perhaps simply continuing previous nomenclature, however, one signatory died in September 1792 and another moved to St. Petersburg during 1792. Therefore, the petition must date from sometime between July 1789 and September 1792. Anik Devriès-Lesure misread a handwritten date on a copy of the petition located in the Bibliothèque nationale de France as "1798," which makes no sense based on the petition's contents. Jean Gribenski clarified Devriès-Lesure's dating error to June 24, 1792, in "Un métier difficile," n. 12.

It was in June 1792 that the petition was finally forwarded to the Committee on Public Instruction from the Assembly, which had actually received it months earlier, on January 2, 1792, the correct dating of the petition. See Hesse, *Publishing and Cultural Politics*, 118n115.

123. Future Conservatoire professors who signed the petition included Berton, Guénin, Vandenbroeck, Bonesi, L. Jadin, X. Lefèvre, LeSueur, Fuchs, Devienne, Blasius, Martini, Rigel, Gebauer, Mereaux, Mozin, Gossec, and Kreutzer.

124. *Pétition adressée à l'Assemblée nationale*, 1. "La propriété étant un des droits les plus sacrés de l'homme, les pétitionnaires soussignés croient qu'il est de leur devoir de vous instruire, *législateurs*, qu'il existe parmi les marchands de musique, un brigandage qui ne tend à rien moins qu'à anéantir la propriété des marchands, auteurs, et éditeurs."

125. *Pétition adressée à l'Assemblée nationale*, 1–2.

126. Barry S. Brook, ed., *The Breitkopf Thematic Catalogue: The Six Parts and Sixteen Supplements, 1762–1787* (New York: Dover Publications, 1966), and "Piracy and Panacea of Music in the Late Eighteenth Century," *Journal of the Royal Musical Association* 102 (1975–6): 13–36.

127. Gribenski identifies the documents with which the petition was submitted in "Un métier difficile," 25.

128. Édouard Gregoir, *Grétry: célèbre compositeur belge* (Bruxelles: Chez Schott, 1883), 150.

129. Gribenski, "Un métier difficile," 25. "Il semble que les grands éditeurs ne souffrent trop du vide juridique: sans doute trouvent-ils plus d'avantages que d'inconvénients dans cette situation, qui permet tous les 'piratages' en autorisant notamment de discrètes mais fructueuse liaisons avec l'étranger, inaccessibles aux 'petits' éditeurs."

130. Gribenski notes these absences, although the absence of Dalayrac I emphasize myself. "Un métier difficile," 25.

131. *Allgemeine Musicalische Zeitung*, iii, 1800–1801, col. 804, quoted in, "Gelinek," *Grove*.

132. Green, *Dedicating Music*, 156.

133. Quoted in Darlow, *Framery*, 283, n. 79. "Les gens de lettres [. . .] auraient rougi de songer à leur intérêt personnel et de chercher à en occuper l'Assemblée un seul instant."

134. Brown, *Literary Sociability*, 153–6. Green also addresses an expectation of sociability among notable composers during this period in *Dedicating Music*, 109–19.

135. Darlow, *Framery*, 283.

136. Brown, *Literary Sociability*, 83.

137. Quoted in Darlow, *Framery*, 283. "De toutes les propriété, la moins susceptible de contestation, celle dont l'accroissement ne peut ni blesser l'égalité républicaine, ni donner d'ombrage à la liberté, c'est sans contredit celle des productions du génie."

138. Letter from André-Ernest-Modeste Grétry et al., undated, BHVP, MS 772, fol. 1, doc. 6. Their reference to the previous act indicates this letter's dating from after the petition by authors and publishers of music. "*Ceux des auteurs soussignés dont les noms se trouvent dans le premier acte ci-dessus mentionné* déclarent ne s'être prêter à cette démarche que par précipitation de confiance et sans en prévoir les suites; mais que ce n'est qu'après une mûre délibération qu'ils ont revêtu la présente de leurs signatures" (emphasis added).

139. Grétry, et al.

140. Grétry, et al.

141. Grétry, et al.

142. "According to modern copyright law, economic rights are earned via an author's originality, usually defined as the result of individual skill, labor, effort and judgement," Rose, *Musical Authorship from Schütz to Bach*, 117, citing Andreas Rahmatian, "The Elements of Music Relevant for Copyright Protection," in *Concepts of Music and Copyright: How Music Perceives Itself and How Copyright Perceives Music*, ed. Andreas Rahmatian (Cheltenham: Edward Elgar Publishing, 2015), 105.

143. Rose, *Musical Authorship from Schütz to Bach*, 117. "There is the notion of moral rights," explains Rose, "whereby authors are entitled to have their names associated with their works, and to object to distorted forms of their works that might detract from their reputation."

144. "Sans approfondir la nature de ce Droit qui n'est autre que celui de représailles exploitée au détriment des auteurs de tous les pays, les signataires pensent qu'au moins ne peut-il s'exercer, qu'il en l'absence de tout propriété naturelle ou légale, et que la présence de pareilles propriétés asséaait radicalement aux yeux de la délicatesse, de la justice et du bon sens toute autre prétention quelconque."

145. Jefferson, *Genius in France*, 43. "The observer has his attention directed to the *experience* of the man of genius, and it is that experience . . . which becomes the object of enquiry and constitutes the focus of analytical interest."

146. Dan Edelstein, *On the Spirit of Rights* (Chicago: University of Chicago Press, 2019), 17.

147. The Physiocrats had also linked property to natural rights. Edelstein, *On the Spirit of Rights*, 185.

148. Gribenski, "Un métier difficile," 26.

149. Hesse, *Publishing and Cultural Politics*, 119.

150. Emmanuel-Napoléon Santini De Riols, *Guide de la propriété artistique et littéraire en France et à l'étranger* (Paris: Le Bailly, 1881), 15, and Ginsburg, "A Tale of Two Copyrights," 45.

151. Translated and quoted in Hesse, *Publishing and Cultural Politics*, 119–20. Gribenski notes the report's significance in "Un métier difficile," 26.

152. Grétry, *De la verité*.

153. Hesse, *Publishing and Cultural Politics*, 120–1. "The only true heir to an author's work was the nation as a whole."

154. Thiollière explains: "The **law of 19–24 Jul 1793** has to the contrary a more general scope. It establishes, in article 1, the principle that "authors of all written genres, composers of music, painters and designers that carve pictures or designs, will enjoy for their entire life exclusive rights to sell, to distribute their works in the territory of the Republic and to relinquish the property in full or in part." It establishes thus a **right to reproduction** to authors for the duration of their life, then to their heirs for five years.

(La **loi des 19–24 juillet 1793** a en revanche une portée générale. Elle pose, dès son article 1er, le principe que "les auteurs d'écrits en tout genre, les compositeurs de musique, les peintres et les dessinateurs qui feront graver des tableaux ou dessins, jouiront durant leur vie entière du droit exclusif de vendre, faire vendre, distribuer leurs ouvrages dans le territoire de la République et d'en céder la propriété en tout ou en partie." Elle consacre donc un **droit de reproduction** aux auteurs pour la durée de leur vie, puis à leurs héritiers pendant cinq ans.)" (emphasis original).

155. Ginsburg, "A Tale of Two Copyrights," 46.

156. Ginsburg notes this citing Edouard Laboulaye's 1858 assessment of Lakanal's report: "one sees that nothing has changed in ideas, nor in legislation: the word *property*, it is true, has replaced that of *privilege*, but this property is still but a charitable grant from society." Quoted and translated in Ginsburg, "A Tale of Two Copyrights," 46.

157. Jefferson, *Genius in France*, 19.

158. Rebecca Dowd Geoffroy-Schwinden, "Music as Feminine Capital in Napoleonic France: Nancy Macdonald's Musical Upbringing," *Music and Letters* 100, no. 2 (2019): 303–4.

159. Gribenski, "Un métier difficile," 27–8. I have added to the genres cited by Gribenski those implicated in operatic genres such as parodies and translations.

160. "Trial and error" is Gribenski's phrase, "Un métier difficile," 30.

161. Boncompain, "Dalayrac, Fortune d'une œuvre," 57.

162. Boncompain, "Dalayrac, Fortune d'une œuvre," 57 and 64. The agency's years ran from August to July and in both 1794–1795 and 1795–1796.

163. Jacques Boncompain, "Les auteurs à livre ouvert pendant la Révolution," *Revue d'histoire du théâtre* 41, no. 161 (1989): 89–98.

164. Hesse, *Publishing and Cultural Politics*, Table 3, 202.

165. Green, *Dedicating Music*, 156–68.

166. See Introduction of Anik Devriès-Lesure, *L'édition musicale dans la presse parisienne au XVIIIe siècle: catalogue des announces*, Science de la musique (Paris: CNRS Éditions, 2005).

167. Green, *Dedicating Music*, 138–73.

168. Gribenski, "Un métier difficile," 29–30, and Ginsburg, "A Tale of Two Copyrights," 1028–30.

169. Bruce R. Schueneman and María de Jesús Ayala-Schueneman, "The Composers' House: Le magasin de musique de Cherubini, Méhul, R. Kreutzer, Rode, Nicolo Isouard, et Boïeldieu," *Fontes Artis Musicae* 51, no. 1 (January–March 2004): 53–73.

170. Jefferson, *Genius in France*, 48.

171. Jefferson, *Genius in France*, 7.

172. Jefferson, *Genius in France*, 19.

173. Jefferson, *Genius in France*, 25.

174. M. H. Abrams, *The Mirror and the Lamp: Romantic Theory and the Critical Tradition* (Oxford: Oxford University Press, 1953).

175. Jefferson, *Genius in France*, 29.

176. Catherine Kintzler, *Condorcet: L'instruction publique et la naissance de citoyen* (Le Sycomore, 1984), 146.

177. Jefferson, *Genius in France*, 35.

178. Kintzler, *Condorcet*, 143–54.

179. Deirdre Loughridge notes the transition from imitative musical aesthetics in the eighteenth century to those that offered a window into a person's—the composer's—soul, in *Haydn's Sunrise, Beethoven's Shadow: Audiovisual Culture and the Emergence of Musical Romanticism* (Chicago: University of Chicago Press, 2016), 51.

180. *Procès-verbaux de L'académie des beaux-arts*, ed. Marcel Bonnaire (Paris: Librairie Armand Colin, 1937), 1:120. "Parce qu'il mettait un démarcation entre le Musicien Artiste, et l'Artisan Musicien."

181. Jefferson, *Genius in France*, 30–1.

182. Annelies Andries has similarly noted that the reception of an opera played a role in the Institute's evaluation of it. Andries, "Modernizing Spectacle: The Opéra in Napoleon's Paris (1799–1815)" (PhD diss., Yale University, 2018), 87.

183. *Procès-verbaux*, 1:122–3.

184. *Procès-verbaux*, 1:123.

185. *Procès-verbaux*, 2:236–8.

186. Jefferson, *Genius in France*, 51.

187. Jefferson, *Genius in France*, 61.

188. See Peter Szendy, *Listen: A History of Our Ears*, trans. Charlotte Mandell (New York, Fordham University Press, 2008), 18–24. Although Szendy interprets the laws of 1791 and 1793 as the first steps toward a paradigm, codified later in the nineteenth century, that gave authors rights over the interpretation of their works, they only granted authors financial compensation for the performance of their works, not artistic rights over the staging of productions. Composers did, however, as I show here, make subtle arguments promoting such performance rights at the time.

189. Michael P. Fitzsimmons, *The Place of Words: The Académie Française and Its Dictionary during the Age of Revolution* (Oxford: Oxford University Press, 2017), 131, 143–4.

190. Gribenski, "Un métier difficile," 28–9.

191. Jean Gribenski, "Un métier difficile," 28–9.

192. See Schueneman and Ayala-Schueneman, "The Composers' House."

193. Hesse, *Publishing and Cultural Politics*, 125.

194. Hesse, *Publishing and Cultural Politics*, 121.

195. Hesse, *Publishing and Cultural Politics*, 124.

196. Brown, *Literary Sociability*, 155.

197. Brown, *Literary Sociability*, 104.

198. Brown, *Literary Sociability*, 155.

Chapter 4

1. Edouard Pommier, *L'art de la liberté: doctrines et débats de la Révolution française* (Paris: Gallimard, 1991).

2. Constant Pierre, *Bernard Sarrette et les origines du Conservatoire national de musique et de déclamation* (Paris: Delalain frères, 1895), 12.

3. Pierre, *Bernard Sarrette*, 13n3.

4. See Chapter 2.

5. Pierre, *Bernard Sarrette*, 18.

6. Mark Darlow, *Staging the French Revolution: Cultural Politics and the Paris Opéra, 1789–1794*, New Cultural History of Music Series (New York: Oxford University Press, 2012), 178.

7. Pommier, *L'art de la liberté*.

8. Pierre, *Bernard Sarrette*, 27. The rebellion took place on August 31, 1790.

9. Document founding municipal school reproduced in Pierre, *Bernard Sarrette*, Appendix 1.

10. Rebecca Dowd Geoffroy-Schwinden, Appendix 1, "Politics, the French Revolution, and Performance: Parisian Musicians as an Emergent Professional Class, 1749–1804" (PhD diss., Duke University, 2015); and Jean-Luc Quoy-Bodin, *L'armée et la franc-maçonnerie au déclin de la monarchie sous la Révolution et l'empire* (Paris: Economica, Edic, 1987).

11. "Lettre de M. Clareton au Comité d'instruction publique," January 24, 1792, F-Pan, D XXXVIII IV, file 24.

12. Michel Noiray, "L'École royale de chant (1784–1795): crise musicale, crise institutionnelle," in *Music Education in Europe (1770–1914): Compositional, Institutional, and Political Challenges*, eds. Michael Fend and Michel Noiray, Musical Life in Europe 1600–1900: Circulation, Institutions, Representation (Berlin: Berliner Wissenschafts-Verlag, 2005), 1:72–3.

13. "L'étude de la musique est une partie de l'éducation moderne, et elle peut devenir une ressource pour les Citoyens qui voudront essayer leurs talens sur nos Théâtres ou dans nos Concerts. Ce bel art fait sur-tout l'agrément de la Société," "Lettre de M. Clareton."

14. Except Puppo, who would become violinist at the Opéra until 1799.

15. See Pommier, *L'art de la liberté*.

16. Even as new plans were formulated, many Old Regime institutions of learning continued to function, though with far fewer resources and lower enrollment. This chaotic educational environment is chronicled in R. R. Palmer, *The Improvement of Humanity: Education and the French Revolution* (Princeton: Princeton University Press, 1985).

17. Palmer, *Improvement of Humanity*, 98–99 and 123.

18. "Pour les professions qu'on peut regarder comme publiques, on doit considérer surtout l'avantage d'en confier l'exercice à des hommes plus éclairés." Condorcet, "Quatrième mémoire sur l'instruction relative aux professions," in *Cinq mémoires sur l'instruction publique,* eds. Catherine Kintzler and Charles Coutel (Paris: Garnier-Flammarion, 1994), 196.

19. Palmer, *Improvement of Humanity*, 83–132.

20. William Doyle, *The Oxford History of the French Revolution*, 2nd ed. (Oxford: Oxford University Press, 2002), 136–58.

21. Timothy Tackett, *When the King Took Flight* (Cambridge, MA: Harvard University Press, 2004).

22. Pierre, *Bernard Sarrette*, 33.

23. Daniel Roche, *Le siècle des lumières en province: académies et académiciens provinciaux, 1680–1789* (Paris: Mouton, 1978).

24. See Chapter 3 on the abolition of corporate privilege during the Revolution.

25. Pierre, *Bernard Sarrette*, 40 and 41n1. Pierre dates the document "Les artistes musiciens de la Garde nationale parisienne à la Convention nationale" to the November 8, 1793, visit to the National Assembly and identifies it as a transcript of the speech Sarrette gave on behalf of his musicians. Original document is "Les artistes musiciens de la Garde nationale parisienne à la Convention nationale," F-Pan, DXXXVIII IV, file 24. "L'intérest [sic.] public, intimement lié à celui des arts, réclame impérativement en leur faveur la protection nationale."

26. "Elle [la Garde nationale] ne peut être considérée comme un rassemblement académique, stagnant dans l'ignorance et la présomption; ce sont des artistes actifs, travaillant sans jalousie et dirigés par le seul désir de porter au dernier degré les connaissances de leur art." Pierre, *Bernard Sarrette*, 41. I have maintained the term *jalousie* from the original French because Sarrette is directly speaking to its productive opposite embodied by his Garde nationale musicians: *emulation*. Darlow explains in *Staging the French Revolution*: "Emulation was defined by Jaucourt in the *Encyclopédie* as "a noble, generous passion which, whilst admiring the merit, possessions and actions of others, attempts to imitate or even surpass them, through courageous effort and honorable virtuous principles." It was diametrically opposed to jealousy and envy as "competitive striving between individuals to determine some rank order or hierarchy based on merit." It was a cornerstone of Revolutionary thinking, especially that of the libertarians, and was a conceptualization of progress as provoked by generous emotions such as admiration and

imitation; this idea was later to become central to the Terror's use of great men as moral example." (103–4).

27. Paola Bertucci and Olivier Courcell, "Artisanal Knowledge, Expertise, and Patronage in Early Eighteenth-Century Paris: The Société des Arts (1728–36)," *Eighteenth-Century Studies* 48, no. 2 (Winter 2015): 160; and Thomas Broman, "The Semblance of Transparency: Expertise as a Social Good and an Ideology in Enlightened Societies," *Osiris* 27, no. 1 (2012): 192.

28. Sarrette used the term *régénération* explicitly. Pierre, *Bernard Sarrette*, 41.

29. See Pommier, *L'art de la liberté*.

30. Palmer, *Improvement of Humanity*, 135.

31. Palmer, *Improvement of Humanity*, 160.

32. Palmer, *Improvement of Humanity*, 132 and 139. On the role of revolutionary festivals in political culture, see Mona Ozouf, *Festivals and the French Revolution*, trans. Alan Sheridan (Cambridge, MA: Harvard University Press, 1988). Catherine Kintzler offers a nuanced explanation of the moral dimension of education in *Condorcet: l'instruction publique et la naissance de citoyen* (Le Sycomore, 1984), 228–38.

33. Jann Pasler, *Composing the Citizen: Music as Public Utility in Third Republic France* (Berkeley: University of California Press, 2009).

34. "Le dernier et le plus intéressant motif d'utilité se trouvera même dans l'emploi de ceux qui, sortant de l'Institut, seront doués d'un talent moins transcendant; au milieu de cette précieuse portion de la société, qui après s'être livrée aux pénibles travaux de l'agriculture, en se délassant célébrera les vertus et les bienfaits de la Révolution sous l'arbre sacré de la liberté." Pierre, *Bernard Sarrette*, 41.

35. "amollie par des jours efféminés dans des salons ou dans des temples . . . des vastes arènes, des places publiques, doivent être désormais les salles de concert d'une people libre. . . . C'est dans une République fondée sur les vertus qua la liberté règne et le règne de la liberté est celui des beaux-arts," Pierre, *Bernard Sarrette*, 40–1.

36. Condorcet, *Cinq mémoires sur l'instruction publique*, ed. Catherine Kintzler and Charles Coutel (Paris: Garnier-Flammarion, 1994), 169. "Ils ne goûtent plus les talents d'un virtuose célèbre, s'ils ne l'entendre pas dans un concert qu'ils ont préparé . . . Ils n'ont pas besoin, pour en jouir, d'un privilège de propriété."

37. See Pommier, *L'art de la liberté*.

38. Kintzler, *Condorcet*, 181–2.

39. See Pommier, *L'art de la liberté*.

40. Darlow, *Staging the French Revolution*, 178.

41. M. Durieu, *Observations sur la diatribe appelée Réponse à la lettre écrite à M. Paesiello*, s.d., New York Public Library, 14. "nous exposent à la risée de nos confrères républicain . . . compromettais notre délicatesse, et qu'il y aurait du danger de nous jeter l'encensoir par le nez."

42. The full speech is reproduced in Pierre, *Bernard Sarrette*, 124–6.

43. Constant Pierre, *Le Conservatoire national de musique et de déclamation documents historiques et administratifs* (Paris: Imprimerie nationale, 1900), 121. "L'empire très réel de la musique."

44. "Empruntée aux écoles d'Italie, malgré la différence de régime entre ces deux établissements." Pierre, *Bernard Sarrette*, 126.

45. Bette W. Oliver, *From Royal to National: The Louvre Museum and the Bibliothèque Nationale* (Lanham, MD: Lexington Books, 2007), 39.

46. Pierre, *Le Conservatoire national de musique*, 123.

47. Palmer, *Improvement of Humanity*, 192.

48. On infighting among the Conservatory faculty in its early years of its founding, see Rebecca Dowd Geoffroy-Schwinden, "Politics, the French Revolution, and Performance," 180–25, and Diane Tisdall, "Pierre Baillot and Violin Pedagogy in Paris, 1795–1815" (PhD diss., King's College London, 2016), 136–65.

49. Kailan R. Rubinoff also emphasizes the elevated position of composers in the institution, "Towards a Revolutionary Model of Music Pedagogy: The Paris Conservatoire, Hugot and Wunderlich's *Méthode de flûte*, and the Disciplining of the Musician," *Journal of Musicology* 34, no. 4 (2017): 48.

50. "Déjà, depuis long-tems, vous aviez destiné une somme de trois cent mille livres aux homme laborieux et sans fortune qui cultivent ces arts utiles que l'orgueil appelait métiers; mais vous avez senti que les sciences sublimes, que les arts fondés sur le beau idéal, et dont l'objet est l'imitation d'une nature d'élite, avaient aussi besoin d'encouragement." *Œuvres de M. J. Chénier, Membre de l'Institut*, ed. M. Arnaud (Paris: Guillaum Libraire, 1826), v:178.

The law had been passed on October 18, 1794, just days before the end to official iconoclasm. Alfred J. Bingham, "Marie-Joseph Chénier and French Culture during the French Revolution," *Modern Language Review* 61, no. 4 (October 1966): 593–600; and Pommier, *L'art de la liberté*, 137.

51. *Œuvres de M. J. Chénier*, v:183. "Les arts sont une propriété nationale; les encouragemens qu'ils réclament sont une dette publique."

52. Pommier, *L'art de la liberté*.

53. *Œuvres de M. J. Chénier*, v: 183.

54. Alain Viala, *Naissance de l'écrivain* (Paris: Minuit, 1985), 75–80; and David Hennebelle, *De Lully à Mozart: aristocratie, musique et musiciens à Paris (XVIIe– XVIIIe siècles)* (Seysell: Champ Vallon, 2009).

55. Pommier, *L'art de la liberté*, 209–10.

56. Letter to the Committee on Public Instruction from François Jean Roussel, 11 brumaire an III [November 1, 1794], F-Pan F^{17} 1210, Pièce 172.

57. Letter from C. Godinot to the Committee on Public Instruction, undated, F-Pan F^{17} 1213, Pièces 68–9.

58. "Le Citoyen Bambini habille compositeur et professeur de musique, excellent citoyen, de famille intéressant, est réduit par des pertes multipliées à la position la plus urgente. Il parait avoir les droits les plus légitimes aux encouragemens qui vont être accordés." Letter from Ginguené, undated (F-Pan, D XXXVIII VII 59).

59. "Aux représentants du peuple composant le Comité d'instruction publique de la Convention nationale," from François Giroust to the Committee on Public Instruction, 28 pluviôse an III [February 16, 1795] (F-Pan, D XXXVIII VII 59).

60. "Aux citoyens représentants du peuple composant la Comité d'instruction publique de la Convention nationale," Letter from the General Council of the Versailles commune to the Committee on Public Instruction, 1 pluviôse an III [January 20, 1795] (F-Pan, D XXXVIII VII 59).

61. Letter from J. Berlioz to the Committee on Public Instruction, 4 pluviôse an III [January 23, 1795] (F-Pan, D XXXVIII VII 59). Though it is difficult to trace the identity of J. Berlioz, he may have been a municipal or departmental administrator writing on behalf of Martini per the procedures outlined in the law passed for social security.

62. Julia Doe, *The Comedians of the King: Opéra Comique and the Bourbon Monarchy on the Eve of Revolution* (Chicago: University of Chicago Press, 2021), 14, 139, and 141.

63. M. Elizabeth C. Bartlet, "Jean-Paul-Gilles Martini," *Grove Music*.

64. Bartlet, "Martini."

65. "Encouragement" here should be read in a strictly revolutionary conception of the term to mean financial subsidy; see Darlow, 124, and "The Opéra during the Terror."

66. Letter to Citizen [Antoine Claire] Thibaudeau from [Stanislas] Champein, 17 nivôse an III [January 6, 1795], F-Pan F^{17} 1210, Pièce 41.

67. Letter to the executive directors from Stanislas Champein, F-Pan F^{17} 1244/A, Pièces 17–19, dos. 423, doc. 11. The letter is contained in a set of documents from year IV, thus the letter must have been sent sometime between 1795 and 1796.

68. Rigade's file is found among the "Sécours des artistes et gens de lettres," in F-Pan, F^{17} 1213, dos. 23, 68–9.

69. Letter from C. Champein to Fourqroy, 20 nivôse an III [January 9, 1795], F-Pan F^{17} 1213, Pièce 57.

70. "Aux représentants du peuple, membre du Comité d'instruction publique," Letter from Janson l'aîné to the Committee on the Public Instruction, with note from colleagues on bottom, undated (F-Pan, D XXXVIII VII 59).

71. Although it lacks an original date, a note on the letter indicates that it was resent on January 9, 1795.

72. He eventually was reimbursed 3,000 *livres* by the Committee on Public Instruction for these services on August 26, 1795. *Procès-verbaux du Comité d'instruction publique*, vi: 590.

73. *Procès-verbaux du Comité d'instruction publique*, "Rapport sur les récompenses à distribuer aux savants et aux artistes, présenté au nom des Comités d'instruction publique et des finances, dans la séance du 27 Germinal, l'an III, par P. C. F. Danou," vi: 88. (April 16, 1795).

74. "Aux citoyens représentans du peuple composant le Comité d'instruction publique," Jean Joseph Rodolphe to the Committee on Public Instruction, floréal an III [late April/early May 1795], F-Pan, D XXXVIII VII 59.

75. Here, Rodolphe is likely referring to his *Théorie de l'accompagnement et composition* (Paris: Naderman, 1785), though he also authored *Solfège, ou nouvelle méthode de musique* (Paris: Dufont et Dupris, 1784/1790).

76. J. Desenne, *Codes général français, contenant les lois et actes du gouvernement publiés depuis l'ouverture des États Généraux au 5 mai 1789, jusqu'au 8 juillet 1815, classés par ordre de matières, et annotés des arrêts et décisions de la Cour de Cassation* (Paris: Ménard et Desenne, fils, 1821), 17: 534.

77. Tisdall, "Pierre Baillot," 136–65.

78. Geoffroy-Schwinden, "Politics, the French Revolution, and Performance," 94–102, and 201–25.

79. Tisdall, "Pierre Baillot," 93, 103, and 113.

80. See for example, École gratuite de musique à Versailles, 1795–1799, F-Pan, F^{17} 1144, file 3.

81. Iris Moon, *The Architecture of Percier and Fontaine and the Struggle for Sovereignty in Revolutionary France* (Oxford and New York: Routledge, 2017).

82. Pasler, *Composing the Citizen*, 94–158.

83. Palmer, *Improvement of Humanity*, 69.

84. Palmer, *Improvement of Humanity*, 64.

85. Palmer, *Improvement of Humanity*, 68.

86. Palmer, *Improvement of Humanity*, 68.

87. Pommier, *L'art de la liberté*.

88. Rafe Blaufarb, *The French Army, 1750–1820: Careers, Talent, Merit* (Manchester: Manchester University Press, 2002). On the bureaucracy achieved early in the Conservatory's existence, Diane Tisdall, "Blood, Sweat, and Scales: The Birth of Modern Bureaucracy at the Paris Conservatoire" (paper, National Meeting of the American Musicological Society, Vancouver, British Columbia, November 5, 2016).

89. On music in service to representational culture during the eighteenth century, especially in France, see T. C. W. Blanning, *The Culture of Power and Power of Culture: Old Regime Europe 1660–1789* (Oxford: Oxford University Press, 2002).

90. Tisdall, "Pierre Baillot," 157–8.

91. Lydia Goehr, *The Imaginary Museum of Musical Works: An Essay in the Philosophy of Music* (1992; repr., New York: Oxford University Press, 2007).

92. Jacques Attali, *Noise: The Political Economy of Music*, trans. Brian Massumi, Theory and History of Literature 16 (1985; repr. Minneapolis and London: University of Minnesota Press, 2003), 55–6.

Chapter 5

1. "Lettre de Bernard Sarrette au Ministre de l'Intérieur," 13 germinal an VII [April 2, 1799], F-Pn, L.A. 99-Scherchen, Pièce 24, doc. 5.

2. Johann Joachim Winckelmann, *History of the Arts of Antiquity*, ed. Alex Potts, trans. Harry Francis Mallgrave (Los Angeles: Getty Publications, 2006), 333.

3. Stendhal, *Correspondance*, eds. Ad. Paupe and P.-A. Chéramy (Paris: C. Bosse, 1908), 2:123, quoted in Francis Haskell and Nicholas Penny, *Taste and Antiquity: The Lure of Classical Sculpture, 1500–1900* (New Haven: Yale University Press, 1981), 91.

4. Lydia Goehr, *The Imaginary Museum of Musical Works: An Essay in the Philosophy of Music* (1992; repr., New York: Oxford University Press, 2007), 157.

5. Vanessa Agnew, *Enlightenment Orpheus: The Power of Music in Other Worlds*, New Cultural History of Music Series (New York: Oxford University Press, 2008), 9.

6. Agnew, *Enlightenment Orpheus*, 171.

7. Edouard Pommier, *L'art de la liberté: doctrines et débats de la Révolution française* (Paris: Gallimard, 1991).

8. Rémy Campos, *Le Conservatoire de Paris et son histoire: une institution en questions; un essai suivi de seize entretiens* (Paris: L'œil d'or, 2016), 12–13; and Antoine Hennion, "L'institution de la musique," in Hennion, ed., *1789–1989: musique, histoire, démocratie* (Paris: Éditions de la Maison des sciences de l'homme, 1992), 1:5–12.

9. Pommier, *L'art de la liberté*, 95. "Le génie des arts se met en marche vers l'avenir en contemplant le passé."

10. Katharine Ellis, *Interpreting the Musical Past: Early Music in Nineteenth-Century France* (New York: Oxford University Press, 2005), 4.

11. David Bell, *The Cult of the Nation: Inventing Nationalism, 1680–1800* (Cambridge, MA: Harvard University Press, 2001).

12. Rafe Blaufarb, *The Great Demarcation: The French Revolution and the Invention of Modern Property* (Oxford: Oxford University Press, 2016), 145. "The ultimate goal was to sell these properties to individuals, not to constitute a vast national patrimony."

13. Pommier, *L'art de la liberté*, 93.

14. Pommier, *L'art de la liberté*, 41 and 126.

15. Pommier, *L'art de la liberté*, 87.

16. Pommier, *L'art de la liberté*, 47.

17. Pommier, *L'art de la liberté*, 52.

18. *Rapport des Commissaires de la commission des monumens chargés par elle de se transporter dans la maison de l'émigré d'Augivillers 10 & 21 avril an II*, April 10–21, 1794, F-Pan, F[17] 1032, file 6.

19. *Procès-verbal de la première séance de M.M. les Commissaires nommés par le comité d'aliénation des domaines nationaux pour l'occuper d'un travail concernans la recherche et la conservation des monuments relatifs aux lettres, aux sciences et aux arts, provenant du mobilier des Maison Ecclésiastiques*, November 8, 1790, F-Pan, F[17] 1032, file 1; and *Au ministre de l'Intérieur sur les dépôts de monuments antiques, de peintre, de sculpture, de physique, de machines, de musique et littéraires qui ont été formés depuis la révolution et dont plusieurs existent encore*, n.d. c. 1793, F-Pan, F[17] 1034, file 11.

20. *Copie des procès-verbal de la neuvième séance du Mardi 18 Janvier 1791*, F-Pan, F[17] 1032, file 1.

21. *Paris le 26 novembre 1792 l'an 1er de la république au Sécrétaire de la Commission des monumens au ministre de l'Intérieur,* F-Pan, F[17] 1032, file 4.

22. Pommier, *L'art de la liberté*, 49–57.

23. See Pommier, *L'art de la liberté*. There was minority dissent toward this practice, see Alexandra Stara, *The Museum of French Monuments 1795–1816: "Killing Art to Make History"* (Surrey and Burlington, VT: Ashgate, 2013), 123–46.

24. Bette W. Oliver, *From Royal to National: The Louvre Museum and the Bibliothèque Nationale* (Lanham, MD: Lexington Books, 2007), 35. Pommier, *L'art de la liberté*, 73n4.

25. *Rapport des Commissaires de la commission des monumens chargés par elle de se transporter dans la maison de l'émigré d'Augivillers.*

26. *Rapport des Commissaires de la commission des monumens chargés par elle de se transporter dans la maison de l'émigré d'Augivillers.*

27. Florence Gétreau, *Aux origines du musée de la musique: les collections instrumentales du Conservatoire de Paris, 1793–1993* (Paris: Réunions des musées nationaux, 1996), 29–31.

28. Andrew McClellan, *Inventing the Louvre: Art, Politics, and the Origins of the Modern Museum in Eighteenth-Century Paris* (Berkeley: University of California Press, 1999).

29. Pommier, *L'art de la liberté*, 127–37.

30. Oliver, *From Royal to National*, 39.

31. Pommier, *L'art de la liberté*, 137.

32. Pommier, *L'art de la liberté*, 139.

33. Catherine Massip, "La bibliothèque du Conservatoire (1795–1819): une utopie réalisée?," in *Le Conservatoire de Paris, 1795–1995: des menus-plaisirs à la Cité de la musique*, eds. Anne Bongrain and Yves Gérard (Paris: Buchet-Chastel, 1996), 118.

34. Getreau, *Aux origines du musée*, 29–31.

35. R. R. Palmer, *The Improvement of Humanity: Education and the French Revolution* (Princeton: Princeton University Press, 1985), 176.

36. M. Louis Tuetey, *Procès-verbaux de la Commission temporaire des arts* (Paris: Imprimerie nationale, 1912), 1:x–xi.

37. Tuetey, *Procès-verbaux*, 1:xxvii.

38. Félix Vicq-d'Azyr, *Instruction sur la manière d'inventorier et de conserver, dans toute l'étendue de la République, tous les objets qui peuvent servir aux arts, aux sciences et à l'enseignement* (Paris: Imprimerie nationale, an II [1793–1794]), 7.

39. Pommier, *L'art de la liberté*, 95.

40. Pommier, *L'art de la liberté*, 209.

41. Pommier, *L'art de la liberté*, 93.

42. Pommier, *L'art de la liberté*, 113–19, and 352–79.

43. Thomas Richards, *The Imperial Archive: Knowledge and the Fantasy of Empire* (London: Verso, 1993), 13.

44. Pommier, *L'art de la liberté*, 223.

45. Goehr, *Imaginary Museum of Musical Works*, 113 and 148.

46. Quoted in Gétreau, *Aux origines du musée*, 29.

47. Cited in Gétreau, *Aux origines du musée*, 31.

48. Pommier, *L'art de la liberté*, 150.

49. Gétreau, *Aux origines du musée*, 32.

50. Gétreau, *Aux origines du musée*, 37.

51. D'Azyr, *Instruction*, 65.

52. D'Azyr, *Instruction*, 65.

53. The inventories are published in *Un inventaire sous la Terreur*, ed. J. Gallay (Paris: Georges Chamerot, 1890). Image in Figure 5.2 is from F-Pan, F^{17} 1054, file 7.

54. Pommier, *L'art de la liberté*, 145.

55. Tuetey, *Procès-verbaux de la Commission temporaire des arts*, 1: xvii–xviii.

56. Tuetey, *Procès-verbaux de la Commission temporaire des arts*, 1:xxix; and "Aux citoyens composant la Commission temporaire des arts," from the Institut National de Musique [Sarrette], quintidi fervidor [thermidor] an deuxième [July 23, 1794], F-Pan, F^{17} 1054, file 1.

57. Tuetey, *Procès-verbaux de la Commission temporaire des arts*, 1:595.

58. "Aux citoyens composant la Commission temporaire des arts." "Les inconvenients qui pourroient resulter . . . si cette collection etoit confiée à un musicien quelconque à un compositeur qui, sous quelques deguisements, ou par quelques substitutions, pourroit en faire en partie sa proprieté pour passer sa muse ingrate aux depends des fleurs du genie de quelques grands hommes . . . en multiplieroit les copies à l'infini."

59. "Aux citoyens composant la Commission temporaire des arts." "Pour le bien public . . . l'intérêt de l'art, autant que pour celui qu'inspirent les hommes celebres qui ont crée des chefs d'œuvres de musique, il importe essentiellement de conserver intactes de garantir de toute atteinte de change et de gaspillage les partitions precieuses dont la nation doit jouir."

60. It is unclear from the letter whether "Blasius" refers to Frédéric, Pierre, or Ignace.

61. Goehr, *Imaginary Museum of Musical Works*, 220–2.

62. Requests located in F-Pan, F^{17} 1054, file 1.

63. Tuetey, *Procès-verbaux de la Commission temporaire des arts*, 1:xxix–xxx. "Dans les sciences et les arts, il y a deux objet principaux à considérer; d'un côté le génie, le talent qui enfantent les chefs-d'œuvre, de l'autre la sagacité et l'érudition qui les contemplent et les comparent. Les uns et les autres ne s'excluent pas toujours, mais rarement se trouvent-ils réunis dans le même individu. Ce sont ces productions du génie et des arts que nous sommes chargés de rechercher et de recueillir de toutes parts. Pour inventorier et soigner des tableaux, rassembler des instruments ou des morceaux de musique, il faut sans doute les connaissances qui y sont propres; mais ces connaissances sont absolument indépendantes du génie qui a su les produire. On peut même assurer qu'il n'y a acune rapport nécessaire entre le talent transcendant des premiers, et les travaux très ordinaires d'un conservateur éclairé. Il faut à la Commission des artistes éclairés sans doute; mais, par-dessus tout, il faut qu'ils puissent y consacrer leur temps presque tout entier, et c'est après s'être assurée qu'en effet les membres désignés peuvent servir utilement la chose publique, qu'elle les a indiqués au Comité d'instruction publique."

64. Goehr, *Imaginary Museum of Musical Works*, 208.

65. Pommier, *L'art de la liberté*, 79.

66. Gétreau, *Aux origines du musée*, 49.

67. Antoine-Barthelemy Bruni, *L'auteur dans son ménage* (Paris: Imbault, 1799), 23. "le plus instruit déplait souvent celui qui sait l'art."

68. Constant Pierre, *Le Conservatoire national de musique et de déclamation documents historiques et administratifs* (Paris: Imprimerie nationale, 1900), 129.

69. Constant Pierre, *Bernard Sarrette et les origines du Conservatoire national de musique et de déclamation* (Paris: Delalain frères, 1895), 144.

70. See Massip, "La bibliothèque du Conservatoire." Eler became librarian on November 20, 1796. Composer and theorist Honoré-François-Marie Langlé replaced him in 1797, serving as librarian until his retirement in 1802. Few sources elucidate the Conservatory library's acquisitions during Langlé's tenure as librarian. Most information on this period comes from the careful bookkeeping of Langlé's successor, the abbé Nicolas Roze.

71. Pierre, *Bernard Sarrette*, 182.

72. This was in some senses an exaggeration of circumstances; pedagogical texts for both music theory and performance proliferated in eighteenth-century France. See Philippe Lescat, *Méthodes et traités musicaux en France 1660–1800* (Paris: Institut de pédagogie musicale et chorégraphique-La Villette, 1991). Diane Tisdall points out, however, that "the variance in technical detail and quality, with no common point of reference, must have been confusing for students" during the eighteenth century, "Pierre Baillot and Violin Pedagogy in Paris, 1795–1815" (PhD diss., King's College London, 2016), 173n18.

73. Ann Jefferson, *Genius in France: An Idea and Its Uses* (Princeton, NJ: Princeton University Press, 2015), 45–61.

74. Cynthia Gessele, "The Institutionalization of Music Theory in France: 1764–1802" (PhD diss., Princeton University, 1989), 298.

75. Gessele, "Institutionalization of Music Theory in France," 187.

76. Pierre, *Bernard Sarrette*, 187: "A côté des musées célèbres que le génie de la liberté forma pour les progrès des sciences et des arts et leur prospérité dans la République, les amis de la gloire nationale verront s'élever aussi celui de la musique: cette nouvelle institution en arrachant à l'oubli les chefs-d'œuvre de toutes les écoles, offrira l'exposition unique des richesses sublimes de cet art, et indiquera à l'histoire sa marche progressive; tout ce que le génie de la musique a produit de grand sera exécuté par le Conservatoire dans des exercice, soit que ces œuvres aient été consacrées au culte, soit qu'elles aient été écrites sous différentes langues ou que le goût du nouveau les ait entièrement éloignées du théâtre [. . .] C'est alors que l'Europe éclairée, appréciant les résultats de cette école, lui marquera avec impartialité la place qu'elle devra occuper près celles d'Allemagne et d'Italie."

77. Jefferson, *Genius in France*, 51.

78. Goehr, *Imaginary Museum of Musical Works*, 241.

79. Goehr, *Imaginary Museum of Musical Works*, 205–6.

80. Goehr, *Imaginary Museum of Musical Works*, 147.

81. Oliver, *From Royal to National*, 35.

82. Oliver, *From Royal to National*, 39.

83. Pommier, *L'art de la liberté*, 209–10.

84. Florence Gétreau, "Un cabinet d'instruments pour l'instruction publique: faillite du projet, ouverture du débat," in *Le Conservatoire de Paris*, ed. A. Bongrain and Y. Gérard, 145.

85. Gétreau, *Aux origines du musée*, 602.

86. Massip, "La bibliothèque du Conservatoire," 118.

87. The first approval was in a letter from July 10, 1798; the second was granted according to the earlier law of 16 thermidor an III.

88. Bernard Sarrette to the Minister of the Interior, 27 brumaire an VII [November 17, 1798], F-Pn, Département de la musique, Sarrette File, Pièce 24, doc. 22.

89. Pommier, *L'art de la liberté*, 342–4.

90. Rebecca Dowd Geoffroy-Schwinden, "The Revolution of Jommelli's *Objets d'art*: Bernard Sarrette's Acquisition of Musical Manuscripts for the Bibliothèque du Conservatoire," in *Moving Scenes: The Circulation of Music and Theatre in Europe, 1700–1815*, eds. Pierre-Yves Beaurepaire, Philippe Bourdin, and Charlotta Wolff, Oxford Studies in the Enlightenment (Oxford: Voltaire Foundation, 2017), 61–76.

91. Jean-François Lesueur to Honoré-François-Marie Langlé, 2 pluviôse an VIII [January 22, 1800], F-Pn, Département de la musique, Mus. L.A. 67.

92. "Le génie de l'étranger ne doit se trouver présent dans notre Conservatoire que pour se voir entouré d'efforts tendant à la surpasser," Letter from Lesueur to Langlé.

93. "Notre conservatoire est françois. N'ayon pas pour but que la perfection de l'école de France." Letter from Lesueur to Langlé.

94. Pommier, *L'art de la liberté*, 104 and 276.

95. Pommier, *L'art de la liberté*, 231.

96. Oliver, *From Royal to National*, 41. The assignment came on July 8, 1794.

97. Quoted in Oliver, *From Royal to National*, 46.

98. Oliver, *From Royal to National*, 47.

99. Oliver, *From Royal to National*, 51.

100. *Projet d'encouragement à accorder aux sciences et arts en Piemont par la République française*, n.d., F-Pan, F^{17} 1278.

101. Herman Lebovics, *Mona Lisa's Escort: André Malraux and the Reinvention of French Culture* (Ithaca: Cornell University Press, 1999), 36.

102. *Pétition d'artistes au Directoire exécutif*, 28 thermidor an IV (August 15, 1796), F-Pan, F^{17} 1279, file 1. Pommier outlines these debates in *L'art de la liberté*, 397–412.

103. Language quoted from *Projet d'encouragement à accorder aux sciences et arts en Piemont*.

104. Luigi Cherubini to the General Director of Public Instruction, 14 messidor an IV [July 2, 1796], F-Pan, originally F^{17} 1279/3/72, now AE/II/1457, part of Archives nationales museum collection. "Seroit il pas possible que comme la peinture, la musique profitai du succès de ses armees."

105. Quoted in Tisdall, "Pierre Baillot," 97.

106. Richard Macnutt, "Early Acquisitions for the Paris Conservatoire Library: Roldophe Kreutzer's Role in Obtaining Materials from Italy, 1796–1802," in *Music Publishing and Collecting: Essays in Honor of Donald W. Krummel*, ed. David Hunter (Urbana: University of Illinois Press, 1994), 168. Macnutt reproduces, in English translation, the letters, which are located in F-Pn, Département de la musique, as part of the Sarrette file, L. A. 99 Scherchen. I quote Macnutt, "Early Acquisitions," rather than the original letters here, because he provides excellent translations from the original Italian. Any changes to Macnutt's translations are noted.

107. Giovachino Caribaldi to Bernardo Mengozzi, November 8, 1797. Macnutt, "Early Acquisitions," 170.

108. Giovachino Caribaldi to Bernardo Mengozzi, 172.

109. Giovachino Caribaldi to Bernardo Mengozzi, 170–173.

110. Data in Table 5.3 based on Macnutt, "Early Acquisitions," 178.

111. Giovachino Caribaldi to Bernardo Mengozzi, 172.

112. Giovachino Caribaldi to Bernardo Mengozzi, 173.

113. Luigi De Rossi to Rodolphe Kreutzer, August 30, 1798. Macnutt, "Early Acquisitions," 173–9.

114. Luigi De Rossi to Rodolphe Kreutzer, 175. Macnutt explains that De Rossi refers to the "Palazzo" rather than the papal chapel, "the Quirinal, the palace in which the Pope lived until Rome became capital of Italy in 1870 and which housed the Papal Chapel—as distinct from the Sistine Chapel, at St. Peter's."

115. Luigi De Rossi to Rodolphe Kreutzer, 175.

116. Luigi De Rossi to Rodolphe Kreutzer, 175.

117. Macnutt suggests that this could be the treaties of Bologna or perhaps related to Napoleon's defeat of the Austrians at Castiglione; however, it was the Treaty of Tolentino in February 1797 that gave the French Commissions access to manuscripts in the Vatican in February 1797 (175n31). See also Oliver, *From Royal to National*, 51.

118. Luigi De Rossi to Rodolphe Kreutzer, 175.

119. Luigi De Rossi to Rodolphe Kreutzer, 175.

120. Data in Tables 5.4a and 5.4b from Macnutt, "Early Acquisitions," 176–8.

121. Luigi De Rossi to Rodolphe Kreutzer, 179.

122. Although Macnutt concludes that De Rossi may not have intentionally coupled these names "Ceri" and Caccini shown in Table 5.4a, but rather grouped them for practicality because he had reached the end of a page, he also speculates that if they were

intentionally paired, then perhaps De Rossi intended to write Peri and not "Ceri." Luigi De Rossi to Rodolphe Kreutzer, 178.

123. *Fête de la liberté et entrée triomphale des objets de sciences et d'arts recueillis en Italie. Programme* (Paris: Imprimerie de la république, thermidor an VI [July 1796]). F-Pan, F^{17} 1279, file 6. Pommier, *L'art de la liberté*, 453.

124. Oliver, *From Royal to National*, 62.

125. Pierre, *Le Conservatoire national*, 136. "Copies de musique pour la formation de la bibliothèque."

126. Letter from Bernard Sarrette to the Minister of the Interior, 15 thermidor an VIII [August 3, 1800], F-Pn, Département de la musique, L.A. Scherchen 99, Pièce 24, doc. 24. "Qui pourroient être utiles à nos musées."

127. Bernard Sarrette to the Minister of the Interior, 15 thermidor an VIII. "Munich et Stagard [sic] renferment une grande quantité d'ouvrages dont la publication est indispensable pour faciliter les progrès de l'art musical."

128. Bernard Sarrette to the Minister of the Interior, 3 fructidor an VIII [August 21, 1800], F-Pn, Département de la musique, L.A.-Scherchen 99, Pièce 24, doc. 23.

129. Bernard Sarrette to the Minister of the Interior, 3 fructidor an VIII.

130. Geoffroy-Schwinden, ""The Revolution of Jommelli's *Objets d'art*," 61–76.

131. Pommier, *L'art de la liberté*, 290–1.

132. Neveu (1756–1808) was a theorist of drawing who trained at the academy and traveled to Italy in 1790. His works had been exhibited at the Salon in 1793 and 1796, and he eventually earned an appointment as professor of drawing at the new École polytechnique. In 1800 and 1801 he was sent to do reconnaissance for France in southern Germany. See Gabriel Vauthier, "Une mission artistique et scientifique en Bavière sous le Consulat," *Bulletin de la Société de l'histoire de l'art français* (1910): 208–50; and Bénédicte Savoy, *Patrimoine annexé: les biens culturels saisis par la France en Allemagne autour de 1800* (Paris: Éditions de la Maison des sciences de l'homme, 2003), 1:470.

133. Bernard Sarrette to Adrien Duquesnoy, 7 fructidor an VIII [August 25, 1800], F-Pn, Département de la musique, Sarrette File, Pièce 24, doc. 8. "Le Conservatoire n'ayant que beaucoup de vieux ouvrages françois qui ne seroient pas bien accueillir je pense."

134. Sarrette to Duquesnoy, 7 fructidor an VIII. "Je ne puis lui répondre que de ne recueillir que ce qui est bon, que ce qui a une réputation généralement consacrée."

135. Sarrette to Duquesnoy, 7 fructidor an VIII. "chefs d'œuvres des grands maîtres."

136. Goehr, *Imaginary Museum of Musical Works*, 103.

137. Pommier, *L'art de la liberté*, 57, 231.

138. Dessalles was part of a pontonier regiment formed in 1794 by General Jourdan after crossing the Rhine to prepare paths further into the Eastern Rhine. Denys de Champeaux, "Les souvenirs du Général Baron de Salle," *Revue de Paris* 1 (1895): 407–37.

139. Von Winter was a composer working with Neveu in Bavaria. See Savoy, *Patrimoine annexé*, 1:55–86; and Anna Amalie Abert and Paul Corneilson, "Winter [von Winter], Peter," *Grove Music Online.*

140. October 4, 1800 (dated 12 vendémiaire, but clearly subsequent to previous letters from jour complémentaires of an VIII). F-Pn, Département de la musique, Sarrette file, Pièce 26, doc. 3. Sarrette's own generic descriptions are maintained.

141. Goehr, *Imaginary Museum of Musical Works*, 241 and 115.

142. Rodolphe Kreutzer to Bernard Sarrette, October 1, 1801. Macnutt, "Early Acquisitions," 179.

143. Macnutt argues that this letter was probably enclosed with the previous October 1 letter. Macnutt, "Early Acquisitions," 180.

144. Rodolphe Kreutzer to Bernard Sarrette, October 20, 1801. Macnutt, "Early Acquisitions," 180.

145. Kreutzer to Sarrette, October 20, 1801, 181.

146. Kreutzer to Sarrette, October 20, 1801, 181.

147. Kreutzer to Sarrette, October 20, 1801, 181.

148. Bruce R. Schueneman and María de Jesús Ayala-Schueneman, "The Composers' House: le magasin de musique de Cherubini, Méhul, R. Kreutzer, Rode, Nicolo Isouard, et Boïeldieu," *Fontes Artis Musicae* 51, no. 1 (January–March 2004): 53–73.

149. Gétreau, *Aux origines du musée*, 35.

150. Kreutzer to Sarrette, October 20, 1801, 183.

151. Kreutzer to Sarrette, October 20, 1801, 181.

152. Kreutzer to Sarrette, October 20, 1801, 181.

153. Mme. Kreutzer to Bernard Sarrette, December 26, 1801. Macnutt, "Early Acquisitions," 184.

154. A letter from Kreutzer in Lyon, written two days after his wife's, corroborates her account. Kreutzer to Sarrette December 28, 1801. Macnutt, "Early Acquisitions," 185.

155. Mme. Kreutzer to Bernard Sarrette, January 11, 1802. Macnutt, "Early Acquisitions," 185.

156. Jean Tarrade, "De l'apogée économique à l'effondrement du domaine colonial (1763–1830)," *Histoire de la France coloniale* (Paris: Armand Colin, 1990) 1:199–314.

157. Todd Porterfield, *The Allure of Empire: Art in the Service of French Imperialism, 1798–1836* (Princeton, NJ: Princeton University Press, 1998). "Official culture promoted the rationale for a foreign policy that became a central focus of national identity in the nineteenth century and well into our own."

158. Pommier, *L'art de la liberté*, 228 and 245.

159. Musicological work on nineteenth- and twentieth-century France reveals how this relationship between music, national identity, and empire unfolded. See Jane Fulcher, *The Nation's Image: French Grand Opera as Politics and Politicized Art* (New York: Cambridge University Press, 1987); Jann Pasler, *Composing the Citizen: Music as Public Utility in Third Republic France* (Berkeley: University of California Press, 2009); and Annegret Fauser, *Musical Encounters at the 1889 World's Fair* (Rochester, NY: University of Rochester Press, 2005).

160. Goehr, *Imaginary Museum of Musical Works*, 148.

161. Étienne-Nicolas Méhul, *Ariodant* (Paris: Janet et Cotelle, 1799).

162. Goehr, *Imaginary Museum of Musical Works*, 174.

Chapter 6

1. Quoted and translated in R. R. Palmer, *The Improvement of Humanity: Education and the French Revolution* (Princeton: Princeton University Press, 1985), 154.

2. Report reprinted in Théodore Regnault, *De la législation et de la jurisprudence concernant les brevets d'invention, de perfectionnement et d'importation* (Paris: Lachevardière fils, 1825), 21. "La nature a tout fait pour nous, mais nous n'avons pas aidé la nature."

3. Rafe Blaufarb, *The Great Demarcation: The French Revolution and the Invention of Modern Property* (Oxford: Oxford University Press, 2016), 146.

4. James Q. Davies, "Creatures of the Air," paper presented at Music and the Body Between Revolutions: Paris, 1789–1848, Columbia University Heyman Center for the Humanities, New York, NY, April 1, 2017; and "Creatures of the Air: Moral Atmospherics and the Enframement of Nature in Mendelssohn's *Elijah*," paper presented at IRCAM, Paris, France, May 30, 2018.

5. Thomas Le Roux, "L'utilité publique et ses débats: les mines et la question des concessions, 1791–1810," paper presented at the conference, Les dynamiques économiques de la Révolution française, sponsored by Institutions et Dynamiques historiques de l'économie et de la société, Conservatoire des Arts et Métiers, June 8, 2018.

6. Jann Pasler, *Composing the Citizen: Music as Public Utility in Third Republic France* (Berkeley: University of California Press, 2009), 66. "Underlying usefulness for the French is not only an explanation of economic exchange, but also a social relationship, an ethical position, and a political belief that, through addressing shared needs, one can build shared interests."

7. Jessica Riskin, *Science in the Age of Sensibility: The Sentimental Empiricists of the French Enlightenment* (Chicago and London: University of Chicago Press, 2002), and E. C. Spary, *Utopia's Garden: French Natural History from Old Regime to Revolution* (Chicago: University of Chicago Press, 2000).

8. *Loi relative aux découvertes utiles et aux moyens d'en assurer la propriété à ceux qui seront reconnus en être les auteurs*, printed in Regnault, *De la legislation*, 135. *Brevets*—the equivalent of the English word "patents"—should not be confused with the French *patentes*, an annual tax paid by people working in certain trades or professions, implemented by the Décret d'Allard, or the *Loi du 2 et 17 mars 1791*. Some writers and scholars, like Regnault, use the words *brevet* and *patente* interchangeably because the concept of patents had been adopted from Britain, and so in these cases it is a French adaptation of the English and not a reference to the tax.

9. Baudry, "Examining Inventions, Shaping Property," 63.

10. *Procès-verbaux du Bureau de consultation des arts et métiers* (Paris: Imprimerie nationale, 1913), 15.

11. 300, 800, and 1500 *livres*, respectively. Jérôme Baudry, "Examining Inventions, Shaping Property: The Savants and the French Patent System," *History of Science* 57, no. 1 (2019): 64.

12. "Loi relative aux gratifications et secours à accorder aux artistes," in Regnault, *De la legislation*, 112.

13. Although technically disbanded in 1796 (see Dominique de Place, "Le Bureau de Consultation pour les arts," 1791–1796," *History and Technology* 5, no. 2 (1988): 139–78), the Committee continued on into the nineteenth century under various names, as shown by Baudry, "Examining Inventions, Shaping Property," n. 18: Bureau consultatif des arts et commerce, Bureau consultatif des arts et métiers, Comité consultatif des arts et métiers, and finally, Comité consultatif des arts et manufactures.

14. Report on the request made by Citizen De Lorthe, March 6, 1793, CNAM, Archives historiques, Dossier P-196, 6.

15. Palmer, *Improvement of Humanity*, 54.

16. Lycée des arts course schedule, April 1793, F-Pan, F^{17} 1143, dos. 1, doc. 10.

17. *Procès-verbaux du Bureau de consultation*, 19.

18. Baudry, "Examining Inventions, Shaping Property," 66.

19. *Tableau des récompenses, gratifications, encouragemens, etc. accordés par le Bureau de consultation des arts et métiers, Depuis le 19 Novembre 1791, jusqu'au 1 Janvier 1793* (Paris: Imprimerie nationale executive de Louvre, an II [1793–4]), F-Pan, F^{17} 1138, dos. 18. "nouvelle méthode pour donner des leçons de musique à un grand nombre d'élèves à la fois."

20. "Report concerning C. Dubos," CNAM, Archives historiques, Cahier 10, Dossier 10-390. In a previous presentation of the instrument in 1787, a review in the *Journal Encyclopédique ou universel* noted that "le *conducteur*, peut, à volonté, par des moyens simples et aisés, presser ou ralentir le mouvement, en suivre avec facilité toutes les diverses variations auxquelles l'expression du chanteur ou d'un exécutant quelconque peut donner lieu; d'où il résulte qu'à ces diverses variations, il peut aussi sans peine soumettre toujours les accompagnemens." November 1787, 7:531.

21. "Report Concerning Citizen Clareton," CNAM, Archives historiques, Cahier 4, Dossier 10-390.

22. "Report Concerning Citizen Clareton," 9.

23. *Procès-verbaux du Bureau de consultation*, 19.

24. Petition from June 8, 1793, *Procès-verbaux du Comité d'instruction publique de l'assemblée legislative*, ed. M. J. Guillaume (Paris: Imprimerie nationale, 1907), 1:489.

25. Letter from Garat to the Committee on Public Instruction, June 23, 1793, *Procès-verbaux du Comité d'instruction publique*, 1:490. "Un motif qui avait porté le Conseil à penser que le Bureau n'avait point fait dans son avis une juste application de la loi du 12 septembre 1791, est qu'il avait d'abord regardé cette invention comme uniquement relative aux arts agréables, et que sous ce rapport il lui avait paru qu'elle n'était point admissible aux récompenses nationales réservées aux découvertes et inventions dans les art utiles, ou arts et métiers."

26. Letter from Garat to the Committee on Public Instruction, *Procès-verbaux du Comité d'instruction publique*, 1:491.

27. Memoir on Stephanopoli, Montu, and Clareton, National Convention, July 19, 1793, *Archives Parlementaires* (Paris: Imprimerie Paul DuPont, 1906), LXIX:208.

28. Here I quote from the table shown in Figure 6.2, which has a column to describe the "objects" awarded.

29. Baudry demonstrates that from its inception through its nineteenth-century iterations, the *brevet*-granting Board prioritized objects over ideas. "Examining Inventions, Shaping Property," 77.

30. Letter from Schnell to the Board, dated April 24, 1793, CNAM, Archives historiques, Dossier P-231.

31. Report on Schnell and Tschirziki, dated July 10, 1793, CNAM, Archives historiques, Dossier P-231, "tous les moyens mécaniques qui tendent à simplifier et à perfectionner les arts d'agrément sont de son ressort."

32. Regnault, *De la legislation*, 112–16.

33. Fourth Report Concerning Citizen De Lorthe, August 16, 1794, CNAM, Archives historiques, Dossier 10-389, 671–7. The Bureau de Consultation's files on Delorthe are located in dossiers 10-389, 10-390, and P-196.

34. Report on the request made by Citizen De Lorthe, March 6, 1793, 3.

35. Design for M. Racicourt's guitar, CNAM, Archives historiques, Dossier P-288, 1807.

36. Fourth Report Concerning Citizen De Lorthe, 16 August 1794, CNAM, Archives historiques, Dossier 10-389, 675.

37. My gratitude to Andrew Pester for pointing this out and for providing me with the phrase.

38. "Bureau des inventaires, mémoires, et rapports concernant les Machines, Arts et Métiers," s.d., F-Pan, F^{17} 1274, doc. 184.

39. "Les Citoyens organists et facteurs d'orgues de Paris, réunis aux Section de Méchanique, Physique, et Musique de la Commission Temporaire des Arts, après avoirs délibéré sur l'utilité des orgues et sur les moyens à prendre pour la conservation de ces instrumens," s.d., F-Pan, F^{17} 1274, doc. 187.

40. "L'utilité de la conservation des orgues dans une païs, ou l'on favorise les arts, peut être considérée sous divers points de vuë," untitled, s.d., F-Pan, F^{17} 1274, doc. 186.

41. Report by Pierre Jobert on the organ at the Abbaye de Salival, September 22, 1794, F-Pan, F^{17} 1054, dos. 4.

42. Claude-Pierre Molard, "Rapport et Projet d'arrêté concernans les bufete [sic] d'orgue de la République," s.d., F-Pan, F^{17} 1274, doc. 189.

43. "Les Citoyens organists et facteurs d'orgues de Paris."

44. "Les Citoyens organists et facteurs d'orgues de Paris." "C'est cependant cet instrument riche et fècond, ce premier de tout les instruments, où le talent de l'artiste constructeur a plan d'une fois ouvert de nouvelles routes au genie de musicien executant." On the "performer's genius" in France at this time, see Mary Hunter, " 'To Play as if from the Soul of the Composer:' The Role of the Performer in Early Romantic Aesthetics," *Journal of the American Musicological Society* 58, no. 2 (2005): 357–98.

45. Molard, "Rapport et Projet."

46. Untitled, s.d., F-Pan, F^{17} 1274, doc. 186. "y puisse les moïens des faire valoire celles de son genie et de produire des effets absolumens inconnus sur tous autre instrumens . . . il dévelope [les idées] du compostieur qui la jouë et on lui doit la célébrité des . . . Couperin, des Charpentiers . . . qui on [illegible] le chemin a ceux qui se distingues aujourdhui."

47. Molard, "Rapport et Projet."

48. Molard, "Rapport et Projet."

49. Molard, "Rapport et Projet."

50. Molard, "Rapport et Projet."

51. Molard, "Rapport et Projet."

52. Memo on the sale of organs, Music section of the [Temporary] Arts Commission, 29 germinal an III [April 18, 1795], F-Pan, F^{17} 1054, dos. 4.

53. Renseignements sur les orgues, ans II–III [1793–5], F-Pan, F^{17} 1054, dos. 4.

54. Letter to the Temporary Arts Commission adjunct to the Committee on Public Instruction, 19 nivôse an III [January 8, 1795], F-Pan, F^{17} 1054, dos. 4.

55. Letter to the Citizens Composing the Temporary Arts Commission, 3 germinal an III [March 23, 1794], F-Pan, F^{17} 1054, dos. 4.

56. Letter from the Commission for Weapons, Powders, and Mining to the Commission for Agriculture and the Arts, 20 ventôse an III [March 10, 1795], F^{17} 1054, dos. 4.

57. To the citizens composing the Temporary Arts Commission, 5 prairial and 13 prairial an III [May 24 and June 1,1795] F-Pan, F^{17} 1054, dos. 4.

58. Memo to the Music Section of the Arts Commission on the sale of organs, 29 germinal an III [April 18, 1795], F-Pan, F^{17} 1054, dos. 4.

59. Letter from Cambry, president of the district of Qimperlé, 29 germinal an III [April 18, 1795], F-Pan, F^{17} 1054, dos. 4.

60. Chiquelier file, CNAM, Archives historiques, Dossier P-230.

61. This prospectus is undated and misplaced in Armand's file, Dossier P-205, CNAM, Archives historiques.

62. Letter to the Minister of the Interior from Charles Désaudray, 7 thermidor an IV [July 17, 1796], F^{17} 1143.

63. *Tablettes de renommée des musiciens, auteurs, compositeurs, virtuoses . . . avec une notice des ouvrages ou autres motifs qui les ont rendus recommandables. Pour servir à l'Almanach-Dauphin* (Paris: Cailleau, 1785).

64. See Jean Mongrédien, *Jean-François Le Sueur: contribution à l'étude d'un demi-siècle de musique française (1780–1830)* vol. 1 (Berne: Peter Lang, 1980) and Philippe Lescat, *Méthodes et traités musicaux en France 1660–1800* (Paris: Institut de pédagogie musicale et chorégraphique, 1991). The publication dates of the *Nouvelle méthode* and *Méthode de violon* are ambiguous. Lescat dates the *Nouvelle méthode* to 1790, Mongrédien dates it to 1794. Lescat dates the *Méthode de violon* to 1794, Mongrédien dates it to 1799. It is likely the Durieu reprinted his works, resulting in multiple editions and publication dates. The *Nouvelle méthode de musique vocale* title extends in later publications and claims to have been "adopted by the National Institute of music, singing, and declamation."

65. Lettre de Durieu, n.d., F-Pan, DXXXVIII 7, no. 59. A subsequent letter in Durieu's file dates this first letter to 18 prairial an III [June 6, 1795].

66. Lettre de Durieu, 22 prairial an III [June 10, 1795], F-Pan, DXXXVIII 7, no. 59.

67. *Procès-verbaux du Comité d'instruction publique*, vi:426–7.

68. The same day, July 18, 1795, the Committee tabled the case of musician called "Champion," perhaps a misspelling of Champein (vi:432). His name does not appear in the remainder of the record.

69. "Copie des attestations rélative à la Méthode du Citoyen Durieu, auteur, professor, et éditeur de musique," 16 messidor an III [July 4, 1795], F-Pan DXXXVIII 7, no. 59.

70. Lettre de Durieu aux Citoyens Membres du Comité d'Instruction publique, 26 messidor an III [July 14, 1795], F-Pan DXXXVIII 7, no. 59.

71. Lettre de Durieu, 3 thermidor an III [July 21, 1795], F-Pan DXXXVIII 7, no. 59.

72. *Procès-verbaux du Comité d'instruction publique*, vi:447.

73. *Procès-verbaux de L'académie des beaux-arts*, ed. Marcel Bonnaire (Paris: Librairie Armand Colin, 1937), 1:vi. The Directory government wrote a letter to the Institute for its inaugural meeting on 3 nivôse an IV [December 24, 1795]: "l'utilité publique était le but auquel devaient tendre tous leurs travaux et que tout devait prendre un nouveau caractère dans le nouvel ordre des choses."

74. Bruno Belhoste, "Condorcet, les arts utiles et leur enseignement," in *Condorcet, homme des Lumières et de la Révolution*, ed. A.-M. Chouillet et P. Crépel (ENS Éditions Fontenay-Saint-Cloud, Fontenay-aux-Roses, 1997), 121–36.

75. Condorcet quoted in Belhoste, "Condorcet," 6. "Les procédés des arts sont les enfants du besoin, on peut en dire autant des méthodes les plus abstraites de la science; mais nous les devons à des besoins plus nobles, à celui de découvrir des vérités nouvelles, ou de mieux connaître les lois de la nature. Ainsi l'on voit dans les sciences des théories

brillantes mais longtemps inutiles devenir tout à coup le fondement des applications les plus importantes, et tantôt des applications très simples en apparence faire naître l'idée de théories abstraites dont on n'avait pas encore senti le besoin, diriger vers ces théories les travaux des géomètres et devenir l'occasion de nouveaux progrès."

76. Condorcet quoted from 1774 in Belhoste, "Condorcet," 55: "Dans ce que j'ai appelé la pratique des sciences, je n'ai point renfermé non plus le génie de la mécanique. Ce génie emploie une géométrie d'une espèce particulière, dont la théorie n'est pas encore écrite, et que chaque grand mécanicien est obligé d'inventer. C'est là ce qui rend les mécaniciens si rares, tandis que les faiseurs de machines sont si communs."

77. Gessele notes especially the work of Bemetzrider. Cynthia Gessele, "The Institutionalization of Music Theory in France: 1764–1802" (PhD diss., Princeton University, 1989), and "The Conservatoire de Musique and National Music Education in France, 1795–1801," in *Music and the French Revolution*, ed. Malcom Boyd (Cambridge and New York: Cambridge University Press, 1992).

78. See Baudry, "Examining Inventions, Shaping Property," 62–80.

79. Regnault, *De la legislation*, 213.

80. *La base de donnée brevets français 19è siècle*, Institution National de la Propriété Industrielle, http://bases-brevets19e.inpi.fr/index.asp, accessed July 12, 2019, côtés 1BA859, 1BA1684, 1BA172, and 1BA331.

81. For one example of many, see *Procès-verbaux de L'académie des beaux-arts*, 2:26. "Arrêté qu'il sera fait un remercîment à l'auteur et que l'ouvrage sera déposé à la bibliothèque."

82. "Aux représentants du peuple, membre du comité d'instruction publique," Letter from Janson l'aîné to Committee on Public Instruction, undated, F-Pan, D XXXVIII 7, no. 59.

83. *Procès-verbaux de L'académie des beaux-arts*, 1:238.

84. *Procès-verbaux de L'académie des beaux-arts*, 1:160.

85. *Procès-verbaux de L'académie des beaux-arts*, 1:161.

86. The fact that Baud's strings were sealed, deposited, and never reopened, allowed Alfred Cohen to provide a detailed analysis of them, published in "A Cache of 18th-Century Strings," *The Galpin Society Journal* 36 (March 1983): 37–48.

87. *Procès-verbaux de L'académie des beaux-arts*, 1:156.

88. *Procès-verbaux de L'académie des beaux-arts*, 1:160.

89. *Procès-verbaux de L'académie des beaux-arts*, 2:49, "L'objet général à considérer dans ce moment et celui qui a dû fixer principalement l'attention de la Commission, c'est l'utilité résultante de l'emploi du procède."

90. *Procès-verbaux de L'académie des beaux-arts*, 2:277–8.

91. *Procès-verbaux de L'académie des beaux-arts*, 2:318.

92. Ollivier and Duplat's names are misspelled in the report, but they are clearly the individuals discussed by Méhul because their brevet applications appear in *La base de donnée brevets français 19è siècle*, Institution National de la Propriété Industrielle, http://bases-brevets19e.inpi.fr/index.asp, accessed July 12, 2019. Ollivier, 1BA179; Duplat, 1BA419; and Bouvier 1BA375.

93. *Procès-verbaux de L'académie des beaux-arts*, 2:319. "n'auront-ils pas le droit de s'oppose à ce que l'on donne de la publicité à leurs procèdes? Voudront-ils même les faire

connaitre à votre Commission? Et si par hasard un de vos com[res] les connaissait, pourrait-il en parler sans s'exposer à porter atteinte au droit de propriété ?"

94. Expositions were held in 1798, 1801, 1802, and 1806, followed by a significant gap until 1819.

95. *Rapport du jury sur les produits de l'industrie française, présenté à S. E. M. de Champagny, ministre de l'intérieur; précédé du procès-verbal des opérations du jury* (Paris: L'imprimerie impériale, 1806), iii–vi.

96. Malou Haine, "Introduction," *Les facteurs d'instruments de musique français aux expositions nationales et universelles au XIXè siècle* (Paris: Institut de recherce en musicologie, 2007), http://www.iremus.cnrs.fr/sites/default/files/introduction.pdf, accessed July 15, 2019, 2. "Il devient impératif de le montrer inventif et de mettre l'accent sur les derniers brevets d'invention."

97. Haine, "Introduction," 6.

98. *Rapport du jury sur les produits de l'industrie française*, 215. "En ajoutant de nouvelles améliorations aux perfectionnemens qu'ils ont déjà introduits dans la construction des harpes, MM. Cousineau contribuent beaucoup à assure à la France la possession exclusive d'une branche de commerce qui devient chaque jour plus importante."

99. Schmidt file, CNAM, Archives historiques, Dossier P-293.

100. Haine, "Introduction," 2.

101. Government budget cuts resulted in layoffs at the Conservatoire in years VIII (September 1799–September 1800) and X (September 1801–September 1802). See Rebecca Dowd Geoffroy-Schwinden, "Politics, the French Revolution, and Performance: Parisian Musicians as an Emergent Professional Class, 1749–1802" (PhD diss., Duke University, 2015), 108–24, and 238; and Diane Tisdall, "Pierre Baillot and Violin Pedagogy in Paris, 1795–1815" (PhD diss., King's College London, 2016), 136–65.

102. "Autrefois le commerce français ne retirait que très peu d'avantages des objets relatifs à la musique; les produits de cette partie de l'industrie nationale étaient nuls pour le fisc." Constant Pierre, *Le Conservatoire national de musique et de declamation documents historiques et administratifs* (Paris: Imprimerie nationale, 1900), 348. Commerce was already a concern when the École royale de chant was founded on December 19, 1783, and its supporters argued that it would provide "a unique means of preserving a *spectacle* so essential in Paris, so useful to the arts, to commerce, and even to his majesty's finances." ("regardant en effet l'établissement de cette école comme l'unique moyen de conserver un spectacle si essentielle dans Paris, et si utile aux arts, au commerce et même au Finances de sa majesté."). Pierre, *Le Conservatoire national de musique* (Paris, 1900), 8. Detractors disagreed, asserting that "wealthy amateurs," not the government, should fund the school. Pierre, *Le Conservatoire national de musique* (Paris, 1900), 17. "Le Conservatoire, par ses propres ressources, peut élever un commerce de musique très considérable." Pierre, *Le Conservatoire national de musique* (Paris, 1900), 17.

103. "La naturalisation des instruments à vent, que l'on est obligé de tirer d'Allemagne, ce qui neutralise en France une branche importante d'industrie et enlève des moyens d'existence à une partie de la nombreuse population de la République." Pierre, *Le Conservatoire national de musique*, 132.

104. Pierre, *Le Conservatoire national de musique*, 347. "Nos pianos maintenant recherchés dans tout l'Europe; leur prix est monté de 1,000 à 2,400 francs; le prix de nos

cors, préférables par leur fini à ceux d'Allemagne, est monté à 300 francs; nos luthiers fabriquent des violons dont la bonté a fait monter le prix ordinaire à 400 francs."

105. Pierre, *Le Conservatoire national de musique*, 348. "L'art qui contribue le plus à procurer de telles ressources au Gouvernement ne peut-il espérer d'obtenir les moyens nécessaires à sa conservation, de laquelle dépendent tous les avantages que les théâtres procurent au commerce national?"

106. Toby Gefland, *Professionalizing Modern Medicine: Paris Surgeons and Medical Science and Institutions in Eighteenth-Century Paris*, Contributions in Medical History 6 (Westport, CT: Greenwood Press, 1980, 83.

107. Palmer, *The Improvement of Humanity*, 197.

108. Edwin L. Dooley Jr., "L'instruction militaire à l'École polytechnique, 1794–1815," *Bulletin de la Sabix* [en ligne] 6 (1990), mis en ligne le 19 avril 2011, consulté le 30 septembre 2016. http://sabix.revues.org/576, 3.

109. Rafe Blaufarb, *The French Army, 1750–1820: Careers, Talent, Merit* (Manchester: Manchester University Press, 2002), and Palmer, *The Improvement of Humanity*.

110. Isabelle Laboulais, "Serving Science and the State: Mining Science in France, 1794–1810," *Minverva* 46 (Spring 2008): 25.

111. For the most recent work on this, see Kailan R. Rubinoff, "Towards a Revolutionary Model of Music Pedagogy: The Paris Conservatoire, Hugot and Wunderlich's *Méthode de flûte*, and the Disciplining of the Musician," *Journal of Musicology* 34, no. 4 (2017): 473–514; and Tisdall, "Pierre Baillot and Violin Pedagogy in Paris, 1795–1815."

112. Laboulais, "Serving Science and the State," 17–19.

113. Laboulais, "Serving Science and the State," 25.

114. Laboulais, "Serving Science and the State," 32.

115. Laboulais, "Serving Science and the State," 33–4.

116. Laboulais, "Serving Science and the State," 27.

117. Laboulais, "Serving Science and the State," 22.

118. Diane Tisdall, "Pierre Baillot," and "Blood, Sweat, and Scales: The Birth of Modern Bureaucracy at the Paris Conservatoire," paper presented at the National Meeting of the American Musicological Society, Vancouver, British Columbia, November 5, 2016).

119. Emmanuel Hondré notes the scientific character of the methods while also labeling them a "propagandistic tool" in, "Les méthodes officiels du Conservatoire," in *Le Conservatoire de musique de Paris: regards sur une institution et son histoire*, ed. Emmanuel Hondré (Paris: Association du Board des étudiants du Conservatoire national supérieur de musique de Paris, 1995), 80. "Les motivations pédagogiques et idéologiques qui ont accompagné la rédaction de ces méthodes dévoilent une nouvelle vision de l'enseignement conçu désormais à mi-chemin entre une 'science' devenue efficace et un formidable outil de propagande."

120. Excluding Nicholas Roze, *Méthode de plain-chant à l'usage des églises de France* (Paris: Magasin de musique [1814]), and Nicholas Roze (attr.), *Méthode de serpent: adoptée par le Conservatoire impérial de musique pour le service du culte et le service militaire* (Paris: Magasin de musique du Conservatoire Impérial de musique, [1814]), because these came much later than the chronological scope of this chapter.

121. On budget cuts, see Geoffroy-Schwinden, "Parisian Musicians as an Emergent Professional Class," 108–24, and 238. For a comparison of Conservatory funding with other institutions, see Palmer, Appendix, *The Improvement of Humanity.* On salary comparisons, see Tisdall, "Pierre Baillot," 154.

122. Geoffroy-Schwinden, "Parisian Musicians as an Emergent Professional Class," 142–4.

123. Kailan R. Rubinoff also notes that the methods sought to subsume the performers into the orchestra in "Towards a Revolutionary Model of Music Pedagogy."

124. Bettina Varwig, "Musical Expression: Lessons from the Eighteenth Century?" *Eighteenth-Century Music* 17, no.1 (2020): 53–72.

125. Mary Hunter identifies this early Romanticism in Baillot's violin method, it appears in other Conservatory method books as well. Hunter, "To Play as if from the Soul of the Composer."

126. Leslie Blasius describes Adam's piano method as a sensationism that led to Romantic epistemologies. Leslie David Blasius, "The Mechanics of Sensation and the Construction of the Romantic Musical Experience," in *Music Theory in the Age of Romanticism*, ed. Ian Bent (Cambridge: Cambridge University Press, 1996), 3–24. On the nativism inherent in some sensationist philosophy, see O'Neal, *The Authority of Experience*, 247.

127. John Tresch, *The Romantic Machine: Utopian Science and Technology after Napoleon* (Chicago: University of Chicago Press, 2012), 12.

128. Tresch, *The Romantic Machine*, 12.

129. Tresch, *The Romantic Machine*, 12.

130. James Q. Davies, *Romantic Anatomies of Performance* (Berkeley: University of California Press, 2014).

131. Tresch, *The Romantic Machine*, 5.

132. Deirdre Loughridge, *Haydn's Sunrise, Beethoven's Shadow: Audiovisual Culture and the Emergence of Musical Romanticism* (Chicago: University of Chicago Press, 2016), 9.

133. Tresch, *The Romantic Machine*, 4–5.

134. Louis Adam, *Méthode de piano du Conservatoire: adoptée pour servir à l'enseignement dans cet établissement* (Paris: Imprimerie du Conservatoire, an XIII [1805]), 2. On entrance exams and levels see Pierre, *Le Conservatoire national de musique*, 229–37.

135. Jean-Xavier Lefèvre, *Méthode de clarinette: adoptée par le Conservatoire pour servir à l'étude dans cet établissement* (Paris: Imprimerie du Conservatoire de musique, an XI [1802–1803]), 114. "Faut-il que l'artiste ait du gout, qu'il soit bon lecteur et qu'il connoise l'harmonie, car au lieu d'ajoute aucune charme d'une pièce de musique il en détruiroit l'effet par l'introduction maladroit de note défectueuses qui n'auroient aucun rapport avec l'harmonie." See also, Étienne Ozi, *Nouvelle méthode de basson: adoptée par le Conservatoire pour servir à l'étude dans cet établissement* (Paris: Imprimerie du Conservatoire, an XI [1803]), 30.

136. Hugot and Wunderlich, *Méthode de flûte du Conservatoire*, 15–16.

137. Heinrich Domnich, *Méthode de premier et de second cor: adoptée pour servir à l'étude dans cet établissement* (Paris: Imprimerie du Conservatoire Impérial de Musique, [1807]), 4. "L'organisation musicale est donc ici la première condition requise; et l'élève qui l'a reçu de la nature doit, avant de poser les lèvres sur une embouchure, avoir acquis par l'exercice du solfège l'habitude de comparer les sons, de mesurer les intervalles, de saisir

les intonations. Si pour les autres instrumens cette étude préliminaire est la plus utile de toutes, pour celui qui nous occupe elle est indispensable."

138. The tuning was based on the piano.

139. This further supports Veilt Erlmann's argument that in eighteenth-century France, the ear was considered as rational as the eye. See *Reason and Resonance: A History of Modern Aurality* (New York: Zone Books, 2014).

140. Joseph Agus et al., *Principes élémentaires de musique; arrêtés par les membres du Conservatoire, pour servir à l'étude dans cet établissement, suivis de solfèges*, 2 vols. (Paris: Imprimerie du Conservatoire de musique, an VIII [1799–1800]), 1.

141. Agus et al., *Principes élémentaires*, 2.

142. Agus et al., *Principes élémentaires*; and Charles-Simon Catel, *Traité d'harmonie: adopté par le Conservatoire pour servir à l'étude dans cet établissement* (Paris: Imprimerie du Conservatoire de musique, an X [1801–1802]).

143. "De deux générations différentes de treize quintes inaltérées chacune," *Principes élémentaires*, 23.

144. *Procès-verbaux de L'académie des beaux-arts*, 3:397. "C'est celui qui paraît destine aux élèves qui, à la pratique voudraient joindre des notions de théorie et de raisonnement."

145. *Procès-verbaux de L'académie des beaux-arts*, 2: 295–6. "La géométrie a voulu soumettre la musique à ses lois, la physique a réclamé en faveur des siennes; mais les praticiens ne pouvant travailler ni en physiciens ni en géomètres, ont senti la nécessité de se dégager des entraves scientifiques, et sont parvenus par de long essais et de nombreuses observations, à se créer des règles indépendantes, en prenant pour base de leur système, l'approbation ou l'improbation de l'oreille."

146. Those that did not require preparation were major, minor, and diminished triads; dominant, diminished, and half-diminished seventh chords; and major and minor ninth chords. Gessele, "The Institutionalization of Music Theory in France," 207n57.

147. *Procès-verbaux de L'académie des beaux-arts*, 3:397. "peu compatible avec un art dans lequel l'oreille est juge souverain."

148. Tresch, *The Romantic Machine*, 12.

149. Domnich, *Méthode de premier et de second cor*, 55 and 83. "Les exercices suivans ont pour objet, non pas d'offrir une série complète des difficultés qui se rencontrent dans la musique écrite pour corn, mais de donner une idée de celles qui peuvent s'y rencontrer."

150. According to Tresch, in Paris "machines and tools were seen as new organs modifying humans' relation to their environment" (5). Musicians' use of instruments correlates saliently here to the "sensual technology" applied by natural scientists in the last quarter of the eighteenth century, as opposed to chemists, who trusted instruments but not the senses, see E. C. Spay, *Utopia's Garden*, 197.

151. Domnich, *Méthode de premier et de second cor*, 5. "Un aussi froid calcul anéantinait toute expression."

152. An example is Hugot and Wunderlich, *Méthode de flûte du Conservatoire*, 56–9.

153. See Hugot and Wunderlich, *Méthode de flûte du Conservatoire*, 61–71; and Domnich, *Méthode de premier et de second cor*, 82.

154. Rubinoff draws a similar conclusion in her study of the flute method in "Toward a Revolutionary Model of Music Pedagogy."

155. Lefèvre, *Méthode de clarinette*, 8.

156. Hugot and Wunderlich, *Méthode de flûte du Conservatoire*, 4.

157. Baillot, Pierre, Pierre Rode, and Rodolphe Kreutzer, *Méthode de violon: adoptée par le Conservatoire pour servir à l'étude dans cet établissement* (Paris: Magasin de musique [du Conservatoire] Faubourg Poissonniere, [1803]), 1.

158. Domnich, *Méthode de premier et de second cor*, 2–3.

159. Domnich, *Méthode de premier et de second cor*; and Frédéric-Nicolas Duvernoy, *Méthode pour le cor suivie de duo et de trio pour cet instrument* (Paris: Imprimerie du Conservatoire de musique, [1802]), vi.

160. Domnich, *Méthode de premier et de second cor*, vii. "Renversement d'harmonie qui n'est motivé, ni préparé, ne fait pas plus d'honneur à l'auteur que de plaisir à l'auditeur."

161. Domnich, *Méthode de premier et de second cor*, i.

162. Domnich, *Méthode de premier et de second cor*, ii.

163. Domnich, *Méthode de premier et de second cor*, iv.

164. Pierre Baillot, Jean-Henri Levasseur, Charles-Simon Catel, and Charles-Nicolas Baudiot, *Méthode de violoncelle et de basse d'accompagnement: adoptée pour servir à l'étude dans cet établissement* (Paris: Imprimerie du Conservatoire Impérial de Musique, [1804]), 1.

165. This view quite clearly corroborates the arguments of Emily I. Dolan, especially *The Orchestral Revolution: Haydn and the Technologies of Timbre* (Cambridge: Cambridge University Press, 2012).

166. Adam, *Méthode de piano*, 229. "Il y a certains traits de violon qui ne peuvent être rendus sur le piano tels qu'ils sont écrits." Many of the methods emphasize each instrument's unique sound that the performer should cultivate. This, again, corroborates Dolan's work on the importance placed on instrumental timbre during this period.

167. Domnich, *Méthode de premier et de second cor*, vii. "On se servait aussi avec succès, il y a quelque années, de deux tons que les Cors mixtes on fait entièrement tomber dans l'oubli; ce sont ceux de *si* bas et d'*ut* à l'octave. Le premier, grave et mélancolique, portait dans les morceaux tristes une teinte sombre, une mélodie sévère, un caractère religieux. Le second, par son timbre aigu, semblait donner à une exécution rapide plus de mouvement et de vie. Ces diverses nuances, en variant les effets d'orchestre, rendaient mieux la pensée des compositeurs; mais faute de premiers et de seconds Cors, les compositeurs sont aujourd'hui privés de tous ces avantages."

168. Hugot and Wunderlich, *Méthode de flûte du Conservatoire*, 4.

169. Baillot et al., *Méthode de violoncelle et de basse d'accompagnement*, 1. "On ne peut y rien changer sans risquer de leur faire perdre leur plus grand avantage qui consiste dans une admirable simplicité, douée de tous les moyens d'expression."

170. Lefèvre, *Méthode de clarinette*, 6.

171. Lefèvre, *Méthode de clarinette*, 114. Ozi, *Nouvelle méthode de basson*, 32.

172. Adam, *Méthode de piano*, 157.

173. Hugot and Wunderlich, *Méthode de flûte du Conservatoire*, 5, and 26–8. Hugot and Wunderlich, *Méthode de flûte du Conservatoire*, 2. "Plusieurs professeurs habiles en ont reconnu l'utilité qui a été confirmée par quinze années d'expérience, nous en adoptons l'usage."

174. Adam, *Méthode de piano*, 149n1.

175. Adam, *Méthode de piano*, 281–21.

176. In "Towards a Revolutionary Music Pedagogy," Rubinoff argues that the "pursuit of technical mastery marked a growing divide between professional and amateur

musicians that only widened over the course of the nineteenth century" (512). In "Pierre Baillot," Tisdall similarly explains, "The days of multi-instrumentalists were over" (108).

177. This event has supported a variety of musicological claims over the past twenty years: about the intimate connections between music and morals during the Revolution, the liaisons between music and sex at the turn of the nineteenth century, and the isolated anecdotes that musicologists have come to fetishize in place of musical scores. See James H. Johnson, *Listening in Paris: A Cultural History* (Berkeley: University of California Press, 1995), 129–32; Michael McClellan, "'If We Could Talk with the Animals': Elephants and Musical Performance in the French Revolution," in *Cruising the Performative: Interventions into the Representation of Ethnicity, Nationality, and Sexuality*, ed. Sue-Ellen Case, Philip Brett, and Susan Leigh Foster (Boulder, CO: NetLibrary, Inc., 1999), n.p.; Jeffrey Kallberg, "Peeping at Pachyderms: Convergences of Sex and Music in France around 1800," in *Fashions and Legacies of Nineteenth-Century Italian Opera*, ed. Roberta Montemorra Marvin and Hilary Poriss (Cambridge: Cambridge University Press, 2010), 133; John Deathridge, "Elements of Disorder: Appealing Beethoven vs. Rossini," in *The Invention of Beethoven and Rossini*, ed. Nicholas Mathew and Benjamin Walton (Cambridge: Cambridge University Press, 2013), 312; and Mary Ann Smart and Nicholas Mathew, "Elephants in the Music Room: The Future of Quirk Historicism," *Representations* 132, no. 1 (Fall 2015): 62–4.

178. Both Johnson and McClellan acknowledge this as a decidedly scientific enterprise.

179. *Décade philosophique, littéraire, et politique*, no. 33, 30 thermidor an VI, 322.

180. *Décade philosophique, littéraire, et politique*, no. 32, 30 thermidor an VI, 257. "Artistes qui armés, non de scalpels et d'instrumens de torture, mais de hautbois, de flûtes et de violons."

181. *Décade philosophique, littéraire, et politique*, no. 32, 20 thermidor an VI, 258. "Cette démonstration vivante, tel qu'on n'en voit pas sur les théâtres anatomiques."

182. *Décade philosophique, littéraire, et politique*, no. 32, 20 thermidor an VI, 257. "Je crois qu'il est plus raisonnable, et surtout plus humain, d'étudier les ressorts et les fonctions de la vie dans la vie même, que de les aller chercher dans la mort, ou dans les convulsions d'un animal expirant."

183. "Pour les philosophes, la chirurgie est la plus utile des sciences médicales, une science qui progresses grâce à la dextérité et l'inventivité des plus grands praticiens. . . . Chirurgiens semblaient nettement plus utiles à l'État que les médecins, du fait des services exemplaires qu'ils rendaient aux armées de la nation." Laurence Brockliss, "L'enseignement médicale et la Révolution: essai de réévaluation," *Histoire de l'éducation* 42 (1989): 79–80.

184. Gefland, *Professionalizing Modern Medicine*, 69.

185. Gefland, *Professionalizing Modern Medicine*, 71.

186. Gefland, *Professionalizing Modern Medicine*, 11.

187. Gefland, *Professionalizing Modern Medicine*, 72.

188. Hugot and Wunderlich, *Méthode de flûte du Conservatoire*, 24–5.

189. Ozi, *Nouvelle méthode de basson*, 27 and 30. "Car on chant avec le basson comme avec la voix."

190. Baillot et al. *Méthode de violoncelle et de basse d'accompagnement*, 133.

191. Domnich, *Méthode de premier et de second cor*, viii.

192. Lefèvre, *Méthode de clarinette*, 7.

193. Hugot and Wunderlich, *Méthode de flûte du Conservatoire*, 6. "l'archet des instrumens à vent."

194. Domnich, *Méthode de premier et de second cor*, 92.

195. An example is Hugot and Wunderlich, *Méthode de flûte du Conservatoire*, 71.

196. Lefèvre, *Méthode de clarinette*, 15. "La manière . . . de respirer . . . doit être subordonnée au rhythme [sic] musical."

197. Hugot and Wunderlich, *Méthode de flûte du Conservatoire*, 4. "La nature donne, par la bonne conformation des lèvres, le premier moyen pour obtenir de beaux Sons sur la Flûte, le travail produit le reste." It continues on page 5 that it is difficult to develop a good embouchure if "l'on n'est doué par la nature des dispositions nécessaire."

198. Duvernoy, *Méthode pour le cor suivie de duo et de trio pour cet instrument*, 24.

199. Domnich, *Méthode de premier et de second cor*, vii. "Il faut y joindre de puissans moyens physiques, une oreille parfaitement organisée, beaucoup de chaleur et d'àplomb [sic]."

200. Duvernoy, *Méthode pour le cor suivie de duo et de trio pour cet instrument*, 5–6. Domnich, *Méthode de premier et de second cor*, 4.

201. Baillot et al. *Méthode de violon*, 162. "C'est le mouvement du sang qui nous a rendu le rythme nécessaire."

202. Baillot et al. *Méthode de violon*, 159. "le matériel du l'expression."

203. Hunter, "To Play as if from the Soul of the Composer."

204. Adam, *Méthode de piano*, n.p.

205. Domnich, *Méthode de premier et de second cor*, 36. "à développer en lui le sentiment musical et à prévenir le dégout qui pourrait résulter d'une étude trop uniforme."

206. Baillot et al. *Méthode de violon*, 158. "tout ce qui tient au mécanisme disparait, et le sentiment règne à sa place . . . faire oublier les moyens dont il se sert pour émouvoir."

207. Hunter, "To Play as if from the Soul of the Composer."

208. Emily Dolan discusses the keyboard's dominance as an interface in music in "Toward a Musicology of Interfaces," *Keyboard Perspectives* 5 (2012): 1–12.

209. It is interesting to note that the horn is omitted here, likely because the technique and technology still caused disagreements about the proper range—the piano method was published two years before the second horn method appeared. Domnich compensates for this omission by offering extensive advice to composers in his horn method. Domnich, *Méthode de premier et de second cor*, 6–16.

210. Adam, *Méthode de piano*, 227. "Un des plus grands avantages qu'on tire du Pianoforte, est de pouvoir exécuter la musique de tous les autres instrumens, et de se rendre compte de toutes les parties qui entrent dans l'harmonie."

211. Adam, *Méthode de piano*, 227. "C'est un de grande jouissance de pouvoir remplacer, par un seul instrument, un orchestra tout entier."

212. Adam, *Méthode de piano*, 1.

213. *Procès-verbaux de L'académie des beaux-arts*, 3:401.

214. Domnich, *Méthode de premier et de second cor*, 68. "L'élève doit s'imposer la loi de rendre strictement les articulations tels qu'elles sont indiquées."

215. Baillot et al. *Méthode de violon*, 162.

216. Baillot et al. *Méthode de violon*, 2. "L'exécution qui doit traduire fidèlement toutes les intentions du compositeur, mais qui ne fait que défigurer les productions de génie lorsqu'elle n'est pas guidée par le sentiment éclairé des convenances."

217. Baillot et al. *Méthode de violon*, 163.

218. Baillot et al. *Méthode de violon*, 164.

219. Baillot et al. *Méthode de violon*, 159: "Chaque compositeur possède un cachet qu'il imprime à tous ses ouvrages, un style qui lui est propre, qui tient à sa manière de sentir."

220. Baillot et al. *Méthode de violon*, 158–64.

221. Baillot et al., *Méthode de violoncelle et de basse d'accompagnement*, 2.

222. Baillot et al. *Méthode de violon*, 3. "Il va chez ses voisins pour y puiser à de nouvelles sources des connaissances dont il revient enrichir sa patrie . . . il accueil [sic] l'étranger avec ce sentiment de fraternité."

223. Baillot et al. *Méthode de violon*, 3.

224. *Procès-verbaux de L'académie des beaux-arts*, 3:400–1.

225. Adam, *Méthode de piano*, 1. "Si les anglais l'on amélioré depuis [its invention by the Germans], les français peuvent se vanter de l'avoir porté à son haut degré de perfection."

226. Pierre, *Le Conservatoire national de musique*, 168.

227. *Procès-verbaux de L'académie des beaux-arts*, 2:264. "juge naturel de tout ce qui concerne la théorie et la pratique de l'art."

228. This is the mission that Framery describes in his report on the Conservatory method books in 1808. *Procès-verbaux de L'académie des beaux-arts*, 3:Appendix II.

229. *Procès-verbaux de L'académie des beaux-arts*, 3:403. "Tels sont, Messieurs, les douze volumes, petit in folio, dont le Conservatoire impérial de musique vous a fait successivement hommage. Ce beau travail de la part de ses membres, suffirait pour démontrer l'utilité de cet établissement, et pour imposer silence à ses détracteurs, qui ont cherché vainement à le décrier, si l'on ne savait que le raisonnement et la raison sont sans pouvoir contre les clameurs de l'envie."

230. M. Durieu, *Observations sur la diatribe appellée Réponse à la letter écrite à M. Paesiello*, s.d., New York Public Library, 3. "Gossec à faire le vil métier de plagiaire."

231. Geoffroy-Schwinden, "Parisian Musicians as an Emergent Professional Class," 151.

232. Durieu, *Observations*, 4. "Je conviens que les ouvrages d'Agus sont bien la propriété de Sarette."

Conclusion

1. These developments in many ways reflect what David Gramit has identified in the case of German music culture in *Cultivating Music: The Aspirations, Interests, and Limits of German Musical Culture, 1770–1848* (Berkeley: University of California Press, 2002).

2. Pierre-Joseph Proudhon, *What Is Property?*, ed. and trans. Donald R. Kelley and Bonnie G. Smith, Cambridge Texts in the History of Political Thought (Cambridge: Cambridge University Press, 1994), 116.

3. Michael Fend and Michel Noiray, eds., *Musical Education in Europe (1770–1914): Compositional, Institutional, and Political Challenges*, 2 vols. (Berlin: Berliner-Wissenschafts Verlag, 2005).

BIBLIOGRAPHY

Unpublished Archival Sources

ARCHIVES NATIONALES DE FRANCE (F-PAN)

Série AE/ II/ 1457
Série AP²⁸⁴ 8
Série D XXXVIII IV, 24, 59
Série F¹⁷ 1032, 1034, 1054, 1138, 1143, 1144, 1210, 1213, 1244/A, 1274, 1278, 1279, 1288

BIBLIOTHÈQUE NATIONALE DE FRANCE, DÉPARTEMENT DE LA MUSIQUE (F-PN)

Mus. L.A. 67
L.A. 99-Scherchen, Pièces 24–26, Sarrette Dossiers

BIBLIOTHÈQUE NATIONALE DE FRANCE, FONDS MAÇONNIQUE (F-PN)

Baylot, FM2-31
Baylot, FM2-33
Baylot, FM2-58bis
Baylot, FM2-89
Baylot, FM2-97
FM2-100 bis
Baylot, FM2-102
Baylot, FM2-104
Baylot, FM2-148
Baylot, FM 153
I Baylot FM 153

BIBLIOTHÈQUE HISTORIQUE DE LA VILLE DE PARIS (BHVP)

MS 722, fol. 1, doc. 4

CONSERVATOIRE NATIONAL DES ARTS ET MÉTIERS, ARCHIVES HISTORIQUES (CNAM, ARCHIVES HISTORIQUES)

Dossier 10-389
Dossier 10-390
Dossier P-196
Dossier P-205
Dossier P-230
Dossier P-231
Dossier P-288
Dossier P-293

Online Database

Dictionnaires d'autrefois. University of Chicago: The ARTFL Project, Summer 2019. https://artfl-project.uchicago.edu/content/dictionnaires-dautrefois

INSTITUTION NATIONAL DE LA PROPRIÉTÉ INDUSTRIELLE

La base de donnée brevets français 19e siècle, http://bases-brevets19e.inpi.fr/index.asp
1BA179
1BA375
1BA419

Periodicals

Allgemeine Musikalische Zeitung
Décade philosophique, littéraire, et politique
Mercure de France
Journal de Paris

Printed Primary Sources

Adam, Louis. *Méthode de piano du Conservatoire: adoptée pour servir à l'enseignement dans cet établissement*. Paris: Imprimerie du Conservatoire, an XIII [1805].

Agus, Joseph et al. *Principes élémentaires de musique; arrêtés par les membres du Conservatoire, pour servir à l'étude dans cet établissement, suivis de solfèges*. 2 vols. Paris: Imprimerie du Conservatoire de musique, an VIII [1799–1800].

Agus, Joseph, et al. *Solfèges pour servir à l'étude dans le Conservatoire de musique* (deuxième partie). Paris: Imprimerie du Conservatoire de musique, an X [1801].

Archives parlementaires de 1787 à 1860, recueil complet des débats législatifs et politiques des Chambres françaises, imprimé . . . sous la direction de J. Mamidal et E Lauren . . . Ier série (1787 à 1799), 47 vols. Paris: [s.p.], 1867–1896.

Baillot, Pierre, Pierre Rode, and Rodolphe Kreutzer. *Méthode de violon: adoptée par le Conservatoire pour servir à l'étude dans cet établissement*. Paris: Magasin de musique [du Conservatoire] Faubourg Poissonnière, [1803].

Baillot, Pierre, Jean-Henri Levasseur, Charles-Simon Catel, and Charles Nicolas Baudiot. *Méthode de violoncelle et de basse d'accompagnement: adoptée pour servir à l'étude dans cet établissement*. Paris: Imprimerie du Conservatoire Impérial de Musique, [1804].

Bruni, Antoine-Barthelemy. *L'auteur dans son ménage*. Paris: Imbault, 1799.

Catel, Charles-Simon. *Traité d'harmonie: adopté par le Conservatoire pour servir à l'étude dans cet établissement*. Paris: Imprimerie du Conservatoire de musique, an X [1801–1802].

De Chabanon, Michael-Paul-Guy. *De la Musique considérée en elle-même et dans ses rapports avec la parole, les langues, la poésie et le théâtre*. Paris: Chez Pissot, 1785.

De Chabanon, Michael-Paul-Guy. *Observations sur la musique*. Paris: Chez Pissot, 1779.

De Chambonnières, Jacques Champion. *Pièces de clavecin, Livre 1*. Paris: Chez Jollain, 1670.

Couperin, François. *Second livre de pièces de clavecin*. Paris: Chez l'auteur, 1717.

Domnich, Heinrich. *Méthode de premier et de second cor: adoptée pour servir à l'étude dans cet établissement*. Paris: Imprimerie du Conservatoire Impérial de Musique, [1807].

Durieu. *Observations sur la diatribe appellée [sic.] Réponse à la lettre écrite à M. Paesiello*. Paris: n.p., n.d.

Duvernoy, Frédéric-Nicolas. *Méthode pour le cor suivie de duo et de trio pour cet instrument*. Paris: Imprimerie du Conservatoire de musique, [1802].

Édit du Roi Concernant le Corps de la Musique du Roi. Paris: n.p., 1782.

Fête de la liberté et entrée triomphale des objets de sciences et d'arts recueillis en Italie. Programme. Paris: Imprimerie de la république, Thermidor an VI [July 1796].

Gossec, François Joseph. *Messe des morts*. Paris: Chez Henry, 1780.

Grétry, André-Ernest-Modeste. *L'ami de la Maison*. Paris: Houbaut, 1772.

Grétry, André-Ernest-Modeste. *La correspondance générale de Grétry, augmentée de nombreux documents relatifs à la vie et aux œuvres du compositeur liégeois*, ed. Georges de Froidcourt. Brussels: Brépols, 1962.

Grétry, André-Ernest-Modeste. *De la vérité, ce que nous fûmes, ce que nous sommes, ce que nous devrions être*. Paris: Chez Ch. Pougens, 1801.

Hiller, Johann Adam, trans. *Über die Musik und deren Wirkungen*. Leipzig: Friedrich Gotthold Jacobäer und Sohn, 1781.

Hugot, Antoine, and Johann Georg Wunderlich. *Méthode de flûte du Conservatoire: adoptée pour servir à l'étude dans cet établissement*. Paris: Imprimerie du Conservatoire, an XII [1804].

Lefèvre, Jean-Xavier. *Méthode de clarinette: adoptée par le Conservatoire pour servir à l'étude dans cet établissement*. Paris: Imprimerie du Conservatoire de musique, an XI [1802–1803].

Loge Neuf Sœurs. *Éloge funèbre du T. R. F. Dalayrac*. Paris: L'imprimerie d' A. Égron, 1810.

Mengozzi, Bernardo et al. *Méthode de chant du Conservatoire de musique: contenant les principes du chant, des exercices pour la voix, des solfèges tirés des meilleurs ouvrages anciens et modernes et des airs dans tous les mouvemens et les différens caractères*. Paris: Imprimerie du Conservatoire de musique, an XII [1803–1804].

Ozi, Étienne. *Nouvelle méthode de basson: adoptée par le Conservatoire pour servir à l'étude dans cet établissement*. Paris: Imprimerie du Conservatoire, an XI [1803].

Pétition adressée à l'Assemblée nationale par les auteurs et éditeurs de musique. Paris: Laurens, aîné, s.d.

Recueil d'Édit, arrêt du conseil du roi, lettres-patentes, mémoires, et arrêts du Parlement, &c. En faveur des Musiciens du Royaume. Paris: Ballard, 1774.

Réglemens [sic.] *de la Loge et Société Olympique.* Paris: n.p., n.d. [c. 1788].

Règlement pour les comédiens français ordinaires du roi. Paris: Ballard, 1781.

Réponse de M. Dalairac à MM. les directeurs de spectacles, réclamans [sic.] *contre deux décrets de l'Assemblée nationale.* Paris: Imprimerie de L. Potier de Lille, 1791.

Rapport du jury sur les produits de l'industrie française, présenté à S. E. M. de Champagny, ministre de l'intérieur; précédé du procès-verbal des opérations du jury. Paris: L'imprimerie impériale, 1806.

Tableau des récompenses, gratifications, encouragemens [sic.], *etc. accordés par le Bureau de consultation des arts et métiers, depuis le 19 novembre 1791, jusqu'au 1 janvier 1793.* Paris: Imprimerie nationale executive de Louvre, an II [1793–1794].

Tablettes de renommée des musiciens, auteurs, compositeurs, virtuoses . . . avec une notice des ouvrages ou autres motifs qui les ont rendus recommandables. Pour servir à l'Almanach-Dauphin. Paris: Cailleau, 1785.

Tablettes royales de renommée ou almanach général d'indication des négocians [sic.], *artistes célèbres et fabricans* [sic.] *des six corps, arts et métiers . . . de Paris et autres villes du royaume.* Paris: Chez Desnois, 1773.

Travenol, Louis-Antoine. *Les Entrepreneurs entrepris, ou complainte d'un musicien opprimé par ses camarades, adressé aux protecteurs et aux protectrices des sciences et des beaux-arts.* Paris: S. Jorry, 1758.

Travenol, Louis-Antoine. *Nouveau catéchisme des Francs-Maçons, Concernant tous les mystères de la Maçonnerie.* "Jerusalem," 1748.

Vicq-d'Azyr, Félix. *Instruction sur la manière d'inventorier et de conserver, dans toute l'étendue de la République, tous les objets qui peuvent servir aux arts, aux sciences et à l'enseignement.* Paris: Imprimerie nationale, an II [1793–1794].

Secondary Sources

Abrams, M. H. *The Mirror and the Lamp: Romantic Theory and the Critical Tradition.* Oxford: Oxford University Press, 1953.

Adams, Sarah. "International Dissemination of Printed Music during the Second Half of the Eighteenth Century." In *The Dissemination of Music: Studies in the History of Music Publishing,* edited by Hans Lenneberg, 21–42. Amsterdam: Gordon and Breach, 1994.

Agnew, Vanessa. *Enlightenment Orpheus: The Power of Music in Other Worlds.* New Cultural History of Music Series. New York: Oxford University Press, 2008.

Alburn, Cary R. "Corpus Juris Civilis: A Historical Romance." *American Bar Association Journal* 562 (1959): 562–642.

Andries, Annelies. "Modernizing Spectacle: The Opéra in Napoleon's Paris (1799–1815)." PhD Dissertation, Yale University, 2018.

Arnaud, Antoine Vincent, ed. *Œuvres de M. J. Chénier, Membre de l'Institut.* Vol. 5. Paris: Guillaum Libraire, 1826.

Arnold, R. J. *Grétry's Operas and the French Public from the Old Regime to the Restoration.* Ashgate Interdisciplinary Studies in Opera. Farnham and Burlington, VT: Ashgate Publishing Limited, 2016.

Ash, Eric H. "Introduction: Expertise and the Early Modern Nation State." *Osiris* 25, no. 1 (2010): 1–24.
Atkinson, Benedict, and Brian Fitzgerald. *A Short History of Copyright: The Genie of Information*. Cham: Springer, 2014.
Attali, Jacques. *Noise: The Political Economy of Music*. Translated by Brian Massumi. Theory and History of Literature 16. Minneapolis and London: University of Minnesota Press, 2003. First published 1985.
Aulard, Alphonse. *Éléments d'instruction civique; suivies des résumés et questionnaires*. Paris: Edouard Cornely, 1902.
Aulard, Alphonse. *Histoire politique de la Révolution française: origine et développement de la démocratie et de la république (1789–1804)*. Paris: Librairie A. Colin, 1901.
Aulard, Alphonse. *Les orateurs de la révolution: L'Assemblée constituante*. Paris: E. Cornély et cie, 1905.
Aulard, Alphonse. *Paris pendant la réaction thermidorienne: recueil de documents pour l'histoire de l'esprit public à Paris*. Paris: L. Cerf, 1898–1902.
Aulard, Alphonse. *Paris sous le Consulat: recueil de documents pour l'histoire de l'esprit public à Paris*. Paris: L. Cerf, 1903–1909.
Aulard, Alphonse. *Patrie, patriotisme avant 1789*. Paris: Au siège de la société, 1915.
Aulard, Alphonse. *La révolution française et le régime féodal*. Paris: F. Alcan, 1919.
Ballot, Charles, ed. "Procès-verbaux du Bureau de consultation des arts et métiers." *Bulletin d'histoire économique de la Révolution*. Paris: Imprimerie nationale, 1913.
Baron, Pierre. "Dental Practice in Paris." In *Dental Practice in Europe at the End of the Eighteenth Century*, edited by Christine Hillam, 113–62. Clio Medical Series. Amsterdam and New York: Rodopi, 2003.
Bartlet, M. Elizabeth C. *Etienne-Nicolas Méhul and Opera: Source and Archival Studies of Lyric Theatre during the French Revolution, Consulate, and Empire*. Heilbronn, Germany: Edition Lucie Galland, 1999.
Baudry, Jérôme. "Examining Inventions, Shaping Property: The Savants and the French Patent System." *History of Science* 57, no. 1 (2019): 62–80.
Beaurepaire, Pierre-Yves. *L'espace des francs-maçons: une sociabilité européenne au XVIIIe siècle*. Rennes: Presses Universitaires de Rennes, 2003.
Becker, Howard S. *Art Worlds*. 25th Anniversary Edition. Berkeley: University of California Press, 2008. First published 1982.
Belhoste, Bruno. "Condorcet, les arts utiles et leur enseignement." In *Condorcet, homme des Lumières et de la Révolution*, edited by A.-M. Chouillet et P. Crépel, 121–36. Fontenay-aux-Roses, Fontenay-Saint-Cloud: Éditions Ecole Normale Supérieure, 1997.
Belhoste, Bruno. *Paris Savant: Capital of Science in the Age of Enlightenment*. Translated by Susan Emanuel. New York: Oxford University Press, 2018.
Bell, David. *The Cult of the Nation: Inventing Nationalism, 1680–1800*. Cambridge, MA: Harvard University Press, 2001.
Benoit, Marcelle. *Musiques de cour: chapelle, chambre, écuri*. La vie musicale en France sous les rois Bourbons 20. Paris: Éditions A. et J. Picard, 1971.
Benoit, Marcelle. *Versailles et les musiciens du roi: étude institutionnelle et sociale, 1661–1733*. La vie musicale en France sous les rois Bourbons 19. Paris: Éditions A. et J. Picard, 1971.

Bernard, Bernhard. "Recherches sur l'histoire de la corporation des ménétriers, ou joueurs d'instruments, de la ville de Paris. Troisième période." In *Bibliothèque de l'école des chartes*, Vol. 5, 254–84. Paris: Librairie Droz, 1844.

Bertucci, Paola. *Artisanal Enlightenment: Science and the Mechanical Arts in Old Regime France*. New Haven: Yale University Press, 2017.

Bertucci, Paola, and Olivier Courcell. "Artisanal Knowledge, Expertise, and Patronage in Early Eighteenth-Century Paris: The Société des Arts (1728–36)." *Eighteenth-Century Studies* 48, no. 2 (Winter 2015): 159–79.

Bingham, Alfred J. "Marie-Joseph Chénier and French Culture during the French Revolution." *Modern Language Review* 61, no. 4 (1966): 593–600.

Blanning, T[imothy] C. W. *The Culture of Power and the Power of Culture: Old Regime Europe, 1660–1789*. Oxford: Oxford University Press, 2002.

Blanning, Tim[othy C. W.]. *The Triumph of Music: The Rise of Composers, Musicians, and Their Art*. Cambridge, MA: Belknap Press of Harvard University Press, 2008.

Blasius, Leslie David. "The Mechanics of Sensation and the Construction of the Romantic Musical Experience." In *Music Theory in the Age of Romanticism*, edited by Ian Bent, 3–24. Cambridge: Cambridge University Press, 1996.

Blaufarb, Rafe. *The French Army, 1750–1820: Careers, Talent, Merit*. Manchester: Manchester University Press, 2002.

Blaufarb, Rafe. *The Great Demarcation: The French Revolution and the Invention of Modern Property*. New York: Oxford University Press, 2016.

Bloechl, Olivia. *Opera and the Political Imaginary in Old Regime France*. Chicago: University of Chicago Press, 2017.

Boncompain, Jacques. "Les auteurs à livre ouvert pendant la Révolution." *Revue d'histoire du théâtre* 41, no. 161 (1989): 89–98.

Boncompain, Jacques. "Dalayrac, fortune d'une œuvre: du droit d'auteur aux droits d'auteur." In *Nicolas Dalayrac: musicien murétain, homme des lumières*, edited by François Karro-Pélisson, 53–64. Muret: Société Nicolas Dalayrac, 1991.

Bonds, Mark Evan. *Wordless Rhetoric: Musical Form and the Metaphor of Oration*. Cambridge, MA: Harvard University Press, 1991.

Bongrain, Anne, and Yves Gérard, eds. *Le Conservatoire de Paris, 1795–1995: des menus-plaisirs à la cité de la musique*. Paris: Buchet-Chastel, 1996.

Bonnaire, Marcel, ed. *Procès-verbaux de L'académie des beaux-arts*. Paris: Librairie Armand Colin, 1937.

Bossenga, Gail. "Estates, Orders, and Corps." In *The Oxford Handbook of the Ancien Régime*, edited by William Doyle, 141–66. New York: Oxford University Press, 2012.

Bossenga, Gail. *The Politics of Privilege: Old Regime and Revolution in Lille*. Cambridge: Cambridge University Press, 1991.

Breckbill, Anita, and Carole Goebes. "Music Circulating Libraries in France: An Overview and Preliminary List." *Music Library Association Notes* 63, no. 4 (June 2007): 764–8.

Brenet, Michel [Marie Bobillier]. "La librairie musicale en France de 1653 à 1790, d'après les Registres de privilèges." *Sammelbände der Internationalen Musikgesellschaft* 8, no. 3 (1907): 401–66.

Brockliss, Laurence. "L'enseignement médicale et la Révolution: essai de réévaluation." *Histoire de l'éducation* 42 (1989): 79–110.

Broman, Thomas. "The Semblance of Transparency: Expertise as a Social Good and an Ideology in Enlightened Societies." *Osiris* 27, no. 1 (2012): 188–208.

Brook, Barry S., ed. *The Breitkopf Thematic Catalogue: The Six Parts and Sixteen Supplements, 1762–1787*. New York: Dover Publications, 1966.

Brook, Barry S. "Piracy and Panacea of Music in the Late Eighteenth Century." *Journal of the Royal Musical Association* 102 (1975–1976): 13–36.

Brown, Gregory S. *A Field of Honor: Writers, Court Culture, and Public Theatre in French Literary Life from Racine to Revolution*. New York: Columbia University Press, 2002.

Brown, Gregory S. *Literary Sociability and Literary Property in France, 1775–1793: Beaumarchais, the Société des Auteurs Dramatiques, and the Comédie Française*. Aldershot, England: Ashgate, 2006.

Boyd, Malcom, ed. *Music and the French Revolution*. Cambridge and New York: Cambridge University Press, 1992.

Campos, Rémy. *Le Conservatoire de Paris et son histoire: une institution en questions. Un essai suivi de seize entretiens*. Paris: L'œil d'or, 2016.

Carroll, Michael W. "The Struggle for Music Copyright," *Florida Law Review* 57, no. 4 (2005): 907–61.

Charles-Dominique, Luc. *Les ménétriers français sous l'ancien régime*. Paris: Klincksieck, 1994.

Charlton, David. *Grétry and the Growth of Opéra-comique*. Cambridge: Cambridge University Press, 1986.

Charlton, David. *Opera in the Age of Rousseau*. Cambridge Studies in Opera. Cambridge: Cambridge University Press, 2013.

Chartier, Roger. *The Cultural Origins of the French Revolution*. Translated by Lydia G. Cochrane. Durham, NC: Duke University Press, 1991.

Cheney, Paul. "Review of Blaufarb, *The Great Demarcation*." *History: Reviews of New Books* 45, no. 3 (June 2016): 70–1.

Chevallier, Pierre. *Histoire de Saint Jean d'Écosse du Contrat Social Mère Loge Écossaise de France à l'orient de Paris*. Paris: Éditions Ivoire-Clair, 2002.

Cohen, Albert. "A Cache of 18th-Century Strings." *The Galpin Society Journal* 36 (March 1983): 37–48.

Cohen, Albert. *Music in the French Royal Academy of Sciences: A Study in the Evolution of Musical Thought*. Princeton, NJ: Princeton University Press, 1981.

Condorcet, Marquis de. *Cinq mémoires sur l'instruction publique*. Edited by Catherine Kintzler and Charles Coutel. Paris: Garnier-Flammarion, 1994.

Cotte, Roger. *La musique maçonnique et ses musiciens*. Braine le Comte: Éditions du Baucen, 1975.

Cowart, Georgia. *The Origins of Modern Musical Criticism: French and Italian Music 1600–1750*. Ann Arbor: University of Michigan Research Press, 1981.

Dachez, Roger. *Histoire de la franc-maçonnerie française*. Paris: PUF, 2003.

Dahlhaus, Carl. *Die Musik des 18. Jahrhunderts*. Laaber: Laaber-Verlag, 1985.

Daston, Lorraine, and Peter Galison. *Objectivity*. New York: Zone Books; Cambridge, MA: Distributed by the MIT Press, 2007.

Darlow, Mark. "Beaumarchais, Framery, and the Society of Dramatic Authors," in *Beaumarchais: homme de lettres, homme de société*, edited by Philip Robinson, 39–55. French Studies of the Eighteenth and Nineteenth Century. Oxford: Peter Lang, 2000.

Darlow, Mark. *Nicolas-Étienne Framery and Lyric Theatre in Eighteenth-Century France*. Studies on Voltaire and the Eighteenth Century. Oxford: Voltaire Foundation, 2003.

Darlow, Mark. "L'effritement du privilège théâtral les débats de 1789–1790." In *L'Opéra de Paris, La Comédie-Française, et L'Opéra-Comique: approches comparées (1669–2010)*, edited by Sabine Chaouche, Denis Herlin, and Solveig Serre, 61–73. Études et rencontres 38, Paris: Publications de l'École nationale des Chartres, 2012.

Darlow, Mark. *Staging the French Revolution: Cultural Politics and the Paris Opéra, 1789–1794*. New Cultural History of Music Series. New York: Oxford University Press, 2012.

Darlow, Mark. *Dissonance in the Republic of Letters: The Querelle des Gluckistes et des Piccinnistes*. London: Modern Humanities Research Association and Maney, 2013.

Davies, James Q. *Creatures of the Air: Music, Atlantic Spirits, Breath*. Chicago: University of Chicago Press, 2022.

Davies, James Q. "Creatures of the Air." Paper presented at Music and the Body between Revolutions: Paris, 1789–1848, Columbia University Heyman Center for the Humanities, New York, NY, April 1, 2017.

Davies, James Q. "Creatures of the Air: Moral Atmospherics and the Enframement of Nature in Mendelssohn's *Elijah*." Paper presented at IRCAM, Paris, France, May 30, 2018.

Davies, James Q. *Romantic Anatomies of Performance*. Berkeley: University of California Press, 2014.

Deathridge, John. "Elements of Disorder: Appealing Beethoven vs. Rossini." In *The Invention of Beethoven and Rossini*, edited by Nicholas Mathew and Benjamin Walton, 305–32. Cambridge: Cambridge University Press, 2013.

De Brossard, Yolande, ed. *Musiciens de Paris 1535–1792*. Paris: J. Picard, 1965.

De Champeaux, Denys. "Les souvenirs du Général Baron de Salle." *Revue de Paris* 1 (1895): 407–437.

De Garidel-Thoron, Mathilde. "Le concert des amateurs à l'Hôtel de Soubise au XVIIIème siècle." Master's Thesis, Université de Paris-Sorbonne—Paris (IV), 1979.

De la Laurencie, L. "Une convention commerciale: entre Lully, Quinault et Ballard en 1680." *Bulletin de la Société française de musicologie* 2, no. 9 (July 1921): 176–82.

De Montbreton Norvins, Jacques Marquet. *Souvenirs d'un historien de Napoléon*. Paris: Furne et cie., 1827.

De Place, Dominique. "Le Bureau de Consultation pour les arts, 1791–1796." *History and Technology* 5, no. 2 (1988): 139–78.

De Riols, Emmanuel-Napoléon Santini. *Guide de la propriété artistique et littéraire en France et à l'étranger*. Paris: Le Bailly, 1881.

DeNora, Tia. *Beethoven and the Construction of Genius: Musical Politics in Vienna, 1792–1803*. Berkeley: University of California Press, 1997.

Desenne, Jean. *Codes Général Français, Contenant les lois et actes du gouvernement publiés depuis l'ouverture des États Généraux au 5 mai 1789, jusqu'au 8 juillet 1815, classés par ordre de matières, et annotés des arrêts et décisions de la Cour de Cassation*. Vol. 17. Paris: Ménard et Desenne, fils, 1821.

Devriès-Lesure, Anik. *L'édition musicale dans la presse parisienne au XVIIIe siècle: catalogue des announces*. Science de la musique. Paris: CNRS Éditions, 2005.

Doe, Julia. *The Comedians of the King: Opéra Comique and the Bourbon Monarchy on the Eve of Revolution*. Chicago: University of Chicago Press, 2021.

Doe, Julia. "*Marie Antoinette et la Musique*: Habsburg Patronage and French Operatic Culture (1770–89)." *Studies in Eighteenth-Century Culture* 46 (2017): 81–94.

Doe, Julia. "Two Hunters, A Milkmaid, and the French 'Revolutionary' Canon." *Eighteenth-Century Music* 15, no. 2 (2018): 177–205.

Dolan, Emily. *The Orchestral Revolution: Haydn and the Technologies of Timbre*. Cambridge: Cambridge University Press, 2012.

Dolan, Emily. "Toward a Musicology of Interfaces." *Keyboard Perspectives* 5 (2012): 1–12.

Dooley, Edwin L., Jr. "L'instruction militaire à l'École polytechnique, 1794–1815." *Bulletin de la Sabix* 6 (1990): 13–21.

Doyle, William. *The Oxford History of the French Revolution*. 2nd edition. Oxford: Oxford University Press, 2002.

Dratwicki, Alexandre. *Un nouveau commerce de la virtuosité: émancipation et métamorphoses de la musique concertante au sein des institutions musicales parisiennes (1780–1830)*. Lyon: Symétrie, 2006.

Duprat, Catherine. *"Pour l'amour de l'humanité": le temps des philanthropes. La philanthropie parisienne des Lumières à la monarchie de Juillet*. Preface by Maurice Agulhon. Vol. 1. Paris: Éditions du Comité des Travaux historiques et scientifiques, 1993.

Edelstein, Dan. *The Enlightenment: A Genealogy*. Chicago: University of Chicago Press, 2010.

Edelstein, Dan. *On the Spirit of Rights*. Chicago: University of Chicago Press, 2019.

Ellis, Katharine. *Interpreting the Musical Past: Early Music in Nineteenth-Century France*. New York: Oxford University Press, 2005.

Erlmann, Veit. *Reason and Resonance: A History of Modern Aurality*. New York: Zone Books, 2014.

Fairleigh, James P. "Lully as *Secrétaire du Roi*." *Bach* 15, no. 4 (1984): 16–22.

Fauser, Annegret. *Musical Encounters at the 1889 World's Fair*. Rochester, NY: University of Rochester Press, 2005.

Fend. Michael "The Problem of the French Revolution in Music Historiography and History." In *Musicology and Sister Disciplines: Past, Present, Future: Proceedings of the 16th International Congress of the International Musicological Society, London, 1997*, edited by D. C. Greer, J. King and I. Rumbold, 239–50. New York: Oxford University Press, 2000.

Fitzsimmons, Michael P. *The Night the Old Regime Ended: August 4, 1789, and the French Revolution*. University Park\: Pennsylvania State University, 2002.

Fitzsimmons, Michael P. *The Place of Words: The Académie Française and Its Dictionary during an Age of Revolution*. Oxford: Oxford University Press, 2019.

Fitzsimmons, Michael P. "Privilege and the Polity in France, 1786–1791." *American Historical Review* 92, no. 2 (April 1987): 269–95.

Fulcher, Jane. *The Nation's Image: French Grand Opera as Politics and Politicized Art*. New York: Cambridge University Press, 1987.

Furbank, P. N. *Diderot: A Critical Biography*. New York: A. A. Knopf, 1992.

Furet, François. *Interpreting the French Revolution.* Translated by Elborg Forster. Cambridge: Cambridge University Press, 1981.

Furet, François. *Marx and the French Revolution.* Translated by Deborah Kan Furet. Chicago: University of Chicago Press, 1988.

Gallay, J., ed. *Un inventaire sous la Terreur: état des instruments de musique relevé chez les émigrés et condamnés.* Paris: G. Chamerot, 1890.

Garrioch, David. *The Making of Revolutionary Paris.* Berkeley: University of California Press, 2002.

Gefen, Gérard. "La franc-maçonnerie, vecteur du classicisme." In *Journée d'étude Hyacinthe Jadin et le classicisme européen*, edited by Denis Le Touzé and Gérard Streletski, 90–100. Lyon: Université Louis-Lumière Lyon 2, Départment de musique et de musicologie, 2001.

Gefen, Gérard. *Les musiciens et la franc-maçonnerie.* Paris: Fayard, 1993.

Gelbart, Matthew. *The Invention of Folk Music and Art Music: Emerging Categories from Ossian to Wagner.* Cambridge: Cambridge University Press, 2007.

Gelfand, Toby. *Professionalizing Modern Medicine: Paris Surgeons and Medical Science and Institutions in the Eighteenth Century.* Westport, CT: Greenwood Press, 1980.

Geoffroy-Schwinden, Rebecca Dowd. "A Lady-in-Waiting's Account of Marie Antoinette's Musical Politics: Women, Music, and the French Revolution." *Women and Music: A Journal of Gender and Culture* 21 (2017): 72–100.

Geoffroy-Schwinden, Rebecca Dowd. "Music, Copyright, and Intellectual Property during the French Revolution: A Newly Discovered Letter from André-Ernest-Modeste Grétry." *Transposition. Musique et sciences sociales* [Online], 7 (2018). Online since September 15, 2018. http:// journals.openedition.org/transposition/2057. doi: 10.4000/transposition.2057.

Geoffroy-Schwinden, Rebecca Dowd. "Politics, the French Revolution, and Performance: Parisian Musicians as an Emergent Professional Class, 1749–1802." PhD Dissertation, Duke University, 2015.

Geoffroy-Schwinden, Rebecca Dowd. "The Revolution of Jommelli's *Objets d'art*: Bernard Sarrette's Acquisition of Musical Manuscripts for the Bibliothèque du Conservatoire." In *Moving Scenes: The Circulation of Music and Theatre in Europe, 1700–1815*, edited by Pierre-Yves Beaurepaire, Philippe Bourdin, and Charlotta Wolff, 61–76. Oxford Studies in the Enlightenment. Oxford: Voltaire Foundation, 2017.

Gessele, Cynthia. "The Institutionalization of Music Theory in France: 1764–1802." PhD dissertation, Princeton University, 1989.

Gétreau, Florence. "Guillaume de Limoges et François Couperin ou comment enseigner la musique hors le Ménestrandise parisienne." In *Musik—Raum—Akkord—Bild: Festschrift zum 65. Geburtstag von Dorothea Gaumann*, edited by Antonio Baldassarre, et al., 163–82. Bern: Peter Lang, 2012.

Gétreau, Florence. *Aux origines du musée de la musique: les collections instrumentales du Conservatoire de Paris, 1793–1993.* Paris: Réunions des musées nationaux, 1996.

Ginsburg, Jane C. "A Tale of Two Copyrights: Literary Property in Revolutionary France and America." Reprinted in *Intellectual Property Law and History*, edited by Steven Wilf, 27–59. Farnham and Burlington, VT: Ashgate, 2012.

Goehr, Lydia. *The Imaginary Museum of Musical Works: An Essay in the Philosophy of Music.* New York: Oxford University Press, 2007. First published 1992.

Goodman, Dena. *The Republic of Letters: A Cultural History of the French Enlightenment.* Ithaca: Cornell University Press, 1994.

Gramit, David. *Cultivating Music: The Aspirations, Interests, and Limits of German Musical Culture, 1770–1848.* Berkeley: University of California Press, 2002.

Green, Emily H. *Dedicating Music, 1785–1850.* Eastman Studies in Music. Woodbridge, UK, and Rochester, NY: Boydell and Brewer and University of Rochester Press, 2019.

Green, Robert A. *The Hurdy-Gurdy in Eighteenth-Century France.* Bloomington: Indiana University Press, 1995.

Goodman, Glenda. *Cultivated by Hand: Amateur Musicians in the Early American Republic.* New Cultural History of Music Series. New York: Oxford University Press, 2020.

Gregoir, Édouard. *Grétry: Célèbre compositeur Belge.* Bruxelles: Chez Schott, 1883.

Gribenski, Jean. "Un métier difficile: éditeur de musique à Paris sous la Révolution." In *Le tambour et la harpe: œuvres, pratiques et manifestations musicales sous la Révolution, 1788–1800,* edited by Jean-Rémy Julien et Jean Mongrédien, 21–36. Paris: Éditions du May, 1991.

Guichard, Charlotte. "Arts libéraux et arts libres à Paris au XVIIIe siècle: peintres et sculpteurs entre corporation et Académie royale." *Revue d'histoire moderne et contemporaine* 49, no. 3 (2002): 54–68.

Guillaume, James, ed. *Procès-verbaux du Comité d'Instruction publique de la Convention.* 8 vols. Paris: Imprimerie nationale, 1891–1907.

Guillio, Laurent. "Legal Aspects." In *Music Publishing in Europe 1600–1900: Concepts and Issues Bibliography,* edited by Rudolph Rasch, 115–38. Berlin: Berliner Wissenschafts-Verlag, 2005.

Habermas, Jürgen. *The Structural Transformation of the Public Sphere: An Inquiry into a Category of Bourgeois Society.* Translated by Thomas Burger. Cambridge, MA: MIT Press, 1991 [1962].

Haine, Malou. *Les facteurs d'instruments de musique français aux expositions nationales et universelles au XIXè siècle.* Paris: Institut de recherce en musicologie, 2007. http://www.iremus.cnrs.fr/sites/default/files/introduction.pdf. Accessed July 15, 2019.

Hanson, Paul. *Contesting the French Revolution.* Chester, UK, and Malden, MA: Wiley-Blackwell, 2009.

Harrison, Bernard. *Haydn: The Paris Symphonies.* Cambridge Music Handbooks. Cambridge: Cambridge University Press, 1998.

Haskell, Francis, and Nicholas Penny. *Taste and Antiquity: The Lure of Classical Sculpture, 1500–1900.* New Haven: Yale University Press, 1981.

Heartz, Daniel. *Music in European Capitals: The Galant Style 1720–1780.* New York: W. W. Norton, 2003.

Hennebelle, David. *De Lully à Mozart. Aristocratie, musique et musiciens à Paris (XVIIe–XVIIIe siècles).* Seyssel: Champ Vallon, 2009.

Hennebelle, David. "Nobles, musique et musiciens à Paris à la fin de l'Ancien Régime: les transformations d'un patronage séculaire (1760–1780)." *Revue De Musicologie* 87, no. 2 (2001): 395–418.

Hennebelle, David. "Un paysage musical de Paris en 1785: les tablettes de renommée des musiciens." *Société française d'histoire urbaine* 26, no. 3 (2009): 89–110.

Hennion, Antoine. "L'institution de la musique." In *Musique, histoire, démocratie, 1789–1989*, edited by Antoine Hennion, Vol. 1, 5–12. Paris: Éditions de la Maison des sciences de l'homme, 1992.

Hesse, Carla Alison. *Publishing and Cultural Politics in Revolutionary Paris, 1789–1810.* Studies on the History and Society of Culture 12. Berkeley: University of California Press, 1991.

Hondré, Emmanuel, ed. *Le Conservatoire de musique de Paris Regards sur une institution et son histoire.* Paris: Association du bureau des étudiants du Conservatoire national supérieur de musique de Paris, 1995.

Horn, Jeff. *Economic Development in Early Modern France: The Privilege of Liberty, 1650–1820.* Cambridge: Cambridge University Press, 2015.

Horn, Jeff. "The Privilege of Liberty: Challenging the Society of Orders." *Proceedings of the Western Society for French History* 35 (2007): 171–83.

Hunt, Lynn. *Politics, Culture, and Class in the French Revolution.* 20th Anniversary Edition. Berkeley: University of California Press, 2004. First published 1984.

Hunter, Mary. "'To Play as if from the Soul of the Composer': The Role of the Performer in Early Romantic Aesthetics." *Journal of the American Musicological Society* 58, no. 2 (2005): 357–98.

Jacob, Margaret C. *Living the Enlightenment: Freemasonry and Politics in Eighteenth-Century Europe.* Oxford: Oxford University Press, 1991.

Jarvis, Katie L. "Exacting Change: Money, Market Women, and the Crumbling Corporate World in the French Revolution." *Journal of Social History* 51, no. 4 (Summer 2018): 837–68.

Jarvis, Katie L. *Politics in the Marketplace: Work, Gender, and Citizenship in Revolutionary France.* New York: Oxford University Press, 2019.

Jefferson, Ann. *Genius in France: An Idea and Its Uses.* Princeton, NJ: Princeton University Press, 2015.

Jerold, Beverly. "Mystery in Paris, the German Connection, and More: The Bérard-Blanchet Controversy Revisited." *Eighteenth-Century Music* 2, no. 1 (2005): 91–112.

Johnson, James H. *Listening in Paris: A Cultural History.* Berkeley: University of California Press, 1995.

Johnson, Victoria. *Backstage at the Revolution: How the Royal Paris Opera Survived the End of the Old Regime.* Chicago: University of Chicago Press, 2008.

Jones, Colin. *The Smile Revolution in Eighteenth-Century Paris.* Oxford: Oxford University Press, 2014.

Julien, Jean-Rémy, and Jean-Claude Klein, eds. *Orphée phrygien: les musiques de la Révolution.* Paris: Éditions du May, 1989.

Julien, Jean-Rémy, and Jean Mongredien, eds. *Le tambour et la harpe: œuvres, pratiques et manifestations musicales sous la Révolution, 1788–1800.* Paris: Éditions du May, 1991.

Jurgens, Madeleine, ed. *Documents du Minutier Central concernant l'histoire de la musique (1600–1650).* 2 vols. Paris: S. E. V. P. E. N., 1967, and Paris: La Documentation Française, 1974.

Kajikawa, Loren. "The Possessive Investment in Classical Music: Confronting Legacies of White Supremacy in U.S. Schools and Departments of Music." In *Seeing Race*

Again: Countering Colorblindness across the Disciplines, edited by Kimberlé Williams Crenshaw, et al., 155–74. Berkeley: University of California Press, 2019.

Kallberg, Jeffrey. "Peeping at Pachyderms: Convergences of Sex and Music in France around 1800." In *Fashions and Legacies of Nineteenth-Century Italian Opera*, edited by Roberta Montemorra Marvin and Hilary Poriss, 132–51. Cambridge: Cambridge University Press, 2010.

Karro, Françoise. "Le musicien et le librettiste dans la nation: propriété et défense du créateur par Nicolas Dalayrac et Michel Sedaine." In *Études sur le XVIIIe siècle: fêtes et musiques révolutionnaires: Grétry et Gossec*, edited by Roland Mortier and Hervé Hasquin, Vol. 17, 9–52. Bruxelles: Éditions de l'Université de Bruxelles, 1990.

Kelly, George Armstrong. "Duelling in Eighteenth-Century France: Archaeology, Rationale, Implications." *The Eighteenth Century* 21, no. 3 (1980): 236–54.

Kennedy, Emmet, et al. *Theatre, Opera, and Audiences in Revolution Paris: Analysis and Repertory*. Westport, CT: Greenwood Press, 1996.

Kintzler, Catherine. *Condorcet: l'instruction publique et la naissance de citoyen*. Paris: Le Sycomore, 1984.

Kretschmer, Martin and Friedemann Kawohl. "The History and Philosophy of Copyright." In *Music and Copyright*, 2nd edition, edited by Simon Frith and Lee Marshall, 21–53. New York: Routledge, 2004.

Kriff, Jean, with Charles Porset. "Saint-Georges." In *Le monde maçonnique des lumières (Europe-Amériques & Colonies): dictionnaire prosopographique*, edited by Charles Porset and Cécile Révauger, 2445. Paris: Honoré Champion Éditeur, 2013.

Kwass, Michael. *Privilege and the Politics of Taxation in Eighteenth-Century France: Liberté, Égalité, Fiscalité*. Cambridge: Cambridge University Press, 2000.

Laboulais, Isabelle. "Serving Science and the State: Mining Science in France, 1794–1810." *Minverva* 46 (Spring 2008): 17–36.

La Gorce, Jérôme. *Jean-Baptiste Lully*. Paris: Fayard, 2002.

Landon, H. C. Robbins. *The Collected Correspondence and London Notebooks of Joseph Haydn*. London: Barrie and Rockliff, 1959.

Le Bihan, Alain. *Francs-Maçons Parisiens du Grand Orient de France (fin du XVIIIe siècle)*. Paris: Bibliothèque nationale, 1966.

Lebovics, Herman. *Mona Lisa's Escort: André Malraux and the Reinvention of French Culture*. Ithaca, NY: Cornell University Press, 1999.

Lefebvre, Georges. *La grande peur de 1789*. Paris: Angré Bruillard, 1932.

Lefebvre, Georges. *La Révolution française*. Paris: Presses universitaires de Frances, 1930.

Leigh, John. *Touché: The Duel in Literature*. Cambridge, MA: Harvard University Press, 2015.

Le Roux, Thomas. "L'utilité publique et ses débats: les mines et la question des concessions, 1791–1810." Paper presented at the conference, Les dynamiques économiques de la Révolution française, sponsored by Institutions et Dynamiques historiques de l'économie et de la société, Conservatoire des Arts et Métiers, June 8, 2018.

Lescat, Philippe. *Méthodes et traités musicaux en France 1660–1800*. Paris: Institut de pédagogie musicale et chorégraphique-La Villette, 1991.

Lever, Evelyne, ed. *Marie-Antoinette Correspondance (1770–1793)*. Paris: Tallandier Éditions, 2005.

Ligou, Daniel. *Histoire des Francs-maçons en France*. Toulouse: Editions Privat, 1987.

Lilti, Antoine. "The Kingdom of Politesse: Salons and the Republic of Letters in Eighteenth-Century Paris." *Republic of Letters: A Journal for the Study of Knowledge, Politics, and the Arts* 1, no. 2 (2009). https://arcade.stanford.edu/rofl/kingdom-politesse-salons-and-republic-letters-eighteenth-century-paris

Lilti, Antoine. *Le monde des salons: sociabilité et mondanité à Paris au XVIIIe siècle*. Paris: Fayard, 2005.

Lilti, Antoine. *The World of Salons: Sociability and Worldliness in Eighteenth-Century Paris*. Translated by Lydia G. Cochrane. New York: Oxford University Press, 2015.

Lister, Warwick. "The First Performance of Haydn's 'Paris' Symphonies." *Eighteenth-Century Music* 1, no. 2 (2004): 289–300.

Loiselle, Kenneth. *Brotherly Love: Freemasonry and Male Friendship in Enlightenment France*. Ithaca: Cornell University Press, 2014.

Loughridge, Deirdre. *Haydn's Sunrise, Beethoven's Shadow: Audiovisual Culture and the Emergence of Musical Romanticism*. Chicago: University of Chicago Press, 2016.

Lowe, Melanie. "Difference and Enlightenment in Haydn's Instrumental Music." In *Rethinking Difference in Music Scholarship*, edited by Olivia Bloechl, Melanie Lowe, and Jeffrey Kallberg, 133–69. Cambridge: Cambridge University Press, 2015.

Mace, Nancy A. "Haydn and the London Music Sellers: Forster v. Longman & Broderip." *Music and Letters* 77, no. 4 (1996): 527–41.

Mace, Nancy A. "Music Copyright in Late Eighteenth and Early Nineteenth-Century Britain." In *Research Handbook on the History of Copyright Law*, edited by Isabella Alexander and H. Tomás Gómez-Arostegui, 139–58. Cheltenham, UK, and Northampton, MA: Edward Elgar, 2016.

Macnutt, Richard. "Early Acquisitions for the Paris Conservatoire Library: Roldophe Kreutzer's Role in Obtaining Materials from Italy, 1796–1802." In *Music Publishing and Collecting: Essays in Honor of Donald W. Krummel*, edited by David Hunter, 167–88. Urbana: University of Illinois Press, 1994.

Maniates, Maria Rika. "'Sonate, que me veux-tu?' the Enigma of French Musical Aesthetics in the Eighteenth Century." *Current Musicology* 9 (January 1969): 117–41.

Mason, Laura. *Singing the French Revolution: Popular Culture and Politics, 1787–1799*. Ithaca and New York: Cornell University Press, 1996.

Massip, Catherine. "La bibliothèque du Conservatoire (1795–1819): une utopie réalisée?" In *Le Conservatoire de Paris, 1795–1995: des menus-plaisirs à la cité de la musique*, edited by Anne Bongrain and Yves Gérard, 117–32. Paris: Buchet-Chastel, 1996.

Mathiez, Albert. *Le dix août*. Paris: Hachette, 1931.

Mathiez, Albert. *La révolution française*. Paris: A. Colin, 1922.

McClellan, Andrew. *Inventing the Louvre: Art, Politics, and the Origins of the Modern Museum in Eighteenth-Century Paris*. Berkeley: University of California Press, 1999.

McClellan, Michael E. "Battling Over the Lyric Muse: Expressions of Revolution and Counterrevolution at the Théâtre Feydeau, 1789–1801." PhD Dissertation, UNC–Chapel Hill, 1994.

McClellan, Michael E. "'If We Could Talk with the Animals': Elephants and Musical Performance in the French Revolution." In *Cruising the Performative: Interventions into the Representation of Ethnicity, Nationality, and Sexuality*, edited by Sue-Ellen Case, Philip Brett, and Susan Leigh Foster, n.p. Boulder, CO: NetLibrary, Inc., 1999.

McClellan, Michael E. "The Italian Menace: Opera Buffa in Revolutionary France." *Eighteenth-Century Music* 1, no. 2 (September 2004): 249–63.

Mongrédien, Jean. *Jean-François Le Sueur: Contribution à l'étude d'un demi-siècle de musique française (1780–1830)*. Vol. 1. Berne: Peter Lang, 1980.

Mongrédien, Jean. *La musique en France des lumières au romantisme (1789–1830)*. Paris: Flammarion, 1986.

Murat, Laure. *The Man Who Thought He Was Napoleon: Toward a Political History of Madness*. Chicago: University of Chicago Press, 2015.

Neubauer, John. *The Emancipation of Music from Language: Departures from Mimesis in Eighteenth-Century Aesthetics*. New Haven: Yale University Press, 1986.

Noiray, Michel. "L'Ecole royale de chant (1784–1795): crise musicale, crise institutionnelle." In *Musical Education in Europe (1770–1914): Compositional, Institutional, and Political Challenges*, edited by Michael Fend and Michel Noiray, Vol. 1, 49–77. Berlin : Berliner Wissenschafts-Verlag, 2005.

O'Neal, John C. *The Authority of Experience: Sensationist Theory and the French Enlightenment*. University Park: The Pennsylvania State University Press, 1996.

Oliver, Bette W. *From Royal to National: The Louvre Museum and the Bibliothèque Nationale*. Lanham, MD: Lexington Books, 2007.

Ozouf, Mona. *Festivals and the French Revolution.* Translated by Alan Sheridan. Cambridge, MA: Harvard University Press, 1988 [1976].

Palmer, R. R. *The Improvement of Humanity: Education and the French Revolution.* Princeton: Princeton University Press, 1985.

Pasler, Jann. *Composing the Citizen: Music as Public Utility in Third Republic France.* Berkeley: University of California Press, 2009.

Pierre, Constant. *Bernard Sarrette et les origines du Conservatoire national de musique et de déclamation*. Paris: Delalain frères, 1895.

Pierre, Constant. *Le Conservatoire national de musique et de déclamation: documents historiques et administratifs*. Paris: Imprimerie Nationale, 1900.

Pierre, Constant. *Les hymnes et chansons de la Révolution: aperçu général et catalogue avec notices historiques, analytiques et bibliographiques*. Paris: Imprimerie Nationale, 1904.

Pierre, Constant. *Le magasin de musique à l'usage des fêtes nationales et du Conservatoire.* Paris: Fischbacher, 1895.

Pierre, Constant. *Musique des fêtes et cérémonies de la Révolution française; œuvres de Gossec, Cherubini, Lesueur, Méhul, Catel, etc*. Paris: Imprimerie Nationale, 1899.

Picon, Antoine. *L'invention de l'ingénieur moderne: L'École des Ponts et Chaussées, 1747–1851*. Paris: Presses de l'École Nationale des Ponts et Chaussées, 1992.

Pinaud, Pierre-François. *Les musiciens francs-maçons, au temps de Louis XVI de Paris à Versailles: histoire et dictionnaire biographique*. Paris: Éditions Véga, 2009.

Pink, Andrew. "A Music Club for Freemasons: Philo-musicae et architecturae societas Apollini, London, 1725–1727." *Early Music* 38, no. 4 (2010): 523–36.

Pommier, Edouard. *L'art de la liberté: doctrines et débats de la Révolution française.* Paris: Gallimard, 1991.

Porset, Charles. *Les philalèthes et les convents de Paris: une politique de la folie.* Paris: Honoré Champion Éditeur, 1996.

Porterfield, Todd. *The Allure of Empire: Art in the Service of French Imperialism, 1798–1836.* Princeton, NJ: Princeton University Press, 1998.

Potts, Alex, ed. "Johann Joachim Winckelmann." In *History of the Arts of Antiquity.* Translated by Harry Francis Mallgrave, 333. Los Angeles: Getty Publications, 2006.

Proudhon, Pierre-Joseph. *What Is Property?* Edited and Translated by Donald R. Kelley and Bonnie G. Smith, Cambridge Texts in the History of Political Thought. Cambridge: Cambridge University Press, 1994.

Quoy-Bodin, Jean-Luc. *L'armée et la franc-maçonnerie au déclin de la monarchie sous la Révolution et l'empire.* Paris: Economica, Edic, 1987.

Quoy-Bodin, Jean-Luc. "L'orchestre de la Société Olympique en 1786." *Revue de Musicologie* 7, no. 1 (1984): 95–107.

Rambaud, Marielle. *Documents du Minutier Central concernant l'histoire de l'art (1700–1750).* 2 vols. Paris: S. E. V. P. E. N., 1964.

Ranum, Patricia. "Lully Plays Deaf: Rereading the Evidence on His Privilege." In *Lully Studies*, edited by John Jajdu Heyer, 15–31. Cambridge: Cambridge University Press, 2000.

Regnault, Théodore. *De la législation et de la jurisprudence concernant les brevets d'invention, de perfectionnement et d'importation.* Paris: Lachevardière fils, 1825.

Richards, Théodore. *The Imperial Archive: Knowledge and the Fantasy of Empire.* London: Verso, 1993.

Riskin, Jessica. *Science in the Age of Sensibility: The Sentimental Empiricists of the French Enlightenment.* Chicago and London: University of Chicago Press, 2002.

Roche, Daniel. *Le siècle des lumières en province: académies et académiciens provinciaux, 1680–1789.* Paris: Mouton, 1978.

Role, Claude. *Marie-Alexandre Guénin.* Maubeuge: Édition Les Amis du Livre, 2003.

Root, Hilton L. *The Fountain of Privilege: Political Foundations of Markets in Old Regime France and England.* Berkeley: University of California Press, 1994.

Rose, Stephen. *Musical Authorship from Schütz to Bach.* Cambridge: Cambridge University Press, 2019.

Rosenfeld, Sophia. "The French Revolution in Cultural History." *Journal of Social History* 52, no. 3 (2019): 555–65.

Rubinoff, Kailan R. "Towards a Revolutionary Model of Music Pedagogy: The Paris Conservatoire, Hugot and Wunderlich's *Méthode de flûte*, and the Disciplining of the Musician." *Journal of Musicology* 34, no. 4 (2017): 473–514.

Sadler, Graham, and Caroline Wood, eds. *French Baroque Opera: A Reader.* 2nd edition Oxon and New York: Routledge, 2017.

Salmen, Walter, ed. *The Social Status of the Professional Musician from the Middle Ages to the 19th Century.* Sociology of Music, no. 1. New York: Pendragon Press, 1983.

Savoy, Bénédicte. *Patrimoine annexé: les biens culturels saisis par la France en Allemagne autour de 1800.* Vol. 1. Paris: Éditions de la Maison des sciences de l'homme, 2003.

Scott, Katie. *Becoming Property: Art, Theory, and Law in Early Modern France.* New Haven, CT: Yale University Press, 2018.

Serre, Solveig. *L'opéra de Paris (1749–1790) Politique culturelle au temps des Lumières.* Paris: CNRS Éditions, 2011.

Sewell, William H., Jr. "Connecting Capitalism to the French Revolution: The Parisian Promenade and the Origins of Civic Equality in Eighteenth-Century France." *Critical Historical Studies* 1, no. 1 (Spring 2014): 5–46.

Sewell, William H., Jr. *A Rhetoric of Bourgeois Revolution: The Abbé Sieyes and What Is the Third Estate?* Durham and London: Duke University Press, 1994.

Sewell, William H., Jr. *Work and Revolution in France: The Language of Labor from the Old Regime to 1848.* Cambridge: Cambridge University Press, 1980.

Shiner, Larry. *The Invention of Art: A Cultural History.* Chicago: University of Chicago Press, 2001.

Simon, Jonathan. *Chemistry, Pharmacy, and Revolution in France, 1777–1809.* Burlington, VT: Ashgate, 2005.

Simon, Julia. *Rousseau among the Moderns: Music, Aesthetics, Politics.* University Park: Penn State University Press, 2013.

Smart, Mary Ann, and Nicholas Mathew. "Elephants in the Music Room: The Future of Quirk Historicism." *Representations* 132, no. 1 (Fall 2015): 61–78.

Smith, Bonnie. *The Gender of History: Men, Women, and Historical Practice.* Cambridge, MA, and London: Harvard University Press, 1998.

Soboul, Albert. *Paysans, sans-culottes, et Jacobins.* Paris: Librairie Clavreuil, 1966.

Soboul, Albert. *Les sans-culottes parisiens en an II: mouvement populaire et gouvernement révolutionnaire.* Paris: Librairie Clavreuil, 1958.

Spang, Rebecca. *Stuff and Money in the Time of the French Revolution.* Cambridge, MA: Harvard University Press, 2015.

Spary, E. C. *Utopia's Garden: French Natural History from Old Regime to Revolution.* Chicago: University of Chicago Press, 2000.

Sterne, Jonathan. *The Audible Past: Cultural Origins of Sound Reproduction.* Durham, NC: Duke University Press, 2003.

Stevenson, David. *The Origins of Freemasonry.* Cambridge: Cambridge University Press, 1998.

Swann, Julian. "Parlements and Provincial Estates," in *The Oxford Handbook of the Ancien Régime*, edited by William Doyle, 93–110. New York: Oxford University Press, 2012.

Szendy, Peter. *Listen: A History of Our Ears.* Translated by Charlotte Mandell. New York, Fordham University Press, 2008.

Tackett, Timothy. *Becoming a Revolutionary: The Deputies of the French National Assembly and the Emergence of a Revolutionary Culture (1789–1790).* University Park: Pennsylvania State University Press, 1996.

Tackett, Timothy. *When the King Took Flight.* Cambridge, MA: Harvard University Press, 2004.

Taïeb, Patrick. "Le Concert des Amateurs de la rue de Cléry en l'an VIII (1799–1800), ou la résurgence d'un établissement 'dont la France s'onorait avant la Révolution." In *Les sociétés de musique en Europe, 1700–192: structures, pratiques musicales et sociabilité*, edited by Hans Erich Bödeker and Patrice Veit, 81–99. Berlin: Berliner Wissenschafts-Verlag, 2005.

Taïeb, Patrick. "L'exploitation commerciale du concert public en l'an V (1797): l'exemple de Charles Barnabé Sageret." In *Organisateurs et formes d'organisation du concert en Europe (1700–1920): institutionnalisation et pratiques*, edited by Hans Erich Bödeker, Patrice Veit, and Michael Werner, 57–82. Berlin: Berliner Wissenschafts-Verlag, 2006.

Taïeb, Patrick. "Suzette au concert Feydeau (1797) ou la vertu déconcertée." In *Le concert et son public:. mutations de la vie musicale en Europe de 1780 à 1914 (France, Allemagne, Angleterre)*, edited by Hans Erich Bödeker, Patrice Veit, and Michael Werner, 403–25. Paris: Éditions de la maison des sciences de l'homme, 2002.

Takats, Sean. *The Expert Cook in Enlightenment France.* Baltimore: Johns Hopkins University Press, 2011.

Talbot, Michael. "The Work-Concept and Composer-Centredness." In *The Musical Work: Reality or Invention?*, edited by Michael Talbot, 168–86. Liverpool Music Symposium I. Liverpool: Liverpool University Press, 2000.

Tarrade, Jean. "De l'apogée économique à l'effondrement du domaine colonial (1763–1830)." *Histoire de la France coloniale*. Vol 1. Paris: Armand Colin, 1990.

Taruskin, Richard. *Music in the Seventeenth and Eighteenth Centuries.* In *Oxford History of Western Music*. Vol. 3. Oxford: Oxford University Press, 2005.

Thiollière, Michel. "IV. Les débats révolutionnaires: droits d'auteur et domaine public." In *Projet de loi relatif au droit d'auteur et aux droits voisins dans la société de l'information*. Rapport n° 308, 2005–2006, fait au nom de la commission des affaires culturelles, déposé le 12 avril 2006, http://www.senat.fr/rap/l05-308/l05-3084.html.

Tisdall, Diane. "Blood, Sweat, and Scales: The Birth of Modern Bureaucracy at the Paris Conservatoire." Paper presented at the Annual Meeting of the American Musicological Society, Vancouver, British Columbia, November 5, 2016.

Tisdall, Diane. "Pierre Baillot and Violin Pedagogy in Paris, 1795–1815." PhD Diss., King's College London, 2016.

Tocchini, Gerardo. "Massoneria, cultura della rappresentazione e mecenatismo musicale nel Settecento." *Studi Storici* 41, no. 2 (Spring 2000): 471–531.

Tresch, John. *The Romantic Machine: Utopian Science and Technology after Napoleon.* Chicago: University of Chicago Press, 2012.

Tschmuck, Peter. "Eighteenth-Century Vienna." In *Copyright in the Cultural Industries*, edited by Ruth Towse, 210–20. Cheltenham, UK, and Northampton, MA: Edward Elgar Publishing, Inc., 2002.

Tuetey, Louis, ed. *Procès-verbaux de la Commission Temporaire des arts.* 2 vols. Paris: Imprimerie nationale, 1912.

Van Allen-Russell, Ann. "'For Instruments Not Intended:' The Second J.C. Bach Lawsuit." *Music and Letters* 83, no. 1 (2002): 3–29.

Vardi, Liana. *The Physiocrats and the World of the Enlightenment.* New York: Cambridge University Press, 2012.

Varwig, Bettina. "Musical Expression: Lessons from the Eighteenth Century?" *Eighteenth-Century Music* 17, no.1 (2020): 53–72.

Vauthier, Gabriel. "Une mission artistique et scientifique en Bavière sous le Consulat." In *Bulletin de la Société de l'histoire de l'art français*, 208–47. Paris: Jean Schemit, 1910.

Viala, Alain. *Naissance de l'écrivain: sociologie de la littérature à l'âge classique*. Paris: Les éditions de minuit, 1985.

Waltham-Smith, Naomi. *Music and Belonging between Revolution and Restoration*. Oxford: Oxford University Press, 2017.

Walton, G. Charles. *Policing Public Opinion in the French Revolution: The Culture of Calumny and the Problem of Free Speech*. Oxford: Oxford University Press, 2009.

Weber, William, ed. *The Musician as Entrepreneur, 1700–1914: Managers, Charlatans, and Idealists*. Bloomington, IN: Indiana University Press, 2004.

Weber, William. *The Rise of Musical Classics: A Study in Canon, Ritual, and Ideology*. New York: Oxford University Press, 1992.

Weisberger, R. William. "Benjamin Franklin: A Masonic Enlightener in Paris." *Pennsylvania History* 53, no.3 (July 1986): 165–80.

Weisberger, R. William. "Parisian Masonry, the Lodge of the Nine Sisters, and the French Enlightenment," *Heredom* 10 (2002): 155–202.

White, Harrison C., and Cynthia A. *Canvases and Careers: Institutional Change in the French Painting World*. Chicago: University of Chicago Press, 1993. First published 1965.

Wilcox, Beverly. "The Music Libraries of the Concert Spirituel: Canons, Repertoires, and Bricolage in Eighteenth-Century Paris." PhD Dissertation, University of California—Davis, 2013.

Wilcox, Beverly. "The Music Libraries of the Paris Concert Spirituel: A Commerce in Masterworks (1734–1778)." *Revue de musicologie* 98, no. 2 (2012): 363–403.

Wildenstein, Georges, ed. *Rapports d'experts, 1712–1791, procès-verbaux d'expertise d'œuvres d'art extraits du fonds du Châtelet, aux Archives Nationales*. Paris: Les Beaux-Arts, Édition d'études et de documents, 1921.

Wills, David. *Killing Times: The Temporal Technology of the Death Penalty*. New York: Fordham University Press, 2019.

Wokler, Robert. *Rousseau on Society, Politics, Music and Language: An Historical Interpretation of his Early Writings*. New York: Garland Publishing, 1987.

Zohn, Steven. "Telemann in the Marketplace: The Composer as Self-Publisher." *Journal of the American Musicological Society* 58, no. 2 (Summer 2005): 275–356.

INDEX

Tables, figures, and examples are indicated by *t*, *f*, and *e* following the page number
Pages in italics indicate illustrations.

A. P. D. R. (Avec privilège du roi), 37
Abel, Charles Frederick, copyright case, 79
Abolition of Privileges, 7–10, 23, 93–94,
    105, 223n59, 246n102
  delineating public from private property
    following, 3, 5, 81, 87–88
Académie des inscriptions et belles-lettres,
    25, 71
Académie d'Opéra, 25
  See also Opéra, the
Académie Française, 4, 71, 110, 160
Académie Royale de musique, 26, 27,
    37–38, 43, 48–49, 182
  See also Opéra, the
academies, 24–33, 176, 209
  abolition of, 108, 118, 128, 166
  Old Regime, 120, 182
  See also universities; *and individual academies*
Academy of Sciences, 33, 37–38, 168,
    182, 184
  See also sciences
Adam, Louis, method book by, 191*t*, 200,
    203–4, 204*f*, 205, 271n126
Advisory Board for Arts and Trades, 168,
    170–80, 183, 209, 265n29
Agnew, Vanessa, 133
Agus, Joseph, method book by, 180–81,
    191*t*, 206–7
Albonèse, Antoine, 124, 126

amateur musicians, 7, 44, 65, 66, 67–69,
    273–74n176
  See also Concert des Amateurs
L'ami de la maison, 58, 60
L'amoureux de 15 ans, 126
*Les amours de Bayard, ou Le chevalier sans peur
    et sans reproche,* 83–85
Amphion, allegory of, 133, 163
Anderson, James, 53
Andries, Annelies, 250n182
anémocorde (instrument), 173–74
Anet, Jean-Baptiste, 43
Apollo Belvedere statue, 132–33
Apollo Society for the Lovers of Music and
    Architecture, 231n15
Ariodant, 163
arrangements/arrangers, 82, 96, 98, 99,
    100, 103, 106
art(s)
  masterpieces, 88, 150, 156
  music as, 16–17, 132–64 (*see also*
    work-concept)
  pleasurable, 124, 167, 172, 174, 180, 200
  regenerating French society through, 113,
    114, 116, 196
  support for, 44, 123
  useful, 33, 45, 46, 81, 88, 124, 167–80, 200
  See also fine arts; freedom: arts connected with
L'art de toucher le clavecin, 34–35

artisans, 24, 33, 49, 182, 221n23
  See also musicians: as artisans and artists
artists, 24, 33, 48, 73, 81, 124
  under Old Regime, 112, 124, 126, 134, 245n83
  property rights petition, 89–93
  savants distinguished from, 67, 143–44, 245n83
  See also musicians: as artisans and artists
artwork, confiscation of. *See* cultural property, confiscation of
Attali, Jacques, 130–31, 242n26
August 4, 1789. *See* Abolition of Privileges
Aulard, Alphonse, 10, 216n45
Austria, 12, 13
  France's war with, 117, 149, 261n117
L'auteur dans son ménage, 259n67
authors, 124, 184
  petition to revolutionary government, 97–104, 98f, 102t, 106
  See also composers; dramatic authors; librettists; method books (Paris Conservatory); playwrights
author's rights, 79–111
  originality as determining factor, 92, 100, 103, 111, 248n142
  petition to revolutionary government regarding, 244n78, 247n122, 247n123, 248n138
  See also composers: rights of; copyright; dramatic authors, rights of; intellectual property; laws, author's rights; music printing, rights of
Avec privilège du roi. *See* A. P. D. R. (Avec privilège du roi)

Bach, Johann Christian, copyright case, 79
Bach, Johann Sebastian, 29, 155t
Bailleux, Antoine, 98f, 99
Baillot, Pierre, method book by, 191t, 203, 204–5, 206, 271n125, 273–74n176
Ballard, Christophe and family, 4, 21, 22, 99
  printing privileges held by, 34, 36, 38, 242n26
Bambini, Felice, 124, 125, 127
Barbier, Luc, 149
Barckhaus, Claude-François de, 69
bassoonists/bassoon, 39, 60, 67, 69
  method book for, 196, 200, 202
Baudin, Pierre-Charles-Louise, 102

Baudry, Jérôme, 265n29
Baumont, Olivier, 29
Beaumarchais, Pierre, 45, 87, 91, 241n16, 244n78
Beaurepaire, Pierre-Yves, 232n30
beaux-arts. *See* arts: pleasurable
Bêche, Jean-Louis, 98f, 99
Becker, Howard, 6
Beethoven, Ludwig van, 3, 12, 13, 100, 106
Berger, François, 39
Bernouilli, Daniel, 198
Berton, Henri-Montan, 98f
Bertucci, Paola, 24, 27, 33, 44, 48–49
biens nationaux (national property), 134, 135, 149
  See also property; property regime, modern; property rights
Bitsch, Jean, 62–63
Blasius, Frédéric, 98f, 115
Blasius, Leslie, 271n126
Blaufarb, Rafe, 5, 9, 14, 15, 215n37, 215–16n38, 216n39, 257n12
Bloechl, Olivia, 8
Bobillier, Marie, 11, 34
Boïeldieu, François-Adrien, 99, 100, 161
Bossenga, Gail, 215–16n38
bourgeois, 54–55, 56, 214n14, 228n158
Bouvier, Antoine, 185, 186
brass instruments, method book for, 197f
  See also individual brass instruments
Brenet, Michel. *See* Bobillier, Marie
brevets. *See* patents (*brevets*)
Brown, Gregory, 83, 87, 97, 101, 110–11, 244n71, 246n102
Bruni, Antoine-Barthelemy, 99, 139–40, 143, 163
Bürckhoffer, J. G., 98f, 99

Cacault, François, 160
Cambini, Giuseppe Maria (Jean-Joseph Cambini), 66, 99, 124
Cambry, Jacque, 178–79
Candeille, Julie, fees collected by, 105–6
Candeille, Pierre-Joseph, 109
capitalism, 6, 11, 13, 67, 209
Capperan, Gabriel, 39
Cardon *jeune*, L., 98f
Caribaldi, Giovachino, 151–52, 153–54
Caroline Louise Queen of Naples (Masonic lodge), 57

Carpani, Giuseppe, 91
Catel, Charles-Simon, 144, 191*t*, 194, 195–96
cello, 36, 200, 202
Censi, Giuseppe, 153
censorship, 12, 34, 94
César *père* and *fils*, 98f, 99
Chabanon, Michel-Paul-Guy de, 71–72, 74, 238n124
Chambonnières, Jacques Champion de, 36
Champein, Stanislas, 105–6, 126–27, 242n34
  author's rights case, 83–87, 91, 101, 267n68
Charles-Dominique, Luc, 28, 32, 44, 222n43, 223n67, 239n131
Charlton, David, 39, 47
chemistry, 45, 228n159
  See also medicine
Cheney, Paul, 15
Chénier, Marie-Joseph, 104, 122, 163
  rewards list, 124, 126, 177, 180
Cherubini, Luigi, 71, 98f, 99, 112, 161
  conserving confiscated musical objects, 142, 144, 150–51
  Inspector at Paris Conservatory, 123, 181
  works by, 69, 74, 100
Chevallier, Pierre, 234n59, 236n91
Chiquelier, Christoph, 179, 180
chords, musical, 52, 196, 272n146
Chrétien, Gilles Louis, 63
church, the, 4, 40, 116, 119, 134, 136
  See also clergy; First Estate; musicians, church
Ciciliani, Filippo, 153
Circé, 69
citizenship, 11, 120, 216n45, 239–40n147
Civil Constitution of the Clergy, 134
Clareton, Jean Joseph
  new method for music lessons, 171–73, 180
  Rue Favart music school proposal, 115–16, 123, 125
clarinet, method book for, 194, 196, 197f, 198, 200–2
class(es), 32, 54–55, 64, 67, 114, 236n92
  See also First Estate; Second Estate; Third Estate
Classical music, 13, 210
Clérambault, Louis-Nicolas, Masonic membership, 232n29

clergy, 3, 26, 34, 54–55, 89, 90, 134, 136
  See also church, the; First Estate
Cohen, Albert, 37, 268n86
Colbert, Jean-Baptiste, 25, 26, 119, 135
Colbertism, 25, 33, 49–50, 148
colonialism, 13, 139, 162–64
  See also imperialism
Comédie-Française
  compensation from, 83, 85–86
  composers pursuing rights from, 26, 89
  and Le Chapelier Law, 92, 95
  Opéra's relationship with, 47, 91
  playwrights affiliated with, 42, 82, 90
  privileges granted to, 4, 39, 45, 87–88
Comédie-Italienne, 85, 91
  composers pursuing rights from, 89–90
  and Le Chapelier Law, 92, 93
  privileges granted to, 4, 39
commerce/commercialization, 84, 110, 168, 185–86, 188, 190
  and industry, 49, 176
  musical privilege and, 33–38
  See also economy
Committee on Liberty of the Press, 88–89
Committee on Public Instruction, 119, 264n13, 267n68
  mission of, 96, 183
  rewards program, 123–28
  service schools established by, 189–90, 190*t*, 192
  See also education
Committee on Public Safety, 118, 121
composers, 48–49, 143, 152*t*, 239n131, 242n21
  as artists, 74, 145–46, 147, 163
  compensation for, 105–6, 106*t*, 107, 126, 241n12
  control by, 82, 83, 224n86, 241n13
  inequity between librettists and, 91, 96
  Masonic memberships, 62–63, 72, 73, 74, 76
  as men of genius, 13, 110
  method books' instructions to, 200, 203, 204–5
  morality and class of, 44, 236n92
  at Paris Conservatory, 123, 254n48
  petitions to government, 97–104, 98f, 102*t*, 106, 244n78, 247n123, 248n138
  privileges registered by, 36–37, 80, 241n14

INDEX | 299

composers (*cont.*)
    professionalization of, 7, 33, 74–76, 111
    property rights sought by, 28, 46, 80, 90, 139, 142
    regulation of, 27, 242n26
    rights of, 79, 80–81, 86–87, 93–97, 103–4, 167, 251n188
    See also and individual composers
Concert de la Loge Olympique, 52, 64, 65, 70, 71, 120, 140, 238n124
    See also Loge Olympique de la Parfaite Estime (Masonic lodge); Olympique (Masonic lodge)
Concert des Amateurs, 44, 65, 66–67, 69, 70, 71, 236n99, 237n105, 238n124
    See also amateur musicians
Concert Spirituel, 39–42, 44, 46
    establishment of, 53, 65
    performances of, 47, 56, 57, 70
    privileges held by, 23, 226n116
Condé, Louis de Bourbon (Comte de Clermont), 53
Condorcet, Marquis de, 86, 120
Condorcet Plan of 1792 for education, 116, 119, 146–47, 182
conductors, 84, 86, 94
    Masonic memberships, 64, 66, 75, 76
Confrérie de Saint-Julien-des-Ménétriers (guild), 24–32
Conservatoire des arts et métiers, 122, 130
    See also art(s); métiers
Consulate government, 108, 165, 192
copyright, 36, 79–80, 96, 105, 130, 240n2, 248n142
    See also author's rights; intellectual property; music printing, rights of
Corbelin, François Vincent, 98f, 99
corporations, 5, 24–25, 27–28, 43, 93, 137
    See also guilds; *ménétriers*
Cotte, Roger, 232–33n39, 234n66
counterfeiters/counterfeiting, 37, 92, 98, 224–25n90
Couperin, Armand-Louis, 84–85, 105, 129, 177, 204
Couperin *le grand*, François
    keyboard suite, 29–33, 31e, 32e, 34, 35f
    privileges acquired by, 24, 27, 36, 49
    struggle for property rights, 48, 62, 83
Cousineau family, 98f, 99, 186, 269n98
Coustos-Villeroy (Masonic lodge), 43, 232n29

craftmanship/crafts, 33, 37, 48
    music as, 174, 177, 179
    See also métiers
Crown, the, 23, 39, 47–48, 116, 119, 126
    privileges granted by, 4, 9, 34, 45, 46, 73, 82, 222n34
    See also individual kings and queens
cultural heritage
    access to, 88, 119
    collective, 3, 109–10, 124
    growing, 33, 166, 186, 188
    interdependence of industry and, 13, 131, 178
    legitimatizing, 10, 209
    See also music, as art; public property
cultural property, confiscation of, 132–64
    German, 155–58, 159t–60t
    inventories of, 135–44, 137f, 141f
    Italian, 149–55, 157, 261n117
    musical instruments, 134, 138–39, 140, 141f, 144, 160
    See also scores, musical, confiscated
culture, 54, 263n157
    agenda of, 179, 205
    military, 115, 130
    Parisian, 8, 69
    regenerating, 112, 138–39
    revolutionary, 11, 217n56
    See also art(s); dance/dancers; music; operas; society

Dahlhaus, Carl, 12
Dalayrac, Nicolas-Marie, 96–97, 105
    Masonic membership, 66, 74
    playwrights organized by, 87, 111
    property rights sought by, 89–90, 93, 99, 101, 107, 110, 131, 167–68, 209, 244n78
    works by, 91, 92, 100
dance/dancers, 25, 26, 27, 28, 30
Darlow, Mark, 13, 88, 94, 114, 232n27, 241n16, 246n107
Daunou, Pierre Claude François, 119, 122, 128
Daunou-Sieyes-Lakanal plan for education, 119
Davies, James Q., 193
Debussy, Claude, 209
De Certeau, Michel, 219n77
Declaration of the Rights of Genius, 104–11, 165
    See also genius

Declaration of the Rights of Man, 9–10, 81, 89, 95, 97, 104, 105
De Lorthe, Gabriel Antoine, 174–75
Demoz, M. Jean François, 38
dentists, professionalization of, 28, 71
　See also medicine
deregulation, 6, 45–46, 88, 94, 166
De Rossi, Luigi, 151, 152*t*, 152–54, 261n114, 261–62n122
Dessalles, Victor Abel, 158, 262n138
Devaux, Georges Jacques, 56–58, 60, 61, 70, 75–76, 234n64
Devienne, F., 98*f*
　Le devin du village, 37
Devriès-Lesure, Anik, 247n122
Dezède, Nicolas, 98*f*
D'Haudimont, Abbé, 124, 125, 171–72, 174
Diderot, Denis, 86, 100, 101, 107
Directory government, 108, 165, 182, 189, 192
doctors, 1, 2, 4, 201
　Masonic memberships, 62, 65, 71
　See also medicine
dodétracorde (instrument), 174
Doe, Julia, 13–14, 47, 242n34
D'Ogny, Claude-François-Marie Rigoley (Comte), 69
Dolan, Emily J., 273n166
Domnich, Heinrich, method book by, 191*t*, 194, 196, 198, 199, 200, 202–4, 275n209
D'Orléans, Louis Philippe II (Duke), 55, 222n40
dramatic authors, 82, 110–11, 126
　petition to revolutionary government, 97–104, 98*f*, 102*t*, 106, 244n78
　See also authors; author's rights; composers; librettists; playwrights
droit d'auteur, 240n2
　See also author's rights
Droit du seigneur, 126
dueling, 51–52, 67, 76, 230n8, 240n154
Dufourny, Léon, 160, 161, 162
Dumanoir, Guillaume, 25
Dumanoir, Michel, 26, 27, 43
Duplat, Jean-Louis, 185, 268n92
Dupont, Nicolas, 176
Durieu, Louis Antoine, 99, 206–7, 209
　method books by, 121, 122–23, 180–81
Duvernoy, Frédéric, method book by, 191*t*, 199, 203

École polytechnique, 130, 189–90
École Royale de chant et de déclamation, 49, 72, 82–83, 97, 115, 123, 127, 128, 190, 269n102
economic privileges, 22, 46
Economist Publishers, 185, 186, 187
economy, 6, 15, 34, 241n13
　fiscal privileges, 22, 46
　free market system, 80, 81, 93
　Old Regime, 27, 236n89
　political, 33, 89, 176, 228n162
　revitalization of, 165, 166, 176, 189, 202
　See also capitalism; commerce/commercialization; industrialization/industry; mercantilism
Edelstein, Dan, 9–10, 15, 219n88, 223n71, 224n74
education, 73, 123, 166, 167, 168, 182
　musical, 113–16, 122, 144, 171
　Old Regime, 144, 252n16
　reforming, 96, 112, 116, 119–20, 146, 181
　role in professionalization, 45–46, 49, 129–30, 189–90
　See also Committee on Public Instruction; method books (Paris Conservatory); professional musicians, education of; *and individual schools*
Eler, André-Frédéric, 259n70
Ellis, Katharine, 133
émigrés, confiscation of property from, 134, 136, 137*f*, 150, 161, 176, 257n12
engineering, 6, 130, 176, 182, 189, 200
　music's affinity with, 166, 190, 196, 198
　See also industrialization/industry; manufacturing; sciences
England, 22, 79–80
　See also Grand Lodge (Masonic lodge, London)
Enlightenment, 71, 192, 239–40n147, 240n154
　philosophers of, 87, 88
　projects of, 208, 209
　tenets of, 13, 15, 33
Erlmann, Veit, 272n139
Estates General, 8, 89
　See also First Estate; Second Estate; Third Estate
Europe, 2, 98, 145
　France's dominance in, 131, 149–51, 155–56, 163

INDEX | 301

Europe (*cont.*)
　Paris as arts capital of, 38, 124
　See also Austria; cultural property, confiscation of; England; France; Germany; Italy
"Les Fastes de la grande et ancienne Mxnxtrxndxsx" (The Splendors of the Great and Ancient Ménétriers), 29–32

Fend, Michael, 12
Ferté, Papillion de la, 49
festivals, 123, 188
　Masonic, 72–73
　national, 126, 165
　public, 176, 177–78
　revolutionary, 11, 94, 113, 114, 118, 121, 154–55
feudalism, 4, 9, 11, 25, 137, 241n14
Figaro, 91
fine arts, 41, 84, 97, 155
　evaluating, 163, 181, 187
　in the French Revolution, 120, 122, 133, 134–44, 147–48
　See also art(s)
First Estate, 8, 54–55, 89, 127
　musician's service with, 125, 178
　privileges concentrated in, 3, 5, 22, 26, 120
　See also clergy; *émigrés*, confiscation of property from
First Republic France, 10, 11, 81, 166
fiscal privileges, 22, 46
Fitzsimmons, Michael P., 220n9
Flachat, Jean-Baptiste, pamphlet by, 96–97
Floquet, Étienne-Joseph, 63–64, 235n77
flute, 28, 201
　method book for, 196, 198, 199, 200, 202
Fournier, Pierre-Simon, 38
Framery, Nicolas-Étienne, 101, 185, 194
　collections agency formed by, 93, 94–95, 105–6, 106t, 110–11, 140, 151
　Masonic membership, 66, 239n132
France, 90, 123, 145
　centralization of, 10, 25, 119
　European dominance by, 131, 162–63
　history of, 133, 135–36, 138–39, 145–46
　national government, 113–14, 117, 121
　See also Crown, the; culture; French Revolution; government; Masonic lodges, French; military; Old Regime France; Paris; society

Francoeur, François, 41, 42
Françoeur, Louis Joseph, Masonic membership, 66
Franklin, Benjamin, Masonic membership, 72, 74
freedom
　arts connected with, 112, 124, 127, 130, 134, 138–39, 155, 208
　before the law, 52, 120
Freemasonry, French, 53–56, 235n72
　demographics of, 232n28, 232n31
　Scottish rite, 54, 63, 238n119
　See also Masonic lodges, French
French Revolution, 146, 149
　agendas of, 10, 13–14, 88, 112, 117, 119–20, 128, 131, 165, 178, 188, 205
　author's rights in, 8, 82–87, 244n71
　culture of, 11, 217n56
　legacy of, 14, 15, 208, 210
　music in, 3, 10–15, 134–44, 209–10, 217n56, 219n90
　origins of, 8–9, 23, 113
　radicalization of, 114, 119, 136
　See also Abolition of Privileges; Reign of Terror; *and forms of government*
Fridzeri, Alessandro Mario Antonio, 124
Fuchs, Georg-Friedrich, 98f, 99
Furet, François, 11

Gallet, André Jean, 60, 61, 113
Garat, Dominique Joseph, 172, 174
Garde Nationale band, 97, 113–16, 118, 123, 252n26
Garrat, Pierre-Jean, Masonic membership, 66
Gaviniés, Pierre, 99
Gebauer, Michel Joseph, 98f, 99
Gefen, Gérard, 58, 232–33n39
Gelinek, Joseph, 98f, 99–100
genius, 45, 88, 104–11, 143, 165, 249n145
　artistic, 73, 127, 133, 163, 177
　composers cultivating, 13, 145
　law protecting, 105, 107, 166
　method book explanation of, 200, 204–5
　musical, 102, 103–4, 145, 147–49, 177, 208–9
　originality a trait of, 107, 108, 111
　See also savants

Germany, 12, 13
  privileges in, 34, 224n80, 229n179, 241n14
  scores confiscated from, 155–58, 159t–60t
Gétreau, Florence, 28, 31, 138, 146
Ginguené, Pierre-Louis, 125, 151, 181
Ginsburg, Jane, 105, 249n156
Giroust, François, 125–26, 180
Gluck, Christoph Willibald Ritter von, 37, 49, 63, 73–74, 127, 155t, 205
Goehr, Lydia, 13, 130, 133, 143, 145–46, 154, 163, 164
  work-concept of, 139, 158
Gossec, François-Joseph, 7, 37, 44, 142, 206–7, 234n64, 238n124
  as director of École Royale de chant, 7, 49
  letters from, 121, 123
  as National Institute reviewer, 108, 109
  at Paris Conservatory, 123, 199, 206
  on property rights, 98f, 99, 127, 225n99
  review of patent applications by, 125, 181, 183, 184–85
  support for Clareton's teaching method, 115, 171–72, 174
government
  combating piracy, 82–83
  national, 113–14, 117, 121
  property rights petition to, 97–104, 98f, 102t, 106
  revolutionary, 1, 9, 87–88, 119
  rewards granted by, 1, 109, 168
  support for musicians, 94–95, 110, 112, 123–28
  theories of, 244n77
  See also citizenship; Crown, the; French Revolution; laws; Old Regime France; taxation/taxes; *and individual Commissions and Committees*
Grand Lodge (Masonic lodge, London), 60, 63, 235n85
  patents and constitutions received from, 53, 55, 56, 57–58, 235n85, 238n119
Grand Orient (Masonic lodge, Paris), 53–54, 55, 63, 232n31, 235n84
Green, Emily H., 236n92, 241n12
Green, Robert A., 29–30
Grétry, André-Ernest-Modeste, 49, 64, 83, 115, 181
  and author's rights, 87, 93, 111, 112
  combating piracy, 82, 83
  compensation for, 96, 105
  dueling story, 51–52, 67, 76
  Inspector at Paris Conservatory, 123, 125, 163, 206
  and Le Chapelier Law, 94–95
  letters from, 14, 90–92, 103
  Masonic membership, 55–56, 70
  Old Regime treatment of artists criticized, 104, 245n83
  pursuing property rights, 89–90, 98f, 99, 100, 101–2, 244n78
  support for Clareton's teaching method, 171–72, 174
  works by, 58, 60, 106
Gribenski, Jean, 47–48, 99, 224–25n90, 247n122
Gruer, Maximilien Claude, 39
Guénin, Marie-Alexandre, 98f, 99, 181, 239n132
Guignon, Jean-Pierre, 42–43, 232n29
guilds, 23, 24–33, 37–38, 100, 120, 232n60
  abolition of, 108, 118, 166
  craft, 33, 37, 48
  hierarchy in, 54–55
  musicians, 27, 32–33, 42–44, 49, 94, 112, 222n43, 222n45
  ownership of privileges, 4, 34
  printers and publishers, 28, 37, 38, 46, 82
  regulations imposed by, 27, 43–44, 45, 84, 86
  weakening of, 10, 28–29, 42–46
  See also corporations; *ménétriers;* Paris Book Guild
Guillard, Nicolas-François, 95
guillotine, 1–2, 9, 117, 166
  See also French Revolution; Reign of Terror
Guillotine, Joseph-Ignace, 1–2
guitar, invention of, 175f

Habermas, Jürgen, 54
Haine, Malou, 186
Hampel, Anton Joseph, method book by, 199
Handel, George Frideric, 37, 158, 159t
harmonists, 27–28, 33, 223n67, 238n119
harmony, 52, 53, 55, 58, 74–76, 100–1
  See also sociability

harp, 183–84, 185, 186
Hassenfratz, Jean Henri, 165, 166, 168, 176, 188
Haüy, René Just, 198
Haydn, Joseph, 3, 12, 13, 64, 68, 74, 100, 205, 217n63)
Hennebelle, David, 44, 48, 225–26n110, 237n105, 246n111
Hesse, Carla, 15, 46, 110
historiography, 2, 10–15, 24, 210, 235n72
    See also France, history of
Hondré, Emmanuel, 270n119
horn, 28, 188, 201
    method books for, 194, 198, 198f, 199, 200, 202, 204, 275n209
Horn, Jeff, 4, 220n9
Hugot, Antoine, method book by, 191t, 198
Hunt, Lynn, 11
Hunter, Mary, 271n125
hurdy-gurdy (*vielle*), 29–30

iconoclasm, 135, 136, 138, 142, 254n51
Imbault, Jean-Jérôme, 63, 99
imperialism, 13, 33, 81, 131, 133, 139, 149–55, 162–63, 210, 224n74
    See also colonialism; nationalism
inalienability, 80, 87, 94, 96, 101, 104, 105
individual rights, 9–10, 12, 166, 186, 205
Industrial Exhibitions (Paris), 186–87, 187f
industrialization/industry
    agenda of, 189–90, 192, 202, 205
    and commerce, 49, 172
    growing, 171, 173, 179, 182, 185, 186
    interdependence of cultural heritage and, 131, 178
    music as, 165–207
    See also capitalism; economy; engineering; manufacturing; mining; public property
Institut de musique. *See* École Royale de chant et de déclamation; National Institute of Music
instrumentalists, 27–28, 73, 74, 75, 94, 106
instruments, 33, 272n150, 273n166
    builders of, 28, 37, 188
    confiscation of, 134, 138–39, 140, 141f, 144, 161
    inventions of, 167, 170–74
    monodic, 27–28, 30
    National Institute's review of, 184–87

technologies of, 2, 37, 176, 179, 198, 200
    See also method books (Paris Conservatory); music, instrumental; Paris Conservatory, library and museum; *and individual instruments*
intellectual property, 15, 86, 130, 186, 205
    See also author's rights; copyright
inventions/inventors
    legal rights, 31, 37, 81, 165–66, 168, 173–75, 205
    mechanical, 37, 167–80, 181–88
    musical, 10, 167, 171–88, 175f, 193
    National Institute's review of applications, 182–87
    rewards for, 168–79, 170f
    Romantic Machine, 188–206
    useful, 1, 97
    See also engineering; manufacturing; technologies, instrument
Isouard, Nicolò, 161, 162
Italy, 123, 261n114
    scores confiscated from, 149–55, 157, 261n117

Jacob, Margaret C., 232n35
Jacquet de la Guerre, Élisabeth, 36
Jadin, Louis, 98f, 99
Janson *l'aîné*, Baptiste-Aimé, 127, 180, 184
Jarvis, Katie, 14–15
Jefferson, Ann, 107, 109, 249n145
Jélyote, Pierre, Masonic membership, 232n29
Jobert, Pierre, 176–77
Johnson, James H., 12
Jommeli, Niccolò, operas by, 154t, 155t, 156–58, 157t

Karro-Pélisson, François, 247n122
keyboard/keyboardists, 27, 28, 33, 43, 72, 239n131
    Couperin's suite for, 29–33, 31e, 32e, 34, 35f
    inventions related to, 173, 174, 179
    method book for, 203, 204
    See also organ/organists; piano
kings. *See* Crown, the; *and individual kings and queens*
Kintzler, Catherine, 107
Kreutzer, Rodolphe, 98f, 144, 151, 153, 158, 160–62

Laboulais, Isabelle, 189–90
Laboulaye, Edouard, 249n156
La Candeur (Masonic lodge), 58–61, 61*f*, 63, 66, 70, 74
Lacépède, Bernard Germain de, 127
La Harpe, Jean-François De, 87, 88, 90, 95, 244n78
La Haye, Étienne-Marie de, 69
Lahoussaye, Pierre, 115
Laïs, Jean-François, 63
Lakanal, Joseph, 104–11, 119, 146–47, 249n156
Lalande, Jêrome de, 72, 127
Langes, Savalette de, 69
Langlé, Honoré François Marie, 72, 127, 147–49, 168, 181, 259n70
Lanzetti, Le Sieur, 36
La Réunion des Arts (Masonic lodge), 56–58, 60, 70, 75, 234n64
law(s), 28, 41, 52, 88, 120, 118, 179, 209
   author's rights, 15, 46, 80–89, 92–96, 101, 103, 105, 242n26, 249n154, 251n188
   government reward system, 1, 124–28, 172, 254n50
   inventors' rights, 1, 37, 81, 165–68, 172–75, 183–85, 205
   musicians' rights, 2–3, 9, 43–44, 55, 79, 81, 83–84, 105, 110, 112
   Old Regime, 126, 166
   printing and publishing, 91, 98, 186
   property, 1, 105, 108–11, 165–68, 170, 172, 174–75, 184, 205, 216n42, 251n188
   tax, 228n158
   See also copyright; genius, law protecting; regulations; *and specific laws*
Law of 19– 24 Jul 1793, 249n154
   See also Declaration of the Rights of Genius
Lebovics, Herman, 150
Lebrun, Jean-Baptiste-Pierre, 136, 146
Le Chapelier Laws, 92–96, 152, 165, 246n102
   January, 92–93, 95–96
   June, 93–94, 246n105
Leclair, Jean-Marie, 43
Le Clerc, Charles Nicolas, 37
Le Contrat Social (Masonic lodge), 65, 74–75
   orchestra of, 69, 70, 73, 236n91, 237n111
Lefebvre, Georges, 11
Lefèvre, Jean-Xavier, method book by, 98*f*, 99, 191*t*, 194, 198, 202
legal privileges, 33, 69, 70
   musical production and, 21–50, 67
   social privileges entwined with, 4, 33, 40–41, 45, 50, 52, 90
Legislative Assembly, 117
Leigh, John, 240n154
Le Moyne, Jean-Baptiste, 95
Le Roux, Thomas, 166
Les Amis Réunis (Masonic lodge), 62–63, 65, 69, 71, 235n72
Les Frères Initiés (Masonic lodge), 72
Les Neuf Soeurs (Masonic lodge), 62, 64, 72, 73, 74, 127, 151
Lesueur, Jean-François, 98*f*, 99, 123, 144, 147–49, 181
lettre patente, 222n36
Lévesque, Pierre, 98*f*, 99
librettists, 89, 91, 92, 93, 96, 105–6
Lilti, Antoine, 54, 234n66, 240n149
Lister, Warwick, 68
Locke, John, 86–87, 101
Loge Olympique de la Parfaite Estime (Masonic lodge), 65, 74, 97
   See also Concert de la Loge Olympique; Olympique (Masonic lodge)
Loi du 30 vendémiaire, 190*t*
Loi du 2 et 17 mars 1791, 264n8
Loi relative aux découvertes. See September 12th law on inventors' rights (*Loi relative aux découvertes*)
Loiselle, Kenneth, 232n26, 239–40n147
Loughridge, Deirdre, 193
Louis, Antoine, 1
Louis de Bourbon (Comte de Clermont, Prince of Condé), 53
Louis XIV (King)
   centralization project, 10, 25, 119
   privileges granted by, 22, 23, 26, 27, 28
Louis XVI (King)
   crises facing, 8, 23, 87
   fate during French Revolution, 116–17, 118
   reforms of 1780s, 46–48, 49
Louvre, 122, 132, 135, 136, 139, 140, 145, 146

Lully, Jean-Baptiste
  ennoblement of, 220n3
  legal battles, 24, 48–49, 83, 112, 129
  privileges acquired by, 23, 25–29, 33–34, 222n34, 222n37, 222n40, 242n26
  Proserpine composed by, 21, 220n2
Lully *fils,* Jean-Baptiste, 21–22, 23
Lycée des Arts, 72, 168, 169f

Macnutt, Richard, 261n114, 261n117, 261–62n122
Magic Flute, The, 54
Maire, A. M., 98f
Malter, François Duval, 47
Mannory, Louis, 226n128
manufacturing, 22, 33–38, 99, 129, 176, 199
  See also engineering; industrialization/industry; inventions/inventors
Marie Antoinette (Queen), 54, 58, 118, 137
Marmontel, Antoine François, 95
Marsenne, Marin, 194
Martini, Giovanni Battista, 98f, 150–51, 180
Martini, Jean-Paul-Gilles, 126
Mason, Laura, 12
Masonic lodges, French
  architects of music memberships, 63–70
  brother servant memberships, 56–63
  free associate memberships, 61, 62–70, 71, 236n91
  hierarchy in, 53, 55, 62, 66, 70, 73
  membership tables, 60, 61f, 62, 64, 66, 70, 234n59
  military connection, 113, 115
  music in, 208, 232n27, 234n67, 237n111
  occasional brother memberships, 56–63
  in Paris, 53–56, 56t, 232n28, 232n31
  savant members, 70–74
  sociability in, 52, 53–56, 67, 232n27, 239–40n147
  talented brother memberships, 63–70
  women's, 54, 58, 65, 232n26
  See also Freemasonry, French; *and individual lodges*
Massip, Catherine, 146–47, 149
Mathiez, Albert, 11
Mayer, Ferdinand, 98f, 99
McClellan, Michael, 92
medicine, 48, 173, 182, 201

  See also chemistry; dentists, professionalization of; doctors; pharmacists/pharmacy; surgeons/surgery
Méhul, Étienne-Nicolas
  evaluation of method books, 194–96
  legal protection initiatives, 99, 112
  Masonic membership, 66, 69–70, 75, 239n145
  as National Institute reviewer, 108, 109, 122
  operas by, 100, 163
  at Paris Conservatory, 123, 144, 181, 206
  publishing house started by, 161
  review of patent applications by, 183, 184, 185, 186, 187, 188, 268n92
ménétriers, 24–33, 43–44, 222n43
  See also corporations; guilds
Mengozzi, Bernardo, 151, 152, 191t, 202
Méon, Jean-François, 181
mercantilism, 25, 45, 48
  See also commerce/commercialization; craftmanship/crafts; economy; trade/trades
Mereaux, Nicolas Jean Lefroid de, 72, 98f
method books (Paris Conservatory), 108, 121–23, 125, 180–81, 184, 191t, 191–206, 195f, 197f, 198f, 209, 267n61, 270n119, 271n123, 273n166
métiers, 28, 122, 124, 130, 223n56
  See also craftmanship/crafts; trade/trades
military, 130, 189, 196
  See also Garde Nationale band; musician-soldiers; Napoleon Bonaparte, military campaigns
mining, 130, 166, 178–79, 186, 189–90, 196
  See also engineering; industrialization/industry
Molard, Claude-Pierre, 176–78, 179, 186, 200
monarchs. *See* Crown, the; *and individual kings and queens*
Mondonville, Jean-Joseph Cassanéa de, 39, 40, 41–42, 46, 56
Mongrédien, Jean, 14
monodists, 27–28, 30, 33, 43, 62
Monsigny, Pierre-Alexandre, 180
Montgeroult, Hélène de, 129
Montu, Anselme, 172, 173, 174
Monuments Commission, 135–38, 142, 147
  See also Temporary Arts Commission

morality/moral rights, 55, 122, 125, 236n92, 248n143, 274n177
Mozart, Wolfgang Amadeus, 3, 13, 54, 74, 100, 160*t*, 205
Mozin *le jeune*, Benoit François, 98*f*, 99
Museum Commission, 122
  See also Monuments Commission; Temporary Arts Commission
music, 12–13, 194, 217n63
  as art, 16–17, 132–64
  as craft, 177, 179
  engineering's affinity with, 166–67, 189–90, 196, 198
  French Revolution's impact on, 3, 10–15, 134–44, 209–10, 217n56, 219n90
  genius of, 102, 103–4, 145, 147–49, 177, 208–9
  instrumental, 70, 74, 85
  masterpieces, 13, 133, 142–43, 145–47, 149, 158, 162, 208
  usefulness of, 75, 81, 110, 114, 165–207
  See also composers; instruments; method books (Paris Conservatory); Old Regime France, music and musicians in; property, music as
musical privileges, 2, 4, 21–50, 35*f*, 56
  granted to music publishers, 22, 33–38, 48, 242n26
  transitioning to musical rights, 87–104
musical production
  French Revolution's changes in, 2–3, 13, 16–17, 105, 133–34, 210
  inventions to improve, 10, 175, 179, 185–86, 188, 193
  legal privileges and, 5, 21–50, 67, 79, 105, 120, 208
  Old Regime, 4, 44, 49–50
  in Paris, 13, 21–50, 105
  Paris Conservatory's monopoly over, 123, 144, 156, 167, 192–93
  professional, 6–7, 110, 130, 133, 164, 188
  See also music-making
  musical work, 97, 103, 142, 193
  See also scores, musical; work-concept
music engraving, 37, 83, 103, 185, 224n86
  See also music printing
musician-masons, 51–76, 97, 232n29, 232–33n39
  professional, 54–55, 57–58, 62–64, 66–74, 236n96

social status of, 52, 56, 63, 65–67, 69, 70, 71, 72, 74–75, 76
  See also Freemasonry, French; Masonic lodges, French; *and individual musician-masons*
musicians, 13, 201
  academy, 27, 32, 49
  as artisans and artists, 27, 44, 69, 74–75, 109, 114, 119, 201, 203
  church, 27–28, 33, 36, 49, 55, 118, 123–27, 222n45
  court, 24, 28, 36, 43–44, 45, 49, 124, 125–26, 222n45
  government support for, 94–95, 110, 112, 123–28
  legal status of, 6, 9, 39, 45–46, 52, 79, 81, 83–84, 112
  in Old Regime France, 6, 167
  orchestra, 48–49, 57–58, 64, 70, 113
  patriotism of, 101, 114, 118, 120–29, 209
  politics of, 10–15
  public service by, 75, 112–31
  rights of, 2–3, 10, 43–44, 81, 83, 86, 93–94, 139, 184, 196
  savant, 24–28, 48–49, 70–74, 108–9, 209
  social status of, 2, 6, 30, 32, 44–46, 49 (*See also* musician-masons, social status of; professional musicians, social status of)
  See also guilds, musicians; *ménétriers*; Old Regime France, music and musicians in; professional musicians; servants, musicians as
musician-soldiers, 112, 113–16, 123
music-making, 7, 22–27, 69, 171, 202
  See also musical production
music ownership. *See* property rights, musicians'
music printing, 96, 185–86
  privileges for, 5, 23, 34–35, 46–47, 82–83, 168, 224n80
  rights of, 79–80, 96, 103, 105, 183, 240n2
  See also author's rights; copyright; guilds, printers and publishers; music engraving; scores, musical
music publishers/publishing
  in Paris, 3, 164
  petition to revolutionary government, 97–104, 98*f*, 102*t*, 106

INDEX | 307

music publishers/publishing (*cont.*)
  privileges granted for, 22, 33–38, 35*f*, 48, 242n26
  rights of, 79–80, 103
  See also composers; guilds, printers and publishers; music printing
music theory, 123, 171, 180, 182, 194–95, 196, 259n72
Naderman, François-Joseph, 98, 98*f*, 99

Napoleon Bonaparte, 108, 205
  military campaigns, 132, 149–51, 155–56, 162–63, 193, 262n138
Napoleonic Civil Code, 105
Napoleon III, 10
National Assembly, 8–9, 88, 117
National Convention, 117–18
National Institute
  establishment of, 108–9, 120, 121–23, 179, 181
  evaluations by, 167, 181–88, 190, 194–95, 205–6, 209, 250n182
National Institute of Music, 118, 122, 136, 138–43, 267n64
  See also Paris Conservatory
nationalism, 17, 133–34, 163
  See also imperialism; patriotism
national rights, 9–10
natural resources, 166, 175–76, 191
natural rights, 15, 80, 219n88
  of composers, 96, 104
  property rights as, 88, 167–68, 249n147
  See also Declaration of the Rights of Man
Naudot, Jacques-Christophe, Masonic membership, 232n29
Navoigille-Julien, Guillaum, Masonic membership, 66, 98*f*
Neveu, François-Marie, 156–58, 262n132, 262n139
New Musicology, 12
New Regime France, 3, 7, 9–10, 16, 106
Nina, ou La folle par amour, 91, 201
nobility, 26, 60, 69, 136, 137*f*, 245n83
  See also émigrés, confiscation of property from; Second Estate
Nochez, Jean-Jacques, 181
Noiray, Michel, 49
Norvins, Jacques Marquet de Montbreton, 66
Le nouveau Don Quichotte, 91

Old Regime France
  archival record of, 10–15
  artists' servitude under, 112, 124, 126, 134, 245n83
  artworks of, 136, 146–47
  educational system, 116, 120, 182, 252n16
  hierarchy of, 52, 54–55, 89, 90, 111
  legal system, 9, 166
  music and musicians in, 4, 6, 21–50, 95, 118, 120, 167, 193, 208, 220n13
  privilege system, 21–22, 27, 50, 73, 89, 90, 93, 105, 111, 137, 168, 180, 187, 205
  sociability in, 7, 82, 125
  social status in, 45, 128n114
  waning days of, 51–52, 239–40n147
Ollivier, François-Henri, 185, 186, 268n92
Olympique (Masonic lodge), 62, 235n84, 235–36n86, 237n111
  orchestra, 64–70, 68*f*, 69, 75
  See also Concert de la Loge Olympique; Loge Olympique de la Parfaite Estime (Masonic lodge)
Opéra, the, 13, 44, 56, 115, 246n107
  Comédie-Française's relationship with, 47, 91
  composers at, 63, 147
  and Le Chapelier Law, 94, 95
  musicians affiliated with, 66, 127–28
  orchestra of, 57, 97
  privileges held by, 4, 23, 25, 32–33, 39, 48, 60–61, 72
  reforms of 1780s, 46–47, 49
opéra comique, 70, 91, 115, 152
operas, 12–13, 96, 126–27, 149, 250n182
  Jommelli's, 156–58, 157*t*
  scores of, 33–34, 155*t*
orchestras, 2, 42, 44, 64, 225–26n110
  method books for, 202, 271n123
  See also individual orchestras
organ/organists, 28, 85, 176–79, 188, 200
  See also keyboard/keyboardists; piano
originality, 86, 92, 100, 104, 107, 108
Orpheus, allegory of, 133, 163
Ozi, Étienne, 69, 191*t*

Paisiello, Giovanni, 91, 100, 155*t*
Palmer, Robert, 130
Paris, 52, 113
  as arts capital of Europe, 38, 124, 133

culture in, 8, 69
Industrial Exhibitions in, 186–87, 187f
insurrection in, 117, 136, 251n8
Masonic lodges in, 53–56, 56t, 232n28, 232n31
municipal government, 113–14, 118, 121
musical production in, 13, 21–50, 105
professional musicians in, 3, 48–49
sociability in, 53–56
See also France
Paris Book Guild, 28, 33, 34, 86
Paris Conservatory, 11, 14, 110, 130, 139, 168, 193, 254n48
   agenda, 123, 133, 149–55, 205
   contributions to industry, 189–92
   curriculum, 127, 144–45, 156, 167
   establishment of, 108, 112, 114, 129, 130–31, 144, 147, 166, 177, 181, 182
   faculty, 69, 72, 97, 123, 128, 133–34, 144, 181
   Inspectors, 123, 167, 181–88, 206
   library and museum, 132, 144–62, 188, 190, 259n70
   mining's similarities to, 189, 190–91
   mission, 133, 145–46, 148, 189, 190, 208
   musicians affiliated with, 7, 60, 155, 188, 196
   music publishing at, 164, 167
   preservation of national monuments by, 144–49
   Romantic Machine, 188–206
   See also method books (Paris Conservatory); National Institute of Music
"Paris" Symphonies (Haydn), 64, 68, 74
Parlements, 22, 28, 37, 220n9
Pasler, Jann, 11, 81, 129, 166, 264n6
patents (*brevets*), 2, 26, 37, 97, 167, 222n36, 264n8, 265n29
   National Institute's review of applications for, 182–88
   See also rewards
patriotism, 45, 67, 83, 110
   of musicians, 101, 114, 118, 120–29, 209
   See also nationalism
patronage/patrons
   aristocratic, 6, 124, 246n11
   dilution of, 48, 69, 225–26n110
   music, 22–23, 42, 44, 56, 67, 120, 121, 237n111
   public, 129–31

"Les pélerines," 29
pensions, 82, 90, 95, 109, 125–26, 179
   See also rewards
performance privileges, 24–33
performance rights, 79, 80, 87, 91, 94–96, 251n188
performers, 48–49, 82, 94
   fees collected by, 106, 107
   Masonic memberships, 74, 75
   method books' instructions to, 200, 203, 259n72, 271n123
   See also dance/dancers; musicians; orchestras; virtuosos; *and individual insturments and players*
Pergolesi, Giovanni Battista, 37, 59, 154t, 155t
Perrin, Pierre, 25–26, 222n34
personal property, 107, 167
   author's and musician's, 10, 40, 42, 80, 92–93, 95, 186
   belonging to the Crown, 39, 46
   privileges as, 215–16n38, 216n39
personal rights. *See* individual rights
Perti, Giacomo Antonio, 150
Petrini, Francesco, 98f, 99
pharmacists/pharmacy, 28, 45, 228n159
   See also medicine
Philalèthes, 235n72
Philidor, François-André Danican, 66, 70
Physiocratism, 45, 219n88, 228n156, 228n162, 249n147
piano, 185, 188
   method books for, 200, 202, 203–4, 204f, 205, 271n126, 275n209
   See also keyboard/keyboardists; organ/organists
Piccinni, Niccolò, 49, 63, 73–74, 155t, 229n129
Pièces de clavecin, 36
Pierre, Constant, 11, 14
Pinaud, Pierre-François, 62, 232–33n39, 234n67
piracy, 82–83, 206
   preventing, 36, 97, 224–25n90
plagiarism, 82, 204, 206–7
playwrights
   petition to revolutionary government, 247n122, 247n123, 248n138
   property rights for, 46, 83–86
   société of, 87, 111, 244n78
   See also authors; dramatic authors

INDEX | 309

Pleyel, Ignace, 83, 186
political privileges, 22
politics, 10–15, 81, 110–11, 166
   See also economy, political
Pollet, Benoit, 98f, 99
Pommier, Edouard, 133, 135, 149, 158
Porthaux, Dominique, 98f, 99
printing privileges. *See* music printing, privileges for
printing rights. *See* author's rights; copyright; music printing, rights of
private property
   music as, 2, 79–111, 112
   public property distinguished from, 3, 5, 9, 10, 81, 87–88
privileges (*privilèges*), 23, 53, 80, 215–16n38, 225n92, 241n7, 241n14
   collective, 93–94
   competition for, 2, 22, 45
   dilution of, 10, 42–50, 87, 89
   for musicians, 2, 56, 79, 226n122
   seigneurial rights differing from, 220n10
   See also Abolition of Privileges; economic privileges; fiscal privileges; legal privileges; musical privileges; music printing, privileges for; music publishing, privileges for; Old Regime France, privilege system; performance privileges; property, privileges as; social privileges; theatrical privileges
professionalism/professionalization, 3–7, 27–28, 33, 75, 120, 228n158
   education's role in, 45–46, 49, 129–31, 189–90
   See also education; method books (Paris Conservatory); National Institute of Music; Paris Conservatory
professional musicians, 13, 273–74n176
   definition of, 2, 6–7
   education of, 110–11, 112, 116, 144–45, 166–67
   French Revolution and, 15, 123
   laws regarding, 43–44, 81
   modern, 209–10
   in Paris, 3, 48–49
   privileges obtained by, 22, 23, 28–29, 48
   reforms of 1780s, 46, 48
   savant, 70–74
   social status of, 28, 71–72, 81, 90

   See also method books (Paris Conservatory); musician-masons, professional; National Institute of Music; Paris Conservatory
property, 14, 100, 101, 215n37
   music as, 2, 75, 79–111, 133–34, 167, 170, 209–10, 220n13
   privileges as, 3–7, 9, 38–42, 47, 88, 96–97, 105, 184, 209–10, 216n39, 249n156
   sacredness of, 95, 103–4
   See also biens nationaux (national property); cultural property, confiscation of; intellectual property; laws, property; private property; public property
property regime, modern, 2–3, 15, 81, 87, 186, 209–10
property rights, 79–111
   legal pursuit of, 46, 80–87
   musicians', 2–3, 9–10, 83, 139, 184
   as natural rights, 15, 167–68
   petition to revolutionary government regarding, 97–104, 98f, 102t, 106
   sacredness of, 97, 105, 186
Proserpine, 21
Proudhon, Peter, 210
public domain, 37, 88, 96, 109, 168, 179, 183
public property, 92–93, 124
   music as, 2, 75, 96, 112, 130–31
   private property distinguished from, 3, 5, 9, 10, 81, 87–88
   See also cultural heritage; industry
public utility, 45, 81, 129, 178, 209
   as criterion for patents and rewards, 182–88
   music as, 129, 166–67, 190
publishers and publishing. *See* guilds, printers and publishers; music publishers/publishing
Puppo, Giuseppe, 115

"Que ne suis-je la fougère?" 59
Quesnay, François, 45, 228n156
Quinault, Philippe, 21

Ragué, Louis-Charles, 98f, 99
Rameau, Jean-Philippe, 100–1, 238n124
   method book by, 194, 196
   musical theories of, 52, 107
   privileges acquired by, 36, 38

Ranum, Patricia, 26, 220n13
Ravel, Maurice, 209
Regnault, Théodore, 264n8
regulations, 25, 46, 83, 97, 105, 209
  guild, 27, 43–44, 45, 84, 86
  See also censorship; deregulation; laws
Reichardt, Johann Friedrich, 108–9
Reign of Terror, 121, 128, 149, 182, 188
  beginning of, 104, 118
  ending of, 122, 124, 126, 144, 176
  See also French Revolution; guillotine
rewards
  Advisory Board for Arts and Trades granting, 171–81
  Committee for Public Instruction granting, 124–28
  government, 1, 109, 124–28, 254n50
  for inventions, 168–79, 170f
  National Institute's review of applications, 182–88
  See also patents (*brevets*); pensions
Rey, Jean-Baptiste, 84–87, 91, 94, 115
rhythmomètres (proto-metronomes), 171, 173
Ribouté, Charles-Henri, poem by, 59, 59e
Richard, Cœur de Lion, 91
Richards, Thomas, 139
Richer, Louis Augustin, Masonic membership, 66
Rigade, André-Jean, 127
rights. *See* Declaration of the Rights of Man; individual rights; music printing, rights of; music publishers/publishing, rights of; national rights; natural rights; property rights
Robespierre, Maximilien, 122
Rochefort, Jean-Baptiste, 84–87, 91, 94
Rode, Pierre, 161
Rodolphe, Jean Joseph, 128, 180, 199, 255n75
Roland, Jean, 136
Romanticism, 12–13, 17, 111, 143, 271n125, 271n126
  See also inventions/inventors, Romantic Machine
Root, Hilton L., 23, 48
Root-Bernstein, Michèle, 47
Rose, Stephen, 34, 80, 81, 224n86, 229n179, 241n7, 241n13, 241n14, 248n143
La rosière de Salenci, 58

Rousseau, Frédéric, 140
Rousseau, Jean-Jacques, 37, 52, 89, 100–1, 107, 148, 244n77
Roussel, François Jean, method book by, 125
Royal Academy of Dance, 25, 27, 30
Royal Academy of Painting, 25, 235n70
Royal Academy of Sculpture, 25, 235n70
Rozier, Pilâtre de, 73
Rubinoff, Kailan R., 254n49, 271n123, 273–74n176

Sabinus, 238n124
Sacchini, Antonio, 49, 127, 154*t*, 155*t*, 160*t*
Saint-Alexandre d'Écosse (Masonic lodge), 238n119
Saint-Charles des Amis Réunis (Masonic lodge), 72
Saint-Charles du Triomphe de la Parfaite Harmonie (Masonic lodge), 70, 238n119
Saint-Georges, Chevalier de (Joseph Bologne), 64–65, 66, 73, 74, 115, 238n124
Saint-Jean d'Écosse du Contrat Social (Masonic lodge), orchestra of, 63–64
Saint-Jean de Palestine (Masonic lodge), 71
Sapho, 126
Sarrette, Bernard
  collecting confiscated musical scores, 156–63
  Garde Nationale band, 97, 113–16, 118, 123, 252n26
  and method books, 200, 203, 205, 206–7
  National Institute proposal, 118–21, 122
  and Paris Conservatory, 123, 132, 133, 139, 163, 178, 186
  political maneuverings of, 129, 130
savants
  artists contrasted with, 24, 143–44
  definitions of, 7, 107, 119, 239n131
  musicians as, 24–28, 48–49, 70–74, 108–9, 209
  See also genius
Schmidt, Tobias, 1–2, 9, 166, 186, 187f
  See also guillotine
Schneitzhoffer, Jacques, 60, 61, 113
Schnell, Jean Jacques, 173–74
Schroetter, J. H., 98f
sciences, 45, 189, 192, 205, 228n159
  music's affinity with, 165–67
  useful, 28, 46, 81, 174, 178, 224n74

INDEX | 311

scientists, 150, 156, 201, 272n150
  Masonic memberships, 65, 72, 127
scores, musical
  confiscation of, 134, 138–39, 144, 148*t*, 152*t*, 153–62, 155*t*, 157*t*, 164, 193
  inviolability and fidelity pertaining to, 3, 13, 92, 104, 108, 109, 111, 142, 204
  National Institute's review of, 108, 109
  as objects, 139, 142, 145, 146–47
  rights to, 96, 103, 104
  sale of, 22, 33, 186, 187, 192
  See also method books (Paris Conservatory)
Scott, Katie, 15
Second Empire France, 10
Second Estate, 8, 125
  confiscation of property from, 134, 150, 257n12
  privileges granted to, 4, 5, 22, 23, 26, 120
  Sieyes's views on, 89, 90
  See also émigrés, confiscation of property from; nobility
Séjan, Nicolas, 127–28
sensationist theory, 28, 191, 192, 193
September 12th law on inventors' rights (*Loi relative aux découvertes*), 167, 172, 174–75, 264n8, 265n25
servants
  artists as, 67, 124, 134, 245n83
  denied admission to Masonic lodges, 55, 67
  musicians as, 6, 23, 41, 44, 56, 58–60, 75, 90, 112–31, 241n14
  La serva padrona, 37, 59
Sewell, William H., Jr., 14, 67, 223n59, 244n77
Shovlin, John, 228n162
Sieber, Jean-George, 83, 99
Sieyes, Emmanuel-Joseph (Abbé), 8, 14, 119, 215n32, 244n77
  writings of, 88–90, 96–97, 102, 104
singers/singing, 64, 94, 106, 202, 205
Smith, Adam, 80, 81, 89
Soboul, Albert, 11
sociability
  in Masonic lodges, 52, 53–56, 67, 232n27, 239–40n147
  in Old Regime France, 7, 82, 125
  See also harmony

social privileges, 22, 51–76
  legal privileges entwined with, 4, 33, 40–41, 45, 50, 52, 90
Société des Amis Réunis (orchestra), 62
Société des Auteurs Dramatiques (guild), 45
Société Olympique, 65, 237n105
society, 3–4, 15, 234n66, 240n149
  regeneration of, 14, 112, 114–16, 119, 133, 138–39, 208
  See also culture
sovereignty, 3, 8–9, 13, 16, 89, 104, 111, 196, 208
  See also Crown, the
Spang, Rebecca, 14, 15
Stamitz, Johann, 37
Statute of Anne (England, 1710), 79
Stendhal, 132
Stephanopoli, Dimo, 172–73
Strasbourg lodge (Masonic lodge), 232n35
string instruments, 43, 173, 174, 175*f*, 185, 268n86
  See also individual string instruments
surgeons/surgery, 2, 28, 71, 166, 201–2
  See also medicine
Surmaine de Missery, Antoine, 174
Szendy, Peter, 251n188

Tablettes de renommée des musiciens (Chantoiseau), 48–49, 56
Talleyrand, Claude-Maurice, 134
Talleyrand Plan of 1791 for education, 116, 119
taxation/taxes, 4, 22, 46, 228n158
technologies, instrument, 2, 37, 176, 179, 198, 200
  See also engineering; industrialization/industry; inventions/inventors
Temporary Arts Commission, 137–44, 138*t*, 145, 146, 147, 149, 161, 163, 176
  See also Monuments Commission
theaters
  compensation from, 86, 91
  deregulation of, 94, 108, 166, 246n102
  See also individual theaters
Théâtre du Monsieur. *See* Théâtre Feydeau
Théâtre Feydeau, 91, 97, 115
theatrical privileges, 4, 24, 26, 42–43, 47, 222n37
Thermidorian Reaction, 122, 144
Third Estate, 4, 8, 54–55, 89, 90, 120

312 | INDEX

Third Republic France, 10–11, 14, 81
Tisdall, Diane, 259n72, 273–74n176
Tocchini, Gerardo, 237n111
Tocqueville, Alexis de, *L'Ancien Régime et la Révolution,* 10
trade/trades, 22, 45, 124, 129, 223n56
　See also craftmanship/crafts; mercantilism
translations, 91–92, 105, 223n56
Travenol, Louis-Antoine, 39–42, 43, 44, 180, 206, 226n122
　attacks on Voltaire, 40–42, 46, 226n128
treaties, 149–50, 151
　of Bologna, 150, 261n117
　of Parma, 149, 157
　of Tolentino, 149–50, 157, 261n117
Tresch, John, 193, 272n150
Troisième Ordre, 29
Tschirziki, Christian, 173–74
Turgot, Anne-Robert-Jacques, Six Edicts, 45

L'union d'amour et des arts, 63
universities, 116, 130, 131, 137
　See also academies
usufructuary rights, 9
　See also property rights
utility, 94, 201, 228n159
　academic, 73, 182–83, 188
　conception of, 33, 97, 264n6
　of inventions, 1–2, 97, 167–80, 179, 185, 187
　of music and musicians, 44, 63, 65, 75, 110, 133, 165–207
　political, 188, 192
　social, 50, 223n71
　See also art(s), useful; public utility; sciences, useful

Variétés-Amusantes (theater), 47
Veillard, Jean-François, 60, 61, 67, 68–69, 113
Viala, Alain, 22–23, 44
Villeneuve, Jérôme Pétion de, 113
violinists/violin, 27, 28, 58, 62–63, 188, 201
　harmonic, 172, 173, 174
　method book for, 198, 199, 200, 202, 203, 204, 205, 206, 271n125
　See also string instruments
Viotti, Giovanni Battista, 66, 75, 236n94
virtuosos, 2, 106, 236n94
　Masonic memberships, 62, 75, 76
Vivetières, Marsolliers de, 91
Voltaire
　Masonic membership, 72, 74
　Travenol's attack against, 40–42, 46, 226n128
Von Winter, Peter, 158, 262n139

Wilcox, Beverly, 39, 226n116
Winckelmann, Johann Joachim, 132
wind instruments, 60, 113, 115, 161, 173, 188
　method book for, 197f, 198, 202
　See also individual wind instruments
women. *See* Masonic lodges, French, female lodges
work-concept, 139, 158, 164
　future-oriented, 133, 146, 149, 154, 164
　See also musical work; scores, musical
writers. *See* authors; composers; dramatic authors; librettists; playwrights
Wunderlich, Johann Georg, method book by, 191t, 198

Zuccarelli, Signor. *See* Champein, Stanislas

www.ingramcontent.com/pod-product-compliance
Lightning Source LLC
Chambersburg PA
CBHW072054290825
31867CB00004B/373